Youth Football:

A Complete Handbook

Youth Football:

A Complete Handbook

Edited by: Jerry Cvengros, M.S.

Youth Sports Institute
Michigan State University
Vern Seefeldt, Ph.D., Director

 Brown & Benchmark

Library of Congress Cataloging in Publication Data:

Cvengros, Jerry
    Youth Football: A Complete Handbook

Cover Design: Gary Schmitt

Executive Editor: I. L. Cooper

Production Manager: Joanne Cooper

Project Coordinator: Jan Edmondson

Copy Editor: Kathy Childers

Library of Congress Catalog Card number: 88-43249
ISBN: 0-697-15191-3

Printed in the United States of America by Brown & Benchmark, 2460 Kerper Boulevard, Dubuque, IA 52001.

10 9 8 7 6 5 4 3 2 1

YOUTH COACHING SERIES

The Youth Coaching Series of books were written to provide comprehensive guides for coaches, parents, and players participating in youth soccer, baseball, football, softball, and basketball.

Developed by the Youth Sports Institute of Michigan State University, these books meet the guidelines established for youth coaches by the National Association for Sport and Physical Education.

Books in the Series:

Youth Baseball
A Complete Handbook (ISBN: 14844)
Skills and Strategies (ISBN: 15196)
Rules of Play (ISBN: 15197)
Effective Coaching (ISBN: 15198)
Training and Conditioning (ISBN: 15199)

Youth Basketball
A Complete Handbook (ISBN: 15183)
Organizing for the Season (ISBN: 15185)
Rules of Play (ISBN: 15186)
Individual Basketball Techniques (ISBN: 15187)
Basic Strategies (ISBN: 15188)
Methods for Effective Coaching (ISBN: 15189)
Sports Medicine and Training (ISBN: 15190)

Youth Football
A Complete Handbook (ISBN: 15191)
Skills and Strategies (ISBN: 15192)
Effective Coaching (ISBN: 15193)
Conditioning and Training (ISBN: 15194)
Rules of Play (ISBN: 15195)

Youth Soccer
A Complete Handbook (ISBN: 14837)
Organizing for the Season (ISBN: 15201)
Methods for Effective Coaching (ISBN: 15202)
Rules of Play (ISBN: 15203)
Individual Techniques for Soccer Field Players (ISBN: 15204)
Individual Techniques for Soccer Goalkeepers (ISBN: 15205)
Basic Strategies of Soccer (ISBN: 15206)
Sports Medicine and Training (ISBN: 15207)

Youth Softball
A Complete Handbook (ISBN: 15200)
Skills and Strategies (ISBN: 16417)
Rules of Play (ISBN: 16418)
Effective Coaching (ISBN: 16420)
Conditioning and Training (ISBN: 16419)

Also available: Program for Athletic Coaches Education (PACE), a program specifically designed by the Youth Sports Institute for interscholastic coaches. (ISBN: 17262)

For more information or to order books in the Youth Coaching Series:
Call: 1-800-338-5578
Write: **Order Department**
        Brown & Benchmark
        2460 Kerper Blvd., P.O. Box 539
        Dubuque, IA 52001

For information on discounts for youth sports groups, contact:
Brown & Benchmark
701 Congressional Blvd., Suite 340
Carmel, IN 46032
(317) 573-6420

Contents

Introduction

Youth Football was written for the beginning level coach of youth ages 8 to 16. The book was designed for coaches who want to improve their teaching effectiveness. The guiding principle of the book was that teaching the skills of football as well as the concepts of offensive and defensive play are fundamental to the development and enjoyment of each participant.

The scope of *Youth Football* ranges from a description of the role of a football coach to guidelines for rehabilitation of football-related injuries. The book is divided into four sections to facilitate the location of information about specific topics. The chapters devoted to physical skills are written with ample illustrations to help the coach gain a clear understanding of the scientific concepts and the skills of football. A comprehensive set of drills for teaching the skills and strategies of football are included.

Youth coaches will find that this book provides many answers to the challenges faced in teaching football skill techniques. Chapters 1 through 6 pertain to the technical instruction of each skill. The remaining chapters address topics such as planning effective instruction, psychology of coaching youth, and working with parents. These topics are not typically found in coaching books. The 22 chapters contain information that meet the guidelines established for youth coaches as described in *Guidelines for Coaching Education: Youth Sports,* prepared by the National Association for Sport and Physical Education.

The authors of each chapter have had extensive experience coaching and teaching. This technical experience, combined with the scientific study of sport, becomes readily apparent by the practical suggestions that you will find in each chapter.

This book is written for the coach, but our ultimate goal is to provide youth with a positive and enjoyable experience in football. It is our hope that all youth will improve their skills, have fun playing and being part of a team, and have their self-esteem enhanced as a result of your coaching.

Jerry Cvengros
Associate Director
Michigan High School Athletic Association

Vern Seefeldt
Director
Institute for the Study of Youth Sports
Michigan State University

Acknowledgments

I wish to thank the following individuals for their assistance in the preparation of this book: Shelley Cvengros, mother of three sons who played football and wife of this former coach—her patience and understanding made 30 years of football a rewarding experience; Steve Cvengros, whose knowledge and understanding of the offensive game and the quarterback position contributed greatly to the content of the book; and Jim Hirn, long-time associate coach whose expertise in the kicking game is surpassed only by his ability to teach the many students who have come under his tutelage.

Randy Bass, of R.A. Bass Photography, Middleville, Michigan, provided the photographs of the action sequences and Eileen Northrup, editorial assistant, typed, edited, and proofread the original and revised versions of the manuscript. Marianne Oren, editorial assistant, generated the diagrams via computer and assisted with the typing of the narrative.

Special thanks to the young men listed below for their contribution during the photo session:

Youth

Luke Bailey	D.J. McClure
Chris Bergall	Michael Monty
Joe Braska	Nicholas Monty
Steve Bretz	Treavor Schmitz
A.J. Keresztes	James Schwartz
Jason Marinelli	Brian Ziel

High School

Andy Backus	Keith Siegmann
Tom Bupp	Bryan Willard
Conrad Keusch	Jerry Cvengros

Key to Symbols Used in Figures

___

Offense

E   = End
T   = Tackle
G   = Guard
C   = Center
QB = Quarterback
FB = Fullback
HB = Halfback
WB = Wingback
SE = Split end
TE = Tight end
FL = Flanker
TB = Tailback
LOS = Line of scrimmage

Ball carrier

or Optional ball carrier

Pulling guard

Center

Offensive player

Defense

N   = Nose guard
DB = Defensive back
LB = Linebacker
R   = Rover
S   = Safety
V   = Defensive player
C   = Cornerback
E   = End
T   = Tackle
H   = Halfback
B   = Back

Kicking

K   = Kicker
P   = Punter
R   = Receiver

Section I
Skills and Strategies

1
Organization of the Offense

Jerry Cvengros, M.S.

QUESTIONS TO CONSIDER

- How will you select a basic offensive scheme?
- How will you determine a balance between running and passing plays?
- What terminology will be used for communication?
- What action in the huddle and on the line of scrimmage will set the play into motion?

INTRODUCTION

One of the first things all coaches must do is to select the offensive philosophy they expect to teach and use in competition. With the exposure of football through television, there is a temptation to be heavily influenced by coaches on the college and professional levels.

In order for youth football coaches to teach offensive football successfully, it is necessary to first understand that football is a fundamental game consisting of blocking, tackling, and ball skill. Practice emphasis should be in teaching these skills well. Football is fun for youngsters because it is a collision sport, and making contact with an opponent or defending himself on the field is necessary.

As a coach, it is necessary for you to teach these skills properly and to place each player in a position relative to size, speed, and ability. Players should be introduced to and taught the basic skills of both offensive and defensive football. Although two-platoon football is the norm professionally, collegiately , and in many high schools, it is advisable in youth leagues that

young players be taught the fundamentals of both offense and defense. There will be plenty of time to specialize as they progress up the football ladder (see Figure 1-1).

Young coaches often fall into the trap of teaching too much offense. Although there is much to learn for players, the game is basically recognition and reaction. When players have to think too much, they tend to hesitate and react slowly. Offenses for youth football should be basic so that players can learn their assignments quickly and thoroughly.

FORMATIONS

The decisions you must make concerning what offense to use revolve around the following:

1. Will you use two tight ends or a split end formation?
2. Will you use a traditional three-running-back offense or two backs plus a wingback or flanker?
3. Will you stack your backs in the I formation

Figure 1-1. Limited squad size results in two-way players.

or split them as in the traditional pro formation?

There are many other options, of course, but we illustrate the basic formations adaptable to youth football.

Formations are by colors, with an accompanying designation when necessary (see Figures 1-2 through 1-5).

WHITE: balanced formation, three running backs or split backs

ORANGE: wing right formation, or flanker right

BLACK: wing left formation, or flanker left

Whenever a split end is necessary to the formation, simply add the word "split" to the color.

BASIC RUNNING PLAYS DIAGRAMED

Selecting plays to be run can be an imaginative procedure, but there must be a basic plan which includes continuity of attack and philosophy. You must always take into consideration the abilities of your players. For purposes of illustration, we have selected 2 basic formations and diagramed those plays usually incorporated in the offense (see Figures 1-6 through 1-15).

THE PASSING OFFENSE

The pass offense should be incorporated using the same basic offensive formations or sets that are used with the running plays. As coach, you should be aware of the routes run by receivers and the methods of delivery by the quarterback.

In general, passing can be categorized into dropback passes, sprintout (rollout) passes, or play action passes.

Dropback Passes

Dropback passing indicates that the quarterback will move directly behind the center. Depending on the route of the receivers, the drop will be either three, five, or seven steps behind the center. At each interval the passer will set up and deliver the ball to the receiver. The actual mechanics of delivery are discussed in Chapter 3 (see Figure 1-16).

Balanced line and backfield formation (white)

LE	LT	LG	C	RG	RT	RE
O	O	O	⊕	O	O	O
				1'	2'	3'
			O			
			QB			
	O		O		O	
	LH		FB		RH	

Figure 1-2. White formation.

(a) Wingback right formation (orange)

O O O ⊕ O O O
        O
O   O   O
             WB

(b) Wingback left formation (black)

O O O ⊕ O O O
              O
O   O
WB

Figure 1-3. Formations.

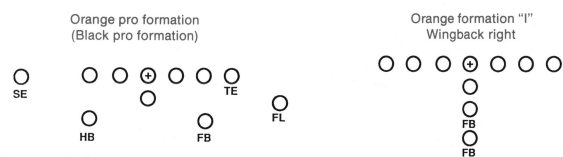

Orange pro formation
(Black pro formation)

SE   HB   FB   TE   FL

Figure 1-4. Pro formations.

Orange formation "I"
Wingback right

FB   FB   WB

Figure 1-5. Orange formation I wingback right.

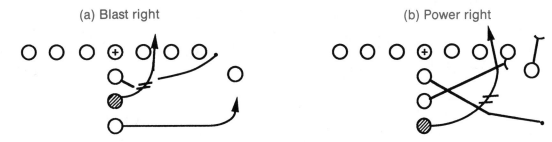

(a) Blast right

(b) Power right

Figure 1-6. Blast right, power right.

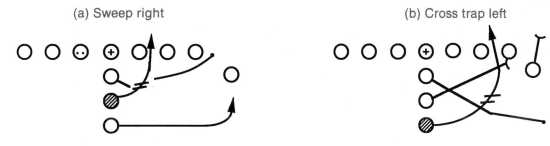

(a) Sweep right

(b) Cross trap left

Figure 1-7. Sweep right, cross trap left.

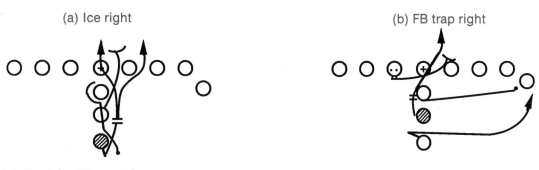

(a) Ice right

(b) FB trap right

Figure 1-8. Ice right, FB trap right.

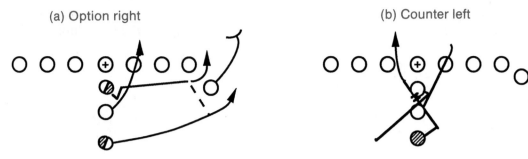

Figure 1-9. Option right, counter left.

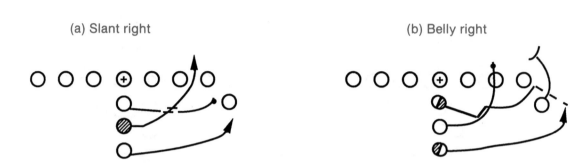

Figure 1-10. Slant right, belly right.

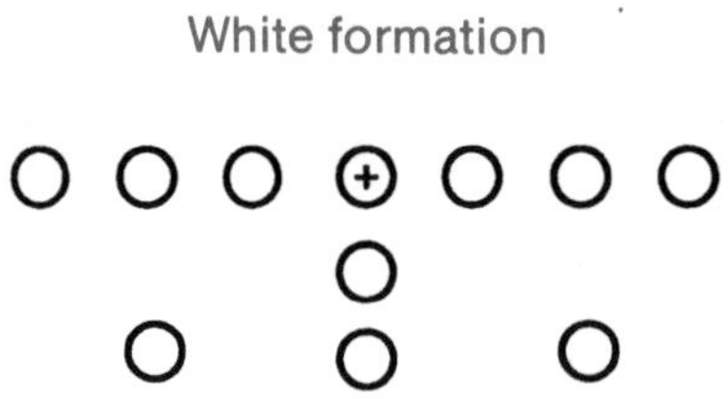

White formation

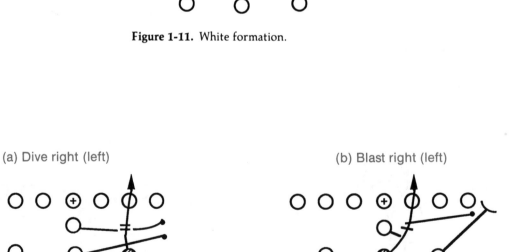

Figure 1-11. White formation.

Figure 1-12. Dive right (left), blast right (left).

(a) Sweep right (left)

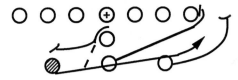

(b) Option right (left)

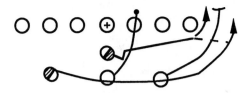

Figure 1-13. Sweep right (left), option right (left).

(a) Power right (left)

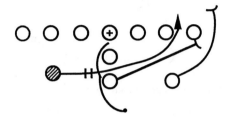

(b) Ice right (left)

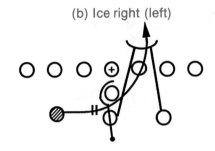

Figure 1-14. Power right (left), ice right (left).

(a) FB trap right (left)

(b) Cross trap left (right)

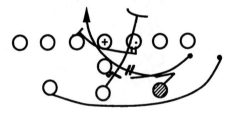

Figure 1-15. FB trap right (left), cross trap left (right).

Sprintout or Rollout Passes

Sprintout or rollout passing indicates a movement by the quarterback away from the center to an area 5-7 yds. behind the offensive tackle (see Figure 1-17).

Play Action Passes

Play action passes incorporate the movement of the backs as in a running play, except that after faking the ball, the quarterback passes to a receiver downfield (see Figures 1-18 through 1-21).

NUMBERING SYSTEM AND OFFENSIVE TERMINOLOGY

There are any number of systems to designate who will carry the ball and the location of where the ball carrier will intersect the line of scrimmage. Whether you use numbers to differentiate the ball carriers and the location or whether word terminology is used depends on what you prefer and how easily you can teach the system. It is necessary for all offensive players, when they break from the huddle, to know instantly their assignments for that

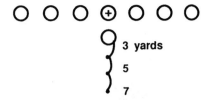

Figure 1-16. Dropback pass.

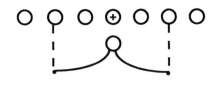

Figure 1-17. Sprintout pass.

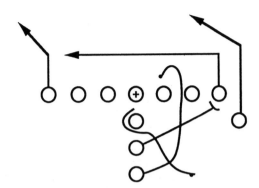

Figure 1-18. Orange power right pass.

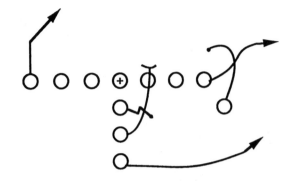

Figure 1-19. Orange option right pass.

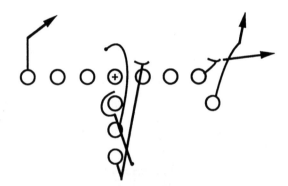

Figure 1-20. Orange ice right pass.

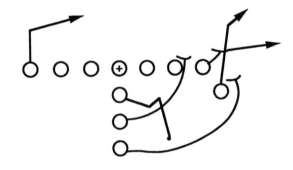

Figure 1-21. Orange belly right pass.

particular play. A confused player cannot react quickly.

Typical System Using Numbers

Numbering holes and running backs is one of the oldest and most widely used systems in existence. Numbering can take many forms, including "odds" and "evens" on either side of the center, or the chronological approach can be used, as illustrated in Figure 1-22.

Holes are numbered directly over the offensive linemen—both to the right or left. "One" and "nine" represent sweep action to the outside of the ends.

A typical huddle call by the quarterback in this formation is "21 sweep." Player action will get the ball to the left halfback who is taught the movement of a sweep right. All players will have appropriate blocking or faking assignments on each play.

Typical System Using Word Terminology

Some coaches have discovered that the numbering system has limitations that makes it difficult for offensive players to learn plays. It is felt that by designating a certain area or hole, a back limited himself to one direction or area and did not take advantage of what the defense might give him through their aggressive pursuit. Backs seldom "ran to daylight" and most times ran to the designated area even if there was no running room. Some have chosen to abandon numbers as our nomenclature, particularly in the running offense, and instead, have adopted a word-only offensive terminology. Players seem to grasp the meaning of descriptive words better than the limitations of a numbering system.

Direction Terminology

Replace numbers to designate holes and direction, and use "right" and "left" to designate direction for the entire team. The ball carrier will wind up either right or left of center initially as his point of attack.

Ball Carrier Designation and Handoff Points

All plays carry a name rather than a number to designate the ball carrier. Names in an offensive scheme might include:

1. Tailback plays: power, sweep, pitch, ice, counter
2. Fullback plays: blast, slant, trap
3. Others: option, reverse

By using this system, ball carriers know immediately who the carrier is by the name of the play. They are taught the proper footwork and handoff techniques that are necessary to get them to the line of scrimmage. Backs and linemen understand the play by virtue of its name and the direction called in the huddle, so there is less chance of forgetting or not hearing the number called.

Backs seem to understand the principle of running to daylight when direction is established as right or left rather than by a single digit number. They realize that their responsibility is to establish direction, square their shoulders with the goal line (line of scrimmage), and find

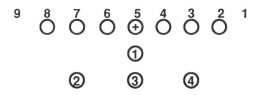

Figure 1-22. Numbering scheme.

the room created by the blocks of their teammates. Backs should not run blindly at a hole designation when there is no running room at that point; rather, all players should understand that running room can be created anywhere along the line of scrimmage. The system determines the ball carrier, direction, and initial blocking assignments. Technique, talent, and alertness determine the success of the play after that.

THE HUDDLE

There are many ways to form a huddle, but they all fall into two categories: the *closed huddle* and the *open huddle*. An example of each is shown in Figures 1-23 and 1-24.

In the closed huddle, everyone lines up with hands on knees, heads up, and eyes focused on the lips of the quarterback.

In the open huddle, linemen stand with hands on knees and heads up. Backs and ends stand with hands at their sides.

The center is responsible for forming the huddle by determining its proper relationship to the line of scrimmage. He should get to a spot exactly 5 or 7 yds. from and directly behind the ball placement. The distance from the ball is the coach's preference. The center should huddle so that all other players can form on his placement. It is necessary for him to establish the huddle position immediately after the ball is placed in position by the official.

It is absolutely necessary to maintain discipline and silence in the huddle so that everyone can hear the play called and any other special instructions that may be given.

The quarterback normally calls the play in the huddle. He does so twice, facing all players so that they can see his lips form the words. He also calls the starting signal twice so that there is no mistake about the starting count.

Generally, the center and wide receivers will leave the huddle after the first call so that they can get to their positions and establish their stances earlier than the other players. The rest of the team will break the huddle and go to their positions after the quarterback calls "Break" and all clap their hands and shout "Go" in unison.

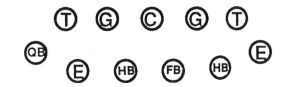

Figure 1-23. Closed huddle.

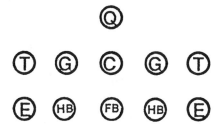

Figure 1-24. Open huddle.

The quarterback will be the last player to position himself before the snap. He normally approaches the center looking over the defense as he places his hands in receiving position under the center's buttocks. Football rules demand that all players, including the quarterback, be set for 1 full second before the snap.

PROCEDURE ON THE LINE OF SCRIMMAGE

The Stance

Some coaches prefer their linemen in two-point stances (standing) having them drop to three-point stances on a predetermined quarterback signal such as "set." It is preferable, however, that you have your linemen come directly to the line of scrimmage and into their three-point stances immediately from the huddle. This enables them to be in their best ready-for-attack position by the time the quarterback reaches the line. It also enables maximum blocking leverage for teams that start on the first sound uttered.

The Signal System

The signal system includes the words or numbers that are called or spoken on the line of scrimmage by the quarterback. Signals initiate the snap from center and all subsequent action.

Do not deal with audibles or automatics on the line of scrimmage. While these sophisticated signals change the huddle-called play at the line of scrimmage, they more often confuse the offensive team rather than produce a successful play.

Some coaches feel that a preset call by the quarterback is necessary to get the attention of all players. Calls like "Set" or "Ready" are very commonplace. Obviously, the ball can also be snapped on either of these commands as well as on a number or another sound.

"Hut" has been a prevalent guttural sound used as a snap count since football began. Some coaches used it for years before changing to "Hit" as a more descriptive word. Often teams move on the first sound uttered by the quarterback when he becomes positioned under center and all players are in a set position.

Typical Signals

Typical play and starting count calls from the huddle to the snap are:

Formation: "Orange"
Play: "Power"
Direction: "Right"
Count: "On two" (the second "Hit")

2
Offensive Line Play

Jerry Cvengros, M.S.

QUESTIONS TO CONSIDER

- What are the characteristics of the basic stances for linemen?
- How do line blocking techniques differ from one another?
- How have rule changes affected blocking techniques?
- What basic drills are useful in teaching the fundamentals of offensive line play?

INTRODUCTION

Once you have established your offensive running and passing plays, terminology, and procedures, it will be necessary for you and your associate coaches to teach the skills and techniques unique to each of the various positions.

In this chapter we describe the characteristics of each of the offensive line positions, along with their basic responsibilities.

We enumerate, step by step, the various types of blocks that you should teach to young football players.

In addition, various drills are presented to aid in your preparation for practices and games.

OFFENSIVE LINE POSITION PLAY

Center

As a coach, you can never overemphasize to the center that his primary assignment is to get the ball to the quarterback without fumbling.

He must count mentally with the quarterback so that the ball reaches the quarterback's hands before the quarterback pulls them from the center's crotch.

The center should be positioned as follows:

- Stance should be balanced with feet parallel and squared away (see Figure 2-1).

    1. Knees are spread as wide as the feet.
    2. Hips are high so that the back is parallel to the ground.
    3. Both arms should extend to the ball, which is positioned laces up and slightly forward of the center's head.

- The right hand should grasp the ball near the front, tilting it slightly upward. The left hand should grasp the rear of the ball and assume most of the center's weight (see Figure 2-2).
- Sweep the ball along the ground forcefully, making an effort to turn the ball so that it slaps into the quarterback's hands parallel to the line of scrimmage with the laces across the quarterback's right fingertips.
- Hold the ball until it is firmly in the quarterback's hands.

Figure 2-1. Center's stance should be balanced with feet parallel and squared away.

Figure 2-2. Grasp the ball with both hands tilting it upward.

- Drive off both feet simultaneously with the snap—all in one movement.
- Bring both hands and arms up into the blocking position as soon as possible after the snap.

Offensive Guards

The offensive guards should be positioned as follows:

- Because they will be expected to pull down and away from the line of scrimmage as well as fire straight ahead, they should place less

weight forward than other interior linemen when they are in their stances.

1. Feet should be in a heel–toe relationship, with the buttocks and back parallel to the line of scrimmage.
2. The fingers of the hand on the ground should be spread open with a minimum of weight on them (see Figure 2-3).

Guards must have speed to run and block on traps and sweeps and quickness to chase linebackers. In addition, they must have the necessary strength to meet defensive linemen that are taller and heavier.

Offensive Tackles

Offensive tackles should be positioned as follows:

- Stance:

1. Feet should be armpit-width apart in a heel–toe stagger with the knees spread and weight on the balls of the feet.
2. Buttocks should be slightly higher than the shoulders. The hand in front of the leg down on the ground should have the fingers open and extended.
3. Weight is pressured slightly forward. The opposite hand rests on the thigh of the leg, with the forearm parallel to the ground.
4. Head should always be up in a bull-like position (see Figure 2-4).

- They should align themselves by looking inside to the center rather than at the guards.

Figure 2-3. Fingers should be spread open with a minimum of weight pressured on them.

This will prevent the bowed-line and keep them on the line of scrimmage.

Tackles normally are the largest players on the team and must be prepared to block the largest defensive players. They will execute the drive, double team, and pass protection blocks as the occasion demands (see Figure 2-5).

BLOCKING TECHNIQUES

Each offensive lineman must be able to handle the defensive player assigned to him in the blocking scheme. Players must understand technique and develop speed and quickness in order to block effectively. In recent years rules have liberalized the use of hands by offensive blockers to the extent that today's players are able to use hands and arms to control defensive players, provided the technique is legal. There are two basic techniques that are allowable when using the hands and arms (see Figure 2-6).

The closed hand or cupped hand technique dictates that the hands must be closed or cupped with the palms not facing the opponent. The elbows may be inside or outside the shoulders, but the forearms may not be extended more than 45 degrees from the body. If the forearms are extended more than this, the hands must be cupped with the palms facing the opponent.

The open hand technique mandates that the hands shall always be in advance of the elbows. The arms must always be within the frame of the blocker's body in the front of the body, at or below the shoulders. When making hand contact with the opponent, the hands and arms must be within the frame of the defensive player's body at the shoulders or below, in front of the body. The hands must be open when the palms are facing the frame of the opponent or when the forearms are extended beyond the 45-degree angle from the body (see Figure 2-7).

High school rules do not allow blockers to swing, throw, or flip the elbow or forearm so that it is moving faster than the blocker's shoulders at the time the elbow, forearm, or shoulder contacts the opponent. The blocker may not initiate contact with his arm or hand above the opponent's shoulder, but he may use his hand or arm to break a fall or maintain his balance.

With the advent of superior protective equip-

Figure 2-4. Buttocks is slightly higher than the shoulders with weight slightly forward.

Figure 2-5. Basic end, tackle, and guard alignment on the line of scrimmage.

Figure 2-6. Today's players may use hands and arms in blocking.

Figure 2-7. The blocker's hands and arms must be within the frame of the defensive player's body at the shoulders or below.

Figure 2-8. Butt or face blocking is a dangerous technique involving a blow with the face mask.

Figure 2-9. Illegal contact can result in disqualification.

ment, it was inevitable that players would begin to take advantage of the rules and use the equipment to their advantage. The helmet, with its advanced styling and secure face protector, has been used as a weapon in both offensive and defensive football. Unfortunately, when used in this manner it can cause injury (see Figures 2-8 and 2-9).

Butt or face blocking is a dangerous technique where the face mask, frontal area, or top of the helmet is driven directly into an opponent and is the primary point of contact either in close line play or in the open field. Use of the helmet in this manner is illegal contact and can result in disqualification of the player. When teaching technique to young players on offense or defense, coaches must stress playing by the rules. Maintaining the safety and welfare of the young player is of primary concern. Equipment is designed to protect the wearer. It is not to be used as a weapon for striking a blow at the opponent.

The Drive Block

The fundamentals of driving the offensive player's body into the defender to either knock him down or make him retreat and circle around the blocker are the same, whether you choose to teach the cupped hand, open hand, or shoulder block.

Starting with the basic head up, heel–toe stance, the offensive player must aim his charge at the chin area of the defender. He should hit off his front foot, bringing the back foot forward and continuing with short chopping steps. His head should remain up in a "bulled" position, working to a position either to the right or left of the opponent in a shoulder block, or within the frame of the opponent if the hand–arm technique is taught (see Figure 2-10).

The first contact must be made with enough of a jolt to stop the defender's forward movement and gain ground from the line of scrimmage. That charge must be made at great speed with a body lift and follow-through. If the block-er slips off the defensive player, he must scramble on the ground, maintaining whatever contact he can to impede the defensive player's path to the ball carrier.

At times, because of the way defensive linemen are positioned, the offensive lineman must extend his body and cut off penetration into the backfield. It will be necessary for him to step first with the foot nearest the direction he's headed, stepping in that direction and making contact with either the reverse shoulder or the open hands in a pushing motion. The effort again is to prevent penetration by filling a gap in the line.

Blocking Downfield

Most levels of football presently have rules limiting blocking below the waist in the open field. Blocking below the waist on the line of scrimmage within the 6-ft. x 8-ft. free-blocking zone is allowed, but in youth football, all other blocking contact must occur initially above the waist. If the initial contact continues downward below the waist, it is allowed. If contact is initiated legally within the frame of a defender who then turns his body, there is no penalty for clipping if the initial contact is maintained.

The downfield block is the same regardless of whether it is executed by a lineman or a back and the object is the same as close-contact interior blocking. The effort is to screen, shield, or block the defender so that he cannot reach the ball carrier. The difficulty results because the defender becomes more elusive in the open field. It is important that the blocker has control of his own body and is able to change direction instantly. He should be taught to keep his feet apart for balance and get as close as possible to the defender before extending his hands and arms legally.

Pass Blocking

Play action pass blocking is designed to simulate a running play and keep the defenders from a hard pass rush. Linemen must be taught to fire out at the defensive linemen the same as they would in the running play. The objective is to jolt the defensive linemen into an upright stance and push off.

Figure 2-10. The head should work to a position to the right or left of the opponent in a shoulder block.

From that point, the blocker must maintain good balance within his stance with flexed knees, extended arms, and head up. The effort then is to keep the defender as far from the offensive lineman's body as possible without actually holding the defender's jersey. The blocker should retreat if necessary, remain tough, and move laterally to maintain relationship with the defender. Teach the body block as a last resort technique to be used only if the blocker is within the legal zone.

Dropback pass blocking is very similar to play action pass blocking except for the initial move. There is no pretense to disguise the play because opponents are expected to recognize a pass instantly. The offensive lineman must set up at the snap in a position to receive contact from the charging defensive player. Contact is met with extended arms, maintaining as wide a gap as possible between the two bodies.

Pulling and Trapping

The principle of pulling and trapping is predicated on the blocker's ability to pivot and run at the same time. Speed is an absolute necessity to get to the defensive player as soon as possible.

Here are some coaching points:

1. Use a short, deliberate pulling step in the pivot (see Figure 2-11).

Figure 2-11. Use a short, deliberate pulling step in the pivot.

2. Work for an inside angle on the defender.
3. Stay low and explode at impact.
4. Keep the head up, back straight, and shoulders level.
5. Make contact with the inside shoulder (right shoulder when going right, left when going left).
6. Drive the defender at least one step.
7. Turn the defender to cut off his pursuit toward your goal line.

Pulling to get in front of the ball carrier on a sweep play to the outside will necessitate a change in the puller's technique. After the initial pivot, the puller will attain a greater depth into the offensive backfield before dropping his inside shoulder and turning upfield.

Double Team Blocking

The double team or two-on-one block indicates a willingness of the offensive team to sacrifice two players to block a defensive player at the point of attack. It is often accompanied with a trap block by a pulling guard.

The post blocker is the offensive player lined up directly across from the defensive player to be blocked. It is his responsibility to make initial contact, stop penetration, and straighten the player upright as much as possible until the drive blocker makes contact.

The drive blocker must close the gap as soon as possible and anticipate a shoulder block. He must drive the defender off the line at a 45-degree angle to the inside toward the center. The first step must be with the foot nearest the defender. The far leg will be used primarily for leverage. The drive blocker must also be prepared to make the first or primary contact if the defender's charge is slanted or directed in his way.

OFFENSIVE LINE DRILLS

All football drills should have a specific purpose. Drills are fashioned to the individual, the group, or the entire team. Drills are designed to increase speed and agility, condition players, teach them how to adjust to contact, and simulate game conditions. Players must learn to control their bodies and discipline themselves to play within the framework of the entire team.

Manufacturers have designed equipment to aid in drills and the teaching of football skills, but most youth coaches and teams don't have access to such coaching aids because they tend to be expensive. If your budget allows, purchase standing cones or pylons for use as markers. Upright blocking dummies are also helpful (see Figure 2-12).

In this section, drills that necessitate a minimum of equipment but that are necessary to improve players' skills are described.

Speed and Agility Drills

Small groups spaced 5 yds. apart face the coach (see Figure 2-13):

- Emphasize forward and backward running with:
  a. proper form—use the crossover step
  b. changing direction—speed is not important in this drill
- Check each player's stance individually and have one or all take off on coach's command.
- Place cones every 5 yds. for 40 yds. Line players up in a single line, and have them weave in and out of the cones, continuing upfield for 40 yards.
- The entire group facing the coach from a three- or four-point stance takes off low and breaks into a forward roll after 3 yds., and comes to their feet in a football position ready to move in any direction.

Contact Drills

To teach the proper techniques of blocking (see Figure 2-14):

- Players line up to practice blocking on dummies held by other players.
- Without dummies, players line up one-on-one with defensive linemen, make active contact on the initial hit, then passively allow the offensive blocker to perfect his technique.
- Coach must critique each player, both on the dummy and the live work—players must always react to coach's command.
- After several repetitions, the entire group can take off in unison on the coach's signal to simulate team takeoff.
- Both the drive block and pass protection block as well as the double team block can be practiced in this drill.
- Coaching points of the drill include:

  1. stress initial fire-out with proper arm and hand contact and leg position
  2. keep head up with rapid movement of feet
  3. keep feet at armpit width and follow through with proper lift
  4. maintain contact until whistle ends drill

- Double team and trap blocking practice can be achieved with two blockers and one dummy.

Figure 2-12. Upright dummies are extremely helpful in teaching blocking techniques.

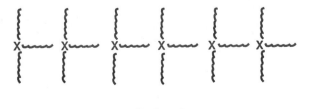

O Coach

Figure 2-13. Speed and agility drills.

O Coach

Figure 2-14. Blocking drills.

- Players should rotate positions so all can get equal work.

    To improve balance, use the contact reaction drill (see Figure 2-15).

- It can be performed individually or as a group.
- Offensive players start from a stance, advance to do a forward roll, and return to a proper ready position.
- Defensive players attempt to push the offensive players off balance.
- Several variations include running backward and changing direction.

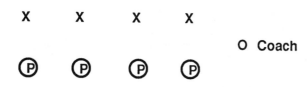

Figure 2-15. Reaction drill.

Team Drills

    To simulate a scrimmage play, use the team takeoff drill (see Figure 2-16):

- Quarterback calls the play in the huddle; the team will break huddle and run to the ball as in a game situation; signals are called at the line of scrimmage and the ball snapped.
- Coaches should check stances and spacing of all positions.
- The goal is for execution by the backs and takeoff in unison by the linemen.
- The entire team should sprint 40 yds. to the goal line.

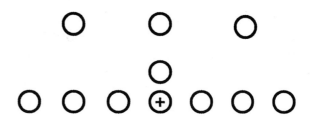

Figure 2-16. Team takeoff drill.

- Variations of the drill include adding seven defensive players holding dummies or shields 5 yds. in front of the offensive linemen. Contact should be made with the dummies in unison with the linemen; players then continue to the goal line.

    For full team playwork:

- Use 11 on 11—offense versus defense.
- Defense is placed in basic alignment (interior linemen hold dummies if possible).
- After reviewing assignments, the entire team breaks huddle and responds to quarterback's commands.
- Defense reacts to ball movement, and makes contact but allows the offense to perfect techniques and run the play successfully.
- Position coaches should monitor their area players, emphasizing proper assignments, speed, technique, and follow-through.
- Players should sprint to the goal line, emphasizing scoring on every play.
- This drill uses a half-line alignment if there aren't enough players for two full teams.
- One variation eliminates defensive backs from the drill.

3
Offensive Backfield Play

Jerry Cvengros, M.S.

QUESTIONS TO CONSIDER

- What skills must the quarterback master?
- Why is the center–quarterback exchange so important?
- What basic passing routes must be learned by the wide receivers?
- What special qualities and skills must running backs possess?

INTRODUCTION

In this chapter, the offensive backfield play is broken down into three distinct positions: the quarterback, wide receiver, and running back.

The primary responsibilities of each position, techniques and maneuvers of each player, and drills necessary for the development of each is given.

THE QUARTERBACK

Every coach should address these questions:

- Does your quarterback's stance ensure safe snaps and ease of transition to ball handling and passing positions?
- How do you teach the young quarterback to hand off, toss, pitch, and fake effectively?
- What drills can you use to increase arm strength, accuracy, and confidence in your passer?

The Center–Quarterback Exchange (The Snap)

Because all plays begin with a snap from center, the importance of the basics cannot be overemphasized. No football team can run a basic dive or a sophisticated pass play if the quarterback can't get the snap properly. The following paragraphs describe the techniques for a right-handed quarterback. For left-handers, just reverse the directions.

Encourage your quarterback to work hard at proper hand position. Have the quarterback place his right hand under the center with the palm facing down and the back of the hand firmly against the center's buttocks with the fingers spread. The depth of the hand will depend on the size of the quarterback and the center.

After getting the right hand comfortably under the center, place the left hand underneath it to form a V beginning at the wrists. The most important part of this hand mesh is the placement of the thumbs. Slide the left hand back just enough to allow the first thumb knuckle to fit into the natural groove of the right thumb (see Figure 3-1). Properly done, and with some pressure, the hands are now secured from the thumbs through the wrists. As with the right fingers, extend the left fingers. Do not, however, allow the quarterback to flex his fingers as he calls the signals. This can be a tipoff to the defense and can also cause injury on a premature snap from the center.

The quarterback's stance begins at ground level. His feet should be at a comfortable shoulder width apart and behind the feet of the center to avoid tangling his feet with the center's. The quarterback's weight should be on the balls of his feet with his right foot slightly back, to perhaps the instep of the left foot. His knees should be bent at about 1 o'clock (see Figures 3-2 and 3-3).

The quarterback should flex his knees to a comfortable level. He should be as tall as the center allows. With his arms slightly bent, his head up, and eyes straight ahead, he is now ready for the snap. The quarterback should remain relaxed, confident, and ready to react—he should not rush the snap!

Reviewing the following checklist helps the quarterback determine if he is ready to receive the snap:

1. hands
2. feet
3. knees
4. arms
5. hips
6. head
7. attitude

Figure 3-2. The quarterback's stance begins at ground level.

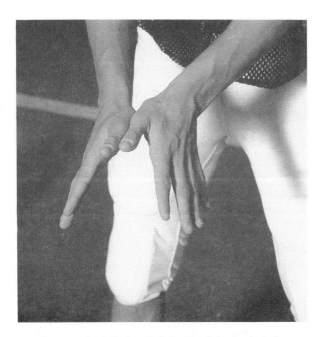

Figure 3-1. The left thumb knuckle slides back to fit into the natural groove of the right thumb.

Figure 3-3. The knees should be bent without strain in the joints.

As the quarterback receives the snap, he should adjust his fingers and with both hands give a little and follow the center as the center charges forward. The quarterback should also at this time begin his footwork and bring the ball into his stomach. Working from the belt buckle, his elbows are close to his sides and his eyes up. He is now ready to hand off, fake, or position himself for passing.

Spend time each day practicing the center snap. Because of its importance, quarterbacks and centers should report 15 minutes early and practice the snap. This extra work will emphasize the fundamentals as well as the work ethic that is necessary for a quarterback to be successful (see Figure 3-4).

Ball Handling

In handing off the ball, the direction, number, and length of steps the quarterback takes vary from play to play. When running from the I formation, the quarterback should step back as deep as possible, and reach and place the ball in the running back's stomach; the deeper the better, as this allows the running back to see the play develop and cut early.

From a full-house backfield or from a split back formation, a premium is placed on angles and often the quarterback will position himself with his back to the line of scrimmage, holding the ball in tight and keeping it hidden as the backs cross and fakes are made.

The fundamentals of the handoff from any set and on any play begin when the ball is received from the center. Teach your quarterback to keep the ball at his stomach and at the proper time reach directly to the ball carrier. Don't allow him to raise the ball in the air. Not only does this cause fumbles, but it shows the defense where the ball is going.

Constantly remind the quarterback to use his eyes to *look* the ball into the runner's stomach. Emphasize seeing the "spot" and placing the ball into the stomach, not slapping it. The quarterback's eyes will help control his steps and because the runner is looking for running room and an area to which he can run, the quarterback must not let the runner look for the ball or feel for the handoff. It is the quarterback's eyes that control the handoff. The runner should not have to worry about receiving the ball if he is in the correct position (see Figure 3-5).

Finally, as the quarterback reaches with both hands, he should release the hand that is closest to the point of contact with the ball carrier's stomach. The other hand (the control

Figure 3-4. Front view of the quarterback and center prior to the snap.

Figure 3-5. The quarterback must not let the runner look for the ball or feel for the handoff.

hand) is released as the runner's arms begin to take control.

Most fumbles that occur at the handoff are the quarterback's fault—the result of poor placement or poor hand–eye coordination. Work diligently with the quarterback to master the handoff and teach him to take pride in this basic skill.

Often from the I formation the quarterback will need to pitch or toss the ball to the tailback. Here, as with the handoff, it is the quarterback's responsibility to give the ball carrier an opportunity to concentrate on the run, not on the ball. Normally he will reverse pivot to the side of the pitch (see Figure 3-6). Once again, the ball moves with the quarterback's directional foot (pitch to the left, step with the left foot) starting from the stomach, to get the proper leverage on the pitch. Traditionally, coaches have taught quarterbacks to use either a spiral pitch or an end-over-end toss. Both of these techniques have drawbacks, however.

With the spiral pitch, quarterbacks tend to fire the ball at the runner, making the catch difficult and dangerous. The ball can easily skip through the runner's hands and cause a significant loss of yardage. The end-over-end toss is more preferable but an overemphasis on revolutions can cause a flip that can easily bounce off a shoulder pad or an extended hand.

Rather than teaching either of those two approaches, teach a dead pitch that doesn't spin

Figure 3-6. The quarterback reverse pivots to the side of the pitch.

or flip but turns over perhaps three to four times in its flight. This should allow for a soft catch and on poor pitches won't bounce wildly or fly beyond the ball carrier's reach.

Finally, to teach a quarterback to become a good ball handler, you should work on faking. Employ these three basic fakes:

1. body position
2. hand fake
3. ball fake

The body position fake is a subtle fake that occurs when the quarterback passes by one of the backs enroute to a handoff. For instance, from a split back offensive set, as the quarterback pivots and the left halfback crosses over to the right, the appearance of a handoff is given. The quarterback then is able to handoff to the right halfback, who is cutting to the left side. An opposing linebacker can be misled because the quarterback keeps the ball in his stomach as the left halfback passes by and the defender must quickly decide if he is to pursue the first motion or the second.

This same play can be used to illustrate the hand fake and ball fake. In the hand fake, as the quarterback pivots on the left foot and opens up to the right, he extends his left hand into the belly of the left halfback and quickly hands the ball to the right halfback with the right hand as the ball carrier passes to the left of the formation. The ball fake can be used in a similar manner. The difference is that in the ball fake both hands are kept on the ball until it is handed off.

In all cases, the effectiveness of the play is a direct result of the appearance of a handoff. Once again, you need to emphasize the eyes. The quarterback's eyes should be on the stomach of the ball carrier to whom the ball is faked and then to the stomach of the true ball carrier. A good faking quarterback can be devastating to the defense. All three types of fakes should be taught and used.

Here is a ball handling checklist your quarterback can use:

1. the handoff
2. the pitch
3. the fake
4. eyes, eyes, eyes

Passing

Quarterbacks come in all sizes and shapes and all have their own preferences when it comes to throwing the football. Teach the proper concepts but don't overcoach. Be consistent and strive for your quarterback to always throw the same way. If he is a successful passer but has a little different style than is explained here, don't worry. If he delivers the ball successfully, leave him alone. Just instruct him to throw the same way all the time.

Coaching the passer involves four major points:

1. the grip
2. the set above the shoulders
3. the follow-through
4. the footwork

The Grip

Individual grips vary from one quarterback to another, but all hold the ball with their fingertips. As the quarterback takes the snap from center, he must adjust his initial grip to the throwing grip. He can do all of his ball handling from a grip that has the two middle fingers on the end of the laces and the little finger extended back for ball control (see Figure 3-7).

Figure 3-7. Strive for a comfortable grip with fingertip control.

His index finger should be extended beyond the striping. The extension of this finger will depend upon the size of his hand. Some quarterbacks extend the index finger to the tip of the ball. In all cases, however, check the quarterback's hand to make sure that there is air between the palm and the ball. This is critical and ensures fingertip control.

The Set

The carry of the ball begins from the stomach and ends with a cradle at shoulder level as the quarterback drops back into the throwing position (see Figure 3-8). Once the quarterback's arms are at shoulder level, have him keep them there. Do not let him drop his hands or arms as he begins his throwing motion.

As the quarterback begins his motion, *two points* are worth mentioning in the set of the ball. *First,* he should raise his arms and cock the ball behind the right ear with his elbows in tight. *Second,* he must now look for his receiver. This is done with his lead (left) shoulder. Think of this lead shoulder as the sight of a rifle. It

Figure 3-8. The quarterback should cradle the ball at shoulder level.

must be pointing at the target. The quarterback should now be set to deliver the ball.

The Delivery

With the ball set and the target sighted, the quarterback is now ready to deliver the ball. The delivery begins with the weight shifted to the right foot and a separation of the left hand from the ball (see Figure 3-9). The left hand should take care of itself. Don't allow the quarterback to aggressively swing his left arm. This will cause a loss of balance in the throwing motion.

With the right wrist firmly locked, allow the right elbow to lead the way. Emphasize a high elbow, one that gets to ear height. The shoulder will follow the elbow into the proper rotation. As the ball leaves the hand, the index finger will be the last finger to lose contact with the ball.

The index finger and the forward motion are the keys to throwing a spiral (see Figure 3-10). As the index finger releases, have the quarterback work on turning the hand and thumb down. The follow-through will then proceed naturally as the right heel comes up from the ground and the right arm swings freely to the inside of the right leg.

The Footwork

As the quarterback gets to the set position, after the dropback, footwork becomes critical. Some coaches teach a five-step drop with three actual steps taken. Steps 4 and 5 come from two "gathering" hops that are taken to get the feet about 6 in. from each other and to transfer the weight to the back foot.

From this position, the quarterback turns his hips to the target (with the shoulders), keeps the knees slightly bent (not stiff), and steps to the target. Do not teach a big stride. The ball should be thrown with the hip and shoulder rotation as well as the arm. A large stride tends to make the ball sail away. Theoretically, the left foot should not even have to step forward; the hips and weight transfer should be suffi-

Figure 3-9. Weight shifts when the left hand separates from the ball.

Figure 3-10. As the index finger releases, the hand and thumb turn down.

cient to provide enough momentum to complete the throw.

Drills

Delivery Drill

Objectives:
1. to concentrate on the delivery
2. to increase arm strength

Procedure:

Take two or more quarterbacks and place them about 10 yds. apart. Have them each kneel on one knee (the knee on the side of the throwing arm) and play catch. Because they are on their knees, you can concentrate on the throwing motion described earlier. Emphasize the starting position, release, and follow-through.

Variations:

Have the passers stand with their feet together and work on the shoulder rotation as they throw (no step is taken here). Later, have the passers put the wrong foot forward and throw. Then have the passers take a normal step (short) and step properly to the target. As you finish the drill, have the passers increase the distance between themselves as they strive to keep the same footwork.

Goalpost Drill

Objectives:
1. to reinforce proper elbow height
2. to attain the proper arch for distance throwing

Procedure:

Line up two quarterbacks 10 yds. away from each side of the goalposts. Have them throw the ball as close to the crossbar as possible while still getting it through the posts. Watch for proper form and short strides.

Variation:

Increase the distance between one of the passers and the goalposts.

Spot Throwing Drill

Objectives:
1. proper form
2. throwing to angles
3. strengthen the throwing arm

Procedure:

This drill simulates game situations. The passer takes a snap from center, takes a short drop, and works on the proper delivery. Have him throw to various spots at various distances downfield. He should throw five in a row to a receiver in one spot before the receiver moves to another location. See Figure 3-11 for the spots.

NOTE: For any drill, keep in mind that throwing many passes a day is the best way for a quarterback to gain accuracy and confidence. Nothing can replace practice and hard work. The closer the drill simulates game situations the better. Always try to have a center snap the ball. If a center is not available, use a manager or do it yourself from a kneeling position.

THE WIDE RECEIVER

The seven basic characteristics every good wide receiver should remember are:

1. Get your feet in position (balanced) to catch the ball.
2. The eyes must catch the ball first, then the hands. Focus on the first 6 in. of the ball. *Remember:* You're a receiver, not a runner. Your responsibility is to catch the ball.
3. Catch the ball with two hands. One-hand catching leads to laziness and dropped balls.
4. After the reception, tuck the ball securely away and head upfield by lowering the upfield shoulder as you begin to run. Getting pads in the upfield direction will help split defenders and take on tacklers.
5. You must hustle on every play, including running plays.
6. Make sure that you know your offense as well as the quarterback.
7. Catch the ball many times each practice. Managers should throw the ball to receivers after they complete routes or as they return to the huddle. A receiver can never get too many repetitions of catching the football.

Figure 3-11. Spot throwing drill.

Basic Fundamentals for the Wide Receiver

Stance

Whether you choose to have your wide receivers use a two-point or a three-point stance, train them to always have their inside foot back. This is one time in football when uniformity is more important than the player's right–left orientation. By always having his inside foot back, the number of steps the receiver takes will be the same regardless of the side of the ball on which he is aligned.

The standing, or two-point, stance allows the player to see the whole field as well as to communicate with the quarterback with hand signals (see Figure 3-12). In this stance, the receiver's shoulders must be parallel with the line of scrimmage. Split ends are considered linemen and must do this. Flankers are considered backs and can line up deeper. Because most receivers should know both positions, they should be consistent in their stance.

The major drawback to the two-point stance is that a player does not get as quick a takeoff as he would from the three-point stance. The three-point stance for the wide receiver is different than a regular three-point taught to interior linemen in that the wide receiver drops the back foot a bit deeper than normal, simulating a track stance. While not providing the broad vision of the two-point stance, it does afford the receiver a quick explosive start.

Patterns

Generally speaking, coaches should teach receivers to count steps rather than yards as they gain depth in the patterns. On muddy fields or in times of stress, counting steps is more accurate than yards and helps the player to know the field better. A three- to four-step route will carry the player 4- to 6-yds. and five to six steps equals about 10 yds.

Here's a basic passing tree (from the right hash mark) (see Figure 3-13):

1. hook (in)
2. in (drag)
3. post*
4. corner (flag)*
5. out
6. curl (out)
7. streak (fly)*

Explanations of All Pass Routes

1. Hook (in):
   At the 4th or 6th step, plant the outside foot

Figure 3-12. The two-point stance allows the player to see the whole field.

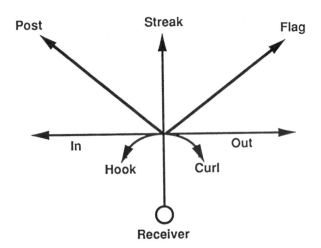

Figure 3-13. Basic passing tree from the right hash mark.

*Deep routes/cuts made at five steps. All others are three- or five-step routes (tree is mirrored at the left hash mark).

and turn the shoulders inside to face the quarterback. Have the hands instantly ready.

2. In (drag):
   At the 4th or 6th step, plant the outside foot and cut to the inside, running parallel to the line of scrimmage, looking for the ball.

3. Post:
   At the 4th or 6th step, plant the outside foot and sprint to the goalpost. Look for the thrown ball soon after the cut.

4. Corner (flag):
   At the 5th step, plant the inside foot and sprint for the corner flag (pylon) or, at the 6th step, plant the outside foot, take three steps to the post, plant the inside foot, and sprint for the corner. (This is a great fake.)

5. Out:
   At the 3rd or 5th step, plant the inside foot and sprint for the sidelines, looking for the ball.

6. Curl (out):
   At the 3rd or 5th step, plant the inside foot and turn the shoulders outside to face the quarterback. Have the hands ready for an early delivery.

7. Streak (fly):
   At the 6th step, plant with the outside foot and fake to the inside with a quick shoulder movement. You want to turn the defender's hips to the inside. Then drive hard with the inside foot and sprint upfield. Work for position between the defender and sideline, looking for the ball to the sideline, away from the defender.

Catching the Pass

By describing particular catches and drills, the following covers the fundamentals of catching the ball.

Emphasize these points:

1. All catches should be made with two hands
2. Catch the ball with the eyes first
3. Catch the ball at its highest point
4. Catch with the hands using the body as a backstop
5. Tuck the ball away before running
6. Don't fumble

The following describes the position of the hands while catching a thrown ball in various ways. After every catch, the ball should be brought into the body and tucked away.

1. Above-the-waist catch (see Figure 3-14):
   With the hands away from the body, the receiver must make a target for the ball by connecting the thumbs and index fingers and forming a diamond shape. Extend the remaining fingers. The finger connections should stop the ball from going through the hands. Remember, use the chest and body as a last resort in catching the football.

2. Below-the-waist catch (see Figure 3-15):
   This catch is very similar to fielding a ground ball in baseball. A basket is formed not by the thumbs but by a connection of the little fingers. On this catch, as in baseball, the body is used as a backstop when the ball is scooped up and into the body.

3. A pass in the dirt (grass):
   To teach complete pass receiving, you must also work on catching poor throws. To catch a ball thrown low and into the dirt, the key is to get low to the ground. Get low to the ground not by bending at the waist but by bending at the knees. If the pass is out in

Figure 3-14. Catching the ball thrown above the head.

Figure 3-15. In catching the ball below the waist, a basket is formed by a connection of the little fingers.

Figure 3-16. Running, over-the-shoulder catch.

front of a running receiver, he can slide to the ball just like a baserunner going into second base.

4. Running, over-the-shoulder catch (see Figure 3-16):
   If the pass is thrown out in front of the running receiver, the hand connection is made with the little fingers. This teaches the receiver to avoid confusion with the arms and will keep him from getting crossed up.

If the pass is thrown behind the receiver, use thumb connections. Although this is difficult at first, as the receiver gets more experience he can move to one-handed catches and pull the ball back into the body as the other hand comes up. This is the one time that one-handed catches are necessary.

Drills

High-Point Drill

Objective:
To develop the habit of catching the ball at the highest point.

Procedure:
The receivers line up at an angle to the goalpost. Individually, they run to a point behind the goalpost where they catch the football at its highest point. The passer throws the football high off the ground by throwing it through the posts and over the crossbar.

Quick Turn Drill

Objective:
To develop quickness, concentration, and to learn to tuck the ball away.

Procedure:
The receivers form a line, arms length apart, with their backs to the passer. One receiver at a time reacts to the quarterback's command. The passer yells right or left, and then throws the ball to the intended receiver. Having heard the command, the receiver turns the appropriate way by whipping that elbow back and pivoting to the passer. The receiver must do this with great quickness as the ball is on its way.
Concentration is the key. Have the receiver get his hands in position and watch the ball travel into his hands. He should tuck the ball

away while taking several steps before returning it to the quarterback.

THE RUNNING BACK

Most football coaches subscribe to the theory that winning teams are running teams. They theorize that in order to pass effectively, you must first be able to run the football, advancing toward the opponent's goal with consistency.

A vocal minority of coaches argue however, that passing effectively opens up the defense and makes the opponent vulnerable to the running game.

Whatever theory you subscribe to, we all might agree that a balanced offensive attack is the most effective weapon and that youth and high school teams generally run the ball more than they pass. Running the football offers the coach and team some assurance that they can advance their efforts and score. A running play allows all 11 players, linemen and backs, to coordinate their efforts in a forward thrust. There is nothing more exhilarating in the game than an all-out effort in the achievement of a first down or to score on a running play.

Qualities of a Running Back

The mark of a great back is not necessarily extraordinary speed. Some of the best running backs at every level of football possess average speed, but they are superior in every other quality of play. Speed can be deceptive. Good backs are capable of turning on bursts and using the change of pace effectively.

A running back must have courage. He carries the football with the knowledge that 11 opposing players want to take him to the ground or separate him from the ball. Whenever necessary, the running back must be prepared to deliver a blow into a tackler while holding onto the ball. His entire team is depending on him to gain yardage and to keep the offensive drive moving.

In this section, we discuss the basic fundamentals of backfield play. Coaches must be prepared to work daily with running backs on the fundamentals and critique the players at all times.

Stance

Basic to every position, a player's stance dictates his first move. He cannot take off with authority without a proper stance, one that is balanced to allow him to go right, left, and straight ahead.

Three-Point Stance (see Figure 3-17)

The most popular stance for runners is the three-point sprinter's stance. The feet should be spread about armpit width apart and pointed straight ahead. Right-handed backs should keep the right foot slightly to the rear of the left foot in the heel–toe relationship. The weight should be balanced on the balls of the feet; knees bent; and back parallel to the ground. The right hand, with fingers open, should be placed on the ground slightly to the inside of the right foot and forward beneath the right shoulder. About a quarter of the back's weight should be placed on the hand so that he can move right or left, as well as forward, with ease.

Figure 3-17. The three-point stance is the most popular backfield stance.

The left hand should rest comfortably on the left thigh. The head must be up with a bull neck and eyes focused straight ahead.

Two-Point Stance (see Figure 3-18)

Although the three-point stance, or the sprinter's stance, is the most widely used stance for straight T and wing T formations, teams employing the I formation must also use the alternate, upright two-point stance for the tailback or deep back in the offensive formation. The tailback normally lines up behind the fullback in the offensive set approximately 1 to 2 yds. deeper. In this position it is necessary to stand upright so that he can see the action in front of him.

The principles of the two-point stance remain similar to the three-point in that the feet are spaced and staggered at the same distances. The knees are slightly bent, back straight, neck bulled, and head up. The back will place both hands on his knees, thighs, or hips—whichever

Figure 3-18. The I-formation tailback usually lines up in a two-point stance.

is most comfortable. From this position he can move forward, right, or left and do the same things he can do from the down stance. It is easier from the two-point stance to view the defense and sense direction with the snap count. However, it is absolutely necessary for the back to focus his vision straight ahead while in this stance. Any peeking at a particular area will tip off the defense as to the location of the play.

Movement

Backs must be able to explode straight ahead on quick-opener plays and be able to step quickly right or left on plays to the outside. Lateral movement can be achieved by stepping directly with the near-side foot or by using a cross-over starting step. Once mastered, both are effective techniques although the direct step is easier to learn and more consistent with the technique used in moving forward. In this move, the back steps with the foot nearest the direction in which he intends to run. He should take a short step first, cross over on his next step, and continue until he comes to the prearranged handoff point. He should then accelerate to full speed, always under control.

RECEIVING THE HANDOFF

In a previous section, the responsibilities and techniques of the quarterback handing off the ball to the running back were described. The action of the quarterback's eyes as he looks the ball into the back's hands was emphasized. It was also pointed out that the responsibility for a successful handoff was primarily the quarterback's.

The running back should not be watching the quarterback or the ball. His head must be up and his eyes should be focused on the direction of his route. In accepting the handoff it is necessary for the back's inside arm to be up in forming the pocket. The outside arm is down with the elbow close to the body.

After receiving the ball in the natural pocket formed by the body and the two arms, the runner must grasp the ball firmly in both hands, protecting it from opponent tacklers (see Figure 3-19). Automatically, the runner should tuck the point of the ball under the armpit snugly and firmly. The bottom of the ball should be

Figure 3-19. After receiving the ball in the handoff, the runner must grasp it firmly in both hands.

Figure 3-20. Grip the ball firmly with fingers over the tip of the ball.

held in the palm of the hand, with the fingers spread over the point of the ball. Continue to protect the ball with both hands until it is securely tucked away and the back has freedom of movement.

It isn't necessary for backs to shift the ball from one arm to the other. Always carry the ball in the outside arm after receiving it in the handoff (see Figure 3-20). This keeps the ball away from inside pressure by the defensive players. Running right, the ball should be in the right arm; to the left, in the left arm. Keep in mind that the fumble is the greatest disaster a running back can suffer. Practice of these basic techniques as well as repetition of drills and playwork should perfect ball carrying skills.

FAKING

Just as faking is important to the play of the quarterback, it is also important for running backs to fake properly. When done cor-

rectly, a faking back will cause defensive players to lose sight of the ball and even tackle the wrong ball carrier at times. Coaches should stress that backs must carry out their fakes on every play.

In some plays the quarterback will actually place the ball in the back's pocket and withdraw it for a handoff to another back. In these cases, the faking back must drop his inside shoulder and hit the line covering up as though he still has the ball. Backs who are not involved in this way will use various faking techniques including leg, hip, and arm movements along with head and eye movements.

BLOCKING

To be a complete football player, the running back must also be a blocker. As noted earlier, football is a complete team game with the offensive assignments of each player designed to complement one another. Running backs are called upon to carry the football, fake, or block for another ball carrier.

Advanced football offensive and defensive schemes are sophisticated to the extent that coaches have designed clever blocks that influence rather than actually move would-be tacklers. Although we consider these skills valuable tools in aiding the offense, we will describe three blocks that are basic and essential to football at every level: the shoulder block, linebacker blocker, and pass protection block.

Shoulder Block

This block is performed by every back at one time or another and is generally designed to aid the ball carrier at the point of attack. In the off-tackle or sweep play to the outside, a blocker leads the ball carrier to the line of scrimmage area where he normally "kicks out" the defensive tackle or end with an inside-out shoulder block. The effort of the blocker is to get to the area as quickly as possible by stepping with the near foot and taking the shortest possible course.

The principles of the block are similar to those of the pulling guard in a lineman's trap block. The back must be low to the ground, head up, and prepared to strike a blow with the forearm and shoulder. Upon impact, the blocker must continue to follow through with an upward thrust, taking short choppy steps and maintaining contact with the defensive player. It is important that the head, at contact, is on the inside between the defensive player and the running back. The neck must be bulled and the head up with the eyes open. The blocker should be running at top speed but under control at impact.

The timing of the play and the movement of the blocker will enable the ball carrier to cut off his block and continue downfield.

Linebacker Block

Isolation plays are generally designed so that the offensive linemen achieve a double team block on the line of scrimmage and leave a linebacker unaccounted for at the point of attack. In these cases, the fullback generally is assigned the task of blocking one of the tougher defensive players on the other team. The design of the play isolates one player for the back to block at the point of attack. Full-house and wing T offenses often have isolation plays in which the halfback has this assignment. In the I formation, the fullback is the primary blocker of linebackers.

It is the blocker's responsibility to get to the area as quickly as possible while running under control. In most plays the route taken will be straight ahead or with a slight veer to the right or left.

There is no need to seek out the linebacker because the backer's "key" or "read" will take him into the play area. There will be a collision. The blocker must keep the head up and eyes open and be ready for the contact. He should approach the block in a higher position than with the shoulder block unless the defensive player lowers himself. He should run through the defender. It is often described as an attempt to "walk on the linebacker's toes." Once contact is achieved, he should follow through and not attempt to position the linebacker; he should drive him straight back and make a seam for the running back.

Pass Protection Block

Running backs are asked to protect the passer at times and as blockers they must accept a hard charge from a defensive end or a blitzing linebacker. On dropback passes by the quarterback, running backs help to form the protective "cup" around the passer, unless they are in the passing pattern. The back must step quickly either right or left, setting up in a football position to meet the oncoming pass rusher. The back should assume the stance with feet aligned with the armpits, knees flexed, and head up. His eyes should be focused on the numbers of the rusher, and his arms and hands should be in front of him to strike a blow at contact. As the bodies meet, the blocker should step into the defender thrusting his open hands into the chest area. He should then regroup and set himself for a second rush from the defender. He must be prepared to shuffle right or left, wherever the player takes him and should always keep in mind where the passer is setting up to throw. It is important that he keep some distance between his body and the defensive player while maintaining contact with open hands. He should keep his head up and his eyes open.

RUNNING TECHNIQUES

It is necessary for running backs to develop several techniques that will help them evade tackles or free themselves while being tackled. There are a number of such techniques and good backs become proficient at using many of them. However it is necessary for the running back to develop his own style, utilizing those techniques that he does well.

Cutting

All backs must learn how to cut while running with or without the ball. Cutting is designed to throw the tackler off balance and should be made when the tackler has his legs crossed or is in a position to tackle the runner. Cutting results in a change of direction and is accomplished by planting the pivot foot hard and changing direction with the other leg. After the cut it is imperative that the ball carrier gets back on track toward the goal line rather than running laterally, parallel to the line of scrimmage.

Change of Pace

Changing the pace of a back's running speed can make the tackler's mission extremely difficult. The running back should always give the impression that he is running at top speed. Then, when the tackle attempt is imminent, he should have the ability to muster a burst of speed and leave the tackler grasping at air.

The Straight Arm

The straight arm or stiff arm is used in close quarters or the open field to ward off tacklers (see Figure 3-21). The runner should thrust out his free arm with an open hand, elbow locked. In most cases the hand will strike the helmet of the tackler, disrupting his move to the ball carrier. Care should be exercised to not grasp the face mask of the opponent.

Drills

Ball Handling Drills (see Figure 3-22)

Divide players into two equal, even-numbered groups. Have each group stand in single file lines facing each other. The first player of one line hands off to the first player in the facing line, who then hands off to the second player in the first line, and so forth until each player either receives or makes a handoff of the football. Each player, after completing his turn, as-

Figure 3-21. The straight arm is a valuable technique in avoiding tacklers.

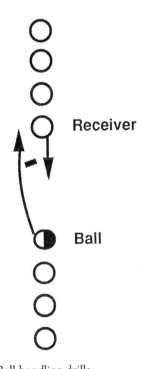

Figure 3-22. Ball handling drills.

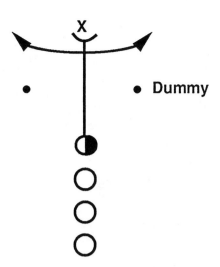

Figure 3-23. Straight arm and sidestepping drill.

width between the lines. Distances can be 1 yd. and then 3 yds., necessitating a pitch and reception by the backs simulating a pitchout or lateral.

Straight Arm and Sidestepping Drill (see Figure 3-23)

Station a defensive player in full equipment beyond two dummies or cones. Opposite him, position a line of ball carriers with footballs. The first player in line runs between the dummies and the defensive player readies himself into a tackling position but does not tackle. The runner uses his free arm to straight-arm the defender as he cuts right or left. If hand-held shields are available, the defensive player can hold one and the ball carrier's straight arm will be delivered into the shield.

Running Technique Drill (see Figure 3-24)

Place dummies or cones 5 yds. apart in a zigzag course. Each back carries the ball straight at the dummy or cone, where he executes a particular evasive technique. When he arrives at the second dummy, he uses a different maneuver. You should be able to teach several ball carrying actions in this one drill.

sumes the same respective position in the opposite line so that the drill can be repeated.

You should check the placement and reception of the ball each time, emphasizing all coaching points. Make sure the lines are far enough apart so that each player can tuck the ball away and then make the handoff to the oncoming player.

This drill can be varied by increasing the

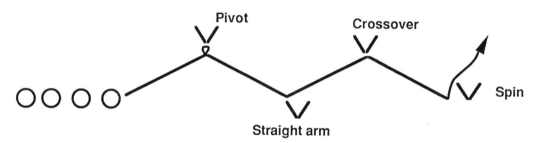

Figure 3-24. Running technique drill.

4
Organization of the Defense

Jerry Cvengros, M.S.

QUESTIONS TO CONSIDER

- How much defense can young football players learn?
- What basic defense is best for youth football?
- Are stunting defenses good for young players?
- What variations are possible in the 52 defense?

INTRODUCTION

Coaches differ on the percentage value defense contributes to the whole of football success, but most agree that championship teams are distinguished by their ability to keep opponents out of their end zone. A strong defensive team is capable of carrying a mediocre offensive team to victory.

There are any number of defenses from which you can choose but you must always be aware of what you can teach and what your players are capable of learning. Young athletes who play offense as well as defense are faced with learning assignments on both sides of the ball. Football players depend on instincts and reaction to keys on defense and will become hesitant if they are forced to learn too much. Defensive football assignments should be minimal so that players can react and play with the reckless abandon necessary to stop the offensive team from maintaining ball possession.

Football defenses are composed of three main units or groups: defensive linemen, linebackers, and secondary personnel.

Defensive linemen think "run" first and react to the blocks of the offensive linemen. As the blockers show pass protection, the linemen become rushers.

Linebackers are responsible for both running and passing plays. They react according to predetermined keys and their position in the alignment to get to the ball.

Defensive secondary personnel always think "pass first," keeping in mind that they never let a receiver beat them deep with a long completion. Backs lend support on running plays, but they should always be aware of their primary assignment: defending the pass.

BASIC DEFENSIVE ALIGNMENTS

Defense alignments are categorized as *odd* or *even*. It doesn't matter how many players are positioned on the line of scrimmage, the determining factor in odd or even alignment is the position of the down linemen in relation to the offensive alignment.

Odd Alignment

A defensive alignment is *odd* when there is a defensive lineman on the line of scrimmage directly over the center (see Figure 4-1).

Even Alignment

A defense alignment is *even* when there is no player on the line of scrimmage directly over the offensive center. The linemen in this alignment are usually positioned over the offensive guards (see Figure 4-2).

INDIVIDUAL LINE POSITIONING

The only rule in football that regulates the position of defensive players states that they must be on their side of the line of scrimmage. Within the context of this rule, coaches may position linemen in a variety of ways prior to the snap:

1. *Head-up* position indicates the player is over the offensive lineman (see Figure 4-3).
2. *Offset* position indicates placement over the inside or outside shoulder of the offensive lineman (see Figure 4-4).
3. *Gap* position indicates that the defensive linemen will avoid lining up on the offensive

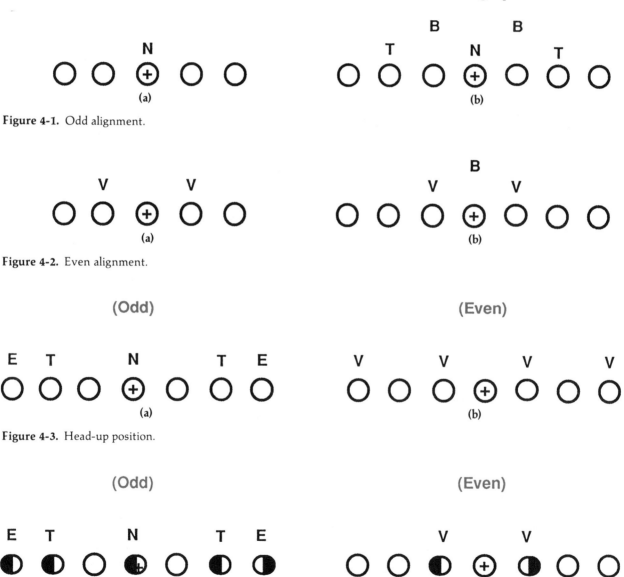

Figure 4-1. Odd alignment.

Figure 4-2. Even alignment.

(Odd)

(Even)

Figure 4-3. Head-up position.

(Odd)

(Even)

Figure 4-4. Offset position.

blocker and will attempt to penetrate through a gap between the offensive players (see Figure 4-5).

Generally speaking, a defensive line will have four to seven men on the line of scrimmage. Although the four-man front as popularized by professional teams has made recent gains in high school football, the more common five- and six-man fronts that are basic to defensive football are described later.

LINEBACKER POSITIONING

As a coach you must determine the number of linebackers you will use and the position of the secondary in relation to the number of linemen and linebackers.

Open Linebackers

In the five-man front, linebackers are usually placed directly over the uncovered offensive linemen (see Figure 4-6).

The defensive *look* that is created is generally called the 52 defense and is backed up by four defensive backs.

In the six-man front, the open linebackers generally are positioned over the tackle area (see Figure 4-7).

This defensive look is called the 62 defense and is backed up by three defensive backs. By dropping the ends back into linebacker positioning, the overall alignment becomes a 4-5 defense.

Stacked Linebackers

Occasionally linebackers are positioned behind defensive linemen rather than directly over offensive linemen. The purposes for doing so vary, but normally this positioning is done to confuse offensive blocking schemes or to protect linebackers who have difficulty meeting offensive blockers one on one. This technique is commonly called *stacking* linebackers or a *stacked* position (see Figures 4-8 and 4-9).

SECONDARY POSITIONING

The defensive secondary is normally aligned as three deep or four deep. More specifically, with two linebackers in an *odd* set, the secondary is normally aligned with four deep backs.

Figure 4-5. Gap position.

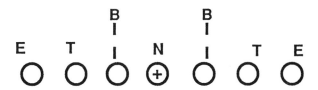

Figure 4-6. Five-man front linebacker placement.

Figure 4-7. Six-man front linebacker placement.

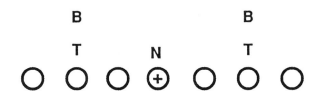

Figure 4-8. Odd-stacked linebackers.

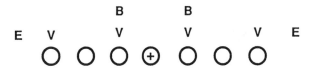

Figure 4-9. Even-stacked linebackers.

An *even* or four-to-six-man defensive front is usually combined with a three-deep secondary unless only one linebacker is used. Three deep backs playing a zone defense divide the playing field into three areas of responsibility in pass defense. Each back is responsible for one-third of the field. The four-deep secondary divides the field into quarters with the same responsibilities.

Man-to-man coverage means just that (see Figure 4-10): one defensive back covers one offensive *eligible* player and is responsible for one person in passing situations.

Of course, defenses become much more sophisticated and are much more intricate than

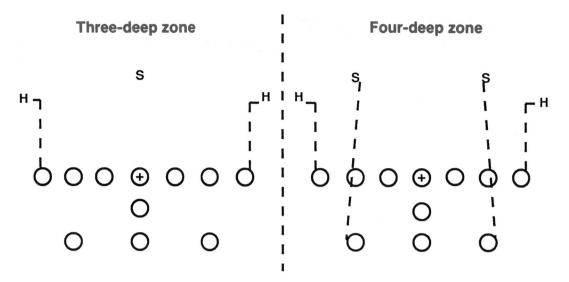

Three-deep zone   **Four-deep zone**

Figure 4-10. Man-to-man coverage.

these basic definitions. Sophisticated offenses necessitate sophisticated defenses. Coaching defensive youth football and young defensive backs, however, should emphasize fundamentals, skills, and techniques rather than a multitude of alignments and assignments.

DEFENSE—A TEAM EFFORT

There are many different team defenses that coaches can use at all levels of football. The chapter on offensive football, however, discussed how youth football coaches are prone to spend much more time teaching the running game rather than the intricacies of the passing game. Because running is basic to any offensive, stopping the run is basic to any defense.

It is important for coaches at all levels to establish a base defense even if they plan on using multiple sets. First and foremost, decide whether you will teach the odd or even concept and then begin placing the players into positions.

Personnel

The decision to use an odd front is usually dictated by personnel, especially the nose guard, where a particularly agile and aggressive player is necessary. Even defenses, especially six- and seven-man fronts, are adaptable to bigger and often slower linemen.

A team with excellent linebackers would do better to utilize a defense which employs many linebacker positions.

A defensive coach should decide which defense fits his personnel and his capability to teach. Selecting a defense used by successful college or professional teams may sound good in principle but may not work in reality. You might not have the personnel to do the things a particular defense necessitates. Successful coaching includes successful placement of personnel.

Strengths and Weaknesses

All coaches must realize that no defense is perfect. No one alignment can provide all the answers to stopping the offensive attack. The field is much too large for a defense to protect the entire area and contain the offense on every play. It is necessary for coaches to understand the strengths and weaknesses of their defensive alignments and to be able to adjust to the strengths of the offensive formation. Being able to react and adjust to situations is as important for the coach as it is for the players. Your players look to you for help whenever they are confused or misaligned. Coaching suggests a knowledge of the strengths and weaknesses of the defense and offense.

Player Awareness

Defense is as much a team concept as offensive football. Players must play within themselves, understanding their areas of responsibility and their awareness of the assignments of their teammates. The more they know about their opponents and the offensive tendencies, the better they will react to each situation.

It is important that you stress basic alignment, areas of responsibility, and reaction to keys for each position.

1. Basic alignment is the exact position of a player just prior to the snap. When offensive formations change, or a new defense is called, each player must know exactly where he is to be aligned (see Figures 4-11 to 4-14).

2. The area of responsibility includes the amount of territory assigned to each position as a primary concern. Secondary concerns include helping players at other positions.

3. Keys are important to all defensive players in the initial reaction at the snap. Every player should have the primary key of focusing on the initial movement of an offensive player. Keys are designed to indicate pass, run, or direction. Your instructions to the defense indicates to them what their reaction should be to every move by their key player (see Figure 4-15).

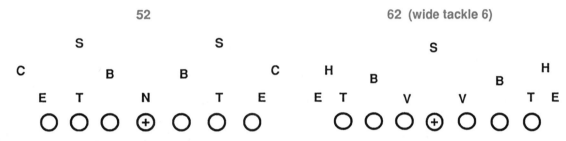

Figure 4-11. 52 - 62 alignment.

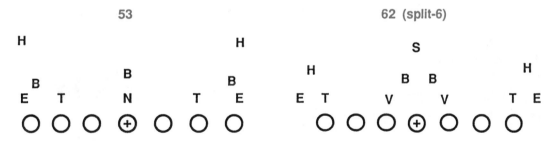

Figure 4-12. 53 - 62 alignment.

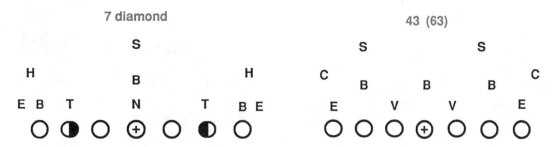

Figure 4-13. 7 diamond - 43 alignment.

52 prevent   Goal line   gap 8

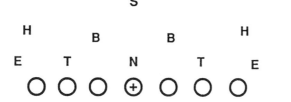

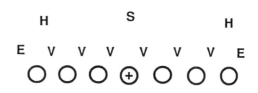

Figure 4-14. 52 prevent - goal line alignment.

Alignment   Movement

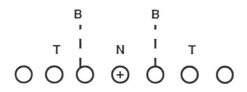

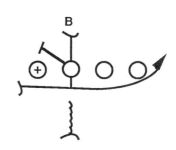

Figure 4-15. Defensive player keys.

In this 52 (odd) defensive alignment, the linebackers are positioned directly over the offensive guards and key their movements on the snap. The backer should be coached to step forward and meet the charge if the guard attacks him, or to meet the block of a charging back if the guard blocks the nose guard.

Linebackers must be able to recognize play development when the guard pulls in one direction or another and to drop into their pass coverage zones when the offensive player shows pass defense.

Keys are valuable to the defense and give the players a necessary edge at the start of every play.

THE 52 DEFENSE

Sometimes referred to as the Oklahoma or 54 defense, the 52 defense contains all the elements of a sound and consistent alignment of personnel. The 52 is possibly the no. 1 high school defense at the present time but also has great favor in collegiate circles. In recent years, professional teams also use variations of the formation although their terminology refers to it as a three-man front with four linebackers.

Whatever it is called, we feel that the odd line positioning with two inside linebackers and

four defensive backs is an excellent alignment to teach youth players (see Figures 4-16 and 4-17).

In evaluating the 52 defense, it becomes immediately apparent that a basic adjustment allows the cornerback on the side of the offen-

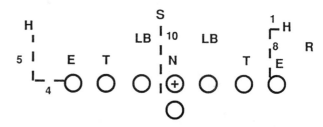

Figure 4-16. The 52 defense.

Figure 4-17. The inside-five players in the 52 defense.

sive formation to rotate closer to the ball and lend immediate strength against the run. As the formation has evolved and coaches have developed specialized athletes, the rover back, monster, or strong safety came into being. Players were switched from side to side, keying on the offensive formation alignment and ball placement on the field. This player is referred to as a *rover*.

Present-day defenses tend to specialize most positions so that the ends, linebackers, and safeties *flip-flop* positions from one side of the ball to the other. The descriptions of the 52 contained herein deal only with switches between the rover and weak-side cornerback.

A basic defensive *package* for youth football coaches will include the 52 defense with adjustments and a gap 8 defense to use near the goal line (see Figures 4-18 and 4-19).

STUNTING AND BLITZING

Although excessive stunting and blitzing on defense is not recommended, it is wise to understand the many possibilities that can come from the 52 alignment. Players in youth football should, however, learn the fundamentals and techniques of their position before they advance to variations. Stunts are designed to confuse offensive blocking assignments, but if not performed properly, the offense could attain a long gain.

Oftentimes stunts involve the nose guard and linebackers (see Figure 4-20).

Another change can be expected between the linebacker and the defensive tackle (see Figure 4-21).

A combination of stunts can be employed between the two linebackers and the five defensive linemen (see Figure 4-22).

A stunt between the linebacker, tackle, and end can be performed or a stunt utilizing just the tackle and end is also possible (see Figure 4-23).

Figure 4-18. Goal line defense.

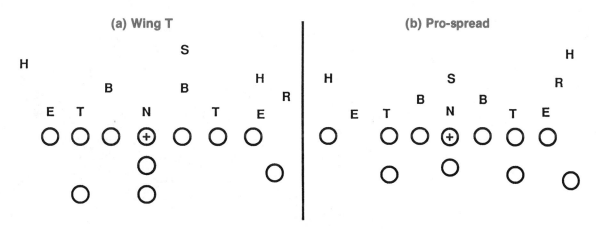

Figure 4-19. 52 adjustments.

Figure 4-20. Defensive stunts involving the nose guard and linebackers.

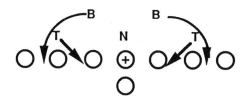

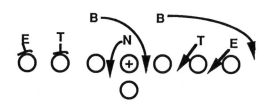

Figure 4-21. Defensive stunts involving the linebacker and defensive tackle.

Figure 4-22. Defensive stunts involving linebackers and defensive linemen.

Figure 4-23. Defensive stunts involving the linebacker, tackle, and end.

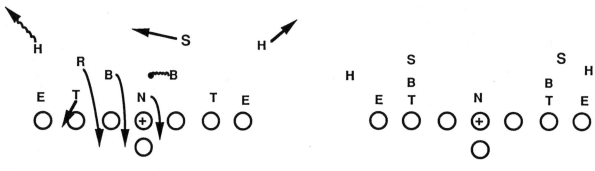

Figure 4-24. Secondary stunts.

Figure 4-25. 52 stack.

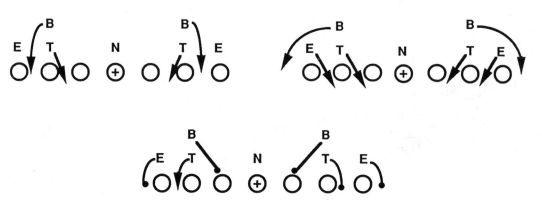

Figure 4-26. 52 stack (stunts).

Safety or rover blitzes are an element of surprise used against the passer. The defense reverts to three-deep zone protection (see Figure 4-24).

There are times when it may be necessary to stack linebackers. Stacking or hiding linebackers directly behind defensive linemen allows ad-ditional variations of stunting and blitzing and makes the linebackers extremely difficult to block (see Figures 4-25 and 4-26).

With all the variations and adjustments, the 52 is one of the most versatile of all de-fenses. It is highly recommended in its basic form for youth football players.

5
Fundamentals of Defensive Football

Jerry Cvengros, M.S.

QUESTIONS TO CONSIDER

- What safety considerations are necessary when teaching tackling techniques?
- What are the differences in the position play of defensive tacklers and the nose guard?
- What basic stunts should be taught?
- What is the linebacker's role in the success of the defense?

INTRODUCTION

Defensive football fundamentals are based, in part, on a knowledge of the opponent's offensive attack. In other words, the player and coach must know what the offensive objective is and then have a defensive plan to neutralize that objective. Basic skills of each defensive position must be taught so that the player can react to all offensive moves and techniques. Reaction is the key work for the defense. Players must learn to neutralize and shed blockers, react to the ball, and tackle.

This chapter describes the types and techniques of tackling for each defensive position as aligned in the 52 defense and gives drills for development of techniques.

TECHNIQUES OF TACKLING

Basic to all defensive players is the technique of tackling—the act of taking the ball carrier to the ground. Some coaches feel that technique is secondary to the prime purpose of bringing down the runner but they forget that without proper technique, the tackle might never be made.

In the early years of football, when equipment did little to protect the players, tackling was usually accomplished by reaching and pulling at the arms and jerseys or by diving and grasping at the ankles. Eventually players engaged in shoulder tackling, using the strength of legs, back, and arms in grasping the runner and "hugging" him to the ground.

Coaches during the fifties and sixties made the face and head a part of football tackling techniques but these procedures are no longer legal in youth and high school play. Players were urged to strengthen neck muscles so that they could lead with their faces into the opponent's numbers (chest area), striking a blow first with head and face mask. The next move, with the arms grasped around the small of the back of the runner, was to squeeze him, lift him and drive him to the ground. The problems with this technique are obvious. Current *National Fed-*

eration Rules refer to it as spearing or butting—an act punishable with a 15-yd. penalty and possible expulsion from the game.

Catastrophic injuries in football often occur during tackling and most frequently to the tackler because of improper and unsafe techniques. Rule-makers, cognizant of the tragedy of catastrophic injury, have been determined to reduce the seriousness of injuries. Teaching proper tackling technique is a primary method of accomplishing this.

The Head-On (Shoulder) Tackle

Although we seldom face ideal one-on-one runner-tackler relationships in a football game, it is necessary to teach tackling in this basic way so that the young player can approach contact with confidence and enthusiasm (see Figure 5-1).

Here's the technique:

1. Keep your eyes on the ball carrier's numbers, just below the chest
2. Position yourself in a good football hitting position: feet are shoulder width apart, knees are flexed, back is straight, arms are free, and head is up
3. Drive your head and face mask into the area of the ball, possibly forcing a fumble

4. Drive your shoulder into the midsection of the ball-carrier
5. Wrap your arms around the runner's back
6. Keep your legs moving and drive up with your chest and shoulders to lift the runner
7. Drive the ball carrier to the ground.

Open Field or Angle Tackle

Most tackles made during a game are angle tackles that necessitate good technique (see Figure 5-2).

The tackler must get his head in front of the ball carrier, driving his shoulder into the side of the runner.

All basic tackling techniques apply except that the tackle is made from the side of the runner and is usually somewhat higher. The tackler must keep his head up, driving through the runner, and wrapping his arms around the body. It is important to keep the legs moving and remain aggressive while delivering the blow.

Tackling Drills

Practicing the technique should be a daily routine, with care taken to prevent injuries while emphasizing all of the basic points. A team that tackles poorly seldom plays well. All play-

Figure 5-1. The shoulder tackle is the safest and most effective way to bring down a ball carrier.

Figure 5-2. The tackler must get his head in front of the ball carrier.

ers should participate in tackling drills and learn the proper techniques.

Form Tackling Drill

Players should be paired according to size and ability and have equal opportunity to perform as runners and tacklers (see Figure 5-3). The drill should be run at 50- to 75-percent speed and be supervised at all times. Emphasize perfect tackling technique.

Players are paired 5 yds. apart facing each other and start on the coach's whistle. The ball carrier proceeds forward, right or left, as directed with a silent command by the coach. The tackler performs a head-on or angle tackle as necessary and is critiqued by the coach. The runner should provide mild resistance and allow the tackler to complete his move. The tackler and runner can switch positions as often as necessary.

Procedure:
1. Start in a football hitting position
2. Keep head and eyes up
3. Key to the runner's belt buckle—not legs or shoulders
4. Keep arms free and "wrap-up" as shoulder impacts ball-carrier
5. Bring legs under body, lift, and follow through with legs
6. Tackler should wind up on top of runner

Variation:
Have the runner jump up as he is tackled, with the tackler shifting him to his shoulder, wrapping his arms around him, and with a good wide base carrying the runner 5 yds.

Sideline Drill—Form Tackling

Pair players according to size and ability and emphasize form at 50- to 75-percent speed.

Set up on the sideline to between the hash mark and sideline (see Figure 5-4).

The runner lines up on the hash mark and heads for the sideline after the coach tosses him the ball. The tackler approaches under control in a football hitting position and practices the angle, sideline tackle by getting his head in front of the runner and driving his shoulder into the side, wrapping his arms around the body. This drill is more appropriate for defensive backs, linebackers, and ends.

DEFENSIVE LINE PLAY

Traditionally, interior linemen are the biggest players on the team and possess superior strength. However, there is truth in the statement that linemen must be aggressive, quick, and able to react to the block of the offensive linemen. The defensive lineman will be blocked at times, but he must withstand the pressure and fight loose from the block and get to the ball carrier.

This section analyzes the play of each defensive lineman in the 52 defense, including the nose guard, tackle, and end. A number of fundamental characteristics, however, apply to each position:

1. Move with the movement of the offensive player. When the closest blocker moves, so must the defensive player. When the blocker's hand leaves the ground, he is moving, signaling the defensive player's move.
2. Deliver a blow to neutralize the blocker's

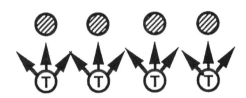

Figure 5-3. Form tackling drill.

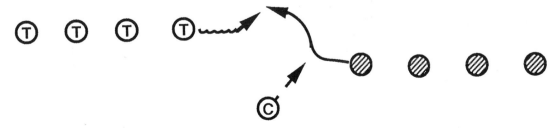

Figure 5-4. Sideline tackling drill.

charge. As this is done the defensive player must "find" the ball and react.

3. Fight pressure through the blocker's head and *never go around him.*
4. Pursue the ball carrier by taking a course that will get you to the ball carrier. Never follow a teammate's path.
5. Tackle! The basis of all good defensive play is good tackling.

Nose (Middle) Guard

In a five-man (odd) defensive line position, the nose guard usually lines up over the center. It is his responsibility to occupy as many offensive linemen as possible and *never* be blocked by only the center. A good nose guard must command respect from the offense and force them to double team at all times. With two linebackers behind him, he must keep the offense from blocking them.

Stance and Alignment (see Figure 5-5)

1. Line up one foot off the ball and, although the distance may vary, have the eyes focus on the ball movement.

Figure 5-5. The nose guard's four-point stance.

2. Use a four-point stance (both hands on the ground), feet nearly parallel, and nose close to the ground.
3. Shoulders should be parallel to the ground and head extended so that the center, guards, and quarterback are visible.
4. Buttocks should be up slightly; knees should be bent and the body ready to uncoil.
5. Feet should be under the body with weight balanced on the balls of the feet and hands.

Movement and Blow

1. Move as the ball moves by using short steps, and strike a blow into the center by using either the forearm or hand shiver technique (see "Defensive Interior Drills"). Key on the center's head.
2. Control the center with the hands and fight in the direction opposite the center's block. Neutralize his charge and be aware of the double team blocks from either of the offensive guards.
3. Keep feet moving and the blocker away from the body.
4. Locate the ball, shed blockers, and make the tackle.

Fighting the Double Team *(If guard blocks down)*

1. Fight the guard's pressure by stepping into him hard.
2. Stay low and hold ground—never stand up.
3. Split the seam, if possible to do so on initial move.
4. Drop the outside leg and seat roll beyond the double team if necessary.

Middle Guard Stunts

As described in a previous chapter, the nose guard is often involved in a stunt with one or both linebackers.

Stunts must be coordinated so that all areas are covered during the predetermined moves. As always, the nose guard watches ball movement and shifts quickly to his area at the snap, using the foot movement taught during practice. Most stunts have the nose guard slanting or looping quickly to either side of the center in an effort to get penetration through the gap between guard and center. It is important to not get caught or hung-up by the center. Movement of the arms, hands, and feet must be extremely quick.

The success of a stunting defense is dependent on the ability and versatility of the middle guard. In many respects he must be a middle linebacker—smart enough to confuse the offense with stunts and tough enough to play in the "pit."

Tackle

Some coaches have described the tackle position as the most important position on the defensive team and extremely important in controlling the offensive running attack.

In ordinary situations, defensive tackles must cope with the biggest and strongest linemen on the offensive team, whose main purpose is to neutralize the big men of the defense and allow ball carriers to run off-tackle. Tackles must be the backbone of the defense.

Defensive tackles must be able to meet the charge of a one-on-one block by the offensive tackle, hold their ground on a double team block, recognize and react to the trap block, and free themselves to rush the passer when the quarterback drops back. Tackles must have superior upper body strength and although it is not necessary to be as quick as the nose guard, good agility and footspeed are valuable skills for the tackle.

Stance and Alignment

1. Line up 1.5 ft. from the ball.
2. Use either a three-point or four-point stance, with the inside foot back and shoulders parallel to the ground.
3. Head should be up in such a position that the tackle can observe linemen on either side of the offensive tackle.
4. Buttocks should be up slightly, knees bent, and the body ready to uncoil.
5. Weight should be distributed between the hands and forward foot.

Movement and Blow

1. Keep eyes focused on the offensive tackle's "down" hand.
2. Move when the offensive tackle's hand moves and step with the inside foot so that feet become parallel.
3. Strike a blow with the forearm or bring both

arms and hands up in a hand shiver into the chest area of the blocker.
4. Read the offensive lineman's block, and control his movements by destroying his charge.

Responsibilities

1. Protect the off-tackle hole and hold ground on the double team block.
2. Rush the passer in your lane. (Do not vary too far inside or outside.)
3. Pursue all plays that go to the opposite side.
4. If no one blocks the defensive tackle, he must turn to the inside, quickly turning his body, staying low, and looking for the pulling guard attempting to trap him. He must deliver a blow with his outside shoulder and forearm and fill the hole.
5. Fight pressure and do not go around the block.
6. Locate the ball and make the tackle.

Defensive Interior Drills

Hand Shiver Drill for the Nose Guard

Objective:
This drill is designed to teach the player to hit out and control the opponent and then look for the ball (see Figure 5-6).

Procedure:
1. Guard moves on the snap and delivers a blow to the center to control the line of scrimmage.
2. React to the blocker's pressure and get to the ball carrier.
3. Drill should be performed at three-quarter speed with the coach evaluating the fine points of each position.

Figure 5-6. Hand shiver drill for nose guard.

Hand Shiver Drill for the Defensive Tackle

Objective:

This drill is also designed to teach the player to control the line of scrimmage and react to the various blocks faced on the line of scrimmage (see Figure 5-7). Because this drill represents two offensive players versus one defensive player, it is necessary for the coach to exercise caution in a controlled setting.

Procedure:

The defensive tackle must deliver a hand shiver blow into the offensive tackle and determine quickly how he is to be blocked. If the end comes down to double team him, he must turn his movement to the end and fight through the double team. If no one blocks him, he must turn inside to meet the trap block from a pulling guard.

End

This position requires players that have many of the same talents as linebackers. They must be agile and strong with good upper body strength and must move quickly to avoid being knocked off their feet.

The defensive end must come across the line of scrimmage quickly and low with legs apart for good balance. At a depth of 2 yds., he must set his feet parallel to the line with his inside leg forward and his outside leg back in a low crouch.

Not only is the end responsible for containment, he is also considered a prime force in pass rushes and thus, he may give ground, if necessary, but he must never go down.

Stance and Alignment (see Figure 5-8)

1. He should take a two-point stance with the inside foot forward in an approximate heel–toe relationship.

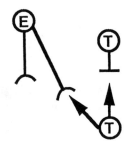

Figure 5-7. Hand shiver drill for defensive tackle.

Figure 5-8. The defensive end lines up in a two-point stance with the inside foot forward.

2. Knees should be flexed.
3. On the offensive tight end side of the ball, the defensive end must line up on the outside shoulder of the tight end. From this position, his play resembles that of a linebacker.
4. On the split end side of the ball, his responsibility is to penetrate and contain.

Technique

1. Take a short jab step forward with the inside foot.
2. Shuffle the second foot into position and react to pressure.
3. Use a hand shiver to meet the blocker. Lock elbows in extended arms with palms forward, jolting into the blocker. An alternate blow is to deliver a forearm to the blocker in an upward motion to the chest area.

Responsibilities

1. Squeeze down if the play develops to the inside.
2. Force the sweep play to the inside unless it

has outside support. In that case, the sweeps should be forced to the outside.

3. In a sprintout pass coming his way, the defensive end must rush from the outside and contain the quarterback.
4. Do not overpursue and leave the area of responsibility. Be ever-mindful of a reverse back to your area.

Defensive ends will meet a variety of blockers during a football game, including offensive ends, pulling guards, and offensive backs. In many cases the type of block is not evident until the last split second. The end needs to determine quickly if the play is a pass or run and whether he is to be blocked out or hooked to the inside.

It is necessary to communicate with teammates, reviewing assignments prior to the snap and warning one another about potential shortcomings of the defense.

Because so much can happen to the end, footwork is extremely important to his development. A defensive end soon realizes that the position of his feet determines his ability to play.

LINEBACKER PLAY AND DRILLS

In many respects the linebacker is to the defense what the quarterback is to the offense. In addition to all of his duties and responsibilities, he must also be a team leader and one of the toughest players. There is no perfect size physically for linebackers because it is impossible to measure the size of a player's desire.

Inside linebackers in the 52 defense can be attacked in a variety of ways. Because of their proximity to the line of scrimmage, they can be blocked by either guards or tackles in the offensive line. Linebackers must also be prepared to step up and meet an offensive back in the isolation play series. Inside backers must pursue to the action on plays to the outside and still be able to react to passes and get into their area of zone coverage.

Linebackers usually lead the team in tackles, partly because of their abilities and partly because the 52 defense is designed to free them to make the tackles. Football is a game of emotion and example. Linebackers should be prime leaders in both areas. Coaches should recognize these characteristics early in the development of young players and harness every source of strength for the good of a team effort.

Stance and Alignment (see Figure 5-9)

1. Take a two-point stance with the outside foot back slightly.
2. Stand in a football position, slightly bent at the waist with the arms out front protecting the knees.
3. Be positioned at least 1 yd. behind defensive lineman.
4. Be positioned eye to eye with the offensive guard.
5. The inside eye of the linebacker should be aligned with the outside eye of the guard.
6. Weight should be slightly forward and on the balls of the feet. Stay off the heels!

Movement and Blow

1. On the snap of the ball use a slight jab step—key to the movement of the guard's head.

Figure 5-9. The youth linebacker should bend slightly at waist with arms out front protecting the knees.

2. Keep the outside leg bent.
3. Be prepared to strike a blow at the blocker with either a lifting forearm shiver or with both hands. The hand shiver is preferable because it enables the linebacker to keep the blocker away from his body. He can then shed the blocker with his hands, find the ball, and make the tackle.

Keys

1. It is necessary to recognize immediately where the play will attack.
2. The offensive lineman will usually take you to the ball.
3. With an aggressive lineman block:
   a. meet the pressure aggressively and neutralize the blocker
   b. locate the ball and pursue
   c. stop if the lineman stops
4. If the guard pulls down the line to either side of the linebacker, the linebacker must go with him, looking for the ball carrier.
5. If the lineman makes a pass protection block, the linebacker drops quickly to the hook zone.

Blitz Movement

The object of the blitz is to destroy offensive blocking schemes while getting penetration into the backfield. Linebackers should be careful to maintain a good football position prior to the snap so that the offense will not recognize the blitz.

Usually the best place to penetrate is through a gap spacing between offensive line positions. The quicker a linebacker moves, the more successful he will be with his blitz action.

Linebacker Drills

Shuffle-Over-Dummies Drill

This is a drill that should be run daily and is designed to perfect footwork and coordination. Dummies are resting on their sides (see Figure 5-10).

Procedure:
1. Bring feet up high.
2. Keep hands moving during the shuffle, with shoulders parallel to the line of scrimmage.
3. Keep eyes on the coach.
4. Finish with a seat roll, then get up.

5. Occasionally execute a tackle on an upright dummy after a seat roll.

Pursuit Drill

This drill (with reaction to a ball carrier) necessitates use of a center, quarterback, and halfback (see Figure 5-11).

Tackling Drills

These described previously in "Tackling Drills" should be a daily routine for linebackers.

Recognition Drill

Procedure:
This drill should be run at half speed. The linebacker will position himself as he would in a game and react to his lineman's key (see Figure 5-12).

The offensive guard (after consultation in

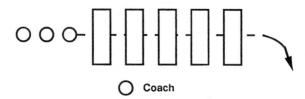

Figure 5-10. Shuffle-over-dummies drill.

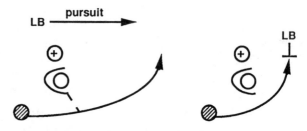

Figure 5-11. Pursuit drill.

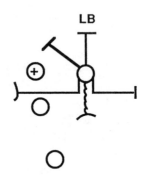

Figure 5-12. Recognition drill.

the huddle) performs any one of the movements illustrated and the linebacker reacts accordingly.

DEFENSIVE SECONDARY PLAY

The 52 defensive alignment allows for four defensive backs—two cornerbacks or halfbacks and two safeties. The safeties are further differentiated into the free safety and the strong safety or rover back (see Figure 5-13).

As a coach, you must evaluate your personnel to determine the qualities necessary to play in the secondary. Running ability and quickness are prerequisites for all secondary positions. Athletes who play in the offensive backfield or wide receiver often perform in the defensive secondary.

It is also necessary that secondary players be able to understand their responsibilities. As the last line of defense between the offense and the goal line, the secondary players must be sure tacklers and must not allow receivers to get behind them on pass patterns.

General Secondary Rules

1. Play every play as a pass first, a run second. Never come up to make a tackle until you are 100 percent sure it is a run.

Figure 5-13. Defensive secondary stance.

2. Keep visual contact with the ball at all times.
3. Communicate. All defenders yell "Pass!" when the ball is being passed and "Ball!" when intercepting. Talk to each other as much as possible.
4. Sprint to the ball. When the ball has been thrown, forget your zone and go to the football.
5. Anticipate the pass. This is the key to a good zone defense. Watch the passer's eyes; they will take you to the ball.
6. Play the ball and not the receiver. Play through the intended receiver with both hands and extended arms in order to avoid pass interference.
7. Intercept the ball at its highest point. Don't wait for the ball to come to you—sprint to it.
8. Always know the down, yardage, and time left in the game.
9. Tackle high. Do not dive for legs in the open field.
10. On the snap of the ball, halfbacks should take one step to the outside.
11. Keys to focus on:
    a. A halfback should not have to key much. He should look through the offensive end or wingback into the football. Using eye control, he must be able to view the offensive players and the ball.
    b. The safety's key is the ball and he must play pass first. He cannot be caught coming up too quickly to make tackles.
    c. Always know your areas of responsibility.

Defensive Backfield Drills

Tackling Drills

Explained earlier in this chapter, tackling drills should be adapted for defensive backfield practice and should be used daily.

Tip Drill

Objective:
This drill is designed to have backs react to the ball, and to coordinate eyes and hands to catch the ball at its highest point (see Figure 5-14).

Procedure:
The coach throws the ball over the head of the approaching player, who jumps and tips the ball

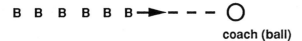

B B B B B B ➤ – – – ⭕
                    coach (ball)

Figure 5-14. Tip drill.

to a trailing player. After catching the ball, the back carries it to the coach.

Players should communicate by yelling "Pass!" when the coach raises the ball to throw and "Ball!" when it is tipped.

Zone Passing Drill

This drill should be performed by three or four backs, an offensive center, and a quarterback (see Figure 5-15).

Procedure:

1. On the snap, the quarterback takes a five-step drop, raising the ball to a passing position.
2. The defensive backs react by taking a drop step, shouting "Pass!" and moving backward in the direction the quarterback faces.
3. The quarterback faces several directions

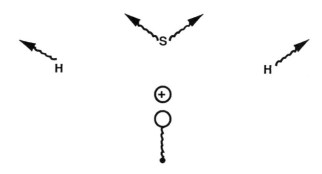

Figure 5-15. Zone passing drill.

quickly, observing the footwork of the backs, who react collectively.

4. The quarterback releases the ball into any of the zones. The backs must yell "Ball!" and go to the area quickly.
5. If the ball is intercepted, the defensive backs react as an escort, carrying the ball back to the goal line.
6. Rover backs and linebackers can be added to this drill.

6
The Kicking Game

Jerry Cvengros, M.S.

QUESTIONS TO CONSIDER
- What is the hidden yardage in football?
- What team kicking concepts should be taught?
- What are the advantages of soccer-type kickers?
- What techniques should be taught to punters?

INTRODUCTION

No area of football is more important than the kicking game. Facets of kicking include the punt and punt return. Kicking is the area of hidden yardage on the field of play. If you can return a punt or kickoff for 10 yds. or more, it is equivalent to a first down for the offensive team. Conversely, if the opponents gain 10 yds. or more on a kick return, it is 10 yds. less they have to cover toward a score. Yardage gained in the kicking game is equivalent to giving up a first down or more.

Probably the most demoralizing plays to a football team in the kicking game are to have a punt blocked and a kick returned for a touchdown. It is necessary to devote serious practice time weekly to every aspect of the kicking game. This chapter concentrates on the individual fundamentals and techniques of punting and placekicking, but it also covers the team aspects of each phase of the kicking game.

KICKOFF COVERAGE

It is imperative to have swift and disciplined personnel on the kickoff team (see Figure 6-1).

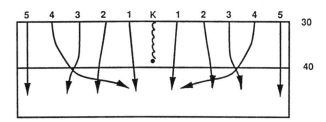

Figure 6-1. Kickoff coverage.

The kickoff is not a time to relax and yet it is not a time to be so aggressive that players forget that they have definite assignments and areas of concern before they converge on the ball carrier.

The entire team will line up on their own 30-yard line facing inside towards the kicker. They should be lined up with hands on knees, ready to sprint in their predetermined lanes. Some coaches prefer to have their players line up in a three-point stance facing straight ahead. The upright stance is preferred, however, so that each player sees the kicker cross his line of vision on the approach to the ball. This is the signal to begin movement downfield. The rules specify that no player may cross the 40-yard line until the kick is made, so it is necessary for the players to gauge their approach with the kicker.

The sprint downfield must be in the assigned lanes until the ball carrier commits himself to his return route. Players must "break down" under control into a football hitting position with their feet shuffling so they can move in either direction.

Once the back has committed to his direction, all players squeeze down and pursue to make the tackle.

The outside coverage must be aware of the cutback to the outside and their overall responsibility of containment. In addition, if the back breaks through they are in a position to pursue from the outside in.

Kickoff coverage personnel should have speed, desire, and courage. Their pride is reflected in forcing a turnover on the coverage or keeping the receiving team from advancing beyond their 30-yard line.

KICKOFF RETURN

There are several ways to run back kickoffs (see Figure 6-2). Some teams work on sideline returns, attempting to build a wall parallel to the sideline for the back to get on track and carry the ball in front of the bench, upfield. Some teams even incorporate a reverse between backs, hoping to confuse oncoming members of the kicking team.

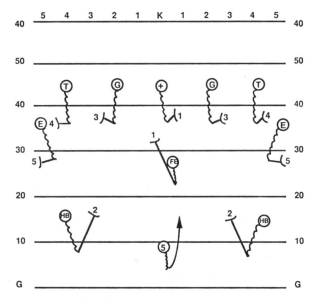

Figure 6-2. Kickoff return.

Probably the easiest return to teach and one of the most consistent is the middle-wedge return. The ball carrier is instructed to advance the ball directly up the middle of the field with each blocker assigned a specific person to block. After the ball is kicked, all players give ground and do not advance until the ball is caught.

High school blocking rules prohibit blocking below the waist or blocking from behind. The object must be to stay in front of the defenders and impede their course to the ball carrier. Hands can be used as long as they are placed within the frame of the defender's body and players don't grasp the arms of the jersey.

The important coaching points on the kickoff return include:

1. Don't fumble!
2. Don't allow the onside kick to succeed!
3. Don't block below the waist (no penalties)!
4. Get yardage upfield!

Although it is the hope of all receiving teams to pop loose and score a quick touchdown, a respectable goal is to advance the ball to the 30-yard line. Anything beyond the 30 can be considered bonus yardage and is a real challenge to the receiving team.

THE SPREAD PUNT (PRO PUNT)

Punting the football to your opponents is usually admission that the offensive drive has stalled and we will be unable to make a first down or score at this time (see Figure 6-3). But it is also a time to take advantage of field position and force the opponent to do something offensively. Consequently, when you must surrender the offense, it is necessary to punt with authority.

We recommend the *spread* or *pro punt* formation. This formation allows for just adequate blocking protection, but it provides the best release for your blockers to become defensive tacklers. The kicker positions himself directly behind the center, approximately 12 yds. deep. The exact position is determined by the center's ability to snap the ball back to the punter. Four players line up on either side of the center. They are chosen according to their ability to run, tackle, and block. They must be willing to discipline themselves for each particular assignment, but they must also have the necessary courage to pursue their tasks with enthusiasm.

The end, tackle, and guard line up on the line of scrimmage, while the inside blocker closest to the center assumes a position 1-2 yds. deeper. The splits are determined by the depth of the punter. The deeper the punter, the wider the splits up front. Each player should position himself quickly with hands on knees, looking to the inside so that he can properly line up on the player immediately to his inside. He should look at the defensive alignment and actually point at the man or gap that he will respond to at the snap. Because the center snaps the ball when everyone is set and he is ready, it is necessary to position and set as soon as possible.

At the snap, the players must step to their areas of responsibility, bringing their arms up to strike a blow on the oncoming linemen. After a 2-second count, the punt should be on its way and the blockers must release and get downfield in their respective lanes to cover the entire width of the field.

The blocking back positions himself 6 yds. deep and to one side of the center. He should survey the entire field and particularly his team to see if they are ready for the snap. At the snap, he should step hard and fast to the right corner to meet any penetration from that side. If a punt is to be blocked, the greatest danger is from the side of the punter's leg. Once the punt is completed, the deep blocker should become a part of the pursuit, advancing downfield behind the front line. The punter will become the safety if the returner breaks away. The punter must maintain a reasonable distance from the front line and adjust his pursuit with the movement of the returner. His assignment is not completed until the play is over.

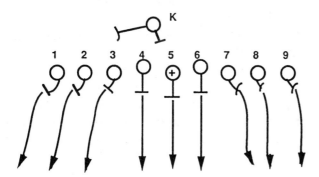

Figure 6-3. Spread punt and coverage.

All Blockers—Zone Block: Step with outside foot
All Blockers—Two-Point Stance: Hands on knees
Center: Snap when ready
Kicker: 12 yds. back
Fullback: Step forward and kick outright (6 yds. back)
Blocking Backs—1 yd. back: Step forward

Splits are determined by the depth of the punter (the deeper the punter, the wider the splits).

Get width coverage responsibilities as you get depth:

1. eight yds. from sideline
2. get to the hash mark
3. between the hash mark and upright
4. to the left upright
5. middle of the crossbar
6. to the right upright
7. between the hash mark and upright
8. to the hash mark
9. eight yds. from the sideline

THE PUNT RETURN

There are several ways to return punts. Once the punt leaves the kicker's foot, every player on the receiving team has a definite role in setting up the sideline wall, allowing the back to run behind the "picket fence."

The return alignment up front should assume a basic 52 defensive alignment. Although the offensive team is lining up in punt formation, until the kick is actually made, you should assume that the play is a fake and that there will be a run or pass. The actions at the snap will determine whether your players will react to a punt or another play.

The middle back positions himself approximately 25 yds. downfield and directly in front of the center. He will be the defensive player who directs traffic and is in a position to recognize a fake if it should occur. Once the ball is kicked, he reacts to the deep penetration—outside of the wall and block the first man who shows to the outside. He, and all blockers, must take care to block above the waist at all times.

The halfback on the outside of the wall makes sure that the ball is caught by the safety (or by himself, if the ball is kicked to him) and then reacts to the first penetrator who shows to the inside of the wall. The opposite halfback makes sure the ball is fielded and checks off penetrators from the backside, then leads the safety on track behind the picket fence.

The players up front on the line of scrimmage have definite assignments before getting to their positions in the wall. The end and tackle on the backside provide a controlled rush on the punter, making sure that he actually punts the ball but also blocking it if possible. The three linemen on the playside make contact and then take the shortest route to the wall. Figure 6-4 shows that the wall is a banana-shaped arc with the players setting up facing the inside and in good football position. The defensive players actually come to them in their positions if the ball is kicked properly and the safety runs the proper course.

Ideally, the safety catches the football and then takes a straight-ahead course for three steps. This tends to make the punting team react inside instead of to the forming wall. The ball carrier then cuts sharply to the outside bellying back slightly to get on track behind the wall. With a halfback leading, the sideline can be an effective way to gain long yardage (the hidden yardage) and place your team in position to score.

Punt Return Right (And Left):

RE	Force end into outside course and get to top of wall
RT	Force tackle to inside and become no. 2 person in wall
RLB	Force inside blocker to inside and become no. 3 person in wall
MB	Give ground, then kick out first person outside
RHB	Block first person inside
LHB	Check inside; the lead back behind the wall can "be an escort"
S	*Catch ball*, step forward 3 yds., get on track

The wall looks like a banana; players are 5 yds. apart (see Figure 6-4).

KICKING TEAM DRILL

Coaches must devote time to the kicking game within the allotted practice schedule every day. After team stretching and warm-up drills, 15 minutes of kicking and coverage drills utilizing all of the areas of the field, hash mark to hash mark, is a necessity. In addition to a review of techniques or assignments, the drill is a good conditioner. It is important that the punter be thoroughly warmed up before he punts for distance.

It isn't necessary for the punt team to huddle on the field. They know in advance what they are going to do, so the players should go directly to their positions from the sideline. Simulating game conditions, you should hold the 11 players on the sideline until the ball is spotted on the field. At your command, the entire team runs onto the field and sets their formation at the ball. The ball is put into play on the punter's command and the center's snap. The blockers react to the snap, hold for two counts, then sprint downfield in their coverage lanes (see Figure 6-5).

Punt receivers are stationed downfield to catch the football. The team adjusts to where the punt takes them and breaks down into a football hitting position when they are within 5 yds. of the receiver. Coaches must check the position of all players at this point.

An added feature of this drill is to have the

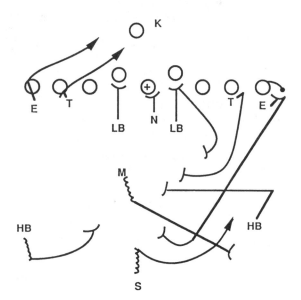

Figure 6-4. Punt return right.

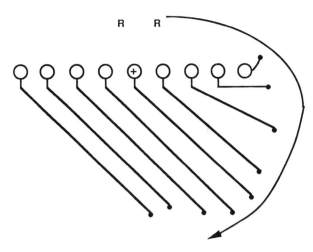

Figure 6-5. Kicking team drill.

receiver–ball carrier advance the ball down the sideline with all 11 players using proper pursuit angles to the ball carrier. Everyone should tag the runner. Backside pursuers (those furthest from the ball carrier) must run under control to prevent the cutback run.

EXTRA POINT BLOCKING

Linemen and corner backs should be positioned in three-point stances or in modified two-point stances with elbows on knees and the feet closer together than in a normal stance (see Figure 6-6).

It is necessary to position quickly because the center snaps the ball when he is ready after getting the "set" call from the holder. As the ball is snapped, each lineman steps to the inside with his near foot while the outside foot remains anchored. As he steps, both arms must come up into a hitting position. The object is to

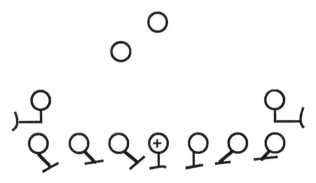

Figure 6-6. Extra point blocking formation.

plug the gap and make yourself as big as possible to prevent penetration.

Both corner blockers must line up close behind the tight end in position to stop the inside corner rush. It is important that neither blocker leaves his position or steps too deep. The most vulnerable rush will come from the inside.

The holder positions himself exactly 7 yds. behind the center, resting on one knee. He should position the tee so that it is in line with the center and accessible to the holder's placement of the ball. The ball's laces should be opposite the kicker.

FUNDAMENTALS OF KICKING

Soccer-Style Free Kicking

In recent years the trend has been to develop soccer-style kickers for kickoffs and extra points. In analyzing the techniques used by soccer kickers, researchers have found that they are able to deliver a greater force to the ball than straight-on kickers. Because of the angle of approach, the kicker increases the total number of muscle groups involved in the kick and is able to generate the force over a greater distance. This results in increased momentum of the kicker's leg and foot at impact, which makes for a longer kick.

Kicking Mechanics

Most soccer-style kickers favor a starting position in which the kicker aligns himself at a 45-degree angle to the ball. This angle is achieved by the kicker taking two paces straight back from the ball and two paces to the right or left of the ball, depending on the kicking foot. This results in a triangle (see Figure 6-7).

Kicker's Stance

The kicker must assume a comfortable stance, with feet about shoulder-width apart. The weight is evenly distributed over both feet. In addition, the feet are aligned in a plane parallel to the kicker's path to the ball. The left foot is slightly forward of the right foot.

When he is ready to begin his approach, the kicker assumes a slight forward lean at the waist, with his left shoulder turned toward the

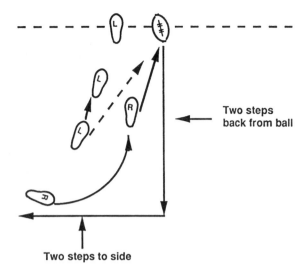

Two steps
back from ball

Two steps to side

Figure 6-7. Soccer-style kicker alignment.

ball. This position enables him to make the rapid transfer of weight and the trunk rotation needed for the soccer-style kick. The kicker's arms are in a relaxed position and his eyes are focused on the bottom half of the ball.

The Approach

The kicker begins the action with a short jab step with his left foot. Next he shifts his weight to his kicking foot as he steps with his right foot. The toes of the right foot should land on the line of approach to the ball. This action allows the hips and the trunk to rotate toward the ball. This second step brings him approximately halfway to the ball.

The third step is an explosive one and accomplishes two important functions:

1. The left hip is rotated so that the toes of the left foot are turned upfield, perpendicular to the crossbar or pointed to the crossbar
2. The left foot should land approximately 6-8 in. to the side of the ball so that the arch of the left foot is on a line with the ball

The placement of the left foot may be the most important part of the kicking sequence. This correct placement allows the kicker's trunk to rotate to a position parallel to the goal post. Also, this allows greater rotation of the right leg during the kick.

Once the left foot is placed, hip and trunk rotation begin simultaneously. The right hip extends forward while the right knee is bent. The kicker is now in position to kick the ball.

The Kick

The right knee leads the foot to the ball. As the right knee passes over the ball, the ankle and foot are flexed. This allows the inside portion of the foot to be swung into the ball.

To prevent excess rotation of the left shoulder, the left arm is brought horizontally across the kicker's chest as the right foot contacts the ball. By this arm action, the kicker's shoulders remain parallel to the goal line. This helps prevent the hooking of the ball that is a common problem of soccer-style kickers.

The Follow-Through

After the ball leaves the foot, the follow-through begins. Though this has no effect on distance or direction (the kick has already been made), it must be considered for the kicker's safety. In making the kick, the kicker has developed a tremendous velocity in the kicking leg. He must now slow this acceleration to prevent damage to the knee and hip.

KICKING GAME TECHNIQUES—PUNTING

Anyone can learn to punt! But to become a successful punter, one must first learn the basic techniques and then practice them over and over again. Developing the balance and timing necessary for success can only be achieved by going through the proper motions literally hundreds of times.

Anyone learning to punt should not be initially concerned with distance. Rather, he should work for consistency. This is the single most important factor in becoming a successful punter—*getting off a fairly good punt every time.* The following is intended to help you teach the skills required to become a consistent punter.

The basic fundamentals of punting that must be mastered are:

1. stance
2. holding and dropping the ball
3. stepping
4. meeting the ball and following through

Though these fundamentals must be studied, discussed, and practiced as separate parts, the punter must consider them as one continuous operation. In no case should the punter think of one specific phase while punting. It should be one complete and fluid motion. Only in practice should this breakdown take place.

Stance

The punter should be relaxed and comfortable in stance. A couple of deep breaths will help the punter to relax. His weight should be evenly distributed over both feet. The feet are in a heel–toe relationship. For a right-footed punter, the left foot will be in front. There should be about a 4-in. spread between the feet. This puts the punter in a ready position and he can move in any direction whenever the snap from center is off line.

The punter must bend at the waist and knees. His arms are extended in front of him at waist height and the palms of the hands are up (see Figure 6-8). Emphasize keeping the ball low and kicking it low.

During the entire punt, the punter's eyes are on the ball. He must see the football from the time the ball is between the center's legs until the ball leaves his foot.

Holding and Dropping the Ball

The punt starts when the center snaps the ball and ends when the ball leaves the punter's foot. At the high school or youth level, the entire punting operation takes about two-and-one-half seconds. During this brief time span, the punter must perform a number of athletic movements in order to make the punt successful.

First, the punter must catch the ball. Because all center snaps are not perfect, he must move to catch the bad snaps and punt them as well as the good snaps. For very poor snaps, a rule to follow is to take a step with the plant foot and kick the ball. This should be done regularly in practice.

With a good snap from center, the kicker looks the ball into his hands. He must keep the ball out in front of him and not bring it into his body. After he catches the ball he should adjust it as he begins stepping forward. As mentioned earlier, the time a punter has is limited and he

Figure 6-8. INCORRECT: This punter's hands are positioned wrong. They should be waist high with palms up.

should use it most efficiently. So, as he begins his steps he adjusts the ball, getting the laces on top with the front of the ball (the nose) pointed slightly down and in (see Figure 6-9). The hands are on the sides of the ball. For a right-footed punter, the right hand is at the rear of the ball and the left hand is a balance at the front of the ball.

In releasing the ball, the punter should develop a level drop. Once the ball is adjusted, it should be kept in the same relative position until it is placed on the instep of the kicking foot. By maintaining the bend at the waist and knees, keeping the arms extended at waist height, and holding the ball with both hands, the punter will improve his chances of making a good drop.

Stepping

For the young punter, a two-step approach is recommended. A two-step movement enables

Figure 6-9. The punter should adjust the ball with laces up and his hands on the sides of the ball.

The cross-over problem develops when the first step is made off to the side. The line drill is helpful in developing a straight ahead approach.

Meeting the Ball and Following Through

To get the maximum force in the punt, the punter must make contact with the football at about knee height. Because the height of players varies, using the knee height as the contact point rather than an arbitrary height of 2 ft. makes more sense. To achieve this, the coach must keep emphasizing bending the waist and knees, and holding the ball at waist level.

Much of the power for the kick comes from extension of the kicking leg. As the second step is made, this kicking leg extends. The toe of the kicking foot is pointed forward and slightly downward. This flattening of the kicking foot then permits the punter to drop the ball onto the instep of the foot. Contact is made low. The kick should be made through the ball. The force of the leg straightening will carry the kicking leg high. The arms, after the drop is made, will be outstretched to the sides and up high. The punter's eyes must stay focused on the football throughout the entire procedure. Once he has kicked the ball, the kicker becomes the safety who directs his team in punt coverage.

The kicking shoe must have a soft and pliable sole. Many shoes have rigid, plastic-type soles which do not permit the punter to flatten his foot.

Line Drills

The use of the line drill with variations helps develop a consistent punter. Using chalk lines helps the punter develop a straight approach.

In the first drill, the punter sets up in the proper position and takes his two-step approach without kicking the ball. Many repetitions can be done in a short period.

In the second drill, the punter practices the drop. Holding the football outside the kicking leg, have the punter take his steps and release the ball to the ground. The ball, if released properly, will bounce up and slightly forward. If the punter is holding the ball in one hand or is just throwing the ball, the drop will not be level and the football will take unusual bounces. Again,

the punter to get the kick off quickly. Also, he uses less than 3 yds. in this action and thus stays well back of the line of scrimmage. Punters who take three or more steps get too close to the line of scrimmage where the defense will have a chance to block the punt. A good rule at the high school and youth level is to get the punt off at least 9 yds. back from the original line. A two-step approach will assure the punter of this relationship.

After catching the ball, the punter takes a short step with the kicking foot and then a normal step with his other foot. As he is stepping and adjusting the ball, he makes his second step and releases the ball.

Coaches must check to see that the punter steps in a straight line. Punters have a tendency to wander either right or left as they step with the ball. Stepping straight allows the punter's blockers to protect him. This also prevents the left foot from crossing over in front of the body.

many repetitions can be done in a short time and the punter will develop a level, consistent drop.

After the punters have worked on the first two basic drills, have two punters stand about 20 yds. apart on a chalk line and kick soft punts to one another. Again, the emphasis is on a proper starting position, a straight ahead approach, a level drop, and a flattening of the kicking foot.

After the punters are familiar with these three drills, they are ready to do some punting for distance. It is wise to avoid kicking for distance in the early part of the training season. If there are several punters practicing at the same time, they will try to impress one another with their distance. This is normal, but it is the coach's responsibility to get them to focus on technique rather than distance. Distance will come with proper technique.

Section II
Effective Coaching

7
Role of the Coach

Paul Vogel, Ph.D.

QUESTIONS TO CONSIDER

- What are the primary roles of a youth football coach?
- What benefits does football offer participants?
- What potential detriments can occur in the presence of inadequate adult leadership?
- What principal goals should a coach seek to achieve?

INTRODUCTION

For young people participating in a football program, the quality and subsequent benefits of their experience is determined largely by their coach. Strong leadership during practices, games, and special events encourages each young person to nurture and develop individual strengths physically, psychologically, and socially. Poor or weak leadership not only inhibits such growth, it actually undermines a youth's existing strengths in these areas.

While it's impossible to provide a totally beneficial experience, as a football coach it is your responsibility to ensure that the benefits gained by each youth far outweigh the detriments. To accomplish this, you must know what these benefits and detriments are, and you must plan each practice and activity carefully to maximize the benefits for each child.

Possible Benefits for Participants

The numerous benefits for youth include:

- developing appropriate skills

- developing physical fitness
- learning appropriate conditioning techniques that affect health and performance
- developing a realistic and positive self-image
- developing a lifetime pattern of regular physical activity
- developing a respect for rules as facilitators of safe and fair play
- obtaining enjoyment and recreation
- developing positive personal, social, and psychological skills (e.g., self-worth, self-discipline, team work, goal-setting, self-control)

Many players achieve significant benefits in at least some of these areas depending on the frequency, duration, and intensity of participation and the quality of coaching leadership.

Many significant benefits can be gained in youth football.

Possible Detriments for Participants

Players are likely to benefit from a football program when the coach sets appropriate objectives in the areas of skill, knowledge, fitness, and personal/social development. If, however, the coach sets inappropriate goals or teaches poorly, detriments may result.

To fully understand the value of a good coach, contrast the benefits listed previously with these possible detriments for the participant:

- developing inappropriate physical skills
- sustaining injury, illness, or loss of physical fitness
- learning incorrect rules and strategies of play
- learning incorrect conditioning techniques
- developing a negative or unrealistic self-image
- avoiding future participation in activity for self and others
- learning to misuse rules to gain unfair or unsafe advantages
- developing a fear of failure
- developing anti-social behaviors
- wasting time that could have been made available for other activities

When incorrect techniques and negative behaviors are learned by young athletes, the next coach must perform the difficult and time-consuming task of extinguishing these behaviors.

To maximize the benefits and minimize the detriments, you must understand your role as a football coach and provide quality leadership.

The benefits of participation relate directly to the quality of leadership.

GOALS FOR THE COACH

As a coach, it is important to:

1. effectively teach the individual techniques, rules, and strategies of the game in an orderly and enjoyable environment
2. appropriately challenge the cardiovascular and muscular systems of your players through active practice sessions and games
3. teach and model desirable personal, social, and psychological skills

Winning is also an important goal for the coach and participants but it is one you have little control over because winning is often con-tingent on outside factors (e.g., the skills of the opposition, calls made by officials). If you concentrate on the three areas mentioned and become an effective leader, winning becomes a natural by-product.

The degree of success you attain in achieving these goals is determined by the extent to which you make appropriate choices and take correct actions in organizing and administering, teaching and leading, and protecting and caring.

Organization and Administration

Effective coaching relies heavily on good organization and administration. Organization involves clearly identifying the goals and objectives that must be attained if you are going to create a beneficial experience (with few detriments) for the participating youths. Steps necessary to organize the season so it can be efficiently administered include:

- identifying your primary purposes as a coach
- identifying goals for the season
- selecting and organizing the season's objectives
- selecting and implementing the activities in practices and games that lead to achievement of the objectives
- evaluating the effects of your actions

Specific information, procedures, criteria, and examples necessary to effectively complete these steps are included in Chapter 8, Chapter 10, and Chapter 15.

Teaching and Leading

Teaching and leading are the core of coaching activity. Principles of effective instruction such as setting appropriate player expectations, using clear instructions, maintaining an orderly environment, maximizing the amount of practice time that is "on task," monitoring progress, and providing specific feedback are included in Chapter 10. This chapter gives you many insights into how you may effectively teach your players. Other important information for teaching and leading young athletes includes motivating your players, communicating effectively, maintaining discipline, and developing good personal and social skills. Coaching guidelines for each of these areas are included in Section II.

The only real control you have over winning and/or losing is the manner in which you plan and conduct your practices and supervise your games.

Because of the influence you have as "coach," your players will model the behaviors you exhibit. If you respond to competition (successes and failures), fair play, officials' calls, and/or spectators' comments with a positive and constructive attitude, your players are likely to imitate that positive behavior. If, however, you lose your temper, yell at officials, or bend and/or break rules to gain an unfair advantage, your players' actions are likely to become negative. When what you say differs from what you do, your players will be most strongly affected by what you do. Negative behavior by players can occur even if you tell them to "be good sports and to show respect to others" and then ignore this advice by acting in a contrary manner. In essence, "actions speak louder than words" and you must "practice what you preach" if you hope to positively influence your players' behavior.

Protecting and Caring

Although coaches often eliminate the potential for injury from their minds, it is important for them to (a) plan for injury prevention, (b) effectively deal with injuries when they occur, and (c) meet their legal responsibilities to act prudently. The information on legal liabilities in Section II, and conditioning youth football players, nutrition for successful performance, and prevention, care, and rehabilitation of common football injuries in Section III, provides the basis for prudent and effective action in these areas.

SUMMARY

Your primary purpose as a youth football coach is to maximize the benefits of participation in football while minimizing the detriments. To achieve this, you must organize, teach, model, and evaluate effectively. Your players learn not only from what you teach but from what you consciously or unconsciously do. You're a very significant person in the eyes of your players. They notice when you're organized and fair, are a good instructor, know the rules, are interested in them or in the win/ loss record, know how to control your emotions, know how to present yourself, and treat others with respect. The choices you make and the actions you take determine how positive the experience is for them.

8
Planning for the Season

Paul Vogel, Ph.D.

QUESTIONS TO CONSIDER

- Why should planning for the entire season precede day-to-day planning?
- What steps should a coach follow when organizing for the season?
- What skills, knowledge, aspects of fitness, and personal/social skills should be included as objectives for the season?
- How should the season be organized to be most effective from a coaching–learning point of view?

INTRODUCTION

Planning for the season involves two basic tasks. First, coaches must select the content that will be the focus of instruction during the season (objectives that involve physical skills, sport-related knowledge, fitness capacities, and personal/social skills). Second, these desired outcomes should be organized into a plan from which practices, games, and other events can be efficiently managed.

What follows provides reasons why season planning is useful and gives you steps necessary to develop a season's plan as well as examples of season objectives. Materials and examples are also provided at the end of this chapter for completing your season plan.

WHY PLAN?

Coaches agree that teaching the skills, rules, and strategies of football are among their primary responsibilities. Most coaches would also

agree that improving the physical condition of the players, promoting enjoyment of the game, teaching good sportsmanship, and attempting to avoid physical and psychological injury are also outcomes they wish to achieve. Many coaches, however, fail to recognize the importance of planning to accomplish these goals.

Achievement of goals and objectives requires effective planning.

Organized practices are vital to maximizing the benefits of football. Disorganized practices often result in players failing to obtain desired skills, knowledge, fitness, and attitudes and often contribute to injuries and inappropriate skills. Organizing your season and planning your practices prior to going on the field can result in the following benefits:

- efficient use of limited practice time
- inclusion of season objectives that are most essential

- appropriate sequence of season objectives
- directing practice activities to the season's goals and objectives
- reduction of the time required for planning
- enhanced preparation of the team for competition
- improved ability to make day-to-day adjustments in practice objectives
- deterrent to lawsuits involving coaches' liability

DEVELOPING A SEASON PLAN

Use these three steps to develop a season plan:

1. Identify the goals and objectives of the season
2. Sequence the season objectives into the pre, early, mid, and late portions of the season
3. Identify practice objectives

The relationship of these three steps to fulfilling your role as the coach and to evaluating the outcomes you desire for your players is illustrated in Figure 8-1.

Identify Goals and Objectives for the Season

Your primary role as coach is to maximize the benefits for your players while minimizing the potential detrimental effects of participation. This alone provides the basis for identifying the specific goals and objectives for your coaching effort. You will affect your players either positively or negatively in each of the following areas:

- physical skills (blocking, kicking, punting, footwork, passing and receiving, offensive strategies, defensive strategies)
- knowledge (rules, tactics, training techniques, terminology, nutrition, safety)
- fitness (muscular strength, endurance, flexibility, aerobic fitness)
- personal/social skills (feelings about football, motivation, discipline, sportsmanship, other character traits)

By thinking of these four broad areas of player outcomes as goals, you are taking the initial step toward fulfilling your major role of "maximizing the benefits" of participation in football and "minimizing the potential detrimental effects of participation" by clearly specifying the objectives for the season.

Although the identification of goals is an important first step, it is the selection of specific objectives within each goal area that provides the direction necessary to organize the season and plan effective practices.

Selecting Skill Objectives

Supplement 8-1 provides you with a list of objectives for each physical skill area. By reviewing the individual techniques listed, you can select objectives that are best for your players. To help with this task, appropriate objectives for players at three levels of play (ages under 10, ages under 12, ages under 14, and ages 14 and over) are suggested. A detailed description of each of these individual techniques as well as progressions for teaching can be found in Section I. The key elements of performance are the basis for assessing players and for focusing your coaching efforts. This information should be reviewed if you do not have a good understanding of these individual techniques.

Selecting Knowledge Objectives

Cognitive outcomes (e.g., knowledge of rules, strategies, and information related to physical conditioning) are important for your players. Rules pertaining to "violations" and "penalties," how to warm up and cool down, what to eat for a pregame meal, and exercises to avoid are all important objectives because they can influence a player's performance. Objectives that include cognitive skills and tactics are listed in Supplement 8-2. You may wish to add to, delete from, or alter the objectives on this list as you determine those that are most appropriate for your team. By identifying these objectives, it's more likely they'll be taught at specific times during the season and at an appropriate level of understanding.

Selecting Fitness Objectives

Generally, your primary concern for athletes in the 6-13 age range should be to develop physical skills, knowledge, and appropriate personal/social skills. This is not to suggest that conditioning is unimportant. It is, however, the studied opinion of many coaches and specialists in growth and development that the specific

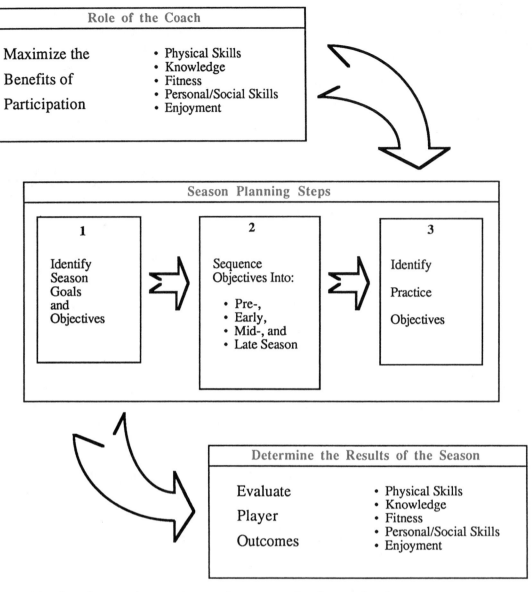

Figure 8-1. A coach's role as it relates to planning the season and evaluating the players.

training designed to promote high levels of sport-related fitness should receive a lower priority at this age. For highly skilled football players 14 years of age and older, a gradually increasing emphasis should be placed on conditioning the muscular and energy production systems. Part of the reason for this recommendation is that when young athletes train for skilled performance, they also obtain conditioning stimuli that are sufficient to cause the body to adapt to the fitness demands associated with learning and performing football skills. As players become highly skilled, conditioning becomes a more important factor for enabling more frequent, more intense, and more enduring appli-

cation of their abilities. Supplement 8-3 includes an overview of fitness objectives you may wish to include in your season plan for older players who are also highly skilled.

For younger players, fitness should be a by-product of learning the physical skills.

Selecting Personal and Social Skill Objectives

A primary objective in the season plan should be to have all players feel increasingly better about their abilities as the season progresses. This should occur not only in the areas of physical skills, knowledge, and fitness, but should also include qualities such as persistence, self-control, tolerance, respect for authority, encouragement of teammates, concentration on the task, commitment to best efforts, and cooperation. Athletes need guidance (modeling, direction, encouragement, gentle rebuking, etc.) to develop such attributes. When achieved, these personal and social qualities contribute to performance in both athletic and non-athletic situations. Moreover, unlike opponents, officials, and/or the "breaks of the game," these qualities are within the control of individual players. The opportunity for individual control has been strongly linked to motivation, and motivation is strongly linked to performance.

Coaches are responsible for developing socially desirable skills in their players.

As a coach, perhaps your most important and lasting contribution is helping your players improve their feelings of self-worth and socially desirable skills. By focusing on controllable qualities such as "effort" versus uncontrollable "outcomes," which are often dependent on others (e.g., an official's call, a "lucky" bounce, the ability of another team), you have a unique opportunity to make a significant and lasting contribution to the personal character of your athletes.

Contributing to team membership is another worthy objective that coaches should set for every player. Athletes, especially those who engage in team sports such as football, must learn to overcome the natural tendency to blame others for a loss or even a bad performance. Players must be taught that their role is to play as well as they can and to think, do, and say those things that can help their teammates do the same. The team will only be as good as its weakest link. Often, an otherwise excellent team performs at a mediocre level due to the dissension created by "putting others down," making excuses, or transferring blame to others.

Coaches should reward effort when they review the accomplishments of the team.

Included in Supplement 8-4 is a listing of several personal and social skill objectives that you may want to incorporate into your season

plan. The listing may be modified and made specific to your players.

Sequence Objectives Into Pre, Early, Mid, and Late Portions of the Season

Once you've identified season objectives for your team, they can be listed on the worksheet provided in Supplement 8-5. While the list may need to be revised as the season unfolds, the objectives should become the basis of your planning for the season.

Categorize the listed objectives into goals you want to achieve in the pre-, early-, mid-, and late-season (see Figure 8-2). Some objectives may be emphasized throughout the season, whereas others may be emphasized in only one division of the season. Photocopy Supplement 8-6 and use it to complete this step of your season plan.

Deciding what objectives should be achieved in the pre-, early-, mid-, and late-season is the basis for all subsequent planning.

Pre-season Objectives

If pre-season activity is possible, it can save you valuable practice time. Many of the objectives pertaining to knowledge of the rules and strategies and some of those involving conditioning can be all, or partially, achieved before formal practice even begins.

Objectives appropriate for the pre-season involve skills, knowledge, fitness capacities, or personal/social skills that can be achieved independently (all or in part) by the player in a safe and efficient manner before the initiation of formal practices. This could include learning the basic rules, violations and penalties, and strategies; obtaining appropriate equipment; and developing strength and aerobic fitness.

Early-season Objectives

The early-season should be devoted to determining how well your players have mastered the fundamental and/or prerequisite objectives you have selected and to teaching, reteaching, or practicing those objectives. Objectives appropriate for the early-season should contain abilities that are prerequisite to attaining other identified objectives. For example, players must be able to run the pattern before they can be expected to run the pattern and catch the ball. This attention to the sequence of skills is particularly important for the inexperienced player, who should spend more time on learning skills typically placed in the early-season division. In addition to objectives associated with physical skills, early-season objectives should include logistical and organizational concerns, safety, strategy, discipline, fitness, socialization, rules of play, and team rules. These are all essential in preparing players for early-season games and to provide a foundation for the rest of the season.

Mid-season Objectives

Mid-season objectives should continue to focus on teaching individual techniques. However, a large share of practice time should be devoted to refining these techniques within the context of game-like drills and controlled scrimmages. Time should be spent combining individual techniques (e.g., catching the ball first, then thinking about running), and integrating these techniques with game strategy. Many of the cognitive, fitness, and personal/social objectives established for the early-season should continue to be emphasized during the mid-season.

Late-season Objectives

Late-season objectives should be focused on the maintenance and refinement of the team's offensive and defensive play. A greater portion of practice time should be spent on small-sided games, game-like drills, and controlled scrimmages. Practices should be organized so fitness levels are maintained and emphasis continues on cognitive and personal and social skills.

Generally, you should focus on single skills in the early-season, skill combinations in the mid-season, and combinations of both within systems of play in the later portion of the season. There are no hard and fast divisions among these three phases of the season (in fact, they should blend or overlap through good transitions). However, you should have them clearly in mind as you view the entire season in terms of what you wish to accomplish and the time in which it must be done.

Identify Practice Objectives

As you place objectives into season divisions and adjust the number of weeks assigned to each division, you will likely find that you have chosen to cover more than your available practice time allows. A good guide in such situations is to devote enough time to the cumulative instruction and practice of each objective so the majority of players are able to make significant improvements on most of the objectives included in the season plan. Merely exposing your team to the individual techniques of the game, without spending sufficient time for them to be learned, results in frustration for you and the players. Your players must receive sufficient instruction, practice, and feedback to master the objectives at an appropriate level for use in a game situation. Accordingly, select, teach, and practice only the objectives that are essential to the game at your team's level of play. You can always add objectives to your plan as it is implemented, but you cannot recover time wasted on objectives that are not achieved or that are inappropriate for your players' level of development.

Select, teach, and practice the key objectives that are essential to your team.

Generally, the allotment of time to physical skill objectives should be based upon the following instructional sequence and distributed across several practices. You should allow time:

1. to introduce the objective—tell the players what you want them to learn and why it is important
2. for the players to try the individual techniques and for you to determine their levels of performance
3. for you to teach the key elements of the individual techniques and for players to practice these elements
4. for skill refinement and automation such that an individual technique can be used in game situations

The time allotment to fitness, cognitive, and personal/social objectives may not be as structured as the allotment for physical skill objectives. Fitness goals may be achieved along

SEASON PLAN WORKSHEET

Coach: _____ **Season:** _____

Goal Areas	Objectives	Season Division			
		Pre	Early	Mid	Late
Physical Skills	Blocking		X	X	X
	Tackling		X	X	X
	Kicking		X	X	X
	Agility		X	X	X
	Ball-carrying		X	X	X
	Throwing		X	X	X
	Receiving		X	X	X
	Centering skills		X	X	X
	Quarterback skills		X	X	X
Knowledge	Rules of the Game				
	penalties	X	X	X	
	scoring	X	X	X	
	timing	X	X	X	
	Strategies				
	offensive			X	X
	defensive			X	X
	kicking game		X	X	
Fitness	Flexibility				
	hip	X	X	X	X
	shoulder	X	X	X	X
	neck	X	X	X	X
		X	X	X	X
	Cardiovascular				
Personal/Social	Personal				
	best effort		X	X	X
	listening		X	X	X
	Social				
	cooperation		X	X	X
	fair play		X	X	X

Figure 8-2. An abbreviated example of a season plan for young football players.

with practice of individual techniques in drills and scrimmages. Similarly, some cognitive, and personal/social objectives may be concomitantly attained during the practice of physical skills. However, some of these objectives may need practice time specifically devoted to them.

Integrating your chosen objectives into a season calendar (see Figure 8-3) will give you a master plan of everything you need to manage your coaching activities. The season calendar converts your plans to practice outlines. The daily entries on the calendar provide a guide from which specific plans can be developed. Supplement 8-7 provides a blank reproducible worksheet that you can use to develop a master plan of practices.

The following list includes examples of entries that can be included on a calender:

- registration dates and deadlines
- date team roster is distributed
- sign-up date for practice time at available facilities
- dates and times for coaches' education meetings
- equipment distribution dates and times
- date and time for parents' orientation meeting
- dates and times for league meetings
- sequential numbers designating practices (e.g., #1 designates first practice)
- practice objectives and time allocations
- game days and times
- tournament dates
- dates and times for special events

The most important part of developing a season calendar is the decision you make about what objectives to include and how much practice time you devote to each objective on a practice-by-practice basis. Using your season plan worksheet, select an appropriate number of objectives listed under "early-season" that you wish to include in your first practice and enter them in the space labeled "practice #1" on your season calendar. This process should be repeated for your second, third, and subsequent practices through the early, mid-, and late-season divisions.

The two most important decisions in planning the season are deciding what objectives to teach and how much time you should spend teaching them.

You will spend less total time planning for your season and practice if you use the approach suggested here than if the task is done practice-by-practice throughout the season. This process will also help you verify which skills you believe are most important as you run out of available practice time and are forced to either exclude objectives from your plan or find other ways to achieve them outside of the normal practice time. In addition to the good feeling and confidence that comes with completing a season calendar, you will have developed the base necessary to systematically change your plans as unexpected events develop. More importantly, you will know before the mid to late portions of the season whether in your initial plan you assigned too much or too little time to some of your early-season objectives. A completed plan that's been implemented and refined is also an invaluable resource for next year's coaching assignment or as a guide for new coaches coming into the program.

SUMMARY

Your role as a coach can be best filled through the leadership and instruction you provide in practice and game situations. Clearly, those coaches who are most effective in helping their players acquire the necessary physical skills, knowledge, fitness, and personal/social skills are those who have clear objectives and who organize to achieve them. Organization of the season by selecting and then teaching objectives in a proper order, and for an appropriate amount of time, is a major step toward helping players acquire the benefits of football.

SEASON PLANNING CALENDAR

Coach __Goodbody__   Team __Falcons__   Month _____

S	M	T	W	T	F	S
	Coaches' education meeting 7:00-9:00 (High School)		Team rosters distributed, sign-up for practice times/fields 7:00-8:00 (Rec Office)			
		Parents' orientation meeting 7:00-8:30 (Elementary School Rm. 10)				
		Practice #1		Practice #2		Practice #3
		Practice #4		Practice #5		Practice #6
		Practice #7		Practice #8		

Figure 8-3. An example of a season planning calendar.

Practice #1

05 Overview of practice
10 Team rules and regulations
05 Warm-up

Review and evaluate:

15 Stance and agility drills
15 Passing and receiving
10 Punting and kicking
05 Snapping and centering
10 Speed timing (40 yds.)
05 Cool-down
05 Handouts: team rules,
    practice and game schedule,
    rules of play

Practice #2

05 Overview of practice
10 Review rules of safety
    (helmet contact)
05 Warm-up

Review and evaluate:

15 Stance and agility drills
10 Huddle and alignment

Practice:

20 Offensive drills
    (blocking, running, handoffs)
20 Team, offensive playwork
10 Team sprints and cool-down

Practice #3

05 Overview of practice
10 Review 3 running plays
05 Team warm-up

Review and evaluate:

15 Stance and agility drills
50 Huddle and alignment

Practice:

20 Offensive drills
20 Defensive drills
20 Offensive team work
10 Sprints and cool-down

Practice #4

05 Overview of practice
10 Review team defense
    and tackling
05 Team warm-up

Review and evaluate:

15 Stance and agility drills
05 Huddle and alignment

Practice:

20 Offensive drills
20 Defensive tackling drills
20 Defensive team alignment
10 Sprints and cool-down

Practice #5

05 Overview of practice
10 Review punting game
05 Team warm-up

Review and evaluate:

15 Stance and agility drills
05 Form tackling

Practice:

20 Team punt and coverage
20 Offensive drills
    (passing and protection)
20 Team passing
10 Sprints and cool-down
10 Review passing offense

Practice #6

05 Overview of practice
10 Review kickoff and returns
05 Team warm-up

Review and evaluate:

15 Stance and agility drills
10 Team tackling (form)

Practice:

20 Team offense scrimmage
    versus defense
20 Defense drills and review
20 Team defense (reaction drills)
10 Sprints and cool-down

Practice #7

05 Overview and questions
05 Warm-up

Review and evaluate:

10 Stance and agility drills
10 Team punt and coverage

Practice:

10 Defensive drills
20 Team defense versus offense
10 Offensive drills
20 Team offense versus defense
10 Goal line offense
05 Cool-down

Practice #8

05 Overview and questions
05 Warm-up

Review and evaluate:

10 Stance and agility drills
10 Team punt and coverage

Practice:

10 Defensive drills
10 Team defense versus
    offense (goal line)
10 offensive drills
20 Team offense versus defense
10 Kickoff and return
05 Cool-down

Centers and quarterbacks
should be dressed and on the
field 15 minutes before the
official start of practice to
practice center-quarterback
exchange. Quarterbacks should
also practice pass drops and
warm up throwing arm by
passing to a stationary receiver.

Figure 8-3 (continued)

Skills and Abilities of Football

PERFORMANCE AREA	SPECIFIC SKILLS	SUGGESTED EMPHASIS			
		Under 10 yrs.	Under 12 yrs.	Under 14 yrs.	14 yrs. and over
Blocking					
	Stance	IT	T	R	R
	Get-off	IT	T	T	R
	Drive	IT	T	T	T
	Double team	IT	T	T	T
	Trap	I	T	T	T
	Sweep	I	T	T	T
	Lb'er	I	T	T	T
	Downfield	I	T	T	R
	Pass	IT	T	T	T
Tackling					
	Straight on	I	T	T	T
	Angle	IT	T	T	T
	Pass rush	I	T	T	T
	Open field	I	T	R	R
Putting ball into play					
	C-QB exchange	IT	T	T	T
	Short–long snaps (punt, p.a.t., f.g.)		I	T	T
Running					
	Stance	IT	T	T	R
	Ball handling/pitches	I	T	T	R
	Running tech	IT	T	T	T
	Ball carrying	I	T	T	R
	Hitting hole	I	T	T	R
	Faking/deception	I	T	T	R
	Cutback			I	T
	Use of interference			I	T
	Body angle			I	T

I = Introduction
T = Teaching
R = Review

Skills and Abilities of Football

PERFORMANCE AREA	SPECIFIC SKILLS	SUGGESTED EMPHASIS			
		Under 10 yrs.	Under 12 yrs.	Under 14 yrs.	14 yrs. and over
Passing					
	Gripping ball	IT	T	R	R
	Footwork	I	T	T	T
	Throwing stance	I	T	T	R
	Throwing tech (delivery/follow-thru)	IR	T	T	T
	Dropback	I	T	T	T
	Sprintout		IT	T	T
	Play action		I	T	T
Receiving					
	Stance/release	IT	T	R	R
	Catching ball	IT	T	R	R
	Hook	IT	T	T	R
	Out	IT	T	T	R
	Post		I	T	T
	Flag		I	T	T
	Drag		I	T	T
	Fly		I	T	T
Kicking					
	Punt	IT	T	T	R
	Kickoff	IT	T	T	R
	P.A.T.		IT	T	T
	F.G.		IT	T	T
Defense play					
Linemen	Stance	IT	T	T	R
	Alignment	IT	T	T	R
	Charge/tech	I	T	T	R
	Responsibilities	I	T	T	T
	Tackling	I	T	T	R
	Pursuit	I	T	T	R
Linebackers	Stance	IT	T	T	R
	Alignment	IT	T	T	R
	Responsibilities/keys	I	T	T	T
	Shuffle	I	T	T	R
	Scrape			I	R
	Reaction run	I	T	I	T
	Tackling	I	T	T	R
	Pursuit	I	T	T	R
Secondary	Stance	IT	T	T	R
	Alignment	IT	T	T	R
	Responsibilities/ coverages	I	T	T	T
	Footwork	I	T	T	T
	Tackling	I	T	T	R
	Pursuit	I	T	T	R

Knowledge Objectives*

PERFORMANCE AREA	SPECIFIC SKILLS	SUGGESTED EMPHASIS			
		Under 10 yrs.	Under 12 yrs.	Under 14 yrs.	14 yrs. and over
Positions					
	Offensive	IT	T	T	R
	Defensive	IT	T	T	R
	Special teams	I	T	T	T
Rules					
	Encroachment	IT	R	R	R
	Delay of game	I	T	R	R
	Illegal motion	I	T	R	R
	Holding	I	T	R	R
	Illegal use of hands	I	T	R	R
	Blocking below waist	IT	T	R	R
	Illegal pass	I	T	R	R
	Ineligible receiver	I	T	R	R
	Personal foul	I	T	T	T
	Unsportsmanlike conduct	IT	T	T	T
	Grasping face mask	I	T	R	R
	Clipping	IT	T	R	R
Nutrition					
	Pregame meal		I	T	R
Conditioning					
	Warm-up		IT	R	R
	Cool-down		IT	R	R
	Stretching	IT	T	R	R
	Light calisthenics		IT	R	R
	Overload			I	T
	Adaptation			I	T
	Progression			I	T

I = Introduction
T = Teaching
R = Review

*Note that these knowledge objectives must be taught. It should not be assumed that young athletes will have learned these just by playing football.

Fitness Objectives*

PERFORMANCE AREA	SPECIFIC SKILLS	SUGGESTED EMPHASIS			
		Under 10 yrs.	Under 12 yrs.	Under 14 yrs.	14 yrs. and over
Muscular strength/power					
	Neck				IT
	Shoulders (back)				IT
	Shoulders (front)				IT
	Upper arm				IT
	Forearm				IT
	Chest				IT
	Abdomen				IT
	Lower leg				IT
	Upper leg				IT
Muscular endurance					
	Neck				IT
	Shoulders (back)				IT
	Shoulders (front)				IT
	Upper arm				IT
	Forearm				IT
	Chest				IT
	Abdomen				IT
	Lower leg				IT
	Upper leg				IT
Muscular flexibility					
	Hamstrings/back	I	T	T	R
	Quads	I	T	T	R
	Arm/shoulder	I	T	T	R
	Lower leg	I	T	T	R
Energy production					
	Aerobic			I	T
	Anaerobic				T

I = Introduction
T = Teaching
R = Review

*Note that progress is made in many of these objectives at the beginning and intermediate levels of play. This development should occur concomitantly through carefully planned practice sessions designed to enhance physical skills. The marks in this chart suggest that coaches should not plan "fitness only" drills for their team until the players have reached approximately 14 years of age and are at the advanced level of play.

Supplement 8-4.

Personal and Social Objectives

PERFORMANCE AREA	SPECIFIC SKILLS	SUGGESTED EMPHASIS			
		Under 10 yrs.	Under 12 yrs.	Under 14 yrs.	14 yrs. and over
Personal					
	Self-worth	R	R	R	R
	Self-control	R	R	R	R
	Coping w/success & failure	R	R	R	R
	Best effort	R	R	R	R
	Persistence	R	R	R	R
	Tolerance	R	R	R	R
	Concentration	R	R	R	R
	Avoiding "excuses"	R	R	R	R
Social					
	Cooperation	R	R	R	R
	Respect for others	R	R	R	R
	Encouraging others	R	R	R	R
	Respect for authority	R	R	R	R
	Team membership	R	R	R	R
	Suppression of "blaming"	R	R	R	R
	Suppression of "put-downs"	R	R	R	R

R = Review

SEASON PLAN WORKSHEET

Coach: _____ **Season:** _____

Goal Areas	Objectives	Season Division			
		Pre	Early	Mid	Late
Physical Skills	Blocking fundamentals				
	Tackling fundamentals				
	Throwing				
	Receiving				
	ball carrying				
	position techniques				
	C - QB exchange				
	Kicking fundamentals				
	Agility skills				
	Coverages				
Knowledge	Rules of the game				
	scoring				
	timing				
	penalties				
	defense and offense rules				
	Strategies				
	offensive				
	defensive				
Fitness	Flexibility				
	leg, hip, shoulder, etc.				
	Strength				
	leg, shoulder, abdominal				
	Cardiovascular: general				
	Speed: sprint work				
Personal/Social	Personal				
	effort				
	listening				
	Social				
	cooperation				
	fair play				
	positive communication				
	(inter-player)				

SEASON PLAN WORKSHEET

Coach: _____   Season: _____

Goal Areas	Objectives	Season Division			
		Pre	Early	Mid	Late

Supplement 8-7.

SEASON PLANNING CALENDAR						
Coach _____ Team _____ Month _____						
S	M	T	W	T	F	S

9
Working Effectively with Parents

Martha Ewing, Ph.D.
Deborah Feltz, Ph.D.
Eugene W. Brown, Ph.D.

QUESTIONS TO CONSIDER

- How can I obtain the information and help needed from parents to do a good job?
- What is my responsibility to the parents of the players on my team?
- How can I avoid the negative influence some parents have on a team or program?
- What are the responsibilities of the players and their parents to this program?

INTRODUCTION

Support and assistance from parents can be very helpful. Some parents, however, through lack of awareness, can weaken the effects of your coaching, and thus reduce the benefits football can provide to their children.

These negative influences can be minimized if you tell parents:

- how you perceive your role as the coach
- the purpose and objectives of the football program
- the responsibilities they and their children have in helping the team run smoothly

Some parents, through lack of awareness, can weaken the effects of your coaching.

The most effective way of communicating the purposes and needs of your program is through a parents' orientation meeting. A parents' orientation meeting can be used to:

- teach parents the rules and regulations of football so they understand the game
- provide details about the season
- provide a setting for collecting and distributing important information

At the parents' orientation meeting, you have the opportunity to ask for their assistance and discuss other items that are specific to the team. A meeting for parents is also an excellent way for them to get to know you and each other. A face-to-face meeting and a few short remarks go a long way toward uniting coaches and parents in a cooperative endeavor that benefits the players. Many potential problems can be eliminated by good communication that begins before the first practice.

CONTENT OF A PARENTS' ORIENTATION MEETING

Parents usually have a number of questions concerning their child's football program. With proper preparation and an outlined agenda, you should be able to answer most questions. A sample agenda is provided. This agenda can be supplemented with items you and/or the parents believe to be important.

Sample Agenda
Parents' Orientation Meeting

1. Introductions
2. Goals of the team and program
3. Understanding the sport of football
4. Dangers and risk of injury
5. Emergency procedures
6. Equipment needs
7. Athletes' responsibilities
8. Parents' responsibilities
9. Season schedule
10. Other

Each agenda item and its relationship to the football program is explained in the following paragraphs.

Introductions

Parents should be informed about who administers the football program. They should become acquainted with the coaches and the parents of the other players. As the coach, you should introduce yourself, briefly describing your background, coaching experience, and reasons for coaching.

The parents should also introduce themselves, identify where they live, and perhaps indicate how long their children have been involved in the program and the objectives that they have for their child's involvement in football. Learning who the other parents are makes it easier to establish working relationships for specific tasks and to initiate sharing of responsibilities (e.g., carpooling and bringing refreshments to games).

Finally, the purpose of the meeting should be explained to communicate important information about each agenda item. If handouts are available, they should be distributed at this time. We suggest that at least one handout, an agenda, be distributed to provide order to the meeting, a sense of organization on your part, and a place for parents to write notes.

Information about the players and their families should be collected (see Supplement 9-1).

A team roster and telephone tree (see Supplement 9-2) could be compiled from the information collected, then typed and distributed to each of the families at another time.

Goals of the Team and Programs

The goals of the sponsoring organization, as well as your personal goals, should be presented. Parents then will be able to judge whether those goals are compatible with their beliefs regarding what is appropriate for their child. Goals that have been identified by young football players as most important are:

• to have fun
• to improve skills and learn new skills
• to be on a team and to make new friends
• to succeed or win

Most educators, pediatricians, sport psychologists, and parents consider these to be healthy goals that coaches should help young athletes achieve. Parents should be informed of the primary goals of the team and the amount of emphasis that will be placed on achieving these goals.

Parents should be informed of the primary goals of the team.

Other areas that should be addressed are your policies on eliminating players, the consequences of missing practices, and recognizing players through awards. You may be asked to answer many questions about how you will function as a coach. Some examples are:

• Will players be allowed to compete if they missed the last practice before a game?
• Will players be excluded from contests or taken off the team if they go on a two-week vacation?
• Will players receive trophies or other material rewards?
• How much emphasis will be placed on rewards?
• Are the rewards given only to good performers or are they given to all participants?

Chapter 11 discusses the issue of appropriate use of rewards. You may wish to comment on several points explained in Chapter 11 as you address this issue.

Understanding the Sport of Football

Many times spectators boo officials, shout instructions to players, or contradict the coach because they do not know the rules or strategies of football. This is particularly true if the rules of play have been modified for younger age groups. Informing parents about basic rules, skills, and strategies may help those who are unfamiliar with football and will prevent some of this negative behavior.

The information may be presented in the form of a film, brief explanation, demonstration of techniques, and/or interpretations. If you'd rather not use the meeting to cover this information, you could invite parents to attend selected practice sessions where a demonstration and/or explanation of positions, rules, and strategies will be presented to the team.

Dangers and Risk of Injury

Parents should be told what they can expect in terms of possible injuries their child may incur in football. As noted in Chapter 16, failure to inform parents of potential injuries is the most frequent basis for lawsuits involving coaches and players.

Tell them, for example, that generally the injuries are confined to sprains, bruises, and contusions, but that there is a possibility for broken bones, concussions, and catastrophic injuries. Supplement 9-3 provides information on sites of injuries in youth football. This information should be reviewed with parents. Let them know if a medical examination is required before their child's participation. If so, tell them what forms or evidence of compliance is acceptable, to whom it must be provided, and when it is due.

Parents should be told what they can expect in terms of possible injuries in youth football.

Tell the parents what will be done to prevent injuries and assure them that the playing/practice area and equipment will be checked to help keep players safe and free from exposure to hazards.

Lastly, the program's policy of accident insurance should be described. Inform parents if the program maintains athletic accident coverage or whether parents are required to provide insurance coverage for injuries that happen during their child's athletic participation.

Emergency Procedures

Have the parents provide you with information and permission necessary for you to function during an emergency. The Athlete's Medical Information Form (Supplement 9-4) and Medical Release Form (Supplement 9-5) were designed for these purposes. You should have the parents complete these forms and keep them with you at all team functions. These forms will provide you with information to guide your actions in an emergency.

Equipment Needs

Explain what equipment the players need and where it can be purchased. Advice on the quality of particular brands and models and an indication of how much parents can expect to pay for specific items is also welcomed by the parents.

If an equipment swap is organized, tell them where and when it will be held. A handout describing proper equipment should be provided. Supplement 9-6 provides a list and guidelines for the selection of football equipment. This supplement could be reproduced and used as a handout to the parents for properly outfitting their child.

Athletes' Responsibilities

The "Bill of Rights for Young Athletes," (Martens and Seefeldt 1979) reminds adults that the child's welfare must be placed above all other considerations. Children and their parents must realize, however, that along with rights, they must meet certain responsibilities. Young athletes must be responsible for:

- being on time at practices and games with all of their equipment
- cooperating with coaches and teammates
- putting forth the effort to condition their bodies and to learn the basic skills
- conducting themselves properly and living with the consequences of inappropriate behavior

These responsibilities should be discussed so parents may help reinforce them at home.

Parents' Responsibilities

Parents of young athletes must assume some responsibilities associated with their child's participation on the football team. This should be discussed at the parents' orientation meeting. Martens (1978) has identified a number of parental responsibilities. You may wish to cover all or a portion of the following responsibilities in the parents' orientation meeting.

- Parents should learn what their child expects from football.
- Parents should decide if their child is ready to compete and at what level.
- Parents should help their child understand the meaning of winning and losing.
- Parents are responsible for disciplining their child and ensuring that their child meets specific responsibilities for participating on the football team.
- Parents should not interfere with their child's coach and should conduct themselves in a proper manner at games.

Parents should also be sensitive to fulfill the commitment they and their child have made to the team. This often requires that parents displace other important tasks in order to get their child to practice on time, publicly support the coach, encourage players to give their best effort, reward players for desirable efforts, and participate in the social events of the team.

Children and their parents must assume certain responsibilities.

If called upon, parents should be willing to assist the coach to carry out some of the many tasks required to meet the needs of the team. If you, as the coach, can anticipate and identify tasks with which you will need assistance, these should be presented to the parents at the orientation meeting.

It is surprising how many parents will volunteer to help you if the tasks are well-defined. See Supplement 9-7 for a description of some qualifications required of assistants and some possible responsibilities. You may not be able to anticipate all the tasks. However, by developing an expectation of shared cooperation at the orientation meeting, parents who are not initially called upon for assistance are more likely to provide help as the need arises.

One conflict that sometimes arises results from parents falsely assuming your responsibility as coach. They may attempt to direct the play of their child and/or others during practices and games. This type of action by a parent undermines your plans for the team. It may also create a conflict in the mind of the athlete as to which set of instructions to follow.

You must inform parents that their public comments should be limited to praise and applause and that you will be prepared to coach the team. There are many ways to coach young athletes and different strategies that can result in success. You should inform parents that, if they disagree with your coaching, you will be open to their suggestions when they are presented in private.

Season Schedule

Fewer telephone calls and memos will be needed later in the season if you prepare and distribute a schedule of events for the season at the orientation meeting. The most efficient way to provide parents with the entire season schedule is with a handout.

The schedule should inform the parents about the length of the season; the dates, sites, and times when practices and games will be held; lengths of practices and games; number of games; number of practices; and other events for the season. Maps and/or instructions about where team events will occur are often helpful.

GETTING PARENTS TO ATTEND AN ORIENTATION MEETING

After you have received your team roster and, if possible, before the first practice, you should make arrangements to schedule a parents' orientation meeting. If you do not personally have sufficient space to accommodate the parents, a room in a neighborhood school usually can be scheduled free of charge for an orientation meeting.

Before scheduling the time and date for the meeting, the parents should be asked about the times that they could attend. This information, as well as items of parental concern for an agenda, can be obtained through a telephone conversation with the parents. Once the time and date have been determined, the parents should be notified about this information by telephone or brief letter.

If a letter is sent, the agenda for the meeting should be included. If possible, this notification should occur about two weeks before the meeting and should be followed by a courteous telephone reminder on the night before the meeting.

In your communication with the parents, you should stress the importance of the meeting and the need for each family to be represented at the meeting.

ORGANIZING THE PARENTS' ORIENTATION MEETING

If you are well-prepared and organized, conducting a parents' orientation meeting will be an enjoyable and useful event. Before this meeting, you should complete the agenda and write down key points you plan to communicate under each item. Next, assemble the handouts that will be distributed at the meeting. At the very least, the handouts should include an agenda for the parents to follow.

Other suggested handouts and forms for distributing and collecting information include: Information on common football injuries, medical examination form (if provided by your program), accident insurance form and information (if provided through your program), athletic medical information form, medical release form, description of proper equipment, list of team assistants and responsibilities, season schedule, telephone tree, and player and parent roster. The items in Supplements 9-1 through 9-7 are suitable for duplication (permission is granted) and could be distributed at the orientation meeting.

FOLLOW-UP ON THE PARENTS' ORIENTATION MEETING

After having conducted the parents' orientation meeting, you should contact the families who were unable to attend and briefly inform them about what was discussed. They should be given the handouts that were distributed at

the meeting, and you should collect whatever information is needed from them. Once your records are completed, you may compile additional handouts (e.g., telephone tree).

Keep the lines of communication open between you and the parents.

No matter how many questions you answer at the parents' orientation meeting, it will not solve all of the problems. Thus, it is important to keep the lines of communication open. You should indicate your willingness to discuss any problems that were not discussed at the first meeting. This might be done with a telephone call or at a conference involving the coach and parent, or the coach, parent, and athlete. Immediately before or after a practice is often an appropriate time to discuss major issues with parents. You could even have another meeting for parents midway through the season to provide an update on the team's progress, to discuss any problems, or to listen to parent's comments. By inviting parents to talk with you, they will become a positive, rather than a negative, influence on the players and the team.

SUMMARY

Parents can be an asset to your program, but some parents can have a negative influence on your program. Communicating to parents about how you perceive your role as the coach, the purpose of the football program, and the responsibilities that they and their children have to the football program can minimize these negative influences. The most effective way to communicate this information is through a parents' orientation meeting. The time and effort you put into developing a well-organized meeting will save you considerably more time and effort throughout the season.

In a parents' orientation meeting, you have the opportunity to explain to parents that they have responsibilities to you and the team, such as deciding if their child is ready to compete, having realistic expectations, disciplining, and not interfering with coaching or playing. Children's responsibilities of promptness, cooperation, commitment, and proper conduct can also be outlined for parents.

In addition, other agenda items can be discussed and information can be gathered at a parents' orientation meeting that may make your job run more smoothly throughout the season. Be sure to discuss such items as danger and risk of injury, equipment needs, emergency procedures, and the season schedule.

The agenda items outlined in this chapter may not cover all the issues you need to address with the parents of your players. Therefore, you must organize a specific meeting that meets the needs of your team.

REFERENCES

Martens, R. (1978). *Joys and sadness in children's sports.* Champaign, IL: Human Kinetics Publishers

Martens, R. & Seefeldt, V. (Eds.). (1979). *Guidelines for children's sports.* Reston, VA: AAHPERD.

SUGGESTED READINGS

American College of Sports Medicine, American Orthopaedic Society for Sports Medicine & Sports Medicine Committee of the United States Tennis Association. (1982). *Sports injuries—An aid to prevention and treatment.* Coventry, CT: Bristol Myers Co.

Foley, J. (1980). *Questions parents should ask about youth sports programs.* East Lansing, MI: Institute for the Study of Youth Sports.

Jackson, D. & Pescar, S. (1981). *The young athletes' health handbook.* New York: Everest House.

Micheli, L.J. (1985). Preventing youth sports injuries. *Journal of Health, Physical Education, Recreation and Dance, 76*(6), 52-54.

Mirkin, G. & Marshall, H. (1978). *The sportsmedicine book.* Waltham, MA: Little Brown, & Co.

Rotella, R.S., & Bunker, L.K. (1987). *Parenting your superstar: How to help your child get the most out of sports.* Champaign, IL: Leisure Press.

Smith, R.E., Smoll, F.L., & Smith, N.J. (1989). *Parents' complete guide to youth sports.* Reston, VA: AAHPERD.

Team Roster Information

	Player's Name	Birth Date	Parents' Names	Address	Phone #'s Home/Work
1.		/ /	————	————	————
2.		/ /	————	————	————
3.		/ /	————	————	————
4.		/ /	————	————	————
5.		/ /	————	————	————
6.		/ /	————	————	————
7.		/ /	————	————	————
8.		/ /	————	————	————
9.		/ /	————	————	————
10.		/ /	————	————	————
11.		/ /	————	————	————
12.		/ /	————	————	————
13.		/ /	————	————	————
14.		/ /	————	————	————
15.		/ /	————	————	————
16.		/ /	————	————	————
17.		/ /	————	————	————
18.		/ /	————	————	————

Telephone Tree

Rules for Passing on Telephone Messages

1. I (coach) will call families 2, 3, and 4.
2. When a family is called, they MUST take responsibility for passing the message on to other families assigned to them.
3. If you cannot make contact with a family assigned to you,
   a. you MUST take that family's responsibility for telephoning others and
   b. you MUST continue to call those families that you could not initially contact.

Athlete's name
Parent's name
Parent's name
Home phone no.
Work phone no.

Rules for Constructing a Telephone Tree

1. Put your name (coach)/family at the trunk of the tree.
2. In boxes 2, 3, and 4, enter information for families who are likely to be available to receive telephone messages.
3. Fill in the remaining boxes in order until all athletes are listed.

Sites of Injuries in Youth Football

Age Group[a]

	Total	0-4 Years		5-14 Years		15+ Years	
		Number	Percent	Number	Percent	Number	Percent
Head and Face	70,238	276	(38%)	24,317	(14%)	45,645	(16%)
Shoulder and Trunk	85,7270	91	(13%)	27,311	(16%)	58,325	(20%)
Arms and Hands	160,926	241	(34%)	75,975	(44%)	84,710	(29%)
Legs and Feet	143,707	111	(15%)	44,896	(26%)	98,700	(34%)
Other	2,422	----	-------	584	-------	1,838	(1%)
Totals	463,020 (100%)	719 ----	(100%)	173,083 (37%)	(100%)	289,218 (63%)	(100%)

	Total All Ages	Age Group 5-14 Years
A. Medically attended injuries, 1980	1,294,800	499,400
B. Hospital emergency room-treated injuries, 1980	463,800	173,100

[a]Distribution of Estimated Football-Related Injuries Treated in U.S. Hospital Emergency Rooms, by Body Part Injured and Age Group of Victim, 1980.

Source: National Electronic Injury Surveillance System, U.S. Consumer Product Safety Commission/EPHA

Athlete's Medical Information
(to be completed by parents/guardians and athlete)

Athlete's Name: _____ Athlete's Birthdate: _____

Parents' Names: _____ Date: _____

Address: _____

(____)_____

Phone No's.: (____)_____ (____)_____ (____)_____
_____(Home)_____ _____(Work)_____ _____(Other)_____

Who to contact in case of emergency (if parents cannot be immediately contacted):

Name: _____ Relationship: _____

Home Phone No.: (____)_____ Work Phone No.: (____)_____

Name: _____ Relationship: _____

Home Phone No.: (____)_____ Work Phone No.: (____)_____

Hospital preference: _____ Emergency Phone No.: (____)_____

Doctor preference: _____ Office Phone No.: (____)_____

MEDICAL HISTORY

Part I. Complete the following:

	Date	Doctor	Doctor's Phone No.
1. Last tetanus shot?	_____		
2. Last dental examination?	_____	_____	_____
3. Last eye examination?	_____	_____	_____

Part II. Has your child or did your child have any of the following?

General Conditions:	Circle one		Circle one or both		Injuries:	Circle one		Circle one or both	
1. Fainting spells/dizziness	Yes	No	Past	Present	1. Toes	Yes	No	Past	Present
2. Headaches	Yes	No	Past	Present	2. Feet	Yes	No	Past	Present
3. Convulsions/epilepsy	Yes	No	Past	Present	3. Ankles	Yes	No	Past	Present
4. Asthma	Yes	No	Past	Present	4. Lower legs	Yes	No	Past	Present
5. High blood pressure	Yes	No	Past	Present	5. Knees	Yes	No	Past	Present
6. Kidney problems	Yes	No	Past	Present	6. Thighs	Yes	No	Past	Present
7. Intestinal disorder	Yes	No	Past	Present	7. Hips	Yes	No	Past	Present
8. Hernia	Yes	No	Past	Present	8. Lower back	Yes	No	Past	Present
9. Diabetes	Yes	No	Past	Present	9. Upper back	Yes	No	Past	Present
10. Heart disease/disorder	Yes	No	Past	Present	10. Ribs	Yes	No	Past	Present
11. Dental plate	Yes	No	Past	Present	11. Abdomen	Yes	No	Past	Present
12. Poor vision	Yes	No	Past	Present	12. Chest	Yes	No	Past	Present
13. Poor hearing	Yes	No	Past	Present	13. Neck	Yes	No	Past	Present
14. Skin disorder	Yes	No	Past	Present	14. Fingers	Yes	No	Past	Present
15. Allergies	Yes	No			15. Hands	Yes	No	Past	Present
Specify:_____			Past	Present	16. Wrists	Yes	No	Past	Present
_____			Past	Present	17. Forearms	Yes	No	Past	Present
16. Joint dislocation or					18. Elbows	Yes	No	Past	Present
separations	Yes	No			19. Upper arms	Yes	No	Past	Present
Specify:_____			Past	Present	20. Shoulders	Yes	No	Past	Present
_____			Past	Present	21. Head	Yes	No	Past	Present
17. Serious or significant ill-					22. Serious or significant in-				
nesses not included above	Yes	No			juries not included above	Yes	No		
Specify:_____			Past	Present	Specify: _____			Past	Present
_____			Past	Present	_____			Past	Present
18. Others:_____			Past	Present	23. Others: _____			Past	Present
_____			Past	Present	_____			Past	Present

Part III. Circle appropriate response to each question. For each "Yes" response, provide additional information.

	Circle one	Additional information

1. Is your child currently taking any medication? If yes, describe medication, amount, and reason for taking. Yes No _____

2. Does your child have any allergic reactions to medication, bee stings, food, etc.? If yes, describe agents that cause adverse reactions and describe these reactions. Yes No _____

3. Does your child wear any appliances (e.g., glasses, contact lenses, hearing aid, false teeth, braces, etc.)? If yes, describe appliances. Yes No _____

4. Has your child had any surgical operations? If yes, indicate site, explain the reason for the surgery, and describe the level of success. Yes No _____

5. Has a physician placed any restrictions on your child's present activities? If yes, describe restrictions. Yes No _____

6. Does your child have any existing and/or past medical or emotional conditions that require special concern and attention by a sports coach? If yes, explain. Yes No _____

7. Does your child have any deformities (e.g., abnormal curvature of the spine, heart problems, one kidney, blindness in one eye, one testicle, etc.)? If yes, describe. Yes No _____

8. Is there a history of serious family illnesses (e.g., diabetes, bleeding disorders, heart attack before age 50, etc.)? If yes, describe illnesses. Yes No _____

9. Has your child lost consciousness or sustained a concussion? Yes No _____

10. Has your child experienced fainting spells or dizziness while exercising? Yes No _____

Part IV. Has your child or did your child have any of the following personal habits?

Personal Habit	Circle one		Circle one or both		Indicate extent or amount
1. Smoking	Yes	No	Past	Present	_____
2. Smokeless tobacco	Yes	No	Past	Present	_____
3. Alcohol	Yes	No	Past	Present	_____
4. Recreational drugs (e.g., marijuana, cocaine, etc.)	Yes	No	Past	Present	_____
5. Steroids	Yes	No	Past	Present	_____
6. Others					
Specify: _____	Yes	No	Past	Present	_____
_____	Yes	No	Past	Present	_____
_____	Yes	No	Past	Present	_____

Part V. Please explain below any "Yes" responses in Parts II, III, and IV or any other concerns that have present implications for my coaching your child. Also, describe special first aid requirements, if appropriate. An additional sheet may be attached if necessary.

_____

_____

_____

_____

_____

_____

_____

Medical Release Form

I hereby give permission for any and all medical attention necessary to be administered to my child in the event of an accident, injury, sickness, etc., under the direction of the people listed below until such time as I may be contacted. My child's name is _____.
This release is effective for the time during which my child is participating in the _____
_____ football program and any tournaments for the 19___/19___
season, including traveling to or from such tournaments. I also hereby assume the responsibility
for payment of any such treatment.

PARENTS' OR GUARDIANS' NAMES: _____

HOME ADDRESS: _____

                     Street   City   State   Zip

                             (____)_____(W)

HOME PHONE: (____)_____ (____)_____(W)

INSURANCE COMPANY: _____

POLICY NUMBER: _____

FAMILY PHYSICIAN: _____

PHYSICIAN'S ADDRESS: _____ PHONE NO. (____)_____

In case I cannot be reached, either of the following people is designated:

COACH'S NAME: _____ PHONE NO. (____)_____

ASS'T. COACH OR OTHER: _____ PHONE NO. (____)_____

SIGNATURE OF PARENT OR GUARDIAN _____

SUBSCRIBED AND SWORN BEFORE ME THIS _____ OF _____, 19 ___

SIGNATURE OF NOTARY PUBLIC _____

Working Effectively with Parents

Guidelines for Selecting Football Equipment

- ### Ball

There are a variety of footballs available for purchase from sporting goods dealers in either rubber or leather in both regulation size and youth league size.

It is recommended that the rubber, youth league football be used by youngsters in pre-high school programs. The ball is easier to handle and allows youth players to perfect ball handling skills.

- ### Shoes

Regulation canvas or leather tennis shoes are acceptable footwear. However, football shoes with molded rubber, half-inch multi-studded cleats are very effective.

- ### Contact equipment

Helmet—Because of the high cost of liability insurance in recent years, few companies remain active in helmet manufacturing. It is necessary to deal with reputable equipment salespeople who have access to the top helmets on the market. Helmets will be either a padded or suspension model and must be equipped with a double bar face mask. Both the helmet and the face mask *must* be NOCSAE approved.

Shoulder pads and hip pads—must be fitted properly in order to assure proper protection.

There is a variety of good protective equipment available from all sporting goods representatives. Coaches and players must inspect their equipment each day to assure proper protection.

Knee pads and thigh pads are standard equipment and must be fitted into the pants.

- ### Clothing

Football pants are normally made of a spandex material that allows a tight fit to the body. Fitted pockets for pads are sewn into the pants at the knees and thighs.

Football jerseys with front and back numbers are usually made of nylon-mesh material.

Descriptions of Team Assistants and Their Responsibilities*

Assistant coach—aids the coach in all aspects of coaching the team during practices and games.

Team manager—keeps game statistics, completes line-up cards, and makes arrangements for practice sites and times; works approximately one hour per week.

Team treasurer—collects fees from players, identifies sponsors, maintains financial records;

*Note that these are only suggestions for assistants and their responsibilities. The way you organize your team may result in the need for different and/or additional assistants.

works approximately five hours at the beginning of the season and a few hours throughout the remainder of the season.

Team doctor/nurse/paramedic—establishes a plan to respond to possible emergencies for each practice and game site, prepares and updates a medical kit, assists the coach in responding to injured players by providing first aid, collects and organizes completed medical history forms and reviews these with the coach, maintains records of completed on-site injury reports and completes a summary of season injuries, delegates other parents to bring ice to games for initial care of certain injuries; works approximately five hours at the beginning of the season and approximately 1/2 hour per week throughout the remainder of the season. Note that only a certified medical doctor, trainer, nurse, or paramedic should assume some of these defined responsibilities. See Chapter 19 for more details.

Team social coordinator—plans team party and team social functions; works approximately five hours per season.

Team refreshments coordinator—contacts parents to assign them the shared expense and responsibilities of providing refreshments at all games (see Chapter 21) works approximately two hours per week.

Team secretary—prepares and duplicates handouts, types, sends out mailings; works approximately 10 hours per season.

10
Planning Effective Instruction

Paul Vogel, Ph.D.
Eugene W. Brown, Ph.D.

QUESTIONS TO CONSIDER

- What four steps can coaches use to systematically instruct their players?
- What guidelines for instruction should be applied to ensure effective instruction?
- What are the features of an effective practice plan?
- What are the characteristics of a good drill?

INTRODUCTION

Effective instruction is the foundation of successful coaching. This is particularly true when you are coaching players in the 6- to 16-year-old age range. Successful results in competition are directly related to the quality of instruction that players have received during practices. Effective instruction requires:

- clear communication of "what" is to be learned (objectives which represent skills, rules, strategies, and/or personal/social skills)
- continual evaluation of players' performance status on the objectives selected
- use of a systematic method of instruction
- application of guidelines for effective instruction
- evaluation and alteration of instruction in accordance with the degree to which players obtain the desired objectives

CLEARLY COMMUNICATING THE CONTENT TO BE LEARNED

The results (or outcomes) of effective instruction can be grouped into three areas.

1. Physical—individual techniques and conditioning
2. Mental—rules, strategies, positional responsibilities
3. Social—personal and social skills

Clearly stated objectives are a prerequisite to effective instruction.

To provide effective instruction, you must identify the teaching objectives for each of these three areas. Players do not learn skills merely through exposure and practice. Rather, they must have specific feedback revealing what they are doing correctly and, equally as important, what they are doing incorrectly. Specific feedback cannot be communicated to your players unless the skill to be learned and its key elements of performance are clearly specified and understood by the coach. By using the suggestions and procedures outlined in Chapter 8, you can be confident that the objectives you include are appropriate for your players. Application of the steps explained in Chapter 8 also results in a systematic plan (pre-season to late-season) for covering the objectives you select. This type of season plan provides a solid base from which effective instruction can occur.

CONTINUALLY EVALUATING THE PERFORMANCE OF PLAYERS

As a coach, it's important to evaluate your players' ability based on the objectives you have selected. Their current status on these objectives determines the instructional needs of the team. The evaluation should include physical, mental, and social content because deficiencies in any one of these areas may preclude successful participation in the sport. For example, the highly skilled football player who lacks motivation may be a liability rather than an asset to the team because of the poor example set for teammates. Also, knowledgeable players who understand the rules and strategies of offense and defense but who lack the skills and fitness to perform as team members must also be evaluated and taught to improve their deficiencies.

To conduct effective practices, you must continually assess players' needs.

The physical, mental, and attitudinal abilities of players who are new to the program or team are usually unknown. And even when accurate records are available from the previous season, considerable changes normally occur in the abilities of returning players. The result is you know very little about many of your players. Accordingly, you may have to spend more time evaluating players' abilities at the beginning of the season. However, evaluations must also occur, skill by skill, practice by practice, throughout the entire season. As their needs change, so should your instructional emphasis.

Assessment of Physical Needs

Performance Assessment

Assess physical skills by carefully observing your players while they participate in individual and small group drills, scrimmages, and/or games. Descriptions of individual techniques, their key elements, and common errors of performance are found in Section I. You must have this information to properly evaluate your players.

In addition to knowledge about how individual techniques of football are performed, the following visual evaluation guidelines help you make accurate observations and assessments regarding physical performance.

- Select a proper observational distance
- Observe the performance from different angles
- Observe activities in a setting that is not distracting
- Select an observational setting that has a vertical and/or horizontal reference line
- Observe a skilled reference model
- Observe slower moving body parts first
- Observe separate key elements of complicated skills
- Observe the timing of performance components
- Look for unnecessary movements
- Observe the full range of motion

Fitness Assessment

Evaluating the fitness of your players requires two levels of assessment; namely, the aerobic and anaerobic energy systems. Precise physiological abilities are difficult to determine because they often require sophisticated measurement apparatus, take a lot of time, and the results are often confounded by players' skills and experience. Due to these complexities, your assessment of fitness should be at a more practical level. For the most part, you should compare individual players with their teammates on the characteristics of energy and muscular system fitness that are explained in Chapter 17. When skill, size, and maturity levels are judged to be similar between players and one is more (or less) fit than the others on a given attribute, you can assume a differential on that attribute. You can then instruct the underdeveloped player on how to make changes. Similarly, when a player cannot keep up with teammates on a series of drills that require either maximum effort or longer, sustained effort, it is prudent to assume that one or both of the energy systems is inadequately trained.

Assessment of Cognitive Needs

Knowledge of strategy, rules, positional responsibilities, and set plays can be evaluated during drills, scrimmages, and games by noting the response of your players to situations that require a decision prior to action. By clearly communicating what you want the players to know in certain circumstances, and then asking questions and observing how they react, you can learn what they know and what skills and knowledge they can appropriately apply.

Assessment of Personal/Social Needs

An assessment of social needs, though subjective, is not difficult. Informally converse with your players and observe their interactions with other team members during practices, games, and informal gatherings to determine what needs exist. Strengthening the personal/social weaknesses of your players, however, may be more difficult than enhancing their performance of individual physical techniques and their knowledge about the game.

As skilled performance is contingent on learning the key elements of each skill, the modification of a negative or interfering attitude requires you to correctly analyze the underlying problem. Ask yourself, the parents, or the player why the behavior in question is occurring. This may require some probing. Often the problem is not related to football. The fact that you care enough about the individual player to invest some time and energy may be all that is needed to reverse or eliminate a negative quality that could become a burden for the individual and the team. Based upon the information obtained, generate a specific strategy for modifying the behavior. The information in Chapters 11 through 14 will help you identify strategies for dealing with important personal/ social skills.

Evaluating the status of players in the physical, mental, and attitudinal areas of performance is necessary in order to obtain insight about how to conduct practices that match your players' needs. Whether your players are performing at low, moderate, or high levels, they can all improve with good instruction.

USING A SYSTEMATIC MODEL FOR INSTRUCTION

Although there are many ways to instruct young football players, the following approach has proven both easy to use and effective in teaching and/or refining skills.

1. Get the attention of the players by establishing credibility
2. Communicate precisely what needs to be learned
3. Provide for practice and feedback
4. Evaluate results and take appropriate action

Step 1: Establish Credibility

Players must direct their attention to the coach before instruction can occur. To encourage this, arrange the players so that each one can clearly see your actions and hear your instructions. Choose where you stand in relation to the players so that you avoid competing with other distractions. Often it's a good strategy to have the players seated or kneeling in front of you as you begin.

Immediately establish the precedent that when you speak, important information is being communicated. Point out that the team cannot maximize its practice opportunity when several people are talking at once.

Establish and maintain the precedent that when you speak, important information is being communicated.

As you begin your instruction, establish the need for competence on a particular physical skill or ability by relating it to some phase of successful team and/or individual play. An excellent way to gain your players' attention and motivate them to want to learn individual techniques is to mention how a local, regional, or national level player or team has mastered the skill and has used it to great advantage. The objective of your introductory comments is to establish the idea that mastery of this skill is very important to individual and team play and that the key elements of its execution are achievable.

The next, and perhaps even more important, task is to clearly establish in the minds of the players that they need to improve their abilities on this skill. This can be accomplished with the following steps:

1. Briefly describe the new skill and then let them try it several times in a quick paced drill
2. Carefully observe their performance and identify their strengths and weaknesses (use the key elements of the skill as a basis for your observations)
3. Call them back together and report your observations

This approach allows you to point out weaknesses in performance on one or more key elements that are common to many, if not all, of the players. Using this approach enhances your credibility and motivates the players to listen to and follow your instructions. Also, your subsequent teaching can be specifically matched to the needs (weaknesses) you observed. Of course, if in observing you determine that your players have already achieved the desired skill level, then you should shift your focus to another skill. This might mean moving on to the next phase of your practice plan.

Step 2: Communicate Precisely What Needs To Be Learned

When you and your players know their status (strengths and weaknesses of their performance) on a particular skill, you have created an environment for teaching and learning. Because individuals learn most efficiently when they focus on one aspect of a skill at a time, it's important to precisely communicate the one key element you want an individual, pair, group, or team to concentrate on. Demonstrate the key element, and explain it, so that all players know exactly what they're trying to achieve.

Individuals learn most effectively by focusing their

practice efforts on one clearly understood element of skilled performance.

When your players are at two or three different levels of ability, you may want to establish two or three instructional groups. This can be accomplished using the following three divisions:

1. Early Learning—focus on learning the key elements of the skill in a controlled situation
2. Intermediate Learning—focus on coordination of all key elements in common situations
3. Later Learning—automatic use of the skill in game-like conditions

Step 3: Provide for Practice and Feedback

Organize your practice time and activities to provide players with:

1. as many repetitions (trials) as possible within the allotted time (minimize standing in lines)
2. specific, immediate, and positive feedback on what they did correctly and then on what they can do to improve. Follow this instruction with some form of encouragement to continue the learning effort.

Repetitions and feedback are essential to players' achievement and are therefore fundamental to effective coaching. You can expect a direct relationship between the gains in players' performances and the degree to which you find ways to maximize these two dimensions of instruction. John Wooden, UCLA basketball coach of fame, was found to provide over 2,000 acts of teaching during 30 total hours of practice, of which 75 percent pertained directly to skill instruction. This converts to more than one incidence of feedback for every minute of coaching activity!

Repeated trials and specific feedback on what was right, followed by what can be improved and an encouraging "try again," produces results.

Feedback can be dramatically increased by using volunteers and/or the players themselves as instructional aids. When instruction is focused on one key element of performance and the important aspects of performing the skill have been effectively communicated to the players, they are often as good, and sometimes better, at seeing discrepancies in a partner's performance as some adults. Thus, working in pairs or small groups can be very effective in increasing both the number of trials and the amount of feedback that individuals get within a given amount of practice time. Also, by providing feedback, players are improving their mental understanding of how the skill should be performed.

Step 4: Evaluate Results and Take Appropriate Action

Evaluation of players' performances must occur on a continuing basis during practices and games. This is the only valid means to answer the question, "Are the players achieving the skills?" If they are, you have two appropriate actions to take:

1. Enjoy it. You're making an important contribution to your players.
2. Consider how you can be even more efficient. How can you get the same results in less time or how can more be achieved within the same time allotment?

If the players are not achieving the instructional objectives, it's important to ask why. Although it is possible that you have players who are very inept at learning, this is seldom the case. First assume that you are using inappropriate instructional techniques or that you simply did not provide enough instructional time. Go through the instructional factors related to effective planning, motivating, communicating, and discipline in this section, and conditioning in Section III, to determine which of the guidelines or steps were missed and/or inappropriately implemented. Then alter your subsequent practices accordingly. Steps for how to complete this type of evaluation are described in more detail in Chapter 15. Continuous trial, error, and revisions usually result in improved coaching effectiveness, which then translates into increased achievement by the players. In those instances where you cannot determine what to alter, seek help from a fellow coach whose teams are consistently strong in the physical skills that are causing difficulty for your play-

ers. This is an excellent way to obtain some good ideas for altering your approach.

APPLYING GUIDELINES FOR EFFECTIVE INSTRUCTION

As you provide for practice and feedback to your players (Step 3), you may wish to use some of the guidelines for instruction that have been found by recent research to be effective in improving student learning. Nine guidelines for effective instruction are named below and described in more detail in Supplement 10-1.

1. Set realistic expectations
2. Structure instruction
3. Establish an orderly environment
4. Group your players according to ability
5. Maximize on-task time
6. Maximize the success rate
7. Monitor progress
8. Ask questions
9. Promote a sense of control

PLANNING EFFECTIVE PRACTICES

If practices are to be effective, they must be directed at helping players meet the objectives defined in the season plan. Objectives are best achieved by using appropriate instructional methods. Instruction is both formal (planned) and informal (not planned) and can occur during practices, games, and special events. Virtually any time players are in your presence, there is potential for teaching and learning.

All coaches, even those who are highly knowledgeable and experienced, are more effective teachers when they organize and plan their instruction. This does not mean that unplanned instruction should not be used to assist your players in learning more about football. In fact, unplanned events that occur often present ideal opportunities to teach important skills. By capitalizing on temporary but intense player interest and motivation, a skilled coach can turn an unplanned event into an excellent learning opportunity. For example, an opponent's offense may prove so effective during a game that your defensive players become highly motivated to learn the tactics necessary to stop such an attack. Often these "teachable moments" are unused by all but the most perceptive coaches.

Features of an Effective Practice

Scheduled practice sessions usually constitute the largest portion of contact between you and your players. Each practice session requires you select both the content of instruction and its method of presentation. To do this effectively and efficiently, each of your practice plans should:

- be based upon previous planning and seasonal organization (see Chapter 8)
- list the objectives that will be the focus of instruction for that practice
- show the amount of time allotted to each objective during the practice
- identify the activities (instructional, drill, or scrimmage) that will be used to teach or practice the objectives
- identify equipment and/or special organizational needs
- apply the guidelines for effective instruction (included in Supplement 10-1)

An effective practice combines the seasonal plan, assessment of your players' abilities, instruction, and an evaluation of practice results. The evaluation portion should be retained even if it means changing future practices to meet the needs of players that may have been unanticipated. The features of an effective practice plan are outlined in Table 10-1. Not all of the features are appropriate for every practice you conduct. There should be a good reason, however, before you decide not to include each feature.

Format and Inclusions in a Practice Plan

Several ingredients that should be included in a practice plan are: the date and/or practice number; the objectives and key points, drills and/or activities; amount of practice time devoted to each objective; equipment needs; and a place for evaluation. The date and/or practice number are helpful to maintain organizational efficiency. The objectives are the reason for conducting the practice and, therefore, must be clearly in mind prior to selecting the activities, drills, games, or scrimmage situations you believe will develop player competence. The key points of each objective you desire to have your players achieve must be clearly in mind. It also helps to have the key points written promi-

Table 10-1. Features of an effective practice.

Features	Coaching Activity
Practice overview	Inform the team about the contents and objectives of the practices (e.g. important new skills, positional play, new drills) to motivate and mentally prepare them for the upcoming activity.
Warm-up	Physically prepare the team for each practice by having them engage in light to moderate aerobic activity sufficient to produce slight sweating. Follow this by specific stretching activities.
Individual skills and drills	Review and practice objectives previously covered.
Small group skills and drills	Introduce and teach new objectives.
Team skills and drills	Incorporate the individual and small group drills into drills involving the entire team.
Cool-down	At the end of each practice, use activities of moderate to light intensity followed by stretching to reduce potential soreness and maintain flexibility.
Team talk	Review key points of the practice, listen to player communications, make announcements, and distribute handouts.

nently on your plan or notes. Supplement 10-2 provides an example plan written to cover the objectives of Practice 5 listed on the season calendar in Chapter 8. In order to communicate the essential features of a practice plan to many readers, this example contains far more narrative than is necessary for most coaches. You need to record only information that will be needed at some later date. Accordingly, phrases, symbols, key words, and other personalized communications will substitute for the more extensive narrative included in the example. A full-sized copy of the practice plan form that you may reproduce is included in Supplement 10-3.

Practice Time

Allotting time for each objective during practices is a difficult but important task for the coach. Sufficient practice time results in the majority of your players making significant improvement on each objective. Although these changes may not be noticeable in a single session, they must occur when considered across all practice sessions devoted to each objective. Assigning too little time may result in players' exposure to individual techniques but often in little change in performance. Keep in mind, however, that practice time must be distributed across several objectives (and/or drills or activities within the practice of a single objective) to keep players' interests high. This is particularly true for younger players who tend to have short attention spans and thus need frequent changes in drills or activities.

Instructional Activities

The selection and implementation of instructional activities, drills, or games should constitute most of each practice session. Players' achievements are directly related to your choices and actions in these important areas. Instructional activities should be conducted in accordance with the guidelines presented in Supplement 10-1. Because most practices are composed largely of drills, you should follow the same guidelines in Supplement 10-1 and develop your drills to include these important features:

- have a meaningful name
- require a relatively short explanation
- provide an excellent context for mastering an objective
- match skill, knowledge, or fitness requirements of football players
- keep the players' "on-task time" high
- are easily modified to accommodate skilled and unskilled players
- provide opportunity for skill analysis and feedback to players

Drills should be written on file cards or paper. It's also helpful to organize drills according to objective, group size (individual, small group, team), possession (offensive and defensive), and position (backs, line, secondary, etc.). When you find a good drill, classify it and add it to your collection. A format for collecting drill information is provided in reproducible form in Supplement 10-4.

Equipment Needs

The equipment needed to conduct a drill or activity should be recorded on the practice plan. It's frustrating and ineffective to discover after you've explained and set up an activity or drill that the necessary equipment is missing. Therefore, after you've planned all the activities for your practice, review them and list the essential equipment needed.

Evaluation

The evaluation/comment portion of the practice plan can be used to highlight ways to alter the practice to accommodate players at unexpected skill levels, or to note changes to be made to improve the plan. It also provides a place for announcements or other information that needs to be communicated to your players.

SUMMARY

Effective instruction is the foundation of successful coaching. It requires practices that include clear communication of what is to be learned, a continuous evaluation of players' performance on the objectives of the practices, a systematic method of instruction, and the use of guidelines for instruction that have been associated with player achievement.

Systematic instruction includes: (a) establishing credibility; (b) providing precise communication of what needs to be learned; (c) providing many practice trials and specific, immediate, and positive feedback; and (d) evaluating the achievement of your players. Use of the guidelines for effective instruction (realistic expectations, structured instruction, order, grouping, maximizing time, success, monitoring, and providing a sense of control) in combination with systematic instruction maximizes the results of your coaching effort.

Guidelines for Effective Instruction

QUESTIONS TO CONSIDER

- What are the nine guidelines for effective instruction?
- How can setting realistic expectations for your players influence their achievement?
- How can you coach players of different ability levels on the same team?
- When players are attempting to learn new things, what success rate motivates them to want to continue to achieve?

Introduction

This supplement provides an overview of nine guidelines for effective instruction. As you plan your practices, this list should be reviewed to help maximize your coaching effectiveness. The nine guidelines are:

1. Set realistic expectations
2. Structure instruction
3. Establish an orderly environment
4. Group your players according to ability
5. Maximize on-task time
6. Maximize the success rate
7. Monitor progress
8. Ask questions
9. Promote a sense of self-control

1. Set Realistic Expectations

The expectations coaches communicate to their players can create a climate for learning that will positively influence player achievement (Rutter et al. 1979). Clear, but attainable, objectives for performance and expenditure of effort for all players on your team will facilitate achievement. As stated in a recent review (Fisher et al. 1980), the reasons associated with this occurrence may be related to the following ideas.

In comparison to athletes for whom coaches hold high expectations for performance, the athletes perceived to be low performers are:

- more often positioned farther away from the coach
- treated as groups, not individuals
- smiled at less

- receive less eye contact from the coach
- called on less to answer questions
- have their answers responded to less frequently
- praised more often for marginal and inadequate responses
- praised less frequently for successful responses
- interrupted more often

Players tend to achieve in accordance with the coaches' expectations.

Coaches and former athletes will be able to understand how even a few of the above responses could reduce motivation and achievement. It is saddening that many capable children are inappropriately labeled as non-achievers on the basis of delayed maturity, poor prior experience, inadequate body size, body composition, and/or many other factors which mask their true ability. Yet, if expectations are low, achievement is likely to be low.

There are at least two important messages in this guideline:

- Expect that, as the coach, you're going to significantly improve the skills, fitness, knowledge of rules and strategies, and attitude of every one of your players during the course of the season.
- Set realistic goals for your players. Make a commitment to help each player achieve those individual goals, and expect improvement.

2. Structure Instruction

Your players' achievements are strongly linked to clear communication of the intended outcomes of instruction (objectives), why the goals and objectives are important (essential or prerequisite skills), and what to do to achieve outcomes (instructional directions) (Bruner 1981; Fisher et al. 1980). Effective instruction is based upon the systematic organization of the content to be taught. The critical steps to take are as follows:

1. Select the essential skills, fitness capacities, knowledge of rules and strategies, and personal/social skills from the many options available
2. Clearly identify the elements of acceptable performance for each objective that you include in your plans
3. Organize and conduct your practices to maximize the opportunity your players have to acquire the objectives by using the effective teaching practices contained in this chapter

3. Establish an Orderly Environment

High achievement is related to the following elements (Fisher 1978):

- an orderly, safe, business-like environment with clear expectations
- player accountability for effort and achievement
- rewards for achievement of expectations

Where such conditions are missing, achievement is low.

The following coaching actions will lessen behavioral problems that interfere with learning and, at the same time, promote pride and responsibility in team membership.

- Maintain orderly and disciplined practices
- Maintain clear and reasonable rules that are fairly and consistently enforced

Caution: strong, over-controlling actions can backfire. Over-control causes frustration and anxiety while under-control leads to lack of achievement. The best of circumstances is a relaxed, enjoyable but business-like environment. The ability to balance these two opposing forces to maximize achievement and enjoyment by keeping both in perspective may be one of your most difficult tasks.

4. Group Your Players

Decisions about the size and composition of groups for various learning tasks are complex, but nonetheless related to achievement (Webb 1980). Typically, in groups of mixed ability, the player with average ability suffers a loss in achievement, while the player with low ability does slightly better. The critical condition for grouping to be effective is to have players practicing at the skill levels needed to advance their playing ability. Typically, this involves groups of similar ability being appropriately challenged. Although this can be difficult to achieve, most effective coaches design practices that maximize a type of individualized instruction.

Your team will have individuals at many levels of ability. While this situation presents a seemingly impossible grouping task, there are some good solutions to this problem:

- When a skill, rule, or strategy is being taught that all your athletes need to know, use a single group for instruction
- As you identify differences in your players' abilities, divide the team and place players of similar ability in small groups when working on these tasks
- When a skill, rule, or strategy is being practiced where individual athletes are at several levels of ability (initial, intermediate, or later learning levels), establish learning stations that focus on specific outcomes to meet each groups' needs

The placement of players into smaller learning groups must be independently decided for each skill, rule, or strategy. A player who is placed at a high level group for practicing individual techniques for passing and catching the ball should not necessarily be placed in a high level group for blocking or tackling techniques. It is important that the following occur at each learning station:

- order is established and maintained (an assistant may be necessary)
- tasks that are to be mastered at each station must be clearly understood

- many opportunities must be provided at each station
- a means for giving immediate, specific, and positive feedback must be established.

5. *Maximize On-Task Time*

Research on the amount of time that athletes are active in the learning process, rather than standing in lines or watching others perform, reveals that actual "engaged" learning time during practices is regularly less than 50 percent of the total practice time, and often falls to 5 or 10 percent for individual athletes. There are several actions you can take to maximize the use of available time.

- Reduce the number of athletes who are waiting in line by using more subgroups in your drills
- Secure sufficient supplies and equipment so that players do not have lengthy waits for their turn
- Reduce the transition time between drills by preplanning practices to minimize reformulation of groups and equipment set-up time
- Use instructional grouping practices that have players practicing skills at their appropriate performance level
- Clearly outline and/or diagram each portion of practice and communicate as much of that information as possible before going on the court
- Complete as many pre and post warm-up/ cool-down activities as possible outside of the time scheduled on the field
- Recruit assistants (parents or older players) to help you with instructional stations under your supervision

Remember: Saving ten minutes a day across 14 weeks of two practices per week equals 280 minutes of instructional time for each player. Time gained by effective organization is available for practicing other skills of the game.

6. *Maximize the Success Rate*

The relationship among successful experiences, achievement, and motivation to learn is very strong (Fisher 1978 and Rosenshine 1983.) The basic message in this research is to ask players to attempt new learning that yields 70% to 90% successful experiences. This level of suc-

cess motivates them to want to continue to achieve. There are two major implications of the finding:

- Reduce each technique, rule, or strategy into achievable sub-skills and focus instruction on those sub-skills
- Provide feedback to the players such that, on most occasions, something that they did is rewarded, followed by specific instructions about what needs more work, and ending with an encouraging "Try again!"

7. *Monitor Progress*

If you organize your practice to allow athletes to work at several stations in accordance with their current abilities and needs, it follows that players often will work independently or in small groups. When players are left to work on their own, they typically spend less time engaged in the activities for which they are responsible. When coaches are actively moving about, monitoring progress, and providing individual and small group instructional feedback, players make greater gains (Fisher 1978). Within this context, you can provide much corrective feedback, contingent praise, and emotionally neutral criticism (not personal attacks or sarcasm) for inappropriate behavior. These actions have a positive influence on both achievement and attitude.

8. *Ask Questions*

Asking questions also relates to player achievement (Brophy 1976). Questions must, however, promote participation or establish, reinforce, and reveal factual data associated with physical skills, rules, or strategies. Use of this teaching technique seems to work best when there is a pause of 3 or more seconds before you ask for a response, at which time the players are cued to think about the answer (Rowe 1974).

9. *Promote a Sense of Control*

Your players should feel that they have some control over their own destiny if they are to reach their potential as football players. This sense of control can be developed by:

- organizing your instruction to result in many successful experiences (i.e., opportunities to provide positive feedback)

- teaching your players that everyone learns at different rates and to use effort and their own continuous progress as their primary guides (avoid comparing their skill levels with those of other players)
- encouraging individual players to put forth their best effort (reward best efforts with positive comments, pats on the back, thumbs up signs, or encouraging signals)

In these ways, players quickly learn that the harder they work and the more they try, the more skillful they will become. At the same time, you'll be eliminating the natural feeling of inferiority or inability that grows in the presence of feedback which is limited to pointing out errors. Although some players develop in almost any practice situation, many potentially excellent players will not continue in an environment where they feel there is no possibility of gaining the coach's approval.

Summary

The information in this supplement provides a base from which effective practices can be developed and implemented. Not all coaches can claim that they use all of these guidelines throughout all of their practice sessions. All coaches should, however, seek to use more of these techniques more frequently as they plan and implement their practices.

REFERENCES

Brophy, J.E., & Evertson, C. (1976). *Learning from teaching: A developmental perspective.* Boston, MA: Allyn and Bacon.

Bruner, J. (1981, August). On instructability. Paper presented at the meeting of the American Psychological Association, Los Angeles, CA.

Fisher, C.W. et al. (1978). Teaching behaviors, academic learning time and student achievement. Final report of Phase III-B, *Beginning teacher evaluation study, technical report.* San Francisco, CA: Far West Laboratory for Educational Research and Development.

Fisher, C.W. et al. (1980). Teaching behaviors, academic learning time and student achievement: An overview. In C. Denham and A. Lieberman (Eds.), *Time to learn.* Washington, D.C.: U.S. Department of Education, National Institute of Education.

Rosenshine, B.V. (1983). Teaching functions in instructional programs. *The Elementary School Journal, 83,* 335-352.

Rowe, M.B. (1974). Wait time and rewards as instructional variables: Their influence on language, logic, and fate control. Part one, Wait time. *Journal of Research in Science Teaching, 11,* 81-94.

Rutter, M. et al. (1979). *Fifteen thousand hours.* Cambridge, MA: Harvard University Press.

Webb, N.M. (1980). A process-outcome analysis of learning in group and individual settings. *Educational Psychologist, 15,* 69-83.

Sample Practice Plan
Eugene W. Brown, Ph.D.

QUESTIONS TO CONSIDER

- How should coaches determine the amount of detail to be included in their practice plans?
- How is a practice plan related to a season planning calendar?
- What are the features of an effective practice?
- How can practice plans help a coach to achieve objectives previously listed for the team?

Introduction

This supplement contains a sample practice plan for football. It is presented as an example of what might be included in a well-organized practice of intermediate level youth players (10 to 13 years of age) conducted by a highly organized coach. This plan illustrates the fifth of eight practices before the first game. Its outline is derived from the procedures outline in the season planning calendar presented in Chapter 8. In addition to the sample practice plan, this supplement contains an overview of the organization and content of the practice plan.

Organization and Content of the Sample Practice Plan

Note that a considerable amount of detail is included in the sample practice plan. This is provided to make it easier to understand the nature of the activities included in the practice. When you prepare a plan for your own use, the level of detail can be substantially reduced. If you're a seasoned coach, you may only need the names of the drills, key coaching points, and a few diagrams. However, most inexperienced coaches will need more detail.

Note that this sample practice plan contains all of the features of an effective practice that are presented in Table 10-1 of this chapter. These features have also been checked at the bottom of the first page of the sample practice plan.

Objectives

The objectives of the sample practice plan should be taken directly from the objectives previously listed by the coach in a season planning calendar in Chapter 8. These objectives, listed in the season planning calendar, may need to be modified slightly because of what the coach was able to cover in previous practices and what the coach has learned from assessing the abilities of the players in previous practices.

Overview of Practice Activities

The overview of practice activities should last only a minute or less. The coach only needs to simply state what is planned for the practice. This helps to mentally prepare and organize the players for the practice. The overview gets the players to "think football" again. Therefore, a good time to respond to players' questions is immediately after the overview.

Warm-up & Stretching

The football-specific warm-ups included in this sample practice plan consist of six aerobic activities. These activities are used to increase the breathing rate, heart rate, and muscle temperature to exercise levels. They also help to reacquaint the athletes to their practice environments and prepare the muscles and joints for stretching activities which follow.

The four stretching activities were selected to maintain flexibility in several muscle groups and joints of the body. On average, approximately 45 seconds can be spent on each of the ten activities included in this phase of the practice. Thus, it is assumed that the players are familiar with each of the ten activities and can quickly change from one to the next. If any of these stretches needs to be taught to the players, more time will be needed for the warm-up session or some activities will need to be excluded.

Teaching Two Skills

The coach must be highly organized to coordinate three drills in the 55 minutes allotted. One way to facilitate this process would be to provide the players with handouts covering the key points at a previous practice and to have the players read the information before the current practice. Players should be encouraged to create a Football Playbook to organize the handouts on skills, strategies, conditioning, and team rules.

Note that the majority of the 55 minutes allotted should be devoted to practice and not to a detailed discussion of the drills. All players can practice each of the skills several times while coaches observe each player and give corrective feedback. Tell players that they have a specific number of minutes for each skill to get as many quality repetitions completed as possible.

Individual Skill Techniques

The drills selected and the manner in which they are conducted should challenge the players to achieve higher levels of performance of individual skills. Selection and conduct should be based upon what the coach has learned from observing the players in previous practices and an understanding of the direction players must proceed to achieve future goals.

While the players are engaged in the practice of individual techniques, the coach(s) should be active in observing performances, providing individual and immediate feedback to the players, and developing ideas about what to include in future practices to improve their level of performance.

If the drills run at a brisk pace, the players may concomitantly enhance their fitness level. The potential for simultaneous enhancement of individual techniques and fitness of players within the same practice activities is an example of economical training.

Cool-Down

In this sample practice plan the same activities are used in the cool-down as were planned for the warm-up and stretching for the beginning of the practice. The cool-down activities could differ from the warm-up activities. The important aspect of the cool-down activities, however, is that they involve the body parts exercised during the practice. This helps clear out waste products built up in the muscle, reduce the pooling of blood in the extremities, reduce the potential for soreness in the muscles, and prevent the loss of flexibility that may accompany intense muscular exercise.

Note that, in an attempt to save time, simple information can be given to the players while they're engaged in their cool-down activities.

Equipment

After coaches plan their practice, they should review each activity to determine what equipment will be needed to carry out the practice. A written list, included on the practice plan, is helpful when coaches are in a hurry to get to practice on time.

Evaluation

The evaluation of the practice should be completed after the practice and before planning the next practice. This evaluation should address (a) the appropriateness of the organization and content of the practice, (b) the success of the coaching methods used, and (c) the degree to which planned objectives (physical skills, tactics, personal and social skills, and fitness) were achieved. This type of evaluation is helpful in improving your coaching methods and in directing future practices to meet the needs of your players.

Summary

The sample practice plan and overview of its organization and content are presented in this supplement to provide guidance and insight to coaches for planning their own practice plans. It is not presented to be directly used by coaches because each team is unique in its needs at any point in time during the season. Therefore, coaches should plan each practice session to meet the specific needs of their players.

PRACTICE PLAN

OBJECTIVES: _To review all phases of punting and offensive game fundamentals_

DATE: _October 18_

#: _5_

TIME	COACHING ACTIVITIES (name, description, diagram, key points)
	Note: Quarterbacks and centers should take field 10 minutes early to practice snaps and warm-up arms for throwing. Punters should do early stretching.
5 min.	<u>Overview of Practice Activities:</u> (1) review punting game including punt coverage (2) repeat fundamental offensive and defensive drills (3) coordinate offensive strategy to be used today
10 min.	<u>Warm-up:</u> (1) Jog length of field and back <u>Team jumping jacks</u> <u>Stretching:</u <u>Warm-up sprints:</u> (1) calf and groin stretch (1) 25 yard knee lifts (2) hurdler's straddle (2) 25 yard crossover (3) trunk and hip stretch (3) 25 yard backward (4) isometrics with partner (4) 25 yard carioca

EQUIPMENT: _Four footballs, cones, hand shields, big bags, whistles, and clipboards._

NOTE: Features of an effective practice include: _√_ practice overview; _√_ warm-up; _√_ individual skills and drills; _√_ small group skills and drills; _√_ team skills and drills; _√_ cool-down; _√_ team talk. (Check the features included in this practice plan.)

EVALUATION: _____

PRACTICE PLAN CONTINUED

TIME	COACHING ACTIVITIES (name, description, diagram, key points)
15 min.	**Team Punting Drill** (1) punt team position, cadence, and snap (2) punt team position, cadence, snap, and punt (3) punt team position, cadence, snap, punt, and coverage (emphasizing: discipline, assignments, lanes and pursuit)
20 min.	**Group Defensive Drills**
20 min.	**Group Offensive Drills**

Group Defensive Drills

Backs
(1) One on one tackling drill
   (stress technique – half speed)
(2) Feet skills drills
(3) Ball skills (interception drill)

Linemen
(1) One on one tackling drill
   (stress technique – half speed)
(2) One on one "shed" technique
   (getting away from blocker)
(3) Pass rush techniques

Group Offensive Drills

Backs
(1) QB.'s and receivers
   (a) warm-up drills throwing
   (b) with center – receive snaps
   (c) throw to basic routes
(2) Running backs
   (a) stance and starts
   (b) practice cuts around cones
   (c) review blocking techniques
      (use hand shields or big bags)
(3) Together – pass offense vs. defensive backs

Linemen
(1) Stance and starts
(2) One on one blocking techniques
   (drive block, double team, pass block)
(3) Together – review assignments vs. defense

PRACTICE PLAN CONTINUED

TIME	COACHING ACTIVITIES (name, description, diagram, key points)
30 min.	**Team Offense vs. Defense**
	(1) Review all phases of offense vs. "passive" defensive team. (Defense will make contact, "wrap up," but no live tackling – all action is full speed.)
	(2) Game-like situation – move ball up and downfield stressing field position, etc..
	(a) long yardage plays
	(b) short yardage plays (goal line offense)
	(c) running and passing game
	(d) stress removal of mistakes from plays and coordination of team efforts
10 min.	**Team Sprints and Cool-down**
	(1) Team sprints by individual groups (backs, q.b. – receivers, linemen) (stress: discipline to cadence, short distance, hard running)
	(2) Return to exercise formation for cool down (stress: proper breathing, stretching)
5 min.	**Group Meeting**
	Review day's activities and team evaluation Reminder of next day's activities

PRACTICE PLAN

OBJECTIVES: _____ DATE: _____

_____ #: _____

_____

_____

_____

TIME	COACHING ACTIVITIES (name, description, diagram, key points)

EQUIPMENT: _____

_____

NOTE: Features of an effective practice include: ___ practice overview; ___ warm-up; ___ individual skills and drills; ___ small group skills and drills; ___ team skills and drills; ___ cool-down; ___ team talk. (Check the features included in this practice plan.

EVALUATION: _____

_____

PRACTICE PLAN CONTINUED

TIME	COACHING ACTIVITIES (name, description, diagram, key points)

DRILL NAME: _____ CLASSIFICATION(S): _____
SOURCE: _____ _____
OBJECTIVES: _____
FACILITIES AND EQUIPMENT: _____ _____

DIAGRAM: DIRECTIONS:

COMMENTS: _____
_____
_____

11
Motivating Your Players

Martha Ewing, Ph.D.
Deborah Feltz, Ph.D.

QUESTIONS TO CONSIDER

- Why do children play football?
- What techniques can you use to minimize the number of "dropouts" from your team?
- What are the four elements of "positive" coaching?
- What can you do to help your players set realistic goals for themselves?

INTRODUCTION

The key to understanding your athletes' motivation is to understand each of their needs. As a coach, you play an important role in determining whether an athlete's needs are fulfilled. Previous research indicates that motivation will be high and young athletes will persist in a sport if their needs are met by that sport. But what are those needs and why do children desire to participate in sports?

WHY YOUNG ATHLETES PARTICIPATE IN FOOTBALL

In order to help your players maintain or improve their motivation in football, you must understand why they participate and why some of them stop participating. Based on interviews with young athletes who participated in a variety of sports, the following reasons for playing were identified and are listed in the order of their importance.

1. To have fun
2. To improve skills and learn new ones
3. For thrills and excitement
4. To be with friends or make new friends
5. To succeed or win

While these research findings provide some insight as to why most children play football, they are only general guidelines. The best information available to you is to learn from the athletes on your team why they are participating in the football program.

To improve your players' motivation, you must know why they participate in football.

WHY YOUNG ATHLETES DROP OUT OF FOOTBALL

Knowing why some youngsters stop playing football can help you find ways to encourage them to continue playing. From a survey of 1,773 young athletes (Youth Sports Institute

1977) who dropped out of football and other sports, we learned that the reason for dropping out was that they did not achieve the goals they set when they initially enrolled to play.

This is not surprising if you consider that their reasons for getting involved in sports represent goals that can only be achieved through participation. When these goals are not being met, withdrawal occurs. Some of the reasons most often cited for dropping out of sports are discussed in the following paragraphs.

Other Interests

Children are often very good at assessing their relative ability in various activities. They may "shop around" and participate in several sports and other activities before deciding which ones provide them the greatest chance of being successful.

Dropping football to achieve in other activities such as music, soccer, swimming, dance, and scouting is acceptable. When children tell you or their parents that they want to pursue other activities, they should be encouraged to do so but welcomed to return to football later if they desire.

Work

Many children who would like to participate in football discontinue because their help is needed at home or they desire to obtain a job. If it is possible, practices and games should be arranged at times that allow all individuals to stay involved. Attempt to find a creative alternative so that having a job does not preclude participation in football. Although much can be learned from work, the lessons that can be learned in sport are also valuable.

Another compelling reason for sports participation during childhood is that this experience may be a prerequisite for successful performance in later years. However, children who find that they must discontinue their participation should be assured that they may return to football at a later time.

No Longer Interested

For many children, playing football is a prestigious achievement. However, once they get involved, some may determine that football is not as glamorous as it first appeared. Although these children may have enjoyed their sport experience, they may decide that other interests are more important and/or enjoyable.

Children with interests in other activities should not be forced by parents or pressured by coaches and peers to continue participation in a football program. Doing so often transforms a normally well-behaved child into one who becomes a discipline problem. Parents and coaches should give children a chance to explore other activities and return to football if they so decide.

Not Enough Playing Time

Children sign up for football because they anticipate the enjoyment and skill development that will result from their involvement. Many young athletes who cited "not playing enough" as a reason for dropping out were telling coaches that they needed more playing time to achieve their goal. These children are not usually asking to be starters or even to play the majority of the time. However, to be told indirectly that they aren't good enough to play during a game can be devastating to a child's feelings of self-worth. Coaches of young athletes need to ensure that a fair and equitable pattern of play occurs both during practices and games.

Skills Were Not Improving

Young athletes want to learn skills and see themselves improving in those skills. Coaches need to recognize that each athlete is different in his/her skill level. Instruction should be designed to help each athlete on the team improve in performance abilities.

It is important to show athletes how they have improved. Too often, young athletes compare their skills to the skills of other athletes rather than their own past performances. This type of comparison is destructive to the self-esteem of unskilled players. Players of all ability levels should be taught to evaluate their performance based on the progress they are making.

Young athletes expect to see improvement in their skills if they are to remain in football.

Did Not Like the Coach

This reason for dropping out may be another way for athletes to tell coaches that they were not playing enough and their skills were not improving. In a study of youth sport participants, the athletes who did not like the coach said they did not like being yelled at, thought the coaches played only their favorite players, and did not think the coaches were fair.

To be effective, coaches must treat young athletes with the same respect that coaches expect from the athletes. It is not necessary or effective to yell at athletes to communicate with them. Avoid all sarcastic and degrading comments. Use a positive approach to create an enjoyable and motivating environment for players to learn and have fun playing the game.

HOW TO HELP MOTIVATE YOUR PLAYERS

Athletes are most highly motivated when they obtain what they seek from their participation in sport. Therefore, motivational techniques that you select should be based on the reasons athletes have for joining the team. The following strategies may help you improve your players' motivation.

Know Why Your Athletes Are Participating

Young athletes differ in their personalities, needs, interests, and objectives for playing football. You must, therefore, get to know your athletes as individuals to determine why they participate. One way to accomplish this is through a team meeting at the start of the season.

Ask your players why they are participating and what their personal objectives are for the season. They may be asked this question before, during, and after practices and special events or whenever you have a chance to talk one-on-one with your players.

Help Your Athletes Improve Skills and Learn New Skills

Skill improvement is a very important reason for joining a football team. Therefore, practice sessions should focus on skill development,

with regular opportunities for players to measure their progress. In addition, you can help athletes set performance goals that are appropriate for them. For example, as young players first learn to throw the football, they should practice throwing the ball a short distance. More advanced players should be encouraged to practice throwing the football a longer distance, at a moving target, from a dropback position, while rolling out, and while being chased by a defensive player. As players improve, they can understand and measure their progress both in practice and in game situations.

Make Practices and Games Enjoyable

As indicated by various studies, young athletes want to have fun. This means they want to play; they do not want to sit on the bench or stand in long lines waiting their turn at a drill. One of the best ways to ensure that practices are enjoyable is to use short, snappy drills that result in all players being involved most of the time. You can also keep your players' interest by incorporating new and challenging drills. Your players may even be able to invent useful drills of their own.

Having a chance to display their skills during a game is an excellent motivator of young athletes.

In games, too, all players can be involved, even if they are sitting on the bench. Team members can be watching the individuals who are playing similar positions to learn from their good techniques or their mistakes. They can also watch for strategies used by the other team. Most importantly, however, they should all have a chance to play in every game. The knowledge that they will have a chance to display their skills during the course of the contest is a primary source of motivation before and after the experience. Players who sit on the bench, unable to test their skills in a game, are not likely to have fun.

Allow Players to be with Their Friends and Make New Friends

Many athletes view their football participation as a chance to be with their friends while doing something they enjoy. Allowing your players to have fun with their friends does not mean your practices have to be disruptive. You can encourage an esprit de corps within the team. Social activities, such as a mid-season pizza party, require more time on your part but may foster rewarding friendships among players and coaches.

Remember, many of your players' friends may be on opposing teams. Encourage athletes to continue their friendships with players on opposing teams and even develop new friendships with opponents.

Help Players Understand the Meaning of Success

Children learn at an early age to equate winning with success and losing with failure. If athletes win a game, they feel good or worthy. If they lose, they feel incompetent or unworthy. This attitude toward winning can be discouraging to players, unless they are always winning. One of your most important roles, therefore, is to help your players keep winning in perspective. One way to accomplish this is to help your players understand that winning a game is not always under their control. For example, after losing a game, you may explain the loss to your team: "We ran the offense well today, but their team played very good defense, so we didn't get as many points as we expected."

Your players also need to know that, although striving to win is an important objective in football, being successful in football also means making personal improvements and striving to do one's best. This attitude can be developed by:

- encouraging maximum effort during practices and games
- rewarding effort
- helping players set important but realistic goals that they can attain and thus feel successful when they are achieved

In helping your players understand the meaning of success, it is also important not to punish them when they fail, particularly if they gave a maximum effort.

Your coaching approach is the factor with the greatest influence on player motivation.

Use the Positive Approach to Coaching

Probably the most important factor that influences your players' motivation is the approach you take in coaching. There are many different styles or approaches used by coaches, but most fall into either of two categories: the negative approach and the positive approach.

- **Negative Approach**

The negative approach is the most visible model of coaching. The negative approach, demonstrated by some professional, college, and even high school coaches, is often highlighted in the media. This approach is one in which the coach focuses on performance errors and uses fear, hate, and/or anger to motivate players.

The negative approach doesn't work very well with young athletes. Constant criticism, sarcasm, and yelling often frustrate young athletes, deteriorate their self-confidence, and decrease their motivation. Remember that young athletes are just beginning to develop their skills, and they have fragile self-concepts.

Focus on correct aspects of performance and use liberal amounts of praise and encouragement.

- **Positive Approach**

The positive approach, in contrast, is one where the coach focuses on the correct aspects of performance and uses plenty of encouragement and praise for the tasks that players perform correctly. When errors occur, a coach who uses the positive approach corrects mistakes with constructive criticism.

A positive, supportive approach is essential when coaching young athletes if high levels of motivation are to be maintained. Key principles for implementing a positive approach to coaching are listed and explained in the following paragraphs.

Key Principles for Implementing a Positive Approach to Coaching (Smoll & Smith 1979)

- **Be liberal with rewards and encouragement.**

The most effective way to influence positive behavior and increase motivation is through the frequent use of encouraging statements and rewards. The single most important difference between coaches whom young athletes respect most and those they respect least is the frequency with which coaches reward them for desirable behaviors.

The most important rewards you can give are free. They include a pat on the back, a smile, applause, verbal praise, or a friendly nod. The greater your use of encouraging statements and rewards, the more your players will be motivated.

- **Give rewards and encouragement sincerely.**

For rewards to be beneficial, they must be given sincerely. It will mean little to your players to tell them they played well if, in fact, they played poorly. This does not mean that you should not give them positive feedback about their performance when they make mistakes. You can point out their errors and at the same time praise them for the plays they performed well. It is important to be positive but also honest.

- **Reward effort and correct technique, not just results.**

It is easy to praise a player who just scored a touchdown, but it is less natural to praise a player who tried hard but missed a tackle. Sometimes, too, we forget to reward correct technique when it does not result in scoring points. It is important, however, to reward players' efforts and the use of correct technique if you want this behavior to continue. An excellent pass to a receiver that is knocked down by a defensive back who makes a spectacular block should be recognized as if the pass was received. Occasionally, spend a few extra minutes with the lesser skilled players, before or after practice, to help them learn the correct techniques. This extra attention and caring will greatly increase their motivation to keep trying.

- **Have realistic expectations.**

Base your rewards and encouragement on realistic expectations. Encouraging your football players to strive for NFL standards, without the feelings of success associated with achieving the many levels of performance leading to such standards, will probably make them feel as though they have failed. It is much easier for

you to give honest rewards when you have realistic expectations about your players' abilities.

Help Players Set Goals

Young athletes learn from parents and coaches that success is equated with winning and failure is equated with losing. Adopting this view of success and failure confuses the players. Let's take, for example, the play of Bill and Tony, members of the winning and losing teams, respectively.

Both boys played about half of the game. Bill's unsporting conduct was noticed quickly by the referee. After a personal foul, the referee cautioned him about his unnecessary rough play. Early in the third quarter, he tackled an opponent after the play was whistled dead and was disqualified from further play due to the flagrant foul. Tony, on the other hand, masterfully used his practiced skills to assist his teammates in scoring and scored his first touchdown of the season. However, since Bill was a member of the winning team, he was able to "laugh-off" his behavior and revel in the success of his team. On the other hand, Tony felt that his efforts were insignificant and worthless and joined his teammates in the disappointment of a 36-28 loss.

As adults, we recognize the inaccuracy of these perceptions. But, our actions at the end of a contest may tell our players that a winning score is what really matters.

Equating success with winning and failure with losing results in mixed messages to the athlete.

Athletes need a way to compare their current performances with their past performances to determine whether they are successful. This can be accomplished through goal setting. You as a coach can help each of your athletes establish individual goals. By doing this, each athlete can regain control over personal success or failure. In addition to removing the mixed messages, remind your players that there are some factors that are out of their control that may determine the outcome of a game. For example, the person your athlete is defending may be playing the best game of his career. Although your athlete is playing very well, there is just no stopping the opposing player. Or, due to injury or illness, a player is forced to play an unfamiliar position. These examples highlight the need to establish goals for personal improvement that are consistent with the objective of winning, but not entirely dependent on their achievement, to maintain player motivation. There are several guidelines for goal setting that can markedly help performance.

Guidelines for Goal Setting

• **Success should be possible for everyone on the team.**

When implementing a goal setting program, each athlete must experience some success. In other words, each athlete should perform at a level that demands a best effort for the existing conditions. Help each athlete realize that effort equals success by focusing rewards on such efforts.

• **Goals under practice conditions should be increasingly more challenging and goals during competition should be more realistic.**

When you set up drills to work on offense or defense, help your players set goals for practice that will challenge each of them to exceed a previous effort. For example, when practicing pass patterns, you may ask your "star" quarterback to complete 7 out of 10 passes in the drill, while another player may be challenged with 4 out of 10. You should not expect the same level of performance in a game because neither you nor the players control all the factors. With this approach, motivation at practice is increased and players have a realistic chance of experiencing self-worth in a game.

• **Goals should be flexible.**

If goal setting is to be effective, goals must be evaluated frequently and adjusted depending on the athlete's success ratio. If an athlete is achieving the set goal, raise the goal to provide a greater challenge and motivation. If the goal is too difficult and the athlete is feeling frustration or failure, the goal should be lowered rather than have the athlete continue to experience failure. Having to lower the level of a goal may also be frustrating. Therefore, it is important to

be as accurate as possible when initially setting goals for individual players.

• **Set individual goals rather than team goals.**

In general, team goals should not be made. This is because team goals are not under anyone's control, and they are often unrealistic. It is too difficult to assess accurately how a team will progress through a season. Will your team improve faster than other teams, at the same pace, or be a latecomer? If you set winning a certain number of games (e.g., 8 of 10 games) as a goal and the team loses their first three games, you cannot achieve the goal even by winning the remaining seven games. This will only cause greater discouragement among team members. Work on individual improvement through goal setting, and let the team's improvement reflect the individual's improvement.

Goal setting can be very effective in improving a player's performance, confidence, and self-worth. To be effective, however, you must know your players well enough to know when they are setting goals that are challenging, controllable, and realistic. In addition, goals must be adjusted to ensure feelings of self-worth.

DEALING WITH COMPETITIVE STRESS

Some coaches believe the best way to motivate a team for competition is to get them "psyched-up" before the game. With young athletes, however, getting psyched-up is not usually the problem; rather, the problem for them is getting "psyched-out."

Competitive stress in young athletes can originate from many sources—the athlete, the teammates, the coach, and the parents. When young athletes were asked what caused them to worry, among the most frequently given answers were:

1. improving their performance
2. participating in championship games
3. performing up to their level of ability
4. what their coach and parents would think or say

Thus, young football players are most likely to be worried about performance failure. This worry about failure may increase players' anxieties, which, in turn, may cause poor performance, and eventually may decrease motivation. Figure 11-1 illustrates this cycle.

A good way to help your players avoid the effects of competitive stress is to reduce their fear of failure. This can be achieved by encouraging them to enjoy the game and to do their best. When your players lose or make a mistake, do not express displeasure; rather, correct their mistakes in a positive way by using the following sequence:

1. Start with a compliment. Find some aspect of the performance that was correct.
2. Tell the player what was wrong and how to correct it.
3. Give another positive statement such as, "Everyone makes mistakes. Keep working at it and you will get it."

This approach allows players to keep practicing their skills without the fear of making a mistake. The following guidelines may be helpful in preventing competitive stress.

Guidelines for Preventing Competitive Stress

- Set realistic goals.
- Use the positive approach when correcting mistakes.
- Eliminate the type of "pep talks" that communicate overemphasis on the game and the outcome.

APPROPRIATE USE OF TEAM TROPHIES, MEDALS, AND OTHER AWARDS*

Anyone who has ever attended a post-season football team party is aware that presenting trophies and awards is a common practice. Young athletes may receive any number of external awards, ranging from small ribbons to large trophies. However, whether it is appropriate to give children these awards is a controversial issue.

The advocates of awards such as medals, trophies, ribbons, certificates, and jackets indicate that they increase the children's desire and

*Much of the material presented in this section has been adapted from Gould (1980).

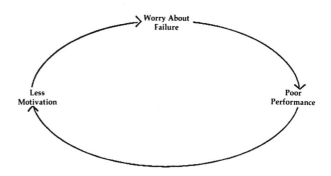

Figure 11-1. A cyclic representation of performance failure.

motivation to participate. Critics, in contrast, suggest that giving rewards to young athletes for activities in which they are already interested turns play into work and decreases their desire to participate. What is the answer: Awards or no awards?

While the advocates and critics of this issue would have us view it as a simple one, researchers have found that no simple answer exists. The purpose of this section is to provide you with information on how and in what situations external rewards influence young athletes' self-motivation to participate in sports.

Understanding Rewards

An activity is defined as intrinsically motivating if an individual engages in that activity for personal interest and enjoyment, rather than for external reasons such as receiving a trophy, money, or publicity. In essence, young athletes are intrinsically motivated when they play for the sake of playing. Until recently, coaches assumed that if external rewards are given for activities that are already intrinsically motivating, the result will be a further increase in intrinsic motivation.

However, research has shown that this is not always the case. The presentation of extrinsic rewards for an already self-motivated activity may result in reduced intrinsic motivation. The following adapted story (Casady 1974) illustrates how rewards can undermine intrinsic motivation.

An old man lived next to an open field that was a perfect location for the neighborhood children's "pick-up" baseball games. Every afternoon the children would come to the field, choose sides, and engage in a noisy game. Finally, the noise became too much for the old man, so he decided to put an end to the games. However, being a wise old man who did not want to stir up trouble in the neighborhood, he changed the children's behavior in a subtle way.

The old man told the children that he liked to hear them play, but because of his failing hearing, he had trouble doing so. He then told the children that if they would play and create enough noise so he could hear them, he would give each of them a quarter.

The children gladly obliged. After the game, the old man paid the children and asked if they could return the next day. They agreed, and once again they created a great deal of noise during the game. However, this time the old man said he was running short of money and could only pay them 20 cents each. This still satisfied the children. However, when he told them that he would be able to pay only 5 cents on the third day, the children became angry and indicated that they would not come back. They felt that it was not worth the effort to make so much noise for only 5 cents apiece.

In this example, giving an external reward (money) for an already intrinsically motivating activity (playing baseball and making noise) resulted in decreased intrinsic motivation in the children. Hence, when the rewards were removed, the amount of participation decreased.

An increasing number of individuals have suggested that this phenomenon also occurs in organized youth sports such as football. In many programs, young athletes are presented with a substantial number of external awards (trophies, jackets, ribbons, etc.) for participating in an already desirable activity. Critics of external awards feel that giving these rewards decreases the youngsters' intrinsic motivation and when the rewards are no longer available, they no longer participate. Thus, external rewards may be one cause of discontinued participation in football.

Effects of Intrinsic Awards

There are two aspects of every reward that can influence a young athlete's intrinsic motivation (Deci 1975). These are:

1. the controlling aspect of the reward
2. the informational aspect of the reward

- **Controlling Aspects of Rewards**

  Extrinsic rewards can decrease intrinsic motivation when they cause players to perceive that their reasons for participation have shifted from their own internal control to factors outside (or external to) themselves. This was illustrated clearly in the story of the old man and the children. The children's reasons for playing shifted from internal factors (fun and self-interest) to external factors (money). Then, when the rewards were diminished, they no longer wanted to play. In essence, the children were no longer participating for the fun of it but were participating solely for the reward. If young football players are made to feel that their primary reason for participating is to receive a trophy or a medal to please their parents, their intrinsic motivation will probably decrease.

- **Informational Aspects of Rewards**

  External rewards can also communicate information to individuals about their competence and self-worth. If the reward provides information that causes an increase in a child's feelings of personal worth and competence, it will increase intrinsic motivation. If it provides no information about self-worth or competence or reduces these feelings about oneself, it will decrease intrinsic motivation.

  Seek to elevate feelings of self-worth in the awards you give.

  A "Most Improved Player" award is a good example of how material rewards can enhance motivation. This award usually tells the player that he/she has worked hard and learned a lot. This award would probably increase intrinsic motivation. Constant failure and negative feedback, however, would decrease a young player's feelings of competence and self-worth and, in turn, would decrease intrinsic motivation. Consequently, you must help children establish realistic goals. When rewards are given, they should be based upon some known criteria (performance, effort, etc.). This helps to ensure that rewards provide the recipients with information to increase feelings of self-worth and competence.

Because most rewards in children's athletics are based upon performance, thus conveying information about the recipient's self-worth, giving external rewards should never undermine intrinsic motivation. However, this may not always be true. Even though external rewards may convey information about a child's sense of personal competence, the child may perceive the controlling aspect as being more important than the information conveyed (Halliwell 1978). Thus, instead of increasing the young athletes' intrinsic motivation, the extrinsic rewards undermine children's interest in sports by causing them to perceive their involvement as a means to an end. They are pawns being "controlled" by the pursuit of winning the reward.

Practical Implications

Extrinsic rewards have the potential to either increase or decrease intrinsic motivation. Two key factors determine which will occur:

1. If children perceive their football involvement as being controlled primarily by the reward (e.g., they are participating only to win the trophy or to please Mom or Dad), intrinsic motivation will decrease. In contrast, if children feel they are controlling their involvement (playing because they want to), then intrinsic motivation will increase.

2. If the reward provides information that increases the young players' feelings of self-worth and competence, intrinsic motivation will increase. If, however, the reward provides no information at all or decreases a person's feelings of competence or self-worth, then intrinsic motivation will decrease.

These findings have important implications for you as the coach. Be very careful about using extrinsic rewards! These rewards should be relatively inexpensive and not used to "control" or "coerce" children into participation in already desirable activities. Moreover, because you play such a vital role in determining how children perceive rewards, you must keep winning in perspective and stress the non-tangible values of participation in football (fun and personal improvement) as opposed to participating solely for the victory or the reward.

The frequent use of inexpensive or "free" rewards will increase player motivation.

One way to increase intrinsic motivation is to give your players more responsibility (more internal control) for decision-making and for rule-making (Halliwell 1978). This could be done by getting input from your athletes about making team rules or letting them help organize practices. Younger players could be selected to lead a drill or favorite warm-up exercise and given some playing time at positions they desire. Older, more experienced players could help conduct practices and make actual game decisions (allowing players to call some plays without interference, for example).

Intrinsic motivation can also be increased by ensuring that when external rewards are given, they provide information that increases your players' feelings of self-worth and competence. The easiest way to accomplish this is to have realistic expectations of the players. Not all children will have a winning season or place first in the league competition. However, some realistic goals can be set with each athlete in terms of improved personal skills, playing time, etc., and the players can be rewarded for achieving their goals. This could be accomplished through the use of "Unsung Hero" and/or "Most Improved Player" awards.

These "official" rewards are not nearly as important, however, as the simple ones that you can give regularly. Remember, some of the most powerful rewards are free (pat on the back, friendly nod, or verbal praise). These rewards should be frequently used to acknowledge each athlete's contribution to the team, personal improvement, or achievement of a personal goal.

Finally, remember that the rewards must be given for a reason that has meaning to your players. Rewards not given sincerely (not based upon some criteria of success) may actually decrease intrinsic motivation. Therefore, coaches must set realistic, attainable goals and reward children when they attain those goals.

SUMMARY

Children play football because they want to improve their skills, have fun, be with friends, and be successful. Children who drop out of football typically do so because one or more of their goals was not met. You can maximize your players' desire to participate, and help prevent them from dropping out, by getting to know them as individuals.

Learn why they are participating. Focus on skill development in practice sessions and make sure the practices are enjoyable. Allow time for friendships to develop by creating a cordial environment both on and off the field. Help players understand the meaning of success and have them set realistic goals.

Using a positive approach to coaching is the most effective way to improve players' performance. Positive coaching also makes playing and coaching more enjoyable. Be sure to reward effort and correct techniques in addition to the results that meet your expectations.

Having realistic expectations of players' performances will provide more opportunities to give rewards. However, when players make mistakes, use the positive approach to correcting errors. The positive approach involves issuing a compliment, correcting the error, and then finishing with another positive statement. Using a positive approach and helping players reach their goals are effective ways to motivate your players toward maximum performance.

Extrinsic rewards have the potential to either increase or decrease intrinsic motivation. Extrinsic rewards are most effective when they are kept in perspective, are inexpensive, and are used to reflect improvements in personal competence. The non-tangible values of participation in football should be stressed, as opposed to participating only for winning or for the reward.

REFERENCES

Casady, M. (1974). The tricky business of giving rewards. *Psychology Today, 8*(4): 52.

Deci, E.L. (1975). *Intrinsic motivation.* New York: Plenum.

Gould, D. (1980). *Motivating young athletes.* East Lansing, MI: Institute for the Study of Youth Sports.

Halliwell, W. (1978). Intrinsic motivation in sport. In W.F. Straub (Ed.), *Sport psychology: An analysis of athlete behavior.* Ithaca, NY: Movement Publications.

Smoll, F.L. & Smith, R.E. (1979). *Improving relationship skills in youth sport coaches.* East Lansing, MI: Institute for the Study of Youth Sports.

Youth Sports Institute (1977). *Joint legislative study on youth sports program, phase II.* East Lansing, MI: Institute for the Study of Youth Sports.

SUGGESTED READINGS

Orlick, T. (1980). *In pursuit of excellence.* Ottawa, Ontario: Coaching Association of Canada.

Singer, R.N. (1984). *Sustaining motivation in sport.* Tallahassee, FL: Sport Consultants International, Inc.

Smoll, F.L., & Smith, R.E. (1979). *Improving relationship skills in youth sports coaches.* East Lansing, MI: Institute for the Study of Youth Sports.

12
Maintaining Discipline

Martha Ewing, Ph.D.
Deborah Feltz, Ph.D.

QUESTIONS TO CONSIDER

- What is the best way to prevent misbehavior?
- Should players be involved in establishing team rules?
- How should team rules be enforced?
- What are the key points of an effective plan for handling misconduct?

INTRODUCTION

Coaches often react to their athletes' misbehaviors by yelling, lecturing, or using threats. These verbal techniques are used because we often do not know what else to do to regain control. Many discipline problems could be avoided, however, if coaches anticipated misbehavior and developed policies to deal with them.

Harsh comments may prevent misbehavior, but they often create a hostile, negative environment that reduces learning and motivation.

PLAN FOR SOUND DISCIPLINE

Although threats and lectures may prevent misbehavior in the short term, they create a hostile, negative atmosphere. Typically, their effectiveness is short-lived. Hostility between a coach and team members neither promotes a positive environment in which it is fun to learn the game of football nor motivates the players to accept the coach's instructions.

Sound discipline involves a two-step plan that must be in place before the misbehaviors occur. These steps are: (1) define team rules, and (2) enforce team rules.

Athletes want clearly defined limits and structure for how they should behave. You can accomplish this without showing anger, lecturing, or threatening. As the coach, it is your responsibility to have a systematic plan for maintaining discipline before your season gets under way. If you have taken the time to establish rules of conduct, you will be in a position to react in a reasonable manner when children misbehave.

Athletes want clearly defined limits and structure for how they should behave.

Define Team Rules

The first step in developing a plan to maintain discipline is to identify what you consider to be desirable and undesirable conduct. This list can then be used to establish relevant team rules. A list of potential behaviors to consider when identifying team rules is included in Table 12-1.

Your players (especially if you are coaching individuals who are 10 years of age or older) should be involved in establishing the rules for the team. Research has shown that players are more willing to live by rules when they have had a voice in formulating them (Seefeldt et al. 1981). This can be done at a team meeting, early in the season. The following introduction has been suggested (Smoll & Smith 1979) to establish rules with players:

"I think rules and regulations are an important part of the game because the game happens to be governed by rules and regulations. Our team rules ought to be something we can agree upon. I have a set of rules that I feel are important. But we all have to follow them, so you ought to think about what you want. They should be your rules, too."

Rules of conduct must be defined in clear and specific terms. For instance, a team rule that players must "show good sportsmanship" in their games is not a very clear and specific rule. What, exactly, is showing good sportsman-

ship? Does it mean obeying all the rules, calling one's own fouls, or respecting officials' decisions? The Youth Sports Institute has adopted a code of sportsmanship which defines sportsmanship in more specific terms (Seefeldt et al. 1981). This code has been reprinted in Table 12-2. You may wish to use some of the items listed as you formulate your team rules.

Players are more willing to live by rules when they have had a voice in formulating them.

Remember, you are a part of the team and you should live by the same rules. You should demonstrate the proper behaviors so the children will have a standard to copy. As a coach, you must also emphasize that behaviors of coaches as seen on television (such as screaming, kicking yard markers, and belittling and embarrassing players) are also examples of undesirable conduct!

Enforce Team Rules

Not only are rules needed to maintain discipline, but these rules must be enforced so reoccurrences are less likely. Rules are enforced through rewards and penalties. Players should be rewarded when they abide by the rules and penalized when they break the rules. The next step, therefore, in developing a plan to maintain discipline, is to determine the rewards and

Table 12-1. Examples of desirable and undesirable behavior to consider when making team rules.

Desirable Behavior	Undesirable Behavior
Making every effort to attend all practices and games except when excused for justifiable reasons	Missing practices and games without legitimate reasons
Being on time for practices and games	Being late or absent from practices and games
Attending to instructions	Talking while the coach is giving instructions
Concentrating on drills	Not attending to demonstrations during drills
Treating opponents and teammates with respect	Pushing, fighting, and/or using abusive language with opponents and teammates
Giving positive encouragement to teammates	Making negative comments about teammates
Bringing required equipment or uniform to practices and games	Forgetting to bring required equipment or uniform to games and practices
Reporting injuries promptly	Waiting till after the team roster is set to report an injury
Helping to pick up equipment after practices	Leaving equipment out for others to pick up

Table 12-2. Youth sportsmanship code.

Area of Concern	Sportsmanlike Behavior	Unsportsmanlike Behavior
Behavior toward officials	No disqualifying arguments	Arguing with officials
	When questioning officials, do so in the appropriate manner (e.g., lodge an official protest, have only designated individuals such as a captain address officials)	Swearing at officials
	Treat officials with respect and dignity at all times	Being ejected from game
	Thank officials after game	
Behavior toward opponents	Treat all opponents with respect and dignity at all times	Arguing with opponents
	Talk to opponents after the game	Making sarcastic remarks about opponents
		Making aggressive actions toward opponents
Behavior toward teammates	Give only constructive criticism and positive encouragement	Making negative comments or sarcastic remarks
		Swearing at or arguing with teammates
Behavior toward spectators	No talking	Arguing with spectators
		Making negative remarks/swearing at spectators
Behavior toward coach	Share likes and dislikes with the coach as soon as possible	
Rule acceptance and infraction	Obey all league rules	Intentionally violating league rules
		Taking advantage of loopholes in rules (e.g., everyone must play, so coach tells unskilled players to be ill on important game days)

penalties for each rule. Your players should be asked for suggestions at this point because they will receive the benefits or consequences of the decisions. When determining rewards and penalties for the behaviors, the most effective approach is to use rewards that are meaningful to your players and appropriate to the situation. Withdrawal of rewards should be used for misconduct. A list of potential rewards and penalties that can be used in football is given in Table 12-3.

The best way to motivate players to behave in an acceptable manner is to reward them for good behavior. When appropriate behavior is demonstrated, comment accordingly or be ready to use nonverbal interactions such as smiling or applauding. Some examples are:

- "We only had nine fouls in that game, that's the fewest we ever had. Way to be!"

- "I know you are all very disappointed in losing this game. I was real proud of the way you congratulated and praised the other team after the game."

- "Do you realize that for our first five practices everyone was dressed and ready to play at 3 o'clock, our starting time? That helped make the practice go better. Keep it up! Let's see if we can make it a tradition!"

Penalties are only effective when they are meaningful to the players. Examples of ineffective penalties include showing anger, giving a player an embarrassing lecture, shouting at the player, or assigning a physical activity (e.g., running laps or doing push-ups). These penalties are ineffective because they leave no room for positive interactions between you and your players. Avoid using physical activity as a form of punishment; the benefits of football, such as

Table 12-3. Examples of rewards and penalties that can be used in football.

Rewards	Penalties
Being a starter	Being taken out of a game
Playing a desired position	Not being allowed to start
Leading an exercise or part of it	Sitting out during practice: • until ready to respond properly • a specific number of minutes • rest of practice or sent home early
Praise from you • in team meeting • to media • to parents • to individual	Dismissed from drills: • for half of practice • next practice • next week • rest of season
Decals	Informing parents about misbehavior
Medals	
Certificates	

learning skills and improving cardiovascular fitness, are gained through activity. Players should not associate these types of beneficial activities with punishment.

Rewards and penalties that are meaningful to your players and appropriate to the situation are most effective.

Sometimes it is more effective to ignore inappropriate behavior if the infractions are relatively minor. Continually scolding players for minor pranks or "horseplay" can become counterproductive. If team deportment is a constant problem, the coach must ask, "Why?" Misbehavior may be the players' way of telling the coach that they need attention or that they do not have enough to do. Coaches should check to see if the players are spending a lot of time standing in lines while waiting for a turn to practice. Try to keep your players productively involved so they don't have time for inappropriate behavior. This is accomplished through well-designed practice plans. A lack of meaningful football activity in your practices could lead to counterproductive or disruptive behavior.

Misbehavior may be the players' way of telling the coach that they need attention or do not have enough to do.

When the rules for proper conduct have been outlined and the rewards and penalties have been determined, they must then be stated clearly so the players will understand them. Your players must understand the consequences for breaking the rules and the rewards for abiding by the rules. Violators should explain their actions to the coach and apologize to their teammates. You must also follow through, consistently and impartially, with your application of rewards for desirable conduct and penalties for misconduct.

Nothing destroys a plan for discipline more quickly than its inconsistent application. Rules must apply to all players equally and in all situations. Thus, if your team is in a championship game and your star player violates a rule that requires that he or she not be allowed to start, the rule must still be enforced. If not, you are communicating to your players that the rules are not to be taken seriously, especially when the game is at stake.

It is impossible to predetermine all rules that may ultimately be important during the season. However, by initiating several rules early in the season, a standard of expected behavior will be established. Positive and negative behaviors that are not covered by the rules can still be judged relative to these established standards and appropriate rewards or punishment can be given.

Key Points to An Effective Discipline Plan

• Specify desirable and undesirable conduct clearly in terms of rules.
• Involve players in establishing the team rules.
• Determine rewards and penalties for rules that are meaningful to players and allow for positive interaction between you and your players.
• Apply rewards and penalties consistently and impartially.

SUMMARY

Although threats, lectures, or yelling may deter misbehavior in the short term, the negative atmosphere that results reduces long-term coaching effectiveness. A more positive approach to handling misbehavior is to prevent it by establishing, with player input, clear team rules and enforcement policies. Use fair and consistent enforcement of the rules primarily through rewarding correct behaviors rather than penalizing wrong behaviors.

REFERENCES

Seefeldt, V. et al. (1981). *A winning philosophy for youth sports programs.* East Lansing, MI: Institute for the Study of Youth Sports.

Smoll, F., & Smith, R.E. (1979). *Improving relationship skills in youth sport coaches.* East Lansing, MI: Institute for the Study of Youth Sports.

13
Communicating With Your Players

Martha Ewing, Ph.D.
Deborah Feltz, Ph.D.

QUESTIONS TO CONSIDER

- How can you send clear messages to your players?
- What is the positive approach to communication?
- What are the characteristics of a good listener?
- How can good communication skills improve your ability to coach?

INTRODUCTION

The most important skill in coaching is the ability to communicate with your players. It is critical to effectively carry out your roles of leader, teacher, motivator, and organizer. Effective communication not only involves skill in sending messages but skill in interpreting the messages that come from your players and their parents.

SENDING CLEAR MESSAGES

Any means you use to convey your ideas, feelings, instructions, and/or attitudes to others involves communication. Thus, when communicating with your players, your messages may contain verbal as well as nonverbal information. Nonverbal messages can be transmitted through facial expressions such as smiling, or through gestures and body movements.

When you send messages to your players, you may, without thinking, send unintentional nonverbal information as well as your intentional verbal message. If your nonverbal message conflicts with what you say, your message will probably be confusing. For example, when you tell your players that they have done a good job and let your shoulders slump and heave a heavy sigh, don't be surprised if your players are less receptive to your next attempt at praise.

Another example of mixed messages occurs when you tell your players they should never question officials' calls and then you denounce an official's decision. If the need should arise to question an official's call, you should ask the official for clarification in a professional manner.

Using a Positive Approach to Communicate

Communication is more effective when you use the positive approach. The positive approach to communication between you and your athletes involves establishing:

- mutual trust
- respect
- confidence
- cooperation

Essential Factors in Sending Clear Messages

• Getting and Keeping Attention

Getting and keeping your athletes' attention can be accomplished by (1) making eye contact with them; (2) avoiding potential distractions, (3) being enthusiastic, and (4) emphasizing the importance of what you have to say. For example, when you want to instruct your players on a new skill, organize them so everything you do is visible to them. Be sure that they are not facing any distractions, such as children playing at the other end of the field. It is also helpful to use a story, illustration, or event that will highlight the importance or focus attention on the instruction that is to follow.

• Using Simple and Direct Language

Reduce your comments to contain only the specific information the player needs to know. For example, when a player makes a mistake in a tackling drill, make sure your feedback is simple, focuses on one error at a time, and contains only information that the player can use to correct the mistake. Keep information simple and specific.

The positive approach to communication is an essential element of good coaching.

• Checking With Your Athletes

Make certain that your players understand what you are saying. Question them so you will know if they understood the key points of your message. For example, let's say you are trying to explain how to run the ball carrier running technique drill. After showing them the drill, you can save time and frustration by asking your players before they practice the drill where they should run, what technique they must perform at each cone, and the route they must take to the concluding station. If your athletes cannot answer these questions, they will not be able to participate effectively in the drill.

• Being Consistent

Make sure your actions match your words. When a discrepancy occurs between what you say and what you do, players are affected most by what you do. "Actions speak louder than words." You need to practice what you preach if you wish to effectively communicate with your players and avoid the loss of credibility that comes with inconsistent behaviors.

• Using Verbal and Nonverbal Communication

Your athletes are more likely to understand and remember what you have said when they can see it and hear it at the same time. Using the previous example, simultaneously demonstrating the ball carrier drill while explaining the key points will result in clearer instructions.

BEING A GOOD LISTENER

Remember, too, that you must be a good listener to be an effective communicator. Communication is a two-way street. Being receptive to your players' ideas and concerns is important to them and informational to you.

Part of good coaching involves listening to your players.

By listening to what your athletes say and asking them how they feel about a point, you can determine how well they are learning. Their input provides you the opportunity to teach what they do not understand.

Essential Factors in Good Listening Skills

• Listening Positively

Players want the chance to be heard and to express themselves. You can encourage this by using affirmative head nods and occasional one- to three-word comments (e.g., "I understand.") while you're listening. The quickest way to cut off communication channels is by giving "no" responses or negative head nods.

• Listening Objectively

Avoid prematurely judging the content of a message. Sincerely consider what your players have to say. They may have good ideas! A good listener creates a warm, non-judgmental atmosphere so players will be encouraged to talk and ask questions.

- ● **Listening With Interest**

Being a good listener means being attentive and truly interested in what your players have to say. Look and listen with concern. Listen to what is being said and how it is being said. Establish good eye contact and make sure your body also reflects your interest in your player's message. Be receptive to comments that are critical of you or your coaching. Criticism is the most difficult communication to accept, but it is often the most helpful in improving our behavior.

- ● **Checking for Clarity**

If you are uncertain of what your athletes are communicating to you, ask them what they mean. This will help to avoid misinterpretation.

Being receptive to your players' thoughts and comments is important to them, and it also provides you with essential information.

SUMMARY

The ability to communicate with your players is critical in your role as a coach. It is a skill that involves two major aspects: speaking and listening. Coaches who are effective communicators get and keep the attention of their players, send clear and simple messages, and check to make sure their message is consistent with their actions. They also have good listening skills, which involve listening positively, helpfully, objectively, and with concern.

SUGGESTED READING

Martens, R. (1987). *Coaches guide to sport psychology*. Champaign, IL: Human Kinetics.

14
Developing Good Personal and Social Skills

Annelies Knoppers, Ph.D.

QUESTIONS TO CONSIDER

- Which personal and social skills should youth football coaches attempt to foster?
- Why are personal and social skills important?
- How can a coach bolster the self-esteem of athletes?
- How important is fun in youth sports?
- What can a coach do to ensure that sport participation is an enjoyable experience for athletes?
- What strategies can be used to help young athletes develop positive interpersonal skills?
- What is sportsmanship and how can it be taught?

INTRODUCTION

Youth sport experiences can play, and often do play, a crucial role in the development of personal and social skills of children. The learning of these skills is different from that of physical skills in the following ways:

- Athletes will learn something about these skills whether or not we plan for such learning. If we do not plan for this learning, however, it is possible that the sport experience will be a negative one for some of the athletes. If we do plan, then it is more likely that the sports experience will be positive. Obviously then, this is different than the learning of physical skills. If you don't teach your players to do a specific sport skill, they will not learn anything about these skills. In con-

trast, at every practice and game, players are learning something about the personal and social skills regardless of planning.
- You as the coach continually model these skills. You may never have to model certain physical skills, but personal and social skills always show.
- The learning of these skills is also different from learning physical skills in that you cannot design many drills for the personal and social skills. These skills are a part of every drill and experience.

Coaches, therefore, can have an influence on children that goes well beyond the sport setting. The extent of this influence is increased when:

- the coach and athletes work together over a long period of time

- the athletes are participating in sport because they want to
- the coach is respected and liked by the athletes

Research has also shown that many parents want their children to participate in sports so their daughters and sons can develop personal and social skills through their sport experiences. Thus, coaches can and should work on the development of these skills in athletes.

The basic skills on which a beginning coach should focus are: self-esteem, fun in sport, interpersonal skills, and sportsmanship. Although self-esteem and interpersonal skills are not solely developed through sport, sport experiences can play a crucial role in the enhancement of these skills. In contrast, having fun in sport and showing sportsmanlike behavior are elements specific to the sport setting. Therefore, the coach is often held responsible for their development.

Regardless of the type of personal and social skills emphasized, the more coaches are liked and respected by the athletes and the more they work to create a positive atmosphere, the more likely it is they will influence the development of those skills in their players. The development of these skills is also likely to be enhanced when there is respect for teammates, opponents, officials, the spirit and letter of the rules, and the sport. Consequently, coaches who are very critical when athletes practice and compete, who are angry after a game or after errors, or who will do anything for a win, should change their ways or get out of coaching. Coaches who are unhappy or angry with athletes who make mistakes or lose contests retard the development of personal and social skills.

PERSONAL AND SOCIAL SKILLS

Self-Esteem

Self-esteem is the extent to which an individual is satisfied with oneself, both generally and in specific situations. The level of your athletes' self-esteem will affect their performance, relationships with others, behavior, enjoyment, and motivation. Thus, self-esteem plays a large part in the lives of your athletes as well as in your own life.

All of the players on your team will have feelings about themselves and their ability to do the things you ask of them. Those feelings were developed through experience. They will tend to behave in a way that reflects how they feel about themselves, making that behavior a self-fulfilling prophecy.

The level of self-esteem in young athletes influences their performance level.

Examples

If Sam feels clumsy when playing the tailback position, he is likely to mishandle the ball frequently, which reinforces for him that he is clumsy.

If adults or kids always laugh at Bill's tackling technique, then he may be very self-conscious about tackling and always miss the tackle.

A combination of a sense of failure and the derisive or negative comments from others can, therefore, lower self-esteem. Luckily, the level of self-esteem is not something that is fixed forever. It can be changed, not overnight nor with a few comments, but over a period of time with a great deal of encouragement. Consequently, enhancing levels of self-esteem requires consistent and daily planning by a coach. Positive changes in the self-esteem of players come about through the implementation of a coaching philosophy that places a priority on this change. Mere participation in sport will not automatically enhance Bill's and Sam's self-esteem; their coach must plan for experiences and develop strategies that promote self-esteem.

- **Show Acceptance of Each Athlete**

Showing acceptance of each athlete means you must take a personal interest in each of your players regardless of their ability, size, shape, or personality. You need to be sensitive to individual differences and respect those differences. Coaches have to accept their athletes as they are. This does not mean that you have to accept or condone all their behaviors and actions. It means you should still show an interest in Tom even though he seems to whine a lot. You can talk to him about his whining, but you still should give him the same amount of attention as the other players, praise him for good behavior, encourage his effort, chat with him about his non-sport life, and compliment him when he does not whine.

You also can show your acceptance of each player by demonstrating an interest in them as people, not just as athletes. Show an interest in their school life and their family as well as in the things they like and dislike. Take the time to make each athlete feel special as both a player and a person. All athletes should know that without them the team would not be such a great place to be.

• React Positively to Mistakes

In practice, be patient. Don't get upset with errors. Instead, focus on the part of the skill that was correctly performed and on the effort made by the player. Give positive suggestions for error correction. Helpful hints on how to do so are given in Chapter 10. Often in games, it is best to let mistakes go by without comment; simply praise the effort and the part of the skill that was performed correctly.

Kids usually know when they make mistakes and do not need an adult to point them out publicly. A coach who constantly corrects errors publicly not only embarrasses the players but may also be giving them too much information. Ask them privately if they know why the error occurred. If they know, then no correction needs to be given. Encourage them also to ask for help when they need it: "Coach, why did I miss that block?" This type of questioning encourages self-responsibility and ensures that an athlete is ready to respond to your helpful suggestions.

• Encourage Athletes

Encouragement plays a vital role in building self-esteem. Coaches can never encourage their athletes enough. Athletes benefit most from coaches who are encouraging. Also, athletes who have supportive coaches tend to like sports more and are more likely to develop a positive self-image in sports. Encouragement is especially crucial for athletes who have low self-esteem, who have difficulty mastering a skill, who make crucial errors in a game, who are not highly skilled, and who are "loners." Encouragement conveys to athletes that the coach is on their side, especially if that encouragement is individualized.

Appropriate Times for Encouragement

- when a skill performance is partially correct
- when things aren't going well (the more discouraging the situation, the more encouragement is needed)
- right after a mistake; focus on the effort, not the error
- when any effort is made to do a difficult task
- after each game and practice; do not let players leave feeling upset or worthless

How to Give Encouragement

In general, give encouragement by publicly naming the athlete so that recognition is directly received for the effort. If an athlete is struggling with something personal, then encourage the athlete privately.

- Publicly acknowledge each athlete's effort and skill as they occur
- Recognize each athlete as they come off the field in either a verbal way: "Good hustle in going for that runner, Jim!" or in a non-verbal way: a smile, pat on the back, or wink
- Praise players who encourage each other
- Monitor your behavior or have someone else observe a practice or game
- Be sincere; make the encouragement both meaningful and specific

Examples

After a player fails to catch a pass, instead of saying "Nice try, John!" say "Way to get open, John! Good hustle!"

After a player fell, instead of saying "I'm sorry you fell, Dan!" say "Way to get back up on your feet so quickly, Dan! I like your determination!"

Before a game, instead of saying "Play well in this game, OK?" say "I want all of you to try to do a little better than you did in the last game. I know you can do it!"

Additional Tips for Enhancing Self-Esteem

- Credit every player with the win
- Applaud physical skills (or parts of them) that were performed correctly
- Praise the use of appropriate social skills and effort
- Be more concerned that each player gets a substantial amount of playing time than whether or not the team wins

- Give special and more attention in practices and games to non-starters
- Give athletes responsibilities; ask for help in setting up team rules and in creating new drills
- Never call athletes by degrading names; poke fun at their physiques, abilities, or gender; or use ethnic, racial, or gender stereotypes or slurs

Examples

Instead of saying (in a derogatory manner), "John runs like a girl!" say "John needs to improve his running."

Instead of saying (in a derogatory manner), "You played like a bunch of sissies!" say "We're going to have to work on being a bit quicker and more assertive!"

Instead of saying, "Paul really looks funny the way he runs down the field!" say "Of all the kids on this team, Paul seems to show the most determination in getting down the field. Good for him!"

FUN IN SPORT

One of the main reasons why youngsters participate in sport is to have fun. Conversely, if they do not enjoy being on the team, players are more likely to drop out. Fun, therefore, is a crucial element in participation. Even though fun occurs spontaneously in sport, each coach should plan carefully to ensure that each athlete is enjoying the sport experience. The following ideas, when put into practice, increase the likelihood that the athletes and you will enjoy the team experience.

A primary reason young athletes participate in sports is to have fun.

- Conduct well-organized practices. Plan so all of the players have the maximum amount of physical activity that is feasible in conjunction with your objectives for a practice. Try to eliminate standing in line and waiting for turns as much as possible. If you have a large group, use the station method to keep all the players busy (see Chapter 10).
- Select drills that are suitable for the skill level of the players.

- Create enjoyable ways of learning skills; use innovative drills and games for practicing fundamental skills; and ask the players for suggestions and innovations.
- Watch the players' faces; if you see smiles and hear laughter, your players are enjoying practice!
- Project fun yourself; tolerate some silliness; avoid sarcasm; and be enthusiastic!
- Use games or drills that end when each person has won or has performed a skill correctly a specific number of times.
- Give positive reinforcement.
- Encourage athletes to praise, compliment, and encourage each other; do not allow them to criticize each other nor use degrading nicknames.
- Make sure athletes regularly change partners in drills.
- Allow each child to learn and play at least two positions, if possible, and to play a lot in every game.
- Keep the atmosphere light; don't be afraid to laugh and to gently joke .
- Smile; show that you enjoy being at practice or at the games. Say, "I really enjoyed this practice!" or "This is fun!"
- Take time to make each athlete feel very special. "The team could not function as well as it does without YOU!"

INTERPERSONAL SKILLS

Since sport involves teammates, opponents, officials, and coaches, it can be a great place to develop good interpersonal, or people, skills. Sport, however, can also be a place where athletes learn poor interpersonal skills. The type of skills that the athletes learn depends on the coach. If you, for example, praise Joe because he encouraged Jeff, then you are reinforcing a positive interpersonal skill and creating a cooperative environment. If you say nothing when you hear Mike call one of the Hispanics on the team Chico, then you are reinforcing a racial slur and an inequitable climate. Just as youngsters need to be taught the proper technique for tackling, they also need to be taught how to relate to others in a way that bolsters self-esteem and sensitivity.

• The Coach as Model

If you want your athletes to develop good people skills, you must consistently model the skills you wish them to develop. If you explain to them that they are not to yell and scream at each other and yet you yell and scream at them, you are giving a conflicting message: "Do as I say, not as I do." Similarly, if you state that your athletes may never criticize each other because it shows lack of respect and yet you criticize officials, you are sending a mixed message.

The greater the inconsistencies in your messages (that is, between what you say and what you do), the less likely that the players will develop good people skills. When you send mixed messages, players are likely to ignore what you say and imitate your behavior. Thus they will yell, scream, and criticize if you yell, scream, and criticize. As part of practice and game plans, therefore, you should give serious thought to the type of behaviors you wish your athletes to show to each other, opponents, officials, and coaches.

The overriding principle that should guide your planning and behavior is to show respect and sensitivity to all others without exception.

What does respectful behavior look like? According to Griffin and Placek, a player who shows respect for others:

- follows rules
- accepts officials' calls without arguing
- compliments good play of others including that of opponents
- congratulates the winner
- plays safely
- says "my fault" if it was
- accepts instruction
- will hold back rather than physically hurt someone
- questions coach and officials respectfully

Players show sensitivity to the feelings of others when they:

- pair up with different teammates each time
- cheer teammates on, especially those who are struggling
- help and encourage less skilled teammates

- stand up for those who are belittled or mocked by others
- are willing to sit out sometimes so others can play
- feel OK about changing some rules so others can play or to make the competition more even
- refrain from using abusive names and stereotypic slurs, and from mocking others

The behaviors mentioned are those you must model, teach, discuss, and encourage to enhance the people skills of your players. When you "catch" your players using these skills, praise them! Praise as frequently, if not more, the use of these skills as you would praise correct physical performance.

However, modeling, teaching, discussing, and encouraging these behaviors is not enough. You must also intervene when players use poor interpersonal skills. If you see such actions and ignore them, you are giving consent and approval.

When should you intervene? Griffin and Placek suggest that you should act when a player:

- criticizes teammates' play
- yells at officials
- pushes, shoves, or trips teammates or opponents
- hogs the ball
- gloats and rubs it in when the team wins
- baits opponents, e.g., "you're no good"
- bosses other players
- will hurt someone just to win
- makes fun of teammates because of their shape, skill, gender, race, or ethnic origin
- calls others names, like "wimp," "stupid," "klutz," etc.
- blames mistakes on others
- complains to officials
- shares a position unwillingly
- ignores less skilled players
- complains about less skilled players
- gets into verbal or physical fights
- uses racial, ethnic, or gender slurs

Obviously, the lists of desirable and undesirable behaviors could be much longer. Their overall theme suggests that everyone should show respect and sensitivity to all people. This includes coaches, officials, teammates, and opponents. Coaches should be firmly committed to this people principle and should try to express it in their coaching.

• Tips for Enhancing People Skills

- Explain the people principle and establish a few basic rules as examples of the principle (e.g., praise and encourage each other).
- Discuss how you feel when you are encouraged and when you are hassled. Ask them how they feel.
- Praise behavior that exemplifies the people principle.
- Work to eliminate stereotypic grouping of players for drills; don't let players group themselves by race, gender, or skill level. They should rotate so all will have a chance to work with everyone else.
- Call the entire team's attention to an undesirable behavior the first time it occurs and explain or ask why that behavior does not fit the people principle.
- Talk to the team about the use of racial jokes and slurs such as calling a Native American "Chief," an Asian American "Kung Foo," and an Hispanic "Taco," and the derogatory use of gender stereotypes such as "sissies," "playing/throwing like a girl," and "wimp." Explain how these behaviors convey disrespect and insensitivity and cannot be tolerated. Remember, too, that often these verbalizations by players echo those they have heard used by adults.
- Assign drill partners on irrelevant characteristics such as birthday month, color of shirt, number of siblings, etc.
- Stress the "one for all and all for one" concept.
- Monitor your own behavior.

SPORTSMANSHIP

Sportsmanship is a familiar term that is difficult to define precisely. When we talk about sportsmanship, we usually are referring to the behavior of coaches, athletes, and spectators in the competitive game setting, especially in stressful situations. Thus, it is easier to give examples of sportsmanlike and unsportsmanlike behaviors than to define sportsmanship. For some examples, see Table 12-2 in Chapter 12.

• Displaying Sportsmanship

Treatment of Opponents

Sportsmanlike behaviors

- At the end of the game, athletes shake hands sincerely with their opponents and talk with them for a while.
- An opponent falls, and George helps him back on his feet.
- John forgets his game shoes, and the opposing team lends him a pair.
- A team brings orange slices and shares them with their opponents.
- After the game, a coach praises the play of both teams.

Unsportsmanlike behaviors

- Frank stomps away in disgust after his team loses.
- An athlete verbally hassles an opponent, saying "You dummy! We're going to run right over you!"
- A player swears after the opponents score.
- After a player on the Stars is tripped by an opposing player, the Stars players decide they have to "get physical" too.

Treatment of Officials

Sportsmanlike behaviors

- The Stars coach saw a Blazers player touch the ball last before it went out of bounds. When the ball is awarded to the Blazers, because the official thought the ball was touched last by a player on the Stars, the Stars coach says nothing.
- The only Stars player who asks the official to explain a call is the captain. When other Stars players have a question, they ask the captain to speak for them.
- When the captain or coach speaks to an official, they do so in a respectful and courteous manner.

Unsportsmanlike behaviors

- The coach of the Stars throws the clipboard to the floor after an official misses a call.
- When an official makes two calls in a row against the Blazers, the coach yells "Homer!"

Reaction to Rules

Sportsmanlike behaviors

- The Stars coach saw a Blazers player step out of bounds before returning to the field to receive a pass thrown by a teammate. When the catch is ruled legal by the official, who did not observe the move out of bounds, the Stars coach says nothing.

Unsportsmanlike behaviors

- The players on the Eagles are taught by their coach how they can break the rules without being detected.
- In order to get play stopped, the coach of the Falcons tells an athlete to fake an injury.
- Jason elbows Matt whenever the official is not looking in their direction.

• Creating a Positive Climate

Because one of the goals of youth sports is to teach sportsmanship, a coach should know in which situations unsportsmanlike actions are most likely to occur. Often these situations are under the control of the coach and by changing them, the likelihood of unsportsmanlike behavior occurring decreases.

Situations when unsportsmanlike behavior is most likely to occur are those in which coaches, parents, and athletes view:

- competition as war rather than as a cooperative, competitive game;
- opponents as enemies rather than as children playing a game;
- abusive language towards opponents and officials as part of the game rather than as disrespectful and intolerant behavior;
- errors by officials as proof that they favor the other team rather than as evidence that officials make mistakes, too;
- winning as the only important part of the game rather than as being only a part of the game; and
- every game as serious business rather than as a playful, fun-filled, and skillful endeavor.

Obviously, then, a coach can decrease the likelihood of the occurrence of unsportsmanlike behavior by viewing youth sport as a playful, competitive, cooperative activity in which athletes strive to be skillful and to win and yet know that neither winning nor perfect performance are required. This type of attitude creates a positive climate and tends to enhance sportsmanship.

• Teaching Sportsmanship

Stress-filled situations are the second type of condition under which unsportsmanlike behaviors tend to occur. These situations are created by the game rather than by the coach. As a coach, therefore, you must teach the athletes how they should behave in these situations. Sportsmanship can be taught.

Role Modeling

Often the behavior of athletes in a stress-filled situation reflects that of their coach. If you stay calm, cool, and collected when the score is tied in the championship game, so will your players. To do so, however, you need to keep the game in perspective, which you can do by answering "no" to the following questions:

- Will the outcome of the game matter a month from now?
- Will it shake up the world if our team wins or loses today?
- Is winning more important than playing well and having fun?

Once you begin to answer "yes" to these questions, the game has become so important to you that you will be more likely to snap at the players and argue with the officials. Perhaps then you should ask yourself whether you should stay in youth sport.

On the other hand, if you can answer "no" to the above questions, you are probably approaching the game from a healthy perspective and are more likely to stay calm, cool, and collected and exhibit good sportsmanlike behavior.

Using the People Principle

If children are to behave in a sportsmanlike manner, they must be told specifically what is expected of them and must be praised for doing so. The people principle that was described in an earlier section requires all to show respect and sensitivity to others.

The people principle is the basic guideline for sportsmanlike behavior.

Use Praise

When athletes follow the people principle, they should be praised.

Examples

Jordan helps his opponent back up to his feet. Coach immediately says, "Way to be, Jordan!"

You know Johnny thinks the official made a mistake, but Johnny says nothing. You immediately say "Way to stay cool, Johnny!"

Eliminate Unsportsmanlike Behaviors

Ideally, when an athlete behaves in an unsportsmanlike way, you should say something immediately, and if possible, pull the child aside. Firmly indicate:

- that the behavior was inappropriate
- how it violates the people principle
- that you expect everyone to follow this principle
- that the athlete will be in trouble if the behavior is repeated
- that you know the athlete will try hard not to do it again

If the behavior is repeated, remind the athlete of the previous discussion and give an appropriate penalty. For examples of penalties see Chapter 12.

If athletes are to develop sportsmanship, you must not tolerate any unsportsmanlike actions. Sometimes it is easy to ignore a youngster's outburst because you feel the same frustration. By ignoring it, however, you are sending the message that at times such behavior is acceptable. Consequently, athletes will not acquire a clear sense of sportsmanship.

Discuss Sportsmanship

Young athletes need to have time to discuss sportsmanship because it is so difficult to define precisely. Team meetings before or after a practice provide a good opportunity for discussion. The following tips should help you facilitate such a discussion:

- Ask opening questions such as "Who can give an example of sportsmanlike behavior? Unsportsmanlike behavior? Why is one wrong and not the other?"
- Read the examples from this section of both types of behaviors, and ask the athletes to label them as sportsmanlike and unsportsmanlike. Ask them to explain their reasoning.
- Encourage role playing. "What would it be like to be an official who is trying to do what's best and to have a coach or players yelling at you?"
- Discuss the relationship between the importance attached to winning and sportsmanship.
- Point out examples from college and professional sports. Ask the players to classify the behaviors and to give a rationale.

During these discussions, refrain from lecturing. Think of yourself as a facilitator who attempts to encourage discussion and an exploration of the people principle.

The extent to which your athletes display or react to sportsmanlike or unsportsmanlike behavior will determine the frequency with which you should hold such discussions at practice. To reinforce these discussions, you should point out examples of both types of behaviors at the brief team meeting after some game. Publicly praise each player who acted in a sportsmanlike manner and remind those who acted otherwise of your expectations. Remember also to continually examine your own behaviors to ensure that you are demonstrating the type of actions in which you want your players to engage.

SUMMARY

The extent to which athletes develop personal and social skills through the sport experience depends a great deal on you. Just as physical skills cannot be mastered without planned and directed practice, neither can personal and social skills be developed without specific strategies and guidelines. If a coach does not plan such strategies nor set guidelines for the development of these skills, then the sports experience may be a negative one for the athletes. They may lose self-esteem, develop a dislike for sport participation, and drop out. Conversely, those athletes who feel good about themselves, their teammates, and the sports experience are more likely to stay in sport. Thus a coach has a responsibility to develop these skills.

REFERENCES

Berlage, G. (1982). Are children's competitive team sports socializing agents for corporate America? In A. Dunleavy et al. (Eds.), *Studies in the sociology of sport.* Fort Worth, TX: Texas Christian University Press.

Coakley, J. (1986). *Sport in society* (3rd ed.). St. Louis, MO: Times/Mirror Mosby.

Griffin, P., & Placek, J. (1983). *Fair play in the gym: Race and sex equity in physical education.* Amherst, MA: University of Massachusetts.

SUGGESTED READINGS

Martens, R. (Ed.). (1978). *Joy and sadness in children's sports.* Champaign, IL: Human Kinetics.

National Coaching Certification Program (NCCP I). (1979). *Coaching theory, level one.* Ottawa, Ontario: Coaching Association of Canada.

National Coaching Certification Program (NCCP II). (1979). *Coaching theory, level two.* Ottawa, Ontario: Coaching Association of Canada.

Orlick, T., & Botterill, C. (1975). *Every kid can win.* Chicago: Nelson Hall.

Tutko, T., & Burns, W. (1976). *Winning is everything and other American myths.* New York: Macmillan, Inc.

Yablonsky, L., & Brower, J.J. (1979). *The little league game.* New York: Times Books.

15
Evaluating Coaching Effectiveness

Paul Vogel, Ph.D.

QUESTIONS TO CONSIDER

- Why evaluate coaching effectiveness?
- What should be evaluated?
- Who should evaluate it?
- What steps can be used to conduct an evaluation?

INTRODUCTION

No individual can coach with 100 percent effectiveness. While beginning coaches who have had no formal coaching education programs, sport-specific clinics, or prior coaching experience are particularly susceptible to using ineffective techniques, experienced professionals have their weaknesses as well. To determine where both strengths and weaknesses exist, beginning as well as experienced coaches should conduct systematic evaluations of their effectiveness.

All coaches can significantly improve their coaching effectiveness by completing an evaluation and then acting on the results.

At least two evaluation questions should be asked:

1. Was the coaching effective in achieving its purpose?
2. What changes can be made to improve the quality of coaching?

The evaluation described herein provides a relatively simple procedure for estimating the effects of your coaching efforts. It will also help you identify ways to improve your techniques.

WHAT SHOULD BE EVALUATED?

Evaluation should be based on more than whether or not you're a good person, worked the team hard, or even had a winning season. The important issue is whether or not you met the objectives identified for your players at the beginning of the season (see Chapter 8), including technique, knowledge, tactics, fitness, and personal-social skills. The worksheet in Figure 15-1 (also included in reproducible form in Supplement 15-1) provides an example of how you can identify what should be evaluated.

Coaching effectiveness should be judged by the degree to which players meet their objectives.

For a discussion on how to use Supplement 15-1, see "Step 2: Collect the Evaluation Data."

WHO SHOULD EVALUATE?

Initially, you should evaluate your own effectiveness. To ensure a broader and more objective evaluation, however, you should have others participate in the evaluation. For example, by using the worksheet illustrated in Figure 15-1, you might rate the majority of your players as achieving one or more objectives in the areas of sport skills, knowledge, tactics, fitness, and personal-social skills. Another person, however, may feel that what you thought was appropriate was in fact an inappropriate technique, an incorrect interpretation of a rule, an improper tactic, a contraindicated exercise, or an improper attitude. Obtaining such information requires courage on your part but it often yields important information to help you improve your coaching effectiveness.

Self-evaluation is a valuable means for improving your coaching effectiveness.

To obtain the most useful second party information, use individuals who meet the following three criteria:

1. They are familiar with your coaching actions.
2. They know the progress of your players.
3. They are individuals whose judgment you respect.

A person fulfilling these criteria could be an assistant coach, parent, official, league supervisor, other coach, local expert, or even one or more of your players.

The evaluation form illustrated in Supplement 15-2 provides another way to obtain information relative to coaching effectiveness as perceived by others. This form can be used for individual players (one form per player) or for the team as a whole (one form for the entire team). The purpose of the form is to obtain information that will reveal areas of low ratings. Follow-up can be completed in a debriefing session with the rater to determine the reasons for low ratings and to identify what can be done to strengthen the ratings. Debriefing sessions with this type of focus have proven to be highly effective in identifying ways to improve programs and procedures.

WHAT STEPS CAN BE USED TO CONDUCT AN EVALUATION?

Four steps can be used to complete an evaluation of your coaching effectiveness. These are:

1. Identify the objectives
2. Collect evaluation data
3. Analyze the evaluation data to identify reasons why some coaching actions were ineffective
4. Implement the needed changes

Step 1: Identify Objectives

The form illustrated in Supplement 15-1 can be used to identify the objectives you have for your players. Simply list the specific sport skills, knowledges, tactics, fitness abilities, and personal-social skills that you intend to develop in your players. Completion of this step clearly identifies what you believe is most important for your players to master and it provides a basis for later evaluation.

A prerequisite to conducting an evaluation of coaching effectiveness is to clearly identify the objectives that you want your players to achieve.

Once the objectives are identified, the remaining evaluation steps can be completed. This step also provides a good opportunity for you to obtain information from others regarding the appropriateness of your season's objectives for the age and experience level of your players.

Once you've identified the objectives, let your players know what they are. Research shows that when players know what they need to learn, they experience improved achievement.

Step 2: Collect the Evaluation Data

The primary source of evaluative data should be your self-evaluation of the results of all or various parts of the season. However, assessments by others, combined with self-assessment, are more valuable than self-evaluation alone. Both approaches are recommended.

Coach **John Smith** Season **Fall** Date **November 1992**

EVALUATION QUESTION:	Did significant, positive results occur on the objectives included in the performance areas listed below?

CATEGORIES / SEASON OBJECTIVES	Dan	Keith	Lee	Rick	Marty	Paul	Doug	Tim	Ross	Randy	Todd	Brandon					Total (% yes)	Other notes
Skills																		
Blocking	Y	Y	N	Y	Y	Y	Y	N	Y	Y	Y	Y					91	EXCELLENT
Tackling	Y	Y	N	Y	Y	Y	Y	N	Y	Y	Y	Y					91	EXCELLENT
Passing	Y	Y	Y	N	Y	Y	N	N	Y	N	Y	Y					83	EXCELLENT
Running	N	Y	N	Y	Y	N	N	N	Y	N	Y	N					66	FAIR
Receiving	N	Y	N	N	Y	N	N	N	Y	N	Y	N					33	NEEDS WORK
Kick-coverage	N	Y	N	N	Y	N	N	N	Y	N	Y	N					33	NEEDS WORK
Knowledge																		
Rules	Y	Y	Y	Y	N	Y	Y	N	Y	Y	N	Y					75	FAIR
Infractions	Y	N	Y	Y	N	Y	Y	N	Y	Y	N	Y					66	FAIR
Penalties	Y	N	Y	Y	Y	Y	Y	N	Y	Y	N	Y					75	FAIR
Nutrition	N	Y	Y	Y	Y	Y	Y	N	Y	N	N	N					58	NEEDS WORK
Defensive Play																		
Alignment	Y	Y	N	N	Y	N	N	N	Y	N	Y	N					42	NEEDS WORK
Reaction	Y	Y	N	N	Y	N	N	N	Y	N	Y	N					42	NEEDS WORK
Pursuit	Y	Y	Y	Y	Y	Y	N	N	Y	N	Y	N					66	FAIR
Footwork	Y	N	Y	Y	Y	Y	Y	Y	Y	Y	Y	N						
Fitness																		
Energy Systems	Y	N	Y	Y	N	Y	Y	Y	N	Y	N	N					58	NEEDS WORK
Muscular Systems	Y	N	Y	Y	N	Y	Y	Y	Y	N	N	N					58	NEEDS WORK
Personal/Social																		
Cooperation	Y	Y	Y	Y	Y	Y	Y	Y	Y	Y	N	N					83	EXCELLENT
Teamwork	Y	Y	N	Y	Y	Y	Y	N	Y	N	N	N					58	NEEDS WORK
Respect	Y	Y	Y	Y	N	Y	N	Y	Y	Y	Y	N					75	FAIR
Sportsmanship	Y	Y	Y	Y	Y	Y	Y	Y	Y	Y	N	N					83	GOOD
Total (% yes)	80	75	60	75	75	75	60	30	90	55	55	30						

EVALUATIVE RESPONSES:	Record your assessment of player outcomes for each objective by answering the evaluative questions with a "Y" ("YES") or "N" ("NO") response.

Figure 15-1. Example of coach's evaluation of players.

- **Completing the Coach's Assessment of Player Performance**

After you have identified objectives and entered them in the first column of the "Coach's Evaluation of Players' Outcomes" form, enter the names of your players in the spaces on the top of the form. Next, respond either Y (Yes) or N (No) to the question, "Did significant improvements occur?" as it relates to each season objective for each player.

Your decision to enter a Y or N in each space requires you to define one or more standards. For example, all of your players may have improved on a particular season objective but you may feel that several of those players did not achieve enough to receive a Y. However, an N may also seem inappropriate. To resolve this difficulty, clarify the amount of player achievement for each objective that you are willing to accept as evidence of a significant positive improvement. There is no exact method of determining how much gain is enough; therefore, you need to rely on your own estimates of these standards. The procedures suggested on the following pages of this chapter allow for correction of erroneous judgments. It is also possible to use a scale to further divide the response options: 0 = none, 1 = very little, 2 = little, 3 = some, 4 = large, and 5 = very large. Given ratings of this type, you may establish 4 and/or 5 ratings as large enough to be categorized as a Y and ratings of 3 or less as an N.

It is important to remember that players who begin the season at low levels of performance on various objectives have the potential for more improvement than players who are near mastery. Players who begin the season at high levels of performance often deserve Y rather than N for relatively small gains.

Injury, loss of fitness, or development of inappropriate sport skills, knowledge, tactics, or personal-social skills are detrimental effects that can occur and should be identified. In this situation the appropriate entry is an N circled to distinguish it from small or slight gains.

You must decide if your players achieved significant gains on the outcomes you intended to teach.

Completion of the coach's evaluation form

will reveal your perception of the degree to which your players achieved important objectives. By looking at one objective across all players as well as one player across all objectives, patterns of your coaching effectiveness will emerge. (This is explained in more detail in Step 3.)

- **Obtaining Information from Selected Other Persons**

To obtain information from others about your coaching effectiveness, use the form in Supplement 15-2. Remember, the form can be used for individual players or for an entire team. Note that the estimates of performance are relative to other players of similar age and gender participating in the same league. When using the form to rate individual players, ask the evaluator to simply place a check in the appropriate column (top 25 percent, mid 50 percent, or bottom 25 percent) for each performance area. When using the form to rate the entire team, estimate the number of players judged to be in each column.

Ratings of players' performance at the end of the season (or other evaluation period) are not very useful without knowing your players' performance levels at the beginning of the season. Changes in performance levels are the best indicators of your coaching effectiveness. To determine change in players' performance, it is necessary to estimate performance before and after coaching occurred. Pre and post ratings may be difficult to obtain, however, because of the time it requires of your raters.

A good alternative is to have the evaluators record pre and post ratings at the end of the evaluation period. For example, if three of your players were perceived to be in the top 25 percent of their peers at the beginning of the season and seven players were perceived to be in that performance category at the end of the season, the net gain in performance would be 4. Your desire may be to have all of your players move into the top 25 percent category during the course of the season. Such a desire is, however, probably unrealistic. Having 50 percent of your players move from one performance level to the next would be an excellent achievement.

It would be nice to look at your evaluations of player performance and the evaluations of their performance by others and see only Y responses or ratings in the top 25 percent. Such a set of responses, however, would not be helpful for improving your coaching effectiveness. An excessive number of high ratings probably signals the use of a relaxed set of standards.

All coaches vary in their ability to change behavior across stated outcome areas and across various individual players on a team. The incidences where individual players do not attain high ratings on various objectives are most useful to reveal principles of coaching effectiveness that are being violated. Accordingly, use standards for your self-ratings (or for the ratings by others) that result in no more than 80 percent of the responses being Y on the "Coach's Evaluation of Player Outcome" or moving from one category of performance to another when rated by others. As you will see in Step 3, ratings that are more evenly distributed among the response options are the most helpful for determining how your effectiveness may be improved.

Use of the form "Evaluation of Player/Team Performance Relative to Others" (Supplement 15-2) provides you with an estimate of changes in player performance as viewed by other persons whose judgment you respect. The relatively broad performance areas upon which the evaluation is based does not, however, provide enough detailed information to fully interpret the data obtained. Simply stated, more information is needed. Additional information can be obtained by using the technique of debriefing.

A debriefing session, based upon the information included in the completed evaluation form, provides a good agenda for discussing potential changes in your coaching procedures with the person who completed the evaluation. The debriefing should include these elements:

- Thank the individual for completing the evaluation form and agreeing to discuss its implications.
- Indicate that the purpose of the debriefing session is to identify both strengths and weaknesses, but that emphasis should be focused on weaknesses, and how they may be improved.
- Proceed through the outcome areas and their corresponding ratings, seeking to understand why each area resulted in large or small gains. For example, if a disproportionate number of the players were rated low relative to their peers on offensive skills, and there were very small gains from the beginning to the end of the evaluation period, you need more information. Attempt to determine what offensive skills were weak and what might be changed to strengthen them in the coming season.
- In your discussion, probe for the things you can do (or avoid doing) that may produce better results. Make a special attempt to identify the reasons why a suggested alternative may produce better results.
- Take careful notes during the discussion. Record the alternative ideas that have good supporting rationales and how they might be implemented.

The information collected in this way is invaluable for helping to identify good ideas for increasing your ability to help players achieve future season objectives.

Coaching strengths are pleasing to hear, but identified weaknesses are more helpful for improving effectiveness.

Step 3: Analyze the Data

The first step necessary to analyze the information collected is to total the number of Y responses entered for each player across all season objectives.

From a coaching improvement viewpoint, it is necessary to have a mixture of Y and N responses across both the objectives and players. It is important that no more than 80 percent of your ratings be Y responses on the coaches' self-evaluation form. Tell other raters that no more than 80 percent of the players can be listed as showing improvement from one performance level to another in their pre/post estimates. It may be necessary to "force" the appropriate number of Y and N responses to meet this requirement.

When you have met the criteria of no more than 80 percent positive answers, divide the number of Y responses by the total number of objectives and enter the percent of Y responses in the row labeled "Total" for each player. Similarly sum the number of Y responses across players for each objective and enter the percent of Y responses in the column labeled "Total" for each season objective.

The pattern of Y and N responses that emerges from "forced ratings" can be very helpful in identifying the season's objectives and/or the kinds of players for which your coaching is most or least effective. By looking at the characteristics of the players who obtained the highest ratings versus those who achieved the lowest ratings, you may obtain good insight into things you can change to be more effective with certain kinds of players. This same type of comparison provides similar insight into how to be more effective in teaching certain objectives.

The real benefits of this kind of analysis come with evaluating the reasons why no or few players received Y responses. Answers to these "Why?" questions reveal changes you can make to improve your coaching effectiveness.

To help you determine why you were (or were not) successful with your coaching in certain player performance areas, a "Checklist of Effective Coaching Actions" was developed (Supplement 15-3). It provides a number of items you can rate that may help you identify ways to increase your coaching effectiveness. For example, if several of your players made insufficient progress in the offensive technique of blocking, you could review the checklist to help determine coaching actions you used (or did not use) that may be related to helping players of similar skill level, fitness, or qualities of character. As you identify coaching actions that may have detracted from player improvement, note these and then alter your subsequent coaching actions accordingly.

- Interpreting Unmet Expectations

The above suggestions provide a systematic method for you to identify ways to improve your coaching ability. There are, however, other ways to interpret lack of achievement. The first and foremost (and nearly always incorrect) is to blame lack of performance on lack of talent or lack of player interest.

Be sure to consider all possibilities for self improve-

ment before accepting other reasons for unmet expectations.

Effective coaches can improve the ability of their players, even those with only average abilities. The most helpful approach you can use to improve your coaching effectiveness is to assume that when the performances of your players do not meet your expectations, the solutions to the problems will be found in your coaching actions. This assumption may prove to be wrong, but you must be absolutely sure that you have considered all possibilities for self-improvement before accepting other reasons for unmet expectations.

If you determine that insufficient players' achievement is not likely to be due to ineffective coaching, it is possible that the expectations you hold for your players are unrealistic. Remember, motivation is enhanced when players perceive that they are improving. Expectations that are too high can have a negative effect on motivation and improvement. Reasonable expectations divided into achievable and sequential steps will result in appropriate standards of performance.

Allotment of insufficient time for teaching and learning the objectives selected for the season can also result in poor players' achievement, even when performance expectations and other coaching actions are appropriate. Players must have sufficient time to attempt a task, make errors, obtain feedback, refine their attempts, and habituate the intended actions before it is reasonable to expect them to demonstrate those actions in competition. Attempting to cover too many objectives within limited practice time is a major cause of insufficient achievement.

If the changes identified to improve coaching effectiveness are not implemented, evaluation is a waste of time.

Step 4: Act on the Needed Changes

The primary reason for conducting an evaluation of your coaching effectiveness is to learn what can be done to improve the achievement levels of your players. Identifying the changes that will lead to improvements, however, is a waste of time if those changes are not implemented. Improvements can occur in planning, instruction, motivation, communication, knowledge of the game, and evaluation. Regardless of your level of expertise, by systematically evaluating your coaching actions, you can find ways to become more effective and more efficient.

SUMMARY

By systematically evaluating players' performance on the intended outcomes of the season, you can estimate the effectiveness of your coaching actions. Limited achievement of players in some performance areas can signal a need to change some coaching actions. Use of the forms and procedures outlined in this chapter will reveal changes you can make to improve your coaching effectiveness. By taking action on the changes that are identified, you can make significant steps toward becoming a more effective and efficient coach.

Coach's Evaluation of Player Outcomes

Coach _____ Season _____ Date _____

EVALUATION QUESTION:	Did significant, positive results occur on the objectives included in the performance areas listed below?		
SEASON OBJECTIVES	Players	Total (% yes)	
			Notes
Total (% yes)			
EVALUATIVE RESPONSES:	Record your assessment of player outcomes for each objective by answering the evaluative questions with a "Y" ("YES") or "N" ("NO") response.		

Supplement 15-2.

Evaluation of Player/Team Performance Relative to Others

Evaluator: _____   Player/Team _____   Season _____

EVALUATION QUESTION:	In comparison with other players in this league, how does the player (or team) listed above perform in the areas listed below?					

PERFORMANCE AREAS	PLAYER OR TEAM PERFORMANCE LEVELS						COMMENTS
	SEASON START			SEASON END			
	TOP 25%	MID 50%	BOTTOM 25%	TOP 25%	MID 50%	BOTTOM 25%	

INDIVIDUAL EVALUATION:
For each performance area, place a check in the top, mid or bottom column to indicate the start and end of the season performance level of the player.

TEAM EVALUATION:
For each performance area estimate the number of players (% or actual numbers) in the top, mid or bottom performance levels at the start and end of the season.

Checklist of Effective Coaching Actions[1]

Introduction

This checklist can be used to identify coaching actions that may be related to player achievement (or lack of achievement) of objectives. It, therefore, serves as an aid to identify the reason(s) why a player(s) did not achieve one or more of your expected outcomes. To use the checklist in this way, read the items in each content category (i.e., coaching role, organization, effective instruction) and ask yourself the question, "Could the coaching actions (or inactions) implied by this item have contributed to the unmet expectation?" Answer the question by responding with a "Yes" or "No." If you wish to rate the degree to which your actions (inactions) were consistent with the guidelines implied by the items, use the 5 point rating scale described below. Items which result in "No" or low ratings suggest that you are in discord with effective coaching practices. The process of seeking answers to specific concerns identified by your reaction to checklist items is an excellent way to obtain information most likely to help you become more effective as a coach.

Directions

Rate the degree to which you incorporate each of the following items into your coaching activities. Check "Yes" or "No" or use the following 5 point scale where: 1 = Strongly Disagree, 2 = Disagree, 3 = Neutral, 4 = Agree, 5 = Strongly Agree.

Item	Rating		
	Disagree		Agree
Coaching Role			
1. My primary purpose for coaching was to maximize the benefits of participation for all of the players.	(NO)	1 2 3 4 5	(YES)
2. The beneficial (individual techniques, knowledge, tactics, fitness, attitudes) and detrimental (time, money, injury, etc.) of participation were constantly in mind during planning and coaching times.	(NO)	1 2 3 4 5	(YES)
3. I communicated through actions and words that I expected each player to succeed in improving his/her level of play.	(NO)	1 2 3 4 5	(YES)

[1] Modified from: Vogel, P.G. (1987). Post season evaluation: What did we accomplish? In V.D. Seefeldt (ed.) *Handbook for youth sport coaches*. Reston, VA: American Alliance for Health, Physical Education, Recreation and Dance.

Organization

4. I completed a plan for the season to guide the conduct of my practices.

(NO)   1   2   3   4   5   (YES)

5. Performance expectations set for the players were realistic and attainable.

(NO)   1   2   3   4   5   (YES)

6. I conscientiously decided which objectives must be emphasized in the pre, early, mid, and late season.

(NO)   1   2   3   4   5   (YES)

7. Objectives for developing my practices were drawn from those identified and sequenced from pre to late season.

(NO)   1   2   3   4   5   (YES)

8. The amount of total practice time allocated to each season objective was sufficient.

(NO)   1   2   3   4   5   (YES)

9. My practices would be characterized by others as orderly, safe, businesslike, and enjoyable.

(NO)   1   2   3   4   5   (YES)

10. Objectives were broken down as necessary to allow players to achieve them in several small steps.

(NO)   1   2   3   4   5   (YES)

Knowledge of the Sport

11. I am familiar with the rationale for each season objective selected and clearly communicated to my players its purpose and described how it is to be executed.

(NO)   1   2   3   4   5   (YES)

12. I was able to identify the key elements of performance necessary for achievement of each season objective.

(NO)   1   2   3   4   5   (YES)

Effective Instruction

13. I clearly communicated (by word and/or example) the key elements to be learned for each objective included in a practice.

(NO)   1   2   3   4   5   (YES)

14. Practice on an objective was initiated with a rationale for why the objective is important.

(NO)   1   2   3   4   5   (YES)

15. Instruction did not continue without players' attention.

(NO)   1   2   3   4   5   (YES)

16. Practice on an objective provided each player with many practice trials and with specific and positive feedback.

(NO)   1   2   3   4   5   (YES)

17. During practice, I regularly grouped the players in accordance with their different practice needs on the season's objectives.   (NO)   1   2   3   4   5   (YES)

18. I used questions to determine if the players understood the objectives and instruction.   (NO)   1   2   3   4   5   (YES)

19. The players sensed a feeling of control over their own learning which resulted from my emphasis of clearly identifying what they needed to learn and then encouraging maximum effort.   (NO)   1   2   3   4   5   (YES)

20. My practices were pre-planned and clearly associated the use of learning activities, drills, and games with the season objectives.   (NO)   1   2   3   4   5   (YES)

21. I evaluated my practices and incorporated appropriate changes for subsequent practices.   (NO)   1   2   3   4   5   (YES)

Motivation

22. My practices and games resulted in the players achieving many of their goals for participation.   (NO)   1   2   3   4   5   (YES)

23. I taught the players how to realistically define success in terms of effort and self improvement.   (NO)   1   2   3   4   5   (YES)

24. An expert would agree, upon observing my practices, that I use a positive, rather than negative, coaching approach.   (NO)   1   2   3   4   5   (YES)

Communication

25. There was no conflict between the verbal and non-verbal messages I communicated to my players.   (NO)   1   2   3   4   5   (YES)

26. I facilitated communication with the players by being a good listener.   (NO)   1   2   3   4   5   (YES)

27. Accepted behaviors (and consequences of misbehavior) were communicated to players at the beginning of the season.   (NO)   1   2   3   4   5   (YES)

28. Players were involved in developing or confirming team rules.   (NO)   1   2   3   4   5   (YES)

29. Enforcement of team rules was consistent for all players throughout the season.   (NO)   1   2   3   4   5   (YES)

Involvement with Parents

30. Parents of the players were a positive, rather than negative, influence on player's achievement of the season objectives.

(NO)   1   2   3   4   5   (YES)

31. I communicated to the parents my responsibilities and the responsibilities of parents and players to the team.

(NO)   1   2   3   4   5   (YES)

Conditioning

32. The intensity, duration, and frequency of the physical conditioning I used was appropriate for the age of the players.

(NO)   1   2   3   4   5   (YES)

33. I routinely used a systematic warm-up and cool-down prior to and after practices and games.

(NO)   1   2   3   4   5   (YES)

34. The physical conditioning aspects of my practices appropriately simulated the requirements of the sport.

(NO)   1   2   3   4   5   (YES)

Injury Prevention

35. I followed all recommended safety procedures for the use of equipment and facilities.

(NO)   1   2   3   4   5   (YES)

36. I did not use any contraindicated exercises in my practices.

(NO)   1   2   3   4   5   (YES)

Care of Common Injuries

37. I established and followed appropriate emergency procedures and simple first aid as needed.

(NO)   1   2   3   4   5   (YES)

38. I had a well stocked first aid kit at each practice and game, including players' medical history information and medical release forms.

(NO)   1   2   3   4   5   (YES)

Rehabilitation of Injuries

39. None of the players experienced a recurrence of an injury that could be attributed to inappropriate rehabilitation.

(NO)   1   2   3   4   5   (YES)

Evaluation

40. I completed an evaluation of player   (NO)   1   2   3   4   5   (YES)
improvement on the season objectives.

41. I identified the coaching actions (or   (NO)   1   2   3   4   5   (YES)
inactions) that appeared most closely
related to unmet player expectations.

42. I made the changes in coaching action   (NO)   1   2   3   4   5   (YES)
needed to improve my coaching effect-
iveness.

16
Legal Liabilities

Bernard Patrick Maloy, J.D., M.S.A.
Vern Seefeldt, Ph.D.

QUESTIONS TO CONSIDER

- In terms of legal liability, what are the coaching duties?
- Against which risks to their players are coaches responsible for taking reasonable precautions?
- Do children who participate in youth sports assume the risk of their own injuries?
- What influence does the age and maturity of the athletes have upon the coach?
- Do coaches' legal responsibilities to their players extend beyond the field of play?
- Are coaches responsible for informing players, parents, and guardians about the risks and hazards inherent in sports?
- What legal responsibilities do coaches have to their players when coaches delegate duties to assistants?

INTRODUCTION

It is inevitable that the role of a coach is expanded beyond that of mere instructor or supervisor when it comes to working with youth sports. Because coaches are the most visible administrators to players, parents, and officials, they are expected to handle anything from correcting player rosters to picking up equipment on the field, from assuaging parents' feelings to arranging transportation for players. While these duties may tax the limits of a coach's patience, they remain very important areas of responsibility.

LEGAL DUTIES

Coaches are subject to certain terms of legal responsibility. However, it would be wrong to assume these legal duties were created by the courts to be imposed on the coaching profession. They are time-honored, recognized obligations inherent in the coaching profession. Thus, they should be termed coaching responsibilities (see Chapter 7). These are responsibilities expected of a coach regardless of pay and regardless of whether the coaching is performed for a school, a religious organization, or a youth sports association.

WHERE DOES COACHING RESPONSIBILITY BEGIN?

The primary responsibility of coaches is to know their players. In that regard it is always important to remember that young athletes are children first, athletes second. The degree of responsibility that coaches owe their teams is measured by the age and maturity of their players. The younger and more immature a player, the more responsibility a coach bears in regard to the instruction, supervision, and safety of that child (see Chapter 18). Additionally, the coach is expected to be aware of any physical or mental handicap that a player may have and must know how to recognize emergency symptoms requiring medical attention (see Chapter 19). A coach in youth sports must always bear in mind that:

- Nine-year-olds participating in organized sport activities for the first time require more instruction and attention than teenagers with playing experience
- A 10-year-old child should not be expected to behave, on or off the playing field, differently than other 10-year-old children
- All children with special needs or handicaps must be identified
- A plan for the emergency treatment of children with special needs and those who sustain injuries should be devised

As will be discussed, coaches do not have to guarantee the safety of their young players. However, they are responsible for taking reasonable precautions against all foreseeable risks that threaten their players. Coaches must realize that those precautions are not measured by what they thought was reasonable, but rather by what was reasonable according to the age and maturity of their players.

Do You Know How to Coach?

The volunteer coach is the backbone of many organized youth activities. Nevertheless, despite good intentions, some degrees of qualifications and certification are necessary for responsible coaching. Therefore, in addition to personal athletic experience and background, coaches should attend programs and seminars on the development of athletic skills, youth motivation, and emergency medical treatment. A coach's responsibility begins with an understanding of current methods of conditioning (Chapter 17), skill development (Section I), and injury prevention and care (Chapters 18 and 19).

Coaches have certain responsibilities that they may not transfer to assistant coaches, parents, or league officials.

In many cases, a youth sports league or association offers classes, materials, or advice on skill development and injury prevention and care. Generally, those associations require some certification or recommendation regarding coaching background, skills, and experience before an applicant is permitted to coach youth sports. Coaches must avail themselves of instructional programs or other information helpful for coaching youth sports. In other words, coaches are responsible for their own incompetencies. A youth sports coach should create a competency checklist:

- Does the youth sports association certify its coaches?
- Does the association require coaches to attend coaching clinics and emergency medical programs?
- Do you know how to identify the necessary individual athletic skills based on size, weight, and age?
- Do you know of any agencies that help identify those skills?
- What steps should you take to become certified in first aid treatment?

Knowledge of your coaching incompetencies is the first step toward seeking a corrective solution.

Coaches must be able to recognize their limitations. Acknowledging that skills, youth motivation, and medical treatment may be different today than when you played is the first step toward becoming a responsible coach.

Where Do Your Coaching Duties Lie?

As noted, youth sports coaches are many things to their teams, parents and guardians, and supporters. Coaching responsibilities extend to areas beyond the football field. These responsibilities require the same effort and devotion as on-the-field duties and may include:

- league or team fund-raising activities
- assisting during registration periods
- talking to interested players and their par-

ents about the league and its athletic and social goals

- providing or planning team transportation to and from practices and games
- attending league or association meetings
- buying, selecting, or maintaining equipment
- maintaining locker rooms, practice and game fields
- supervising players during pre-practice and post-practice periods

What Misconceptions Do Many Coaches Have?

There are two common misconceptions regarding youth sports. The first is that children participating generally assume the risk of their own injury; the second, that the role of the coach is severely limited by legal liability.

The legal defense of assumption of risk as it applies to sports is very specific. An athlete assumes the risk of injury from dangers inherent to the sport itself. In other words, it is recognized that injuries occur, especially in contact sports such as football (e.g., an intense collision between an offensive and defensive player, the injury of a player on the field resulting from a non-intentional hit).

Many risks confronting athletes are not inherent to the sport, however; rather, they're the result of improper instruction, supervision, or equipment (e.g., protective equipment or pads that are defective or have been poorly fit, lack of instruction in athletic skills).

The interpretation of *assumption of risk* is complicated when it is applied to youth sports because young athletes require careful supervision regarding their own welfare. The concept that young athletes must assume the responsibility for their injuries sustained in practices or games must be contrasted with whether or not the coach or other adult supervisors were negligent in their instruction and supervision of the activity. In such a comparison it is unlikely that responsibility for *assumption of risk* will serve as a viable excuse.

When an injury occurs in youth sports, the coach's responsibility is considered a much greater factor than the assumption of risk by the player.

Fortunately, most coaches inherently understand the limitations involved in *assumption of risk*. The motivation for many youth coaches is the involvement of their own children in sports. And, like most parents, those coaches accept injury as a natural risk of the sport, but they will not tolerate an injury resulting from lack of proper skill development or poor equipment.

Youth sport coaches should concern themselves less with whether adhering to these responsibilities is good legal protection, and more with the thought that their actions represent the standards expected of youth sport coaches. Actually, the areas of expertise legally required of coaches can serve as measures of qualification and certification. Youth sport leagues and conferences realize that coaches must adhere to legal principles of liability not merely to protect the league and the coach from costly litigation but also to ensure that children continue to participate in athletics. It's very doubtful that parents would continue to support youth sports that were plagued by poor coaching, lack of supervision, or poor medical treatment procedures. In short, these imposed responsibilities are good business practices for youth sports.

COACHING RESPONSIBILITIES

As a youth football coach you have many responsibilities beyond teaching your players to pass, catch and kick a football. Your coaching responsibilities are: providing proper instruction, providing reasonable supervision, warning of hazards and risks, providing competent personnel, preventing and caring for injuries, providing safe equipment, and selecting participants. Each of these responsibilities are discussed in subsequent sections.

Providing Proper Instruction

A coach must teach the physical skills and mental discipline or attitude required to play football (see Sections I and II). You must enhance the development of those skills while reducing the chance of injury. Specifically, volunteer coaches, who represent that they can teach the sport or activity, must be aware of the rules of safety and know how to teach the proper methods of conditioning. For example, when young players are injured, coaches should be prepared to competently assess whether:

- the conditioning or skill drills are realistic for players of young or immature years
- video, film, or written materials, in addition to on-field instruction, would improve instructional techniques
- the players are taught the correct way to wear equipment
- all the players, starters and substitutes, have been given the same amount of time, instruction, and practice on the correct methods of play, conditioning, and the rules
- conditioning techniques and skill drills are current
- coaching methods are accurately evaluated by the league
- parental comments and concerns have been integrated into the coaching instruction
- provision has been made in coaching instruction for learning-disabled and mentally or emotionally handicapped children who participate
- criticism or comments regarding coaching instruction are met with a positive response

The foregoing list consists of some expectations a parent or guardian has of a coach. While those expectations impact heavily on liability, they more accurately serve as guidelines by which youth sports coaches can evaluate their instruction. Again, a youth sports coach must remember that the age and immaturity of the players are key factors to instructional techniques. The coach must be sensitive to the outside environment in which a young player lives, as well as the sports environment created by the coach. Only then can you ensure a youngster the full benefit of your instruction (see Chapter 7).

Providing Reasonable Supervision

A coach is responsible for the reasonable supervision of the players. There is little question that this responsibility starts on the field of play during all practices and games. Again, the scope of this responsibility depends on the age and maturity of the players. The younger the player, the greater the degree of responsibility a coach must take for the player's safe supervision.

In youth sports, a coach's supervisory responsibility may extend to times and places other than the field. In some instances, this may include managing parents or guardians and supporters as well as the players and assistant coaches. A coach's checklist of potential supervisory functions should question:

- Is there a supervisor available for a reasonable time before and after practice?
- Have parents or guardians advised who will pick up their children after practices and games?
- Who is assigned to remain with the players until all have been called for, according to instructions provided by parents or guardians?
- How are parents or guardians notified of practice and game times, dates, and places?
- Who is responsible for player transportation to and from games?
- Are substitute players supervised off the field during games?
- Are players allowed off the field during practice for bathroom or other personal comforts? If so, how are those players supervised?

Many youth sports leagues or associations have a rule that coaches are responsible for the behavior of team parents, guardians, and fans. Such a rule becomes very important in those instances where parents believe their child has been slighted on the field during play, or off the field from lack of play. Coaches should recognize that their conduct can incite parents, guardians, and supporters. A coach must ask:

- Have team and league rules regarding parental involvement, the rules of play, and rules regarding team participation been communicated to parents and guardians?
- Do parents and guardians know my coaching philosophy and team goals?
- Have the team and parents and guardians been notified that only the coach is permitted to discuss a decision with an official?

The coach's role in supervision of the football field can be eased by holding a parents' orientation meeting at the start of the season (see Chapter 9). The parents have a right to know what to expect of the coach. Also, the meeting prepares parents to become actively involved with other parents in stopping any unruly conduct. Again, the supervisory responsibility starts with coaches who conduct themselves in the spirit of good sportsmanship. It also includes a coach's support of game officials in order to defuse angry parents, guardians, supporters, or players.

Warning About Hazards and Risks

A coach is responsible for informing players, parents, and guardians about the risks and hazards inherent to football. Obviously, it's not expected that coaches will dissuade parents and guardians from permitting their youngsters to participate. By the same token, a coach's experience and knowledge helps to assure parents and guardians that the greatest care possible will be taken for the well-being of their children.

The age and maturity of the players play a major role in the degree of risk from playing football. Older, more experienced children may face a greater risk of injury from football simply due to the more sophisticated style of play. However, those children and their parents or guardians already should be fairly well-versed in the risks of football. Therefore, they don't need the same information and assurances as parents and guardians whose children are younger and have never participated.

The coach must inform athletes and parents of the potential dangers inherent in playing youth football.

The youth league or association may provide information regarding sports hazards, but the responsibility to warn parents and athletes remains a very important coaching duty (see Chapter 18). Therefore, a coach would be well-served to provide parents, guardians, and players with as much information and materials as possible regarding football at registration, as well as during the season. The coach must be prepared to instruct or advise:

- how many injuries his or her teams with similar age and experience have suffered, and what types of injuries occurred
- what types of equipment, clothing, or shoes are not recommended or permitted for play
- how equipment should properly fit

- what written, video, or audio materials are available that will instruct parents and guardians about the sport and its risks
- what style, conduct, or manner of play is to be avoided due to the likelihood of injury to the player or an opponent
- what conduct or manner of play is not permitted under the rules
- whether the field and facilities have been inspected for hazards and determined to be safe for play

Hosting a parents' orientation meeting prior to the first game is an excellent way to describe your role in the prevention and care of their children's injuries.

Providing Competent Personnel

We've already examined the coach's responsibility to provide quality instruction. Also, we have examined many of the attendant roles and duties that coaches must provide with that instruction. In many cases, the sheer numbers of players and responsibilities demand that a coach have some assistance. It is not unusual for a coach to delegate some of those coaching or supervisory duties to assistant coaches or parents (see Supplement 9-7). However, the coach must ensure that the people who are assisting are competent. Obviously, having a responsible coach is of little value if the players are subject to the directions of incompetent assistants. Therefore, in a coach's absence, an assistant coach or aide must be able to provide the same responsible instruction and supervision as the players and parents expect from the head coach. It is wise, then, for a coach to learn:

- whether the league or association certifies assistant coaches
- what policies the league or association has regarding the use of parents for supervision, transportation, or instruction
- whether assistant coaches have any hidden past regarding child abuse, or other conduct that constitutes a threat to children
- whether there is any reason to suspect an assistant's or aide's coaching competency
- whether teenagers may be qualified as assistants with coaching and supervisory duties

It is a coach's responsibility to determine

whether assistant coaches and team aides are qualified to step into the coach's shoes.

Preventing and Caring for Injuries

There are few areas that demand as much attention as the prevention and care of injuries (see Chapters 18, 19, and 20). It is not uncommon to find youth sports programs conducting football practices without qualified medical personnel or knowledgeable athletic trainers readily available. In those instances, the first attendant to an injured player is usually the coach or teammates. The coach's responsibility is to recognize when immediate medical treatment is required and to ensure that assistant coaches and teammates do not attempt to touch, move, or help the injured player. Obviously, the care of injuries can be a very confusing task.

Many problems in the initial care of athletic injuries might be solved if coaches were required to qualify as emergency medical technicians, or to have some type of comparable training in first aid and health care. In the absence of those qualifications, however, coaches must use their best discretion, based on experience. Obviously, those deficiencies are compounded in youth sports where most of the coaches are volunteers.

In addition to recognizing when emergency medical help is needed, a coach must be able to recognize symptoms of ongoing problems. If a player has a disease, diabetes for instance, the coach has the responsibility for checking with the player's parents about medication, learning how to recognize the symptoms of shock or deficiency, and what type of emergency treatment to request.

A coach must also be aware of the effects a conditioning program may have on players (see Chapter 17). For instance, if practices are conducted during hot weather, a coach should provide ample water (see Chapter 21), change the time of practice to early morning or late afternoon, learn the symptoms of heat stroke or exhaustion, and learn how to provide for immediate care (see Chapter 18).

It's impossible to categorize all the areas of concern for injuries that a coach may face. However, there are precautions that you can take to ensure that your responsibilities have been reasonably met:

- Attend league-sponsored programs dealing with athletic injuries
- Check with local health authorities, local hospitals, and coaching associations to learn about the availability of emergency medical care at the field
- Implement a plan for the immediate notification of parents or guardians in case their child is seriously injured
- Do not attempt unfamiliar care without emergency medical competency or ability
- Identify players with specific medical handicaps before the season and prepare reasonable emergency plans in case of sudden illness
- Do not permit players who have suffered injuries requiring medical attention to play or participate until their return to practice and competition has been approved by a physician
- Notify parents or guardians of any minor injuries occurring to, or complaints by, their children

It is wise to document the circumstances of a serious injury (see Chapter 19). In many cases, a written report shows that coaches have reasonably met their responsibility. Such a report is also helpful to medical personnel in the subsequent treatment of an injury. The documentation should include:

- a record of all facts surrounding the injury including who, when, and where the injury occurred and the injured player's responses
- a list and description of the equipment involved, if any
- a list of those who witnessed the injury
- a record of actions taken in response to the injury prior to the arrival of medical personnel

When completed, provide copies of the injury report to the attending physician, the medical response personnel, and the league or association. Be sure to keep a copy for your own files.

Providing Equipment

A coach must take reasonable care to provide the team with proper and safe equipment (see Supplement 9-6). You should know the various types and brands of equipment, master the proper maintenance procedures, and learn to outfit players properly and safely. Generally, you are not responsible for equipment defects unless you're directly involved in the manufacture of equipment. However, you are expected to know whether or not the proper equipment is being used, or if it is defective, and to ensure that defective equipment is not distributed to players. A coach must take reasonable care to:

- select or recommend the proper equipment for the sport
- select or recommend specific types of equipment for specific uses
- properly fit players
- verify that old equipment has been properly reconditioned or recertified for use
- disallow players who are not properly equipped and dressed to participate in practices or games
- have knowledge of league or association rules regarding proper dress and equipment
- instruct players and parents on the proper maintenance of sports equipment in their possession
- utilize a written inventory for reporting and tracking the repair of damaged equipment
- become aware of manufacturers' recommendations and warnings

Selecting Participants

A football coach is obligated to protect the health and safety of players during practices and games. The potential for injuries to occur in football is reduced when players are matched according to size, age, and playing experience. Injuries that occur when players are mismatched in terms of body size and playing experience are more likely to be viewed as the result of irresponsible teaching and supervision rather than as an inherent risk of playing football.

Coaches should protect players by following these guidelines:

- Never permit an injured athlete to compete in practices and games
- Never allow athletes who are out of condition to compete
- Never place players in drills in which there is

the potential for mismatches in physical conditioning, chronological age, and/or skill level.

SUMMARY

A youth sports coach cannot guarantee a child's safety. Legally, a coach is responsible for reasonably foreseeing risks and hazards to the players.

For example, if a youth sports group uses a field that has permanent benches installed near the sidelines, a coach should recognize the foreseeable risks to players and supervise, instruct, and/or warn of those dangers.

Some consider this foreseeability factor as a legal precept. However, it is predicated on knowledge and experience of football. Therefore, its true application is not in legal theory but in the real world of sports.

The curricular objectives for youth sports coaches are defined in the following reference: *Guidelines for Coaching Education : Youth Sports*, National Association for Sport and Physical Education, 1986. The Guidelines identify the competencies that coaches of young athletes should possess or acquire. The competencies are listed under five categories of content within the general title of "Scientific Bases of Coaching." An outline of the content follows:

Curricular Objectives for Youth Sport Coaches

Scientific Bases of Coaching

A. Medical-Legal Aspects of Coaching

Every young athlete should be provided a safe and healthful environment in which to participate. The coach should have basic knowledge and skills in the prevention of athletic injuries, and basic knowledge of first aid.

Every youth sports coach should:

1. Demonstrate knowledge and skill in the prevention and care of injuries generally associated with participation in athletics
2. Be able to plan and coordinate procedures for the emergency care of athletes
3. Be knowledgeable about the legal responsibilities of coaching, including insurance coverage for the coach and athlete
4. Recognize and insist on safe playing condi-

tions and the proper use of protective equipment

5. Be able to provide young athletes with basic information about injury prevention, injury reporting, and sources of medical care

B. Training and Conditioning of Young Athletes

Every youth sport athlete should receive appropriate physical conditioning for sports participation. The coach should use acceptable procedures in their training and conditioning programs.

Every youth sports coach should:

1. Be able to demonstrate the basic knowledges and techniques in the training and conditioning of athletes
2. Recognize the developmental capabilities of young athletes and adjust training and conditioning programs to meet these capabilities
3. Know the effects of the environmental conditions (e.g., heat, cold, humidity, air quality) on young athletes and adjust practice and games accordingly
4. Be able to recognize the various indications of over-training, which may result in injury and/or staleness in athletes, and be able to modify programs to overcome these consequences

C. Psychological Aspects of Coaching

A positive social and emotional environment should be created for young athletes. The coach should recognize and understand the developmental nature of the young athlete's motivation for sport competition and adjust his/her expectations accordingly.

Every youth sports coach should:

1. Subscribe to a philosophy that emphasizes the personal growth of individuals by encouraging and rewarding achievement of personal goals and demonstration of effort, as opposed to overemphasis on winning
2. Demonstrate appropriate behavior of young athletes by maintaining emotional control and demonstrating respect to athletes, officials, and fellow coaches
3. Demonstrate effective communication skills such as those needed to provide appropriate feedback, use a positive approach, motivate

athletes, and demonstrate proper listening skills

4. Emphasize and encourage discussion of matters concerning the display of sportsmanship in competitive and noncompetitive situations
5. Be sufficiently familiar with the principles of motivation, including goal setting and reinforcement, in order to apply them in constructive ways
6. Be able to structure practice and competitive situations to reduce undue stress, and/or to teach young athletes how to reduce any undue stress they experience related to performance

D. Growth, Development, and Learning of Youth Athletes

Youth athletes should have positive learning experiences. The coach should have a knowledge of basic learning principles and consider the influence of developmental level on the athlete's performance.

Every youth sports coach should:

1. Recognize the physical and cognitive changes that occur as children develop and how these changes influence their ability to learn sports skills
2. Concentrate on the development of fundamental motor and cognitive skills that lead to improvement of specific sports skills
3. Understand the physical and cognitive differences manifested by early and late maturers

E. Techniques of Coaching Young Athletes

Every young athlete should have the opportunity to participate regularly in a sport of his/her choosing. The coach should provide guidance for successful learning and performance of specific sport techniques, based on the maturity level or proficiency of the athlete.

Every youth sports coach should:

1. Know the key elements of sport principles and technical skills and the various teaching styles that can be used to introduce and refine them
2. Recognize that young athletes learn at different rates and accommodate these differences by flexibility in teaching styles

3. Be able to organize and conduct practices throughout the season in order to provide maximal learning
4. Be able to select appropriate skills and drills, and analyze errors in performance
5. Be able to provide challenging but safe and successful experiences for young athletes by making appropriate modifications during participation
6. Understand why rules and equipment should be modified for children's sports

Implementation

These guidelines are considered the minimum levels toward which youth sport coaching education programs should strive. To cover the topics of Sections A-D requires at least three hours of clinic time plus additional home study. Another three hours should be devoted to the techniques of coaching session.

Presentations developed for the scientific bases of coaching (Sections A-D) should be as sport specific as possible. The frequent use of audiovisual aids such as videotapes, films, overheads, and slides is helpful. Presentations should be short, with numerous practical examples as well as opportunities for practical exercises and questions. Having materials (e.g., books, pamphlets, self study exams) available for the coaches to study either prior to or following the clinic is essential for adequate coverage of the topics.

For additional information about youth sport coaching education materials and organizations, write the Youth Sports Coalition Steering Committee, 1900 Association Drive, Reston, VA 22091.

REFERENCES

Berry, R., & Wong, G. (1986). *Law and business of the sports industries.* (Vol. II, pp. 227-302, 320-341). Dover, MA: Auburn House.

Clement, A. (1988). *Law in sport and physical activity.* (pp. 27-61). Indianapolis, IN: Benchmark Press.

Maloy, B. (1988). *Law in sports: Liability cases in management and administration.* Indianapolis, IN: Benchmark Press.

National Association for Sport and Physical Education. (1986) *Guidelines for Coaching Education.* Reston, VA: Youth Sports.

Responsibility is also Part of the Game. *Trial,* 13, 22-25, January, 1977.

Schubert, G. et al (1986). *Sports law.* (pp. 220-231). St. Paul, MN: West Publishing Co.

Seefeldt, V. (1985). Legal liability. In P. Vogel & K. Blase (Eds.), *AHAUS associate coaches manual: Fundamentals of coaching youth ice hockey.* (pp. 167-174). East Lansing, MI: Institute for the Study of Youth Sports.

Wong, G. (1988). *Essentials of amateur sports law.* (pp. 336-350). Dover, MA: Auburn House Publishing Co.

Section III
Conditioning and Training

17
Conditioning Youth Football Players

Jean Foley, Ph.D.
Paul Vogel, Ph.D.
Eugene W. Brown, Ph.D.
Karen Garchow, M.A.

QUESTIONS TO CONSIDER

- What are the energy production systems and how important are they to performance in football?
- What are muscular strength, power, endurance, and flexibility and how important are they to performance in football?
- What are the five principles of training that should be used when conditioning youth football players?
- What are interval training, circuit training, and weight training and how can they be used to enhance the conditioning of your athletes?

INTRODUCTION

Aerobics, anaerobics, strength, power, and endurance are some of the many terms that may lend confusion to your understanding of sport conditioning. The goals of this chapter are to provide you with an understanding of the basic principles of conditioning and how these principles apply to football. The information will provide you with a more detailed understanding of the process involved in conditioning so that you can appropriately integrate these concepts into your coaching.

Sport conditioning is the participation in physical activity, intended to enhance the energy production and muscular systems of the body, which may supplement and improve the performance of learned sport skills in future play.

ENERGY PRODUCTION SYSTEMS

Anyone who has played or watched football knows that much energy is required to participate in the game. Sport scientists have discovered that the body can produce energy for physical activity by two different systems—the aerobic system and the anaerobic system. Muscle cells, which use the energy, can only store enough reserves for a few seconds of all-out exercise. When this immediate energy supply is used up, new energy is generated by one of these two energy "refill" systems.

Aerobic System

The aerobic system is sometimes called the "endurance" system. In this system, food, the body's fuel, is converted into energy in the presence of oxygen. The aerobic system functions during long-duration, low-intensity exercise. This type of activity allows the body plenty of time to react effectively to the energy needs of the working muscle.

The aerobic system is very efficient because it converts fuel into energy with relatively little waste and produces little unnecessary heat. The aerobic system can function for extended periods of time because it can produce energy from fats, carbohydrates, and protein.

Protein is not a major source of energy for exercise except in cases of extreme starvation.

Carbohydrates are stored in a limited supply in the muscles and liver, and can be used for both aerobic and anaerobic work.

Fats can be used only by the aerobic system. The virtually unlimited supply of this fuel, stored as adipose tissue or fat, is the basis for the long-term functioning of the aerobic system.

In football, conditioning the aerobic system is a necessary base for energy system conditioning. The reasons for this are twofold:

1. **Football has an endurance component.**

The football player with a well-conditioned aerobic system is not as susceptible to fatigue toward the end of a contest. The delayed onset of fatigue in an aerobically fit athlete can also be a factor in determining how much high quality work can be accomplished during lengthy practice sessions and games.

2. **The body learns to "spare" carbohydrates.**

As the aerobic system is trained, the body learns to use more fat for fuel and to conserve carbohydrates for high-intensity (anaerobic) activities.

Anaerobic System

High-speed or sprint-type activities require a refilling of the muscle cells' energy supplies at a faster rate than is possible by the aerobic system. In this situation, energy production switches over to a special, faster operating system that converts carbohydrates into energy without using oxygen. This system is called anaerobic, meaning "without oxygen." As with any emergency procedure, there are trade-offs that must be made. In order to gain the advantage of quicker replenishment of energy supplies, the anaerobic system suffers two limitations:

1. **Reduced energy yield.**

For each sugar (carbohydrate) unit consumed, the anaerobic system can produce only three basic energy units. On the other hand, the aerobic system can produce 39 energy units from each sugar unit. Therefore, the aerobic system yields 13 times more energy (per fuel unit utilized) than the anaerobic system.

2. **Lactic-acid build-up.**

The anaerobic system produces a byproduct called lactic acid that is not produced by the aerobic system. This chemical quickly builds up in fast-working muscles, causing temporary fatigue, discomfort, and impaired performance. The only way the body can get rid of lactic acid is to slow down and use the aerobic system to convert the lactic acid into usable fuel.

The anaerobic system can produce energy at high speed for about 30 to 90 seconds or at a moderate speed for about 90 seconds to three minutes before the oxygen debt forces the body to slow down so it can switch to the aerobic system. After a recovery period, the anaerobic system can be turned on again to give another short burst of high-speed work. This alternating of sprint work and recovery periods can be continued only until the body's stores of carbohydrates are used up or until the lactic acid removal system can no longer keep up with the rate of anaerobic work.

The energy production system responds to anaerobic training in three major ways:

1. By learning to tolerate larger amounts of lactic acid

The body physiologically adapts to tolerate larger amounts of lactic acid. Therefore, high-intensity work can be maintained for longer periods of time.

2. By reducing the recovery period

The body adapts by reducing the recovery time required before the anaerobic system can be used again.

3. By increasing the rate at which the anaerobic system can operate

Training adaptations increase the speed at which the system can produce energy.

A summary of the two energy production systems is presented in Figure 17-1.

USE OF THE ENERGY SYSTEMS IN FOOTBALL

Now that the basic principles of the energy production systems have been presented, let's look at the sport of football and determine where its requirements fit on the energy scale from aerobic to anaerobic. In analyzing the relative importance of the two energy systems in football, the main concept to keep in mind is that performance time and effort determine the extent to which the aerobic, anaerobic, or both systems are called upon.

Football generally can be considered a sport that places a relatively high demand on the anaerobic system and a moderate demand on the aerobic system. The anaerobic system is used during the high-intensity work of each play. The

Energy Production Systems	Characteristics
Aerobic	• produces energy from fuel with oxygen • can use fats, carbohydrates, or protein for fuel • high energy yield per fuel unit • no lactic acid produced • slow rate of energy production
Anaerobic	• produces energy from fuel without oxygen • can only use carbohydrates for fuel • low energy yield per fuel unit • produces lactic acid as a byproduct • fast rate of energy production

Figure 17-1. Energy production summary.

aerobic system is used during recovery between the short bursts of activity and during longer periods of low-intensity work. Thus, it is important to condition both of these energy systems to be prepared best for the various demands of football.

MUSCULAR SYSTEM

In addition to requiring large amounts of energy, football calls upon the muscles to produce forces for various activities. Passing the ball requires upper arm strength while blocking requires explosive power by the legs so the opponent can be effectively moved backward.

Muscles can produce force only by shortening or contracting. All muscle forces, therefore, are pulling forces and not pushing forces. For example, if you forcefully bend (flex) your knee, the muscles in the back of the thigh (hamstrings) are active. On the other hand, forcefully straightening (extension) the knee results in contraction of the muscles in the front of the thigh (quadriceps). Almost all muscles in the body operate in this paired fashion. As one muscle (or muscle group) shortens to pull a body part in a particular direction, the paired muscle (or muscle group) relaxes and allows the movement to take place. To cause movement in the opposite direction, the muscles simply reverse their roles. If it is desirable to hold a body part in a fixed position, both muscles in the pair exert force to stabilize the joint.

When planning to condition the muscular system for football, several factors need to be addressed. In addition to the "muscle pair" concept, the components of muscular power, endurance, and flexibility; age and ability level of the players; and the specific muscular needs for participation in the sport must be carefully considered. These factors are covered in the sections that follow.

Muscular Power

The force that a muscle can apply is called muscular strength. In football, many of the movements not only require large muscular forces, but these forces must be exerted during short periods of time. This concept of rate of application of muscular force is called muscular power.

Muscular Endurance

Power is the high-intensity component of muscular conditioning. There is also a low-intensity aspect, the muscular endurance component. Muscular endurance refers to the ability of a muscle to exert a sub-maximal force for a prolonged period of time.

Scientists have shown that there are actually different types of muscle fibers within a muscle. Some of these fibers, called fast-twitch or white fibers, are used primarily for brief, powerful muscular movements. Other fibers, called slow-twitch or red fibers, are mainly used for longer, low-intensity movements. As with the aerobic and anaerobic energy systems, the power and endurance components of the muscular system require different types of conditioning.

Flexibility

Flexibility refers to the range of motion of a joint or the range through which the muscle groups can move the bones of a joint without causing injury.

Stretching exercises, used as part of a conditioning program to maintain or increase flexibility, are often ignored by coaches and athletes. However, flexibility exercises are an important component of a football conditioning program. They may reduce the occurrence of certain injuries and enhance the performance of certain techniques.

• Reducing injury potential

When muscles are worked hard, there is a temporary breakdown in their tissue. This breakdown is quickly repaired, but the muscle fibers become shortened unless they are stretched. A shortened, inflexible muscle on one side of the joint won't be able to readily stretch when its muscle pair on the opposite side of the joint fully contracts. The result may be a muscle tear (strain) or damage to the connective tissues of the joint (sprain). Flexibility exercises may reduce the occurrence of these types of injuries.

• Enhancing performance

Lack of flexibility may inhibit or prevent the performance of certain techniques. For example, limited trunk flexibility may retard a receiver's ability to catch a pass thrown just within reach. This is only one of the many examples of the influence of flexibility on performance.

USE OF THE MUSCULAR SYSTEM IN FOOTBALL

Picture again a typical game of football. How would you rate the three muscular factors of power, endurance, and flexibility in terms of their importance to successful performance? (See Figures 17-2 and 17-3) Clearly, most of the actions in football can be characterized as powerful movements. Along with powerful, high-force action comes a high risk of injury, so flexibility should also be a high priority in conditioning for football. Finally, for the same reasons aerobic fitness is necessary in conditioning the energy systems for football, a muscular endurance base is required by the repetitive nature of the movements.

How to Condition for Football

Now that we have examined conditioning, we can turn to the problem of how to develop programs to promote the kind of conditioning needed for football.

You should now have a basic knowledge of the underlying concepts of conditioning. The contrasts between the aerobic and anaerobic ends of the energy production continuum have been described. Three critical aspects of the muscular system continuum (power, endurance, and flexibility) have been explained. Both the energy production systems and the muscular system have been analyzed in relation to their specific applications to football. Now we come to the practical application of this information. How can you as a coach use the discoveries of the sport scientists to develop better football players?

Five Principles of Training

The following five principles of training should be used as guidelines for conditioning both the energy production and muscular systems.

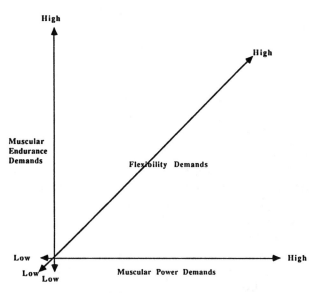

Where should the various positions in football be placed?

Figure 17-2. Graph showing the continuum of the muscular system demands.

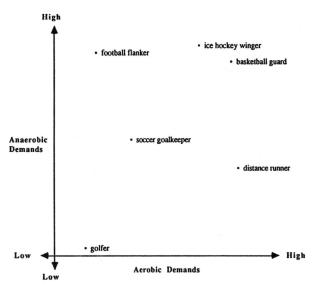

Figure 17-3. Graph, with examples by sport and position, of the aerobic/anaerobic continuum.

1. Warm-Up/Cool-Down

Before beginning a training session or game, use jogging, calisthenics, football-specific exercises, and stretching to prepare the body for more strenuous activity. A program for accomplishing this goal, as well as cooling down the body after strenuous exercise, is outlined in Supplement 17-1. Warm-up activities increase the breathing rate, heart rate, and muscle temperature to exercise levels. Warm-up also causes cartilage pads in the joints to absorb fluids, thereby increasing their shock-absorbing capabilities. It is a period in which the athlete becomes more aware of his surroundings (the field, bleachers, etc.) and gradually reacquainted with the demands of more vigorous activity to follow. Providing the opportunity for your athletes to become aware of their surroundings and sensitive to the demands of the sport are important factors in reducing the potential for injury.

Proper warm-up can thus improve performance and reduce the likelihood of injury to the athlete. Note that the warm-up should not be used as a conditioning period. Having your players exercise too hard during warm-ups defeats the purpose of this period and may cause, rather than prevent, injuries. Stretching exercises are appropriate after a warm-up.

As the age of the athlete group increases, a greater amount of time is needed to warm up for exercises. Seven-year-olds may only need five minutes to warm up, whereas 18-year-olds may need as much as 10 to 15 minutes of warm-up exercises. It is, however, important to include a warm-up interval before practices and games even with the youngest athletes because this proper approach to training is more likely to persist as they grow older.

After a workout session or game, the body should be cooled down. This process should include light, aerobic activity (e.g., jogging) to help the body clear out any remaining lactic acid from the muscles and to reduce the pooling of blood in the extremities. This will reduce soreness and speed the recovery process in preparation for the next day's activities. The cool-down should also be followed by stretching exercises, as emphasized earlier, to help maintain flexibility.

2. Overload

In order to cause a change to take place in the energy production and muscular systems, a stress must be applied to these systems. Repeatedly demanding more than usual of a bodily system causes the system to respond by changing to a state in which it can more easily handle that stress. Overload does not mean placing an impossibly heavy work load on the system, but rather, asking the system to work harder than it is normally accustomed to doing, without reaching a work load at which injury may occur.

Regulation of the overload is the basis of all conditioning programs.

There are five factors that can be manipulated to produce an exercise overload within a workout:

- *Load*

This is the resistance to muscular force. It can be the body, a body part, or any object, such as a weight, which is to be moved. Systematic variation of resistance (load) can be used to create an exercise overload to enhance the development of muscular strength.

- *Repetitions*

This is the number of times muscular force is applied in moving a load. Conditioning of the aerobic energy-production system and enhanced muscular endurance result from progressively increasing the number of repetitions of muscular contraction.

- *Duration*

This is the length of time muscular force is applied in performing a set (bout) of repetitions. Similar to a systematic increase in repetitions, increasing duration of exercise can be used to enhance the aerobic energy-production system and muscular endurance.

- *Frequency*

The rate of exercise (number of repetitions for a given time unit) is the frequency. As frequency increases, exercises shift from having a conditioning effect on the aerobic energy-production system and muscular endurance to having a conditioning effect on the anaerobic energy-production system and muscular power.

- *Rest*

The recovery interval between bouts of exercise, during which a muscle or muscle group is moderately inactive to inactive, is the rest pe-

riod.* Note that rest for the anaerobic system also may occur when the frequency of exercise is reduced so the demands of the exercise are placed upon the aerobic system.

3. Progression

The overload principle must be applied in progressive stages. Conditioning must start with an exercise intensity the body can handle, allowing time for recovery from the physical stress before progressing to an increased work level. Overloading your athletes too rapidly or failing to allow sufficient time for them to recover between workouts can cause injury or illness rather than enhance their fitness.

A good example to keep in mind is the method by which muscles get stronger. A training overload actually causes a temporary breakdown of the muscle fibers, which are then repaired to an even stronger state. If the muscles are overloaded again before the repair period is over, the result may be further damage instead of adaptation. Coaches should be familiar with the signs of overtraining as outlined in Chapter 18 and should monitor their athletes closely to make sure they are progressing at a rate their bodies can handle.

4. Specificity

In order to activate the energy production systems, the muscular system must also be activated. Even though this relationship exists, it is important to carefully consider the desired nature of conditioning when selecting physical activity to achieve these goals.

Physical exercises have specific conditioning effects. Stretching the hip joints will have little, if any, influence on increasing the power of the muscles that move these joints. Exercises to strengthen the calf muscles will not increase the strength of the stomach muscles. Similarly, a well-conditioned gymnast is not likely to possess the type of fitness required for football. Thus, when planning a conditioning program, it is important to first assess the demands of football on your players in order to select exer-

---

*Longer rests are required for short, high-intensity exercise bouts. Shorter rests are required for long, low-intensity exercise bouts.

cises and manipulate the overload factors to help condition your players to meet these specific demands.

The specific components of the energy and muscular systems can be conditioned by application of the following general guidelines to overload these systems. However, these guidelines must be applied in conditioning the energy and muscular systems associated with the specific demands of football.

Training the Energy Production Systems

- Aerobic system—use endurance activities involving moderate exercise intensity of large body segments or the whole body. Some examples include swimming laps, running, and bicycling long distances. Running is more desirable for football than the other aerobic activities because it has a more specific training effect for the sport.
- Anaerobic system—use "sprint" type activities involving very intense exercise of large body segments or the whole body. The same exercises, as listed for aerobic training, are appropriate activities for anaerobic training. However, distances must be reduced and the intensity increased. Sprinting pass patterns would have a more specific training effect for football. By performing sprinting pass patterns, players would be developing their techniques along with anaerobic conditioning.

Training the Muscular System

- Power—use exercises, by specific muscle groups, involving the rapid application of relatively large forces and few repetitions.
- Endurance—use exercises, by specific muscle groups, involving the application of relatively small forces and many repetitions.
- Flexibility—use slow and sustained (six to 30 seconds) stretching of specific muscle groups to the point of slight discomfort. Don't bounce!

5. Reversibility

It is not enough to plan and carry out a developmental conditioning program. Once an athlete's body attains a certain fitness level, a maintenance program is necessary to prevent the conditioning benefits from being lost.

Studies on athletes have shown that even starting players will experience a decrease in fitness level during the competitive season unless provisions are made to maintain conditioning throughout the season. The maintenance program does not have to be as frequent or as intense as the build-up program, but without a minimal program of this type, the hard-earned fitness will gradually be lost.

METHODS FOR CONDITIONING

Regulation of the exercise overload is the basis for all conditioning programs. As previously stated, this can be accomplished by manipulating the factors of load, repetition, duration, frequency, and rest. There are three distinct training methods that can be used to effectively manipulate these factors to enhance conditioning. These methods are *interval training, circuit training,* and *weight training.*

1. Interval Training

This type of training was first used in training runners. Interval training, however, has been used in many sports, including football. Interval training involves a period of vigorous exercise followed by a recovery period. It functions by using aerobic and anaerobic activities to condition the energy production systems. By gradually increasing the duration, intensity, and number of exercise bouts and by decreasing the rest interval between bouts, an overload can be achieved.

Interval training can be adapted to football by alternating bouts of intense practice on basic skills, such as blocking, with recovery periods. In fact, a series of practice sessions can be structured with an interval training basis. The first session would consist of relatively low-intensity exercises of short duration with relatively long rest intervals; whereas, in subsequent practice sessions, the exercise intensity and duration would be increased and the number and duration of rest intervals would be decreased. It should be noted that in interval training, rest periods can be used for rest, water breaks, strategy sessions, team organization, and light aerobic activity.

The specific conditioning components enhanced by an interval training program depend upon the nature of the exercises included in the program. A systematic interval training program can improve the energy production systems (aerobic and anaerobic) as well as the strength and endurance of specific muscle groups that are exercised. A year-round interval training program for highly skilled and motivated players who are 14 years of age or older is included in Supplement 17-2.

2. Circuit Training

This type of training involves participation in a variety of activities in rapid succession. These activities are conducted at various locations (stations) around the football field. The team is divided so that an equal number of players are at each station. When the circuit begins, all players attempt to perform their best at the tasks assigned to each station within a set time. Successive stations should differ in the demand they place on the body. For example, an intense arm exercise should not be followed by a passing drill. Recovery occurs as the groups rotate, within a specified time interval, to the next station and as subsequent stations differ in their demands upon the body.

In circuit training an exercise overload is produced by:

- increasing the number of stations in the circuit
- increasing the number of repetitions or work intensity at one or more stations
- increasing the time for exercise at each station
- increasing the number of times the circuit is completed
- decreasing the recovery period between stations

The variety of activities that can be included in a circuit provides the opportunity to be flexible in creating different and specific exercise overloads as well as simultaneously enhancing skill. Supplement 17-3 contains an example of a football training circuit and recording form, which can be photocopied as is, as well as a blank form upon which you can implement your own

training circuit to meet the specific needs of your players.

3. Weight Training

This type of training involves the lifting of weights to produce an exercise overload. In weight training, a variety of sub-maximal lifts are performed to produce increased strength, power, and endurance in the specific muscle groups that are exercised. In general, weight training involves applying the "Five Principles of Training" to produce increases in muscular strength.

Following the "Five Principles of Training," the first part of a weight training routine is the warm-up and stretching program. The weight resistance is the overload, which is increased in a progression as the athlete's workout record indicates gains in strength. Analysis of the strength requirements of football (specificity) has resulted in the list of exercises outlined in Supplement 17-2. The cool-down and post-lifting stretching routine decreases muscle soreness and prevents loss of flexibility. Finally, once strength gains are achieved, the maintenance program must be used to avoid reversal of strength increases acquired during the developmental program.

In weight training, an exercise overload can be produced by varying the:

- exercise load
- number of repetitions per set
- frequency of exercise during each set
- number of sets
- length of rest interval between exercise sets

The exercise load determines the number of repetitions of an exercise an athlete can perform during each set. Generally, no fewer than eight repetitions per set of each exercise are recommended when attempting to increase muscular strength for football. However, if increased muscular endurance is the goal of a particular weight training exercise, (a) the load should be decreased to permit a much greater number of repetitions, (b) the number of sets should be increased to three or more, and (c) the rest intervals between sets should be decreased. On the other hand, if increase in muscular power is the goal, this can be achieved by rapidly and repeatedly lifting a relatively heavy load 8 to 12 repetitions per set.

It should be noted that it is possible to train some muscle groups to increase power and others to increase endurance. The degree to which either component increases depends upon the specific nature of the overload condition.

Several factors should be carefully considered before engaging your players in a weight training program. These factors include:

- Age of the athletes

A weight training program for football is not recommended for players under 14 years of age.

- Level of interest

A weight training program is not an essential element for participants in a recreational league. However, a weight training program can be beneficial to highly skilled players who are interested in participating in a very competitive league.

- Availability of facilities and equipment

Sites and equipment for weight training may not be accessible. Before encouraging your athletes to participate in a weight training program, some investigation of availability is needed.

- Availability of qualified adults

Before encouraging your players to participate in a particular weight training program, a qualified adult must be available to supervise the weight room and to provide instruction in proper spotting and performance techniques for each of the suggested exercises.

Because of the great variety of weight training equipment and the availability of many books and guides to weight training, only general guidelines are presented here. A suggested program of weight training exercises appropriate for the highly skilled football player who is 14 years of age or older is included in Supplement 17-2. These exercises can be done using either free weights or weight machines. The guidelines given cover training schedules and how to fit a weight training program into the overall plan of the season. Specific techniques

and explanations of weight training exercises can be found in manuals available in most local bookstores. Some references are:

- *Strength Training by the Experts* by Daniel P. Riley (2nd edition, Leisure Press, 1982). Covers a variety of equipment, including free weights, Nautilus, and Universal. Explains which muscle groups are used in each exercise.
- *Weightlifting for Beginners* by Bill Reynolds (Contemporary Books, 1982). Designed primarily for free weights and at-home weight training.

ECONOMICAL TRAINING

The relative importance of conditioning for football must be put into perspective with the importance of meeting the cognitive, psychosocial, strategy, and sport techniques needs of your players. As a football coach, you must address all of these needs, to varying degrees, during practices and games. However, because of the limited amount of time available to meet the needs of your players, whenever possible, you should plan activities that simultaneously meet needs in more than one area. This approach is referred to as economical training. If practice sessions are carefully planned, it is possible to devise activities that simultaneously meet needs in more than one area. For example, the intensity, duration, and structure of a tackling drill could be organized to enhance components of conditioning and strategy, as well as techniques of tackling.

It is easier to get 14-year-olds in condition to play than it is to make up for the years in which they were not taught the techniques of the game.

The concept of economical training is presented here because many coaches erroneously set aside blocks of time within their practices for conditioning-only activities. Push-ups, sit-ups, sprints, and distance running are typical of what is included in these conditioning-only blocks of time. With youth players who have not achieved a high level of mastery of the techniques of the game, conditioning-only activities are not recommended. Practice time needs to be spent on learning the techniques and strategies of the game of football, with conditioning an accompanying outcome as the result of planned economical training. As players develop a higher level of mastery of the techniques of football, conditioning-only activities could be included in practices. However, they should be made as closely related to football as possible.

SUMMARY

In this chapter you have learned how the energy and muscular systems work, how they are used in football, and how to condition these systems. Although separate conditioning-only workouts were not recommended for the under-14 age group, guidelines were given for incorporating the principles of training into the regular practices for the double purpose of skill improvement and enhanced conditioning (economical training). Athletes begin to require and benefit from supplementary programs for conditioning the energy and muscular systems around the age of 14. Examples of such programs have been provided, with guidelines for varying the training at different points in the year. Suggested schedules and workout routines to guide this training are provided in the supplements.

A basic knowledge of the scientific principles of physical conditioning will help you design effective practices and training sessions. It will also help you communicate to your athletes the importance of each type of conditioning activity you use. Conveying this understanding to your players will not only make them more knowledgeable, but will also help them develop good lifelong habits and attitudes towards exercise and fitness.

SUGGESTED READINGS

Fox, E.L. (1979). *Sports physiology*. Philadelphia: W.B. Saunders.
Lamb, D.R. (1984). *Physiology of exercise* (2nd ed.). New York: Macmillan.
Sharkey, B. (1984). *Physiology of fitness* (2nd ed.). Champaign, IL: Human Kinetics Publishers.
Stone, W.V., & Knoll, W.K. (1978). *Sports conditioning and weight training*. Boston: Allyn and Bacon.

Supplement 17-1.
Warm-Up, Cool-Down, and Stretching Activities for Football

Introduction

The players' preparation for each practice and game should begin with a warm-up session and should be followed by a cool-down period. Warm-up and cool-down activities should be conducted at light to moderate intensities and should be followed by stretching exercises.

Warm-up

Warm-up activities should be performed to increase the breathing rate, heart rate, and muscle temperature to exercise levels. These are done to prepare the body for the demands of subsequent strenuous activities. Additionally, warm-ups enhance the players' awareness for their surroundings. Warm-ups can also be used as a valuable introduction in setting the tone of the players' attitude toward the activity to follow. Warm-ups for sport should involve the regions of the body upon which more intense exercise demands will be placed during training for and participation in the sport. Thus, with football, virtually all regions of the body should be prepared. The following categories included some examples of warm-ups that can be used for football.

Light Aerobic/General Warm-ups

- Jogging
- Jogging in place
- Jumping jacks

Light Aerobic/Football-Specific Warm-ups

- Center-quarterback exchange

- Passing drills using various types of pass routes

Body Region-Specific Warm-ups

- Neck rolls—The head is rolled from shoulder, to chest, to opposite shoulder, and the procedure is reversed and repeated. (Note: Do not make complete head circle. There is potential for compression of the vertebrae when the neck is hyperextended.)
- Shoulder circles—With arms horizontal and to the side of the body, small circular rotations of the arms are made. These circles are gradually increased. This pattern is then repeated; however, the arms are rotated in the opposite direction.
- Trunk circles—While standing with the feet shoulder-width apart and the hands on the hips, the trunk is moved in a circular manner. (Note: Avoid an excessive arch of the low-back by keeping the head in an upright position.)

Stretching

Stretching should be performed by slowly and gently extending each muscle group and joint to the point of slight discomfort. This position should be held for 6-30 seconds. The stretch should then be released and repeated in the same manner two or more times. Bouncing or fast, jerky movements are inappropriate in that they activate the muscles' stretch reflex mechanism and, therefore, limit rather than enhance flexibility.

Stretching exercises, used as part of a football conditioning program to maintain or increase flexibility, may reduce the occurrence of certain injuries, such as muscle strains and joint sprains, and may enhance performance of certain techniques. Because football involves virtually all major muscle groups and joints of the body, a variety of flexibility exercises, targeted at these regions, should be a part of each pre- and post-practice and game. The following flexibility exercises are some examples that are appropriate for football.

- Calf stretch—With the legs straddled in a forward–backward alignment, the knee of the back leg is bent while the entire sole of the back foot maintains contact with the ground. By switching the position of the feet, the other calf is stretched.
- Kneeling quad stretch—From a kneeling position, the hip is pressed forward. By switching the positions of the legs, the other quadriceps muscle and hip joint are stretched. Note that this exercise also stretches the trunk.
- Seated straddle (groin stretch)—From a seated position with the legs straddled, the trunk is moved forward. The head should be kept upright to reduce pressure on the lower back.
- Butterfly (groin stretch)—In a seated position, place the soles of the feet together with the knees bent no more than 90 degrees. Grasp the ankles with the hands and apply pressure with the elbows to the inside of the legs to rotate the legs outward. Keep the back straight with the head in an upright position.
- Trunk and hip stretch—From a supine position, both arms are placed 90 degrees from the trunk. The head is turned toward one of the outstretched arms while bringing the opposite leg (90 degrees from the trunk) over the midline of the body and toward the ground. This exercise should be performed on both sides.
- Shoulder stretch—Bend the elbow and position the arm behind the head. The hand of the opposite arm grasps the bent elbow and slowly pulls it toward the midline of the trunk. To stretch the other shoulder, the roles of the arms are switched.

Cool-Down

The importance of cooling down has not received sufficient emphasis among coaches of young athletes. Cool-down sessions are infrequently used to end a practice session and are rarely used following a game. A cool-down period helps to:

- clear out lactic acid accumulated in the muscles
- reduce the pooling of blood in the extremities

- prevent the loss of flexibility that may accompany intense muscular exercise

Like the warm-up, cool-down activities should include movements similar to those included in the practice or game. Thus, the warm-up and stretching activities, previously listed, are appropriate for the cool-down. Have your athletes perform the cool-down exercises first, then the stretching activities.

Supplement 17-2.
Year-Round Conditioning Program

Introduction

This supplement contains information on a year-round conditioning program. It is directed at conditioning the energy production system, through a program of interval training, and the muscular system, through a weight training program. This year-round program is appropriate for the highly motivated player who is 14 years of age or older. It is for players who have chosen to concentrate on football and wish to maximize their performance through enhanced conditioning on a year-round basis. This program is NOT for beginning players and/or players below the age of 14 years who would derive greater benefit by devoting their time to learning and perfecting the techniques of football.

Interval Training Program

Interval training is a method for developing the anaerobic energy-production system while maintaining and/or enhancing a previously established base of aerobic fitness. This type of training uses alternating periods of short-duration, high-intensity anaerobic ("sprint" type) exercises with longer periods of moderate-to low-intensity aerobic exercises.

The training outlines provided in this supplement can be used with different modes of exercise, depending on individual preference and the availability of equipment and facilities. Jogging, running, and/or bicycling are modes of exercise suggested for interval training in football. Specific distances are not indicated in this supplement because of the variety of exercises possible and because of variations in individual fitness. All players should, however, maintain a record of distances covered on individual forms provided in this supplement so their progress can be assessed. Distance records can be kept in yards, meters, miles, kilometers, blocks, or laps.

An important concept to keep in mind when planning an interval training program is that the program should progress to a point where it places a similar aerobic and anaerobic demand on the athlete as that of a hard-played game of football. This type of work load in an interval training program conditions the athletes to the demands they will be confronted with during competition. Regulation of the duration and intensity of exercise, as well as the rest intervals, are the components of an interval training program that can be manipulated to achieve the desired exercise levels.

The interval training program included in this supplement is divided into five phases. These phases are briefly described and followed by forms that can be used by athletes to keep records of their progress.

- Pre-season Aerobic/Anaerobic Transition Program —This four-week program is used to prepare athletes for high intensity anaerobic conditioning after they have developed a good aerobic fitness base (see Table 17-1s).
- Pre-season Anaerobic Developmental Interval Training Program —This is an eight-week program to be started 10 weeks before the first game (see Table 17-2s). The program should be preceded by anaerobic training and

the four-week "Aerobic/Anaerobic Transition Program."

- In-Season Anaerobic Maintenance Program—This program should be completed once, a week starting two weeks before the first game and continuing through the end of the season (see Table 17-3s).
- Post-Season Aerobic Program—This program involves rhythmical, low intensity aerobic activities such as jogging, running, and bicycling for three days per week to enhance aerobic fitness (see Table 17-4s).
- Post-Season Anaerobic Maintenance Program—This program should be done once a week to maintain anaerobic fitness levels during the aerobic phase of off-season conditioning (see Table 17-4s).

Weight Training Program

Weight training for football should focus on the development of muscular power, or the ability to quickly exert large muscular force. The load should be lifted explosively, then returned to the starting position slowly. Generally, the larger muscle groups should be exercised first. Also, the same muscle groups should not be exercised in succession. Table 17-5s contains weight-lifting exercises that can be used to meet the specific requirements of football. They are arranged in an appropriate order.

Since the weight training exercises listed can be done using a variety of equipment, details of technique and an explanation of procedures for each exercise will not be given here. Many good guides for weight training are available in local bookstores. A few examples of such guides that contain explanations of correct technique and details for each specific exercise are:

- *Sports Conditioning and Weight Training* by William J. Stone and William A. Kroll (Allyn & Bacon, 1978). This book is designed to offer sound, systematic training programs for those who wish to apply strength and conditioning techniques to specific sports.
- *Strength Training by the Experts* by Daniel P. Riley (2nd edition, Leisure Press, 1982). This book covers a variety of lifting equipment, including free weights, Universal equipment, and Nautilus equipment, and explains which muscle groups are used in each exercise.

- *Weightlifting for Beginners* by Bill Reynolds (Contemporary Books, 1982). This book is designed primarily for free weights and at-home weightlifting.

Year-round conditioning for muscular power can be divided into three parts: pre-season (developmental), in-season (maintenance), and post-season (developmental). Pre-season and post-season workouts have improvement in muscular power as their goals. In-season workouts are done less frequently and should be used to maintain the muscular fitness developed during the off-season.

Pre-season Weight Training

Athletes new to weight training should start a developmental program at least three months before the first competition. Overloaded muscles require about 48 hours to repair and recover sufficiently, so a lifting schedule of three days per week with a minimum of one day off between workouts will give best results.

For the first one to two weeks, the athlete should do one exercise 8-12 times (repetitions), then move on to the next exercise until each exercise in the weight training program has been covered. This series of repetitions of each exercise is called a set.

The appropriate weight load or resistance is a load the athlete can lift properly a minimum of eight times, but is not so light that it can be lifted more than 12 times. Some experimenting with weight loads will be necessary to determine correct starting weights for each exercise. Once these weight loads are determined, they should be recorded on the "Weight Training Program Checklist" included in this supplement (see Table 17-6s).

During this first phase of the weight training program (two weeks), the athlete should master the proper lifting technique and work through the initial muscle soreness that accompanies learning the correct weight loads. After this initial phase, the work can be increased to two sets while maintaining the initial weight levels for 8-12 repetitions per exercise. Two sets of the same exercise are completed before the next exercise is done. This second phase also lasts two weeks.

Table 17-1s. Pre-Season Aerobic/Anaerobic Transition Program.

(To be started 10 weeks before the first game)

Name_____

The information at the top of each week's schedule specifies a suggested duration and intensity of the workout for that week. Space is provided for a coach or player to write an alternate workout for each week. The frequency of workouts is three per week, on an every-other-day basis. Each workout should be preceded and followed by stretching exercises. Work intensity is specified in terms of percentage of effort as follows:

LM	= Light to Moderate	**50% of maximum** effort*
H	= Hard	**80% of maximum** effort
S	= Sprint	**100% of maximum** effort

For example, **3x(2:H,2:LM)** means do three sets of (two minutes at 80% of effort followed by two minutes at 50% of effort). For each workout completed, record the **date** and the **total distance covered.**

		Pre-season Aerobic/Anaerobic Transition Program		
WEEK		**Day 1**	**Day 2**	**Day 3**
1	[9:LM,3x(2:H,2:LM),9:LM] alternate workout: [		]	
	Date:			
	Distance:			
2	[7:LM,4x(2:H,2:LM),7:LM] alternate workout: [		]	
	Date:			
	Distance:			
3	[5:LM,5x(2:H,2:LM),5:LM] alternate workout: [		]	
	Date:			
	Distance:			
4	[3:LM,6x(2:H,2:LM),3:LM] alternate workout: [		]	
	Date:			
	Distance:			
		TOTAL TIME FOR EACH WORKOUT = 30 MINUTES		

*If the intensity of the hard and sprint portions of the exercise intervals cannot be maintained, the athlete should reduce the intensity of the light to moderate intervals.

(To be started 10 weeks before the first game)

Name_____

The information at the top of each week's schedule specifies a suggested duration and intensity of the workout for that week. Space is provided for a coach or player to write an alternate workout for each week. The frequency of workouts is three per week, on an every-other-day basis. Each workout should be preceded and followed by stretching exercises. Work intensity is specified in terms of percentage of effort as follows:

LM	= Light to Moderate	**50% of maximum** effort*
H	= Hard	**80% of maximum** effort
S	= Sprint	**100% of maximum** effort

For example, **4x(:20S,2:LM)** means do four sets of (20 seconds at maximum effort followed by two minutes at 50% of effort). For each workout completed, record the **date** and the **total distance covered**.

Pre-season Anaerobic Developmental Interval Training Program				
WEEK		**Day 1**	**Day 2**	**Day 3**
1	[4:LM,2x(1:H,2:LM),4x(:20S,:40LM),4:LM]			
	alternate workout: [			]
	Date/Distance			
2	[4:LM,2x(1:H,2:LM),5x(:20S,:40LM),4:LM]			
	alternate workout: [			]
	Date/Distance			
3	[4:LM,2x(1:H,2:LM),6x(:20S,:40LM),4:LM]			
	alternate workout: [			]
	Date/Distance			
4	[4:LM,2x(1:H,2:LM),7x(:20S,:40LM),4:LM]			
	alternate workout: [			]
	Date/Distance			
5	[4:LM,3x(1:H,2:LM),8x(:20S,:40LM),4:LM]			
	alternate workout: [			]
	Date/Distance			
6	[4:LM,3x(1:H,2:LM),9x(:20S,:40LM),4:LM]			
	alternate workout: [			]
	Date/Distance			
7	[4:LM,3x(1:H,2:LM),6x(:10S,:20LM),2:LM,6x(:10S,:20LM),4:LM]			
	alternate workout: [			]
	Date/Distance			
8	[4:LM,3x(1:H,2:LM),8x(:10S,:20LM),2:LM,8x(:10S,:20LM),4:LM]			
	alternate workout: [			]
	Date/Distance			

*If the intensity of the hard and sprint portions of the exercise intervals cannot be maintained, the athlete should reduce the intensity of the light to moderate intervals.

Table 17-3s. In-Season Anaerobic Maintenance Program.

(To be started two weeks before the first game)

Name_____

A suggested workout is provided at the top of the In-Season Aerobic Maintenance Program form. Space is provided for the coach or player to write an alternate workout. The frequency of workouts is one per week. Workouts should be completed at the end of a practice but not on a day before a game. Each workout should be preceded and followed by stretching exercises. Intensity is specified in terms of percentage of effort as follows:

LM	= Light to Moderate	**50% of maximum effort***
H	= Hard	**80% of maximum effort**
S	= Sprint	**100% of maximum effort**

For example, **3x(2:H,2:LM)** means do three sets of (two minutes at 80% of effort followed by two minutes at 50% of effort). For each workout completed, record the **date** and the **total distance covered.**

In-Season Anaerobic Maintenance Program					
[2:LM,2x(1:H,2:LM),2x(:20S,:40LM),8x(:10S,:20LM),4:LM]					
alternate workout: [ ]					
MONTH	**WEEK**				
	1	**2**	**3**	**4**	**5**
1 Date:					
Distance:					
2 Date:					
Distance:					
3 Date:					
Distance:					
4 Date:					
Distance:					
5 Date:					
Distance:					

*If the intensity of the hard and sprint portions of the exercise intervals cannot be maintained, the athlete should reduce the intensity of the light to moderate intervals.

Table 17-4s. Post-Season Aerobic and Anaerobic Maintenance Program.

(To be started two to four weeks after the last game)

AEROBIC PROGRAM

Aerobic capabilities should be developed during the post-season to provide the base for building the more intense anaerobic work capacity required for top performance during the season. Aerobic work combined with muscular strength/power work on alternate days is a good variation from the typical season routine. In the post-season time period, the development of aerobic capacity and muscular strength/power become primary, rather than secondary, objectives.

Begin three days of aerobic activity (dribbling, jogging and running, bicycling, or other rhythmical, low intensity, long duration activities) alternated with three days of weight training. Progress up to 40 minutes of continuous aerobic activity and then work on increasing the speed or intensity at which the 40 minutes of work is done. Each workout should be preceded and followed by stretching exercises. Record the date and workout time on the Year-Round Conditioning Checklist in the portion of the checklist devoted to Post-Season.

ANAEROBIC MAINTENANCE PROGRAM

A suggested workout is provided at the top of the Post-Season Anaerobic Maintenance Program form. Space is also provided for the coach or player to write an alternate workout. The post-season anaerobic maintenance program should be done once a week. It should not be completed on the same day as an aerobic workout. Each workout should be preceded and followed by stretching exercises. Intensity is specified in terms of percentage of effort as follows:

LM	= Light to Moderate	**50% of maximum** effort*
H	= Hard	**80% of maximum** effort
S	= Sprint	**100% of maximum** effort

For example, **4x(:20S,:40LM)** means do four sets of (20 seconds at maximum effort followed by 40 seconds at 50% of effort). For each workout completed, record the **date** and the **total distance covered.**

Post-Season Anaerobic Maintenance Program						
[4:LM,2x(1:H,2:LM),4x(:20S,:40LM),4x(:20S,:40LM),4:LM]						
alternate workout: [ ]						
MONTH		**WEEK**				
		1	**2**	**3**	**4**	**5**
1	Date:					
	Distance:					
2	Date:					
	Distance:					
3	Date:					
	Distance:					
4	Date:					
	Distance:					

*If the intensity of the hard and sprint portions of the exercise intervals cannot be maintained, the athlete should reduce the intensity of the light to moderate intervals.

Table 17-5s. Conditioning activities for football players.

Order	Exercise	Comment
1	Neck flexion	This exercise can be done on specially designed weight machines or can be accomplished by wrapping a towel around the forehead and having a partner provide resistance.
2	Squat lift	The angle at the back of the knee should not be allowed to become less than 90 degrees. An upright position of the head should be maintained, and the back should be kept as close to vertical as possible throughout the lift. Trained spotters must be used. If using free weights, wrap a towel or foam pad around the center of the bar to lessen the discomfort of the bar across the back of the neck.
3	Bench press	Trained spotters must be used.
4	Bent knee sit-ups	A weight can be held high on the chest and/or the sit-up can be done on an incline to increase resistance. The feet should be held down by a partner or restraining structure.
5	Finger flexion	Grip strength exercises can be done with a spring hand gripper.
6	Hip abduction	This exercise can be done on a specially designed weight machine or by having a partner provide resistance. Both legs should be exercised.
7	Bent over row	The head should be supported, and the back should be in a horizontal position.
8	Neck extension	This exercise can be done on specially designed weight machines or can be accomplished by wrapping a towel around the head and having a partner provide resistance.
9	Hip abduction	This exercise can be done on a specially designed weight machine or by having a partner provide resistance. Both legs should be exercised.
10	Toe rise	If using free weights, wrap a towel or foam pad around the bar to lessen the discomfort of the bar across the back of the neck. Trained spotters must be used. A block of wood can be used under the toes to increase the range through which the muscles must exert force in lifting the body.
11	Arm curl	A rocking motion of the body should not be used to aid the arms in lifting the resistance.
12	Knee flexion	
13	Lat pull-down	Keep the hips extended and do not use hip flexion to aid in the pull-down motion.
14	Back hyperextension	A partner or restraining structure is needed to hold the legs down.
15	Knee extension	
16	Reverse forearm curl	

In the third phase, three full sets are done during each workout. Three full sets of 8-12 repetitions on an exercise are completed, then the next exercise is done. This phase should last for eight or more weeks and should end about two weeks before the first competition. It is during this third phase that weight levels are adjusted upward as strength increases. This information is summarized in Table 17-7s.

When 12 repetitions of a given exercise have been completed for each of the three sets for two successive workouts, the weight load for that exercise can be increased to the next level for the following workout. The athlete

Table 17-6s. Weight Training Program Checklist.

Name _____

INSTRUCTIONS:

- Record the weight load only when there is a change in load.
- Record the number of repetitions for each set (example: 12/10/10)
- Increase the weight load when you have done 12 repetitions for each of three sets for two consecutive workouts.
- Use a smaller load increase if you cannot do a minimum of eight repetitions per set at a new load.

Date		Neck flexion	Squat lift	Bench press	Bent knee sit-up	Finger flexion	Hip abduction	Bent over row	Neck extension	Hip adduction	Toe rise	Arm curl	Knee flexion	Lat pull-down	Back hyperextension	Knee extension	Reverse forearm curl
	WT.																
	REPS.	/ /	/ /	/ /	/ /	/ /	/ /	/ /	/ /	/ /	/ /	/ /	/ /	/ /	/ /	/ /	/ /
	WT.																
	REPS.	/ /	/ /	/ /	/ /	/ /	/ /	/ /	/ /	/ /	/ /	/ /	/ /	/ /	/ /	/ /	/ /
	WT.																
	REPS.	/ /	/ /	/ /	/ /	/ /	/ /	/ /	/ /	/ /	/ /	/ /	/ /	/ /	/ /	/ /	/ /
	WT.																
	REPS.	/ /	/ /	/ /	/ /	/ /	/ /	/ /	/ /	/ /	/ /	/ /	/ /	/ /	/ /	/ /	/ /
	WT.																
	REPS.	/ /	/ /	/ /	/ /	/ /	/ /	/ /	/ /	/ /	/ /	/ /	/ /	/ /	/ /	/ /	/ /
	WT.																
	REPS.	/ /	/ /	/ /	/ /	/ /	/ /	/ /	/ /	/ /	/ /	/ /	/ /	/ /	/ /	/ /	/ /
	WT.																
	REPS.	/ /	/ /	/ /	/ /	/ /	/ /	/ /	/ /	/ /	/ /	/ /	/ /	/ /	/ /	/ /	/ /
	WT.																
	REPS.	/ /	/ /	/ /	/ /	/ /	/ /	/ /	/ /	/ /	/ /	/ /	/ /	/ /	/ /	/ /	/ /
	WT.																
	REPS.	/ /	/ /	/ /	/ /	/ /	/ /	/ /	/ /	/ /	/ /	/ /	/ /	/ /	/ /	/ /	/ /
	WT.																
	REPS.	/ /	/ /	/ /	/ /	/ /	/ /	/ /	/ /	/ /	/ /	/ /	/ /	/ /	/ /	/ /	/ /
	WT.																
	REPS.	/ /	/ /	/ /	/ /	/ /	/ /	/ /	/ /	/ /	/ /	/ /	/ /	/ /	/ /	/ /	/ /
	WT.																
	REPS.	/ /	/ /	/ /	/ /	/ /	/ /	/ /	/ /	/ /	/ /	/ /	/ /	/ /	/ /	/ /	/ /
	WT.																
	REPS.	/ /	/ /	/ /	/ /	/ /	/ /	/ /	/ /	/ /	/ /	/ /	/ /	/ /	/ /	/ /	/ /
	WT.																
	REPS.	/ /	/ /	/ /	/ /	/ /	/ /	/ /	/ /	/ /	/ /	/ /	/ /	/ /	/ /	/ /	/ /
	WT.																
	REPS.	/ /	/ /	/ /	/ /	/ /	/ /	/ /	/ /	/ /	/ /	/ /	/ /	/ /	/ /	/ /	/ /
	WT.																
	REPS.	/ /	/ /	/ /	/ /	/ /	/ /	/ /	/ /	/ /	/ /	/ /	/ /	/ /	/ /	/ /	/ /
	WT.																
	REPS.	/ /	/ /	/ /	/ /	/ /	/ /	/ /	/ /	/ /	/ /	/ /	/ /	/ /	/ /	/ /	/ /
	WT.																
	REPS.	/ /	/ /	/ /	/ /	/ /	/ /	/ /	/ /	/ /	/ /	/ /	/ /	/ /	/ /	/ /	/ /
	WT.																
	REPS.	/ /	/ /	/ /	/ /	/ /	/ /	/ /	/ /	/ /	/ /	/ /	/ /	/ /	/ /	/ /	/ /
	WT.																
	REPS.	/ /	/ /	/ /	/ /	/ /	/ /	/ /	/ /	/ /	/ /	/ /	/ /	/ /	/ /	/ /	/ /

Table 17-7s. Pre-season developmental weight training program.

Phase	Duration	Reps	Sets	Days/Week	Comments
1	2 weeks	8-12	1	3	Maintain starting resistance level.
2	2 weeks	8-12	2	3	Maintain starting resistance level.
3	8 or more weeks	8-12	3	3	Increase resistance levels as strength gains are made.

should be able to do a minimum of eight repetitions for each of the three sets at the new weight level. If this is not possible, a smaller weight increase is indicated.

In-Season Weight Training

Strength improvement is the goal of the preseason weight training developmental program. Maintenance of the increased strength is accomplished by a scaled-down in-season weight training program that should begin about two weeks before the first game. If weight training is done only during the preseason period, the strength gains will gradually be lost as the season progresses. Research has shown that a weight training maintenance program of one to two workouts per week will prevent the reversal of strength gains. Performance will not be hampered by in-season weight training if three general rules are followed:

- Lifting should be limited to once or twice a week, with two to three days between weight training workouts.
- Do not schedule weight training workouts for the day before or the day of a game.
- Maintain the resistance at the last load level where 12 repetitions for all three sets could be done. Do not increase weight loads during in-season workouts. Use pre- and post-season periods for strength improvement with strength maintenance as the goal of the in-season workouts.

The workout program itself remains the same as in Phase 3 of the developmental program. The same series of exercises is followed, with 8-12 repetitions per exercise, for a total of three sets. As long as the athlete lifts at least once every four days and does not increase the weight load, there should be no muscle soreness or undue fatigue that will interfere with performance during games.

Post-Season Weight Training

Once the competitive season is over, players can again focus on achievement of higher strength levels. A post-season break from training of at least two weeks can be followed by a return to the program outlined in Phase 3 of the preseason developmental program (see Table 17-2s). Three-set workouts, three times per week, can be continued throughout the off-season months. The "Weight Training Program Checklist" can be used to determine when weight loads should be increased. After the first year in which players build up gradually through the one-set and two-set phases during the preseason developmental program, Phase 1 and 2 should not be needed.

Year-round conditioning program

The year-round conditioning program contains two components. They are: (a) an interval training program for conditioning the aerobic and anaerobic energy-production systems, and (b) a weight training program for conditioning the muscular system (see Tables 17-8s through 17-10s). These components are integrated into a year-round conditioning program (see Table 17-11s).

Table 17-8s. Year-Round Conditioning Checklist.

Name _____

(Mark the date of each completed workout in the box.)

PRE-SEASON

	AEROBIC/ANAEROBIC TRANSITION PROGRAM AND WEIGHT TRAINING PROGRAM (Phases 1 and 2 or 3)					
WEEK	TRANSITION WORKOUT	WEIGHT TRAINING	TRANSITION WORKOUT	WEIGHT TRAINING	TRANSITION WORKOUT	WEIGHT TRAINING
1						
2						
3						
4						

PRE-SEASON

	DEVELOPMENTAL INTERVAL TRAINING PROGRAM AND WEIGHT TRAINING PROGRAM (Phase 3)					
WEEK	INTERVAL TRAINING	WEIGHT TRAINING	INTERVAL TRAINING	WEIGHT TRAINING	INTERVAL TRAINING	WEIGHT TRAINING
5						
6						
7						
8						
9						
10						
11						
12						

(After 12th week, begin **in-season maintenance programs** (intervals once per week, weights one to two times per week)

Table 17-9s. Year-Round Conditioning Checklist.

Name _____

IN-SEASON MAINTENANCE PROGRAMS

Place a check in the box corresponding to the month and week for each time you complete the interval and weight workout.

WEEK

MONTH	1		2		3		4		5	
	Wts.	Interval	Wts.	Interval	Wts.	Interval	Wts.	Interval	Wts.	Interval
1										
2										
3										
4										
5										
6										

Table 17-10s. Post-Season Conditioning Checklist.

Name _____

Mark the date of each workout in the corresponding box. For aerobic workouts, record the distance covered and the total time of the workout.

WEEK	Aerobic	Weights	Aerobic	Weights	Aerobic	Weights	Anaerobic Maintenance
1							
2							
3							
4							
5							
6							

Table 17-10s (continued) **POST-SEASON CONDITIONING CHECKLIST**

WEEK	Aerobic	Weights	Aerobic	Weights	Aerobic	Weights	Anaerobic Maintenance
7							
8							
9							
10							
11							
12							
13							
14							
15							
16							
17							
18							
19							
20							
21							
22							
23							
24							
25							
26							
27							
28							
29							
30							

Table 17-11s. Overview of year-round conditioning program.

Time	Interval Training Activity for Conditioning the Energy Production System*	Weight Training Activity for Conditioning the Muscular System**
Pre-season (start 14 weeks prior to first game)	Complete the Pre-season Aerobic/Anaerobic Transition program (four weeks).	New lifters complete the Pre-season Weight Training Program by beginning with four weeks of introductory weight training (Phase 1 and 2) and then starting the Post-Season Weight Training Program (Phase 3).
	Complete the Pre-season Anaerobic Developmental Interval Training Program (eight weeks).	Continuing lifters complete the Post-Season Weight Training Program.
In-Season (two weeks prior to first game until last game)	Participate in interval training as part of regularly scheduled practices. Complete the In-Season Anaerobic Maintenance Program.	Complete the In-Season Weight Training Maintenance Program.
Post-Season (two to four weeks after last game until 14 weeks before first game of next season)	Complete three days/week of aerobic activity (dribbling, jogging and running, or bicycling). Complete the Post-Season Anaerobic Maintenance Program.	Complete the Post-Season Weight Training Program.

*Note that all conditioning sessions should be preceded by warm-up and stretching and followed by cool-down and stretching (see Supplement 17-1).

**Descriptions of these activities are included in this supplement.

Circuit Training Program

Introduction

This supplement contains an example of a football training circuit and recording form (see Table 17-12s). These forms can be photocopied and duplicated on the front and back of a 5 x 8" card. Also included in this supplement is a blank form (see Table 17-13s) upon which you can write your own training circuit to meet the specific needs of your players.

Using a Training Circuit

A training circuit can be implemented one to three times per week during the season. The number of times per week you have your players engage in a training circuit should vary according to the number of games scheduled for a given week, the physical demands of an in-season interval training and weight training program, and other activities included in your practice. You should not have your players perform a circuit the day before or the day of a game.

The requirements for performance and scoring each station need to be thoroughly explained to the players. Players need to be informed that the correct performance of each station is as important as the number of repetitions. After all the players understand each of the items in the complete circuit, you may have them perform a partial circuit of four or five stations and then increase the number of stations by one on subsequent days until all stations of the training circuit are performed.

The prescribed time for exercise and for the rest interval, during which the players write their scores on their recording forms and rotate from one station to the next, should be controlled to create an exercise overload. The first day the team performs the entire circuit, 30 seconds of exercise and 20 seconds rest between each station might be appropriate. This results in an eight-station circuit that can be completed in 6 minutes and 20 seconds. Gradually the exercise interval should increase and the rest interval should decrease. You will need to judge what is the appropriate exercise/rest interval ratio for your players.

Table 17-12s. Example of a five-station football training circuit and recording form on two sides of a 5 x 8″ card.

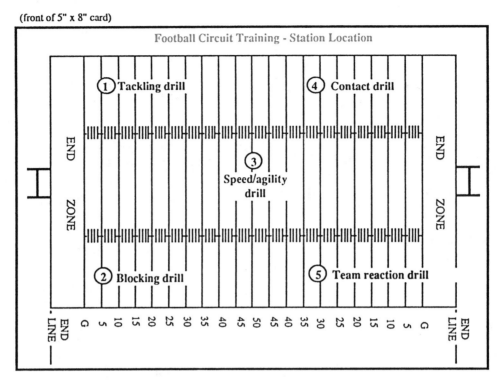

(front of 5" x 8" card)

Football Circuit Training - Station Location

① Tackling drill   ④ Contact drill

③ Speed/agility drill

② Blocking drill   ⑤ Team reaction drill

5 Stations-
(3 to 4 minutes
Rotate clockwise)

1. Tackling drill
2. Blocking drill
3. Speed/agility drill

4. Contact drill
5. Team reaction drill

(back of 5" x 8" card)

Football Circuit Training - Recording Form													
Name:													
Date (mo./day)													
Exercise/Rest interval (seconds)													
STATIONS	Performance Scores												
Tackling drill													
Blocking drill													
Speed & agility drill													
Contact drill													
Team reaction drill													

Table 17-12s (continued)

Station	Description	Equipment
Tackling drill	Players will line up, one-on-one, facing each other approximately 5 yds. apart in a "breakdown" football hitting position. One side of players will be designated ball carriers while the other will be tacklers. On the coach's command, the players will advance toward each other at three-quarter speed. The tackler will make contact, wrapping his arms around the ball carrier, lifting him off the ground and carrying him 5 yds. The ball carrier should be passive and not resist the tackler. Stress proper form: head up, feet apart, upward lift, and arm wrap. Ball carriers and tacklers will alternate assignments.	None
Blocking drill	Players will line up much the same as they did in the tackling drill except that they should be in a three-point stance about 1 yd. apart. One side will be designated blockers while the other will be defensive players. On the coach's command, the blockers will make contact with the defensive players, executing a prearranged type of block. The defensive player, after the initial contact, will then allow the offensive player to move him back 3-5 yds. The players will switch assignments alternately. Stress proper contact, form, techniques, and follow-through.	None
Speed and agility drill	Players must line up single file in 2-3 separate lines facing the coach. The coach will call players into action by specifying one of several running activities. Players will continue 20 yds. in one direction, stop and re-form for directions to return to their original positions. Drills include high knee action, crossover stepping, carioca steps, and backward running. Stress form rather than speed at all times.	None
Contact drills	Players will line up in separate lines with one player out front facing the rest approximately 5 yds. away. The player facing the line should be in a football hitting position with his arms free in front of him. On the coach's command, one player after another will approach the single player making shoulder contact with a solid forearm blow to the chest-shoulder area. The objective is to make solid contact, with each player having a turn out front. Stress balance, reaction, and strength. The single defensive player attempts to "shed" the contact as quickly as possible. Players should alternate shoulders to avoid stress to one side.	None

Table 17-12s (continued)

Station	Description	Equipment
Team reaction drill	Players will line up in a hitting position facing the coach, waiting for commands. Coach will shout "breakdown" to get the players into their hitting position with arms in front of their bodies, knees bent, and eyes looking ahead. Other commands that signal movement from the players are: right, left, down, up. Stress attention, form, quickness, spirit. Players should shout "go" after each of the coach's commands.	None

Table 17-13s. Recording form to photocopy and complete.

(front of 5" x 8" card)

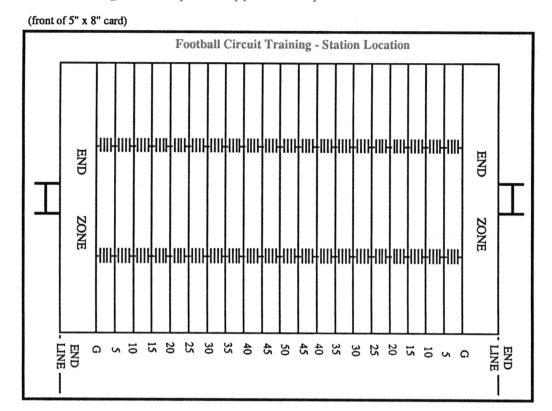

(back of 5"
x 8" card)

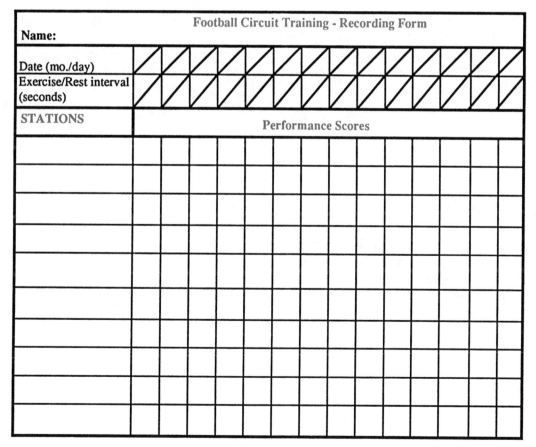

18
Prevention of Common Football Injuries

Rich Kimball, M.A.
Eugene W. Brown, Ph.D.
Wade Lillegard, M.D.
Cathy Lirgg, A.T.C.

QUESTIONS TO CONSIDER

- What role does equipment and apparel play in the prevention of football related injuries?
- How can the facilities be made safer for football?
- What effect can warm-ups, cool-downs, and conditioning have on preventing injuries?
- What role does teaching players safety, appropriate football techniques, and proper drills have in injury prevention?
- What injury prevention techniques can be implemented over the course of a season?

INTRODUCTION

Football involves the application of large muscular forces and physical contact at all levels of the game. Each collision presents an opportunity for an injury to occur. However, if you follow several steps aimed at preventing injuries, you can make football a safer game.

As a youth football coach, you are responsible for doing everything reasonable to provide participants the opportunity to compete in an environment that is healthy and safe.

INJURY PREVENTION TECHNIQUES

Equipment and Apparel

A large amount of equipment is necessary in football to protect against injury. A properly equipped and attired football player is less likely to be injured. All equipment must be well-fitted, including helmets, shoulder pads, pants, hip pads, and shoes. If a player must wear glasses, safety lenses or glass guards should also be required. In addition, a properly fitting mouth guard is required.

Parents should be informed during a pre-season parents' orientation meeting about appropriate equipment and apparel for their children. They should be made aware that: (a) if eyeglasses are essential for their child to play, they should be safety glasses worn with a safety strap; (b) their child's shoes should fit properly and have the appropriate non-skid sole; (c) jewelry is not appropriate at practices or games; and (d) gum chewing is prohibited.

At the start of the first practice, you should reinforce what you told the parents about appropriate equipment and apparel and determine if:

- all players are properly attired
- optional equipment (e.g., eyeglasses, mouth guards) fits properly

This type of inspection should be carried out regularly.

Facilities

Inspection of a practice or game facility for safety hazards is the responsibility of the adults in charge. For practices, the coach is responsible for the safety of all facilities. For games, both the officials and coaches are responsible. Therefore, you or your assistant must inspect the facilities before permitting your players to participate in practices and games. Whoever is responsible for inspecting the facilities should arrive approximately 10 minutes before the players to carry out the inspection.

If a safety hazard is present, it must be avoided by either relocating, rescheduling, restricting the activity, or removing the hazard.

There are three categories of safety hazards associated with facilities. These are field conditions, structural hazards, and environmental hazards. Safety hazards that are not easily rectified must be reported to the league and/or program administrators. If corrections are not made quickly, you should resubmit your concerns in writing. Do not play in facilities that you consider hazardous to your athletes!

- Field Conditions

Some fields and open areas are improper for football. Often fields have bumps, rocks, and holes, which are dangers as well as detracting from the skill of playing the game. Other fields that have playable conditions can quickly change from one that is safe to one that is dangerous. These changing conditions are usually associated with an excessive buildup of water and mud from rain, excessively hard surfaces, and objects unknowingly left in the field.

- Structural Hazards

The football field should be free of obstacles near boundary lines (e.g., bleachers, water fountains, equipment bags) and free of extraneous objects or debris on the field that might threaten the safety of the participants. The playing area itself should be a smooth, grassy surface. The goal post's main support(s) should be padded.

- Environmental Hazards

When playing on football fields lightning is an environmental condition that can be extremely hazardous. No matter how important a practice or game may seem to be, it is not worth the risk of an injury or a fatality due to environmental hazards. Other extreme weather conditions such as high winds, hail, high temperatures, humidity, cold, snow, and rain need to be cautiously evaluated as potential safety hazards. Insufficient light is another environmental condition that could be hazardous.

Activity should not be permitted to continue under the threat of lightning or any other environmental hazard.

Management of Practices and Games

Every physical activity that occurs during practices and games has some potential to result in an injury. Injuries that do occur are the result of interactions between the situation in which the activity occurs and the physical status of the player. In addition to having an influence over the equipment, apparel, and facilities in reducing the risk of injuries, you have a major influence over the physical activities of your players during practices and games. There are several steps you can take to properly manage the physical activities to reduce the rate and severity of injuries. These steps include:

Teaching Safety to Players

Whenever appropriate, inform your players about the potential risks of injury associated with performing certain football activities and methods for avoiding injury. For example, teach correct blocking and tackling techniques so that injuries are not sustained by hard passes that are made when players are close together, or by incorrectly placing the hands when receiving the ball.

The key to teaching safety to your players is to prudently interject safety tips in your instruction whenever appropriate.

Warming Up

A warm-up at the beginning of your team's practices and before games provides several important benefits. If the field is not immediately available for your team's use, warm-ups (i.e., stretching exercises) can start in the locker room. Specific warm-up suggestions are included in Chapter 17 under "Warm-Up, Cool-Down," and "Stretching Activities for Football." When warm-ups and stretching are completed, the skill-oriented drills on your practice plan or the formal drills before the game may begin. A warm-up period:

- increases the breathing rate, heart rate, and muscle temperature to exercise levels
- reduces the risks of muscle pulls and strains
- increases the shock-absorbing capabilities of the joints
- prepares players mentally for practices and games

Teaching Appropriate Techniques

The instructions you provide during practices on how to execute the skills of football have an influence on the risks of injuries to your players as well as to their opponents. Teach your players the proper ways to perform football techniques, and avoid any temptation to teach how to intentionally foul opponents.

First, an improper technique often results in a greater chance of injury to the performer than does the correct execution. Acceptable techniques in sports usually evolve with safety as a concern.

Second, techniques involving intentional fouls should never be taught or condoned. Coaches who promote an atmosphere in which intentional violent fouls are acceptable should be eliminated from the youth football program. You should promote fair and safe play in practices and games with strict enforcement of the rules. Encourage skill as the primary factor in determining the outcome of the game.

Selecting Proper Drills

Drills that you select or design for your practices and the ways in which they are carried out have an influence on the risks of injuries for your players. Drills should be selected and designed with safety as a primary feature. Before implementing a new drill into your practice, several safety questions should be considered.

- Is the drill appropriate for the level of maturation of the players?
- Are the players sufficiently skilled to comply with the requirements of the drill?
- Are the players sufficiently conditioned to handle the stress of participation in the drill?
- Are other, less risky drills available to achieve the same practice results?
- Can the drill be modified to make it less risky and yet achieve the desired training result?

Conditioning

High intensity work is part of the game of football. How well your players can handle fatigue determines how well they perform during the latter part of a contest. Is there, however, any relationship between fatigue and injury? The following sequence of events draws an association linking fatigue with an increased potential for injury (see Figure 18-1).

In addition to improving performance, every conditioning program should be designed to minimize fatigue and the potential for injury. Being "in shape" can postpone fatigue and its detrimental effects. By progressively intensifying your practices throughout the season, you can produce a conditioning effect that can be an important deterrent to injury (see Chapter 17.)

Coaches must also be aware that older players who engage in intense, frequent practices and games may need time off as the season wears on. It is possible to overtrain, and predis-

Athlete becomes fatigued

↓

Skilled performance is reduced

↓

Concentration becomes difficult

↓

Reactions slow down

↓

Judgment becomes impaired

↓

Faulty decisions are made

↓

Injuries may result

Figure 18-1. How fatigue is linked to an increased potential for injuries.

pose to, rather than prevent, injuries. Injuries caused by overtraining have grown to represent an increased portion of reported sports injuries. Some telltale signs of overtraining include:

- elevated resting heart rate
- poor performance
- loss of enthusiasm
- depression
- higher incidence of injury
- longer time to recover from injury

Antidotes to overtraining include time off from practice, shorter practices, alternating intense practices with lighter workouts, or any combination of these suggestions. Overtraining is not usually a problem when players are practicing two or three times a week, unless they are also: (a) playing two or more games per week, (b) playing on more than one football team, or (c) playing on a different sport team during the same season.

• Avoiding Contraindicated Exercises

Over the past several years, researchers and physicians have identified a list of exercises that are commonly used by coaches but are potentially harmful to the body. These are called contraindicated exercises. This information has been slow in reaching coaches and their players. Table 18-1 contains a list of these exercises and how contraindicated exercises can be modified to eliminate their undesirable characteristics. Also included in Table 18-1 are substitute football exercises that accomplish the same purpose in a safer manner.

• Cooling Down

There are few feelings more uncomfortable than finishing a vigorous workout, sitting down for a while, then trying to walk. Muscles in the body tighten during periods of inactivity following hard work.

To minimize the stiffness that usually follows a workout, and the soreness the following day, take time to adequately cool down at the end of practice. A gradual reduction of activity (the reverse of the warm-up procedure) facilitates the dissipation of waste products associated with muscular activity. Letting the body cool off gradually may not prevent injuries, but the players may experience less discomfort and be better able to function at high levels during the next workout (see Chapter 17, "Warm-up, Cool-Down," and "Stretching Activities for Football.")

SUMMARY

This chapter has focused on three areas in which you can exert an influence to reduce the potential number and severity of injuries in football. The first area involves your insistence that your players wear appropriate apparel and protective equipment. Avoiding safety hazards associated with the facilities (field conditions, structural hazards, and environmental hazards) is the second area. Management of practices and games is the third area. Proper management includes teaching your players safety, appropriate football techniques, and proper drills; and conducting practices that include warming up, conditioning, and cooling down exercises but exclude known contraindicated exercises. Safety and injury prevention should be a primary factor to consider in whatever plans you make for your football team. You will be more than compensated for the extra time and effort required to

Table 18-1. Contraindicated exercises and alternatives.
This table contains an outline of information on contraindicated exercises associated with the knee and spine. Safer alternative exercises that achieve the same objectives as the sample contraindicated exercises are provided.

I. PROBLEM AREA: KNEE JOINT

A. Problem Activity—Hyperflexion (over flexion)

Contraindicated Activities	Intended Purposes of Activities	Safer Alternatives
1. Hurdler's stretch 	Stretch the hamstring (back of thigh)	Seated straight leg stretch  Standing bent knee thigh pull  Lying hamstring stretch 
2. Deep knee bend 	To develop quadriceps (front of thigh), hamstrings, gluteal (buttocks), and back muscles	Half squat or half knee bend 

I. PROBLEM AREA: KNEE JOINT (continued)

A. Problem Activity—Hyperflexion (over flexion)

Contraindicated Activities	Intended Purposes of Activities	Safer Alternatives

3. Lunge

Wall sit

4. Landing from jumps

5. Deep squat lift

6. Squat thrust

I. PROBLEM AREA: KNEE JOINT (continued)

A. Problem Activity—Hyperflexion (over flexion)

Contraindicated Activities	Intended Purposes of Activities	Safer Alternatives
7. Lying quad stretch (back lying position from hurdler's stretch)	Stretch quadricep muscles	Kneeling thigh stretch

8. Double leg lying quad stretch

9. Standing one leg quad stretch

B. Problem Activity—Hyperextension (over extension)

Contraindicated Activities	Intended Purposes of Activities	Safer Alternatives
10. Standing toe touch	Stretch the hamstring muscles	Seated straight leg stretch

I. PROBLEM AREA: KNEE JOINT (continued)

B. Problem Activity—Hyperextension (over extension)

Contraindicated Activities	Intended Purposes of Activities	Safer Alternatives

11. One leg standing hamstring stretch

Standing bent knee thigh pull

Lying hamstring stretch

C. Problem Activity—Twisting or forcing knee joint into unnatural position

Contraindicated Activities	Intended Purposes of Activities	Safer Alternatives

12. Hurdler's stretch—see Contraindicated
    Activity 1.

13. Standing one leg quad stretch   Stretch quadricep muscles   Seated straight leg stretch

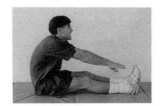

C. Problem Activity—Twisting or forcing knee joint into unnatural position

Contraindicated Activities	Intended Purposes of Activities	Safer Alternatives

14. Hero

Standing bent knee thigh pull

Lying hamstring stretch

15. Standing straddle groin stretch

Stretch inner thigh (groin) muscles

Seated straddle groin stretch

Butterfly

Lying groin stretch

Elevated legs straddle groin stretch

A. Problem Activity—Forceful hyperflexion of cervical (neck) region

Contraindicated Activities	Intended Purposes of Activities	Safer Alternatives

16. Yoga plough

Stretch back and neck muscles

Standing bent knee thigh pull

17. Shoulder stand

Alternate yoga plough (Note that when lifting legs from the floor to assume this position, the knees should initially be bent.)

Supine tuck

Half neck circle

B. Problem Activity—Hyperextension of the spine

Contraindicated Activities	Intended Purposes of Activities	Safer Alternatives
18. Wrestler's bridge	Stretch neck muscles	Half neck circle

19. Full neck circle

20. Partner neck stretch

21. Donkey kick	Stretch abdominal muscles	Kneeling thigh stretch

22. Full waist circle		Reduced waist circle

II. PROBLEM AREA: SPINE (continued)

B. Problem Activity—Hyperextension of the spine

Contraindicated Activities	Intended Purposes of Activities	Safer Alternatives
23. Back bend 		
24. Back arching abdominal stretch 		
25. Donkey kick (see Contraindicated Activity 21)	Strengthen gluteal muscles	Half squat or half knee bend 

C. Problem Activity—Excessive lumbar curve or hyperextension of the low back

Contraindicated Activities	Intended Purposes of Activities	Safer Alternatives
26. Straight leg sit-ups 	Strengthen abdominal muscles	Bent knee sit-up 
27. Double leg lifts 		Reversed sit-up 

implement the suggestions found in this chapter by the comfort of knowing that you have done as much as you can to assure that your players will have a safe season.

REFERENCES

Rutherford, G., Miles, R. Brown, V., & MacDonalkd, B. (1981). *Overview of sports related injuries to persons 5-14 years of age.* Washington, DC: U.S.Consumer Product Safety Commission.

Seidel, B.L., Biles, F.R., Figley, G.E., & Neuman, B.J. (1980). *Sport skills.* Dubuque, IA: W.C. Brown.

SUGGESTED READINGS

American College of Sports Medicine, American Orthopaedic Society for Sports Medicine & Sports Medicine Committee of the United States Tennis Association. (1982). *Sports injuries—an aid to prevention and treatment.* Coventry, CT: Bristol-Myers Co.

Jackson, D., & Pescar, S. (1981). *The young athletes health handbook.* Everest House.

Lane, S. (1990). Severe ankle sprains. *The Physician and Sportsmedicine, 18,* 43-51.

Micheli, L.J. (1985). Preventing youth sports injuries. *Journal of Health, Physical Education, Recreation and Dance, 76*(6), 52-54.

Mirkin, G., & Marshall, H. (1978). *The sportsmedicine book.* Little, Brown, & Co.

19
Care of Common Football Injuries

Eugene W. Brown, Ph.D.
Rich Kimball, M.A.
Wade Lillegard, M.D.

QUESTIONS TO CONSIDER

- What are the steps to take in an emergency medical situation?
- What items belong in a well-stocked first aid kit?
- What procedures should you follow when a minor injury occurs?
- What information should you have about your players in case they become injured?

INTRODUCTION

Chris has the ball and is racing toward the end zone. An opponent rushes in and attempts to tackle Chris. Both players are going full speed and a violent collision occurs. Chris lies motionless on the field. The official, sensing the likelihood of an injury, immediately signals Chris's coach onto the field to tend to the injured player.

Watching from the bench, the first, and normal, reaction of a coach is to be frightened by the possible outcome of this violent collision. The sinking feeling in the stomach and the "Oh, no!" message sent out by the brain when Chris went down have been felt by most coaches at some point in their careers.

If this, or some similar situation confronted you, what would you do? Are you prepared to act appropriately? As a coach of a youth football team, it is your obligation to be able to deal with such an emergency. Before your first practice, you should:

- obtain medical information on your players
- establish emergency procedures
- prepare to provide first aid

You must not rely on the likelihood that a serious injury will not occur to the players on your team as an excuse for not being prepared to handle an emergency situation!

ESSENTIAL MEDICAL FORMS

Prior to the first practice, completed Athlete's Medical Information forms (see Figure 19-1) and Medical Release forms (see Figure

213

Figure 19-1.

Athlete's Medical Information
(to be completed by parents/guardians and athlete)

Athlete's Name: _____ Athlete's Birthdate: _____

Parents' Names: _____ Date: _____

Address: _____

Phone No's.: (____)_____ (____)_____ (____)_____
             (Home)   (Work)   (Other)

Who to contact in case of emergency (if parents cannot be immediately contacted):

Name: _____ Relationship: _____

Home Phone No.: (____)_____ Work Phone No.: (____)_____

Name: _____ Relationship: _____

Home Phone No.: (____)_____ Work Phone No.: (____)_____

Hospital preference: _____ Emergency Phone No.: (____)_____

Doctor preference: _____ Office Phone No.: (____)_____

MEDICAL HISTORY

Part I. Complete the following:

	Date	Doctor	Doctor's Phone No.
1. Last tetanus shot?	_____		
2. Last dental examination?	_____	_____	_____
3. Last eye examination?	_____	_____	_____

Part II. Has your child or did your child have any of the following?

General Conditions:	Circle one		Circle one or both		Injuries:	Circle one		Circle one or both	
1. Fainting spells/dizziness	Yes	No	Past	Present	1. Toes	Yes	No	Past	Present
2. Headaches	Yes	No	Past	Present	2. Feet	Yes	No	Past	Present
3. Convulsions/epilepsy	Yes	No	Past	Present	3. Ankles	Yes	No	Past	Present
4. Asthma	Yes	No	Past	Present	4. Lower legs	Yes	No	Past	Present
5. High blood pressure	Yes	No	Past	Present	5. Knees	Yes	No	Past	Present
6. Kidney problems	Yes	No	Past	Present	6. Thighs	Yes	No	Past	Present
7. Intestinal disorder	Yes	No	Past	Present	7. Hips	Yes	No	Past	Present
8. Hernia	Yes	No	Past	Present	8. Lower back	Yes	No	Past	Present
9. Diabetes	Yes	No	Past	Present	9. Upper back	Yes	No	Past	Present
10. Heart disease/disorder	Yes	No	Past	Present	10. Ribs	Yes	No	Past	Present
11. Dental plate	Yes	No	Past	Present	11. Abdomen	Yes	No	Past	Present
12. Poor vision	Yes	No	Past	Present	12. Chest	Yes	No	Past	Present
13. Poor hearing	Yes	No	Past	Present	13. Neck	Yes	No	Past	Present
14. Skin disorder	Yes	No	Past	Present	14. Fingers	Yes	No	Past	Present
15. Allergies	Yes	No			15. Hands	Yes	No	Past	Present
Specify:_____			Past	Present	16. Wrists	Yes	No	Past	Present
_____			Past	Present	17. Forearms	Yes	No	Past	Present
16. Joint dislocation or					18. Elbows	Yes	No	Past	Present
separations	Yes	No			19. Upper arms	Yes	No	Past	Present
Specify:_____			Past	Present	20. Shoulders	Yes	No	Past	Present
_____			Past	Present	21. Head	Yes	No	Past	Present
17. Serious or significant ill-					22. Serious or significant in-				
nesses not included above	Yes	No			juries not included above	Yes	No		
Specify:_____			Past	Present	Specify: _____			Past	Present
_____			Past	Present	_____			Past	Present
18. Others:_____			Past	Present	23. Others: _____			Past	Present
_____			Past	Present	_____			Past	Present

Figure 19-1 (continued)

Part III. Circle appropriate response to each question. For each "Yes" response, provide additional information.

		Circle one		Additional information
1.	Is your child currently taking any medication? If yes, describe medication, amount, and reason for taking.	Yes	No	
2.	Does your child have any allergic reactions to medication, bee stings, food, etc.? If yes, describe agents that cause adverse reactions and describe these reactions.	Yes	No	
3.	Does your child wear any appliances (e.g., glasses, contact lenses, hearing aid, false teeth, braces, etc.)? If yes, describe appliances.	Yes	No	
4.	Has your child had any surgical operations? If yes, indicate site, explain the reason for the surgery, and describe the level of success.	Yes	No	
5.	Has a physician placed any restrictions on your child's present activities? If yes, describe restrictions.	Yes	No	
6.	Does your child have any existing and/or past medical or emotional conditions that require special concern and attention by a sports coach? If yes, explain.	Yes	No	
7.	Does your child have any deformities (e.g., abnormal curvature of the spine, heart problems, one kidney, blindness in one eye, one testicle, etc.)? If yes, describe.	Yes	No	
8.	Is there a history of serious family illnesses (e.g., diabetes, bleeding disorders, heart attack before age 50, etc.)? If yes, describe illnesses.	Yes	No	
9.	Has your child lost consciousness or sustained a concussion?	Yes	No	
10.	Has your child experienced fainting spells or dizziness while exercising?	Yes	No	

Part IV. Has your child or did your child have any of the following personal habits?

Personal Habit	Circle one		Circle one or both		Indicate extent or amount
1. Smoking	Yes	No	Past	Present	
2. Smokeless tobacco	Yes	No	Past	Present	
3. Alcohol	Yes	No	Past	Present	
4. Recreational drugs (e.g., marijuana, cocaine, etc.)	Yes	No	Past	Present	
5. Steroids	Yes	No	Past	Present	
6. Others					
Specify: _____	Yes	No	Past	Present	
_____	Yes	No	Past	Present	
_____	Yes	No	Past	Present	

Part V. Please explain below any "Yes" responses in Parts II, III, and IV or any other concerns that have present implications for my coaching your child. Also, describe special first aid requirements, if appropriate. An additional sheet may be attached if necessary.

_____
_____
_____
_____
_____
_____
_____

19-2) for all athletes must be in the possession of the coach. The Athlete's Medical Information form provides essential information about whom to contact during the emergency as well as a comprehensive overview of past and current medical conditions that may have implications for coaching and/or emergency care. The Medical Release form is a mech-anism by which parents and guardians can give permission to the coach and/or someone else to seek medical attention for their child. If the parents or guardians of an injured athlete cannot be contacted, this signed and notarized form is an essential element in the process of providing emergency medical attention.

Note that for most athletes their responses will be negative to a high proportion of the questions on their medical information forms. Therefore, an Athlete's Medical Information Summary form (see Figure 19-3) that parallels the Athlete's Medical Information form has been developed for transcribing any essential information. This summary, as well as the Medical Release, can be printed on the front and back sides of a 5 x 8-in. card. One completed card for each athlete must be present at all team events.

Another essential medical form is the On-Site Injury Report form (see Figure 19-4). This information may be helpful to provide some guidance for medical care and may be very important if any legal problems develop in connection with the injury.

The final form that the coach must have is the Emergency Plan form (see Figure 19-5). This form provides guidance for handling an emergency and is discussed in the next section.

EMERGENCY PLAN FORM

The Emergency Plan form provides directions to a number of people in helping them to carry out their assigned responsibilities in an emergency. One completed form is needed for each of these individuals. The form also contains space for inserting site-specific emergency information. The following paragraphs describe the procedures associated with the Emergency Plan form.

Before the first practice, a number of responsible individuals must be assigned roles to carry out in an emergency. These roles are:

coach, attending to an injured athlete, attending to the uninjured athletes, calling for emergency medical assistance, and flagging down the emergency vehicle. Note that when a medical emergency occurs, all assignments must be simultaneously activated.

For most agency sponsored and for many school sponsored sports, a physician or athletic trainer are not present to assist the coach in handling the medical aspects of an emergency. Thus, after taking charge of the situation and alerting individuals with assigned tasks, the coach is likely to be the person to attend to the injured athlete. The steps in attending to the injured athlete are presented in Figure 19-5 under section B. In order to provide emergency care, knowledge and skill in cardiopulmonary resuscitation (CPR), controlling bleeding, attending to heat stroke, attending to shock, and use of an allergic reaction kit are essential. This knowledge and skill should be obtained through Red Cross courses offered in most communities. When emergency medical personnel arrive, responsibility for the injured athlete should be transferred to these professionals. The 5 x 8-in. card that includes the Medical Release should be presented to the emergency medical personnel. If the parents or guardians are not available, the person designated on the Medical Release form (usually the coach) must accompany the injured athlete to the medical center.

If the coach is attending the injured athlete, the uninjured athletes should be directed to a safe area within voice and vision of the coach. The responsibilities assigned to the person in charge of the uninjured athletes is presented in Figure 19-5 under section C. A "rainy day" practice plan could have been prepared and available for an emergency or an accepted procedure for dismissing the uninjured athletes could be used.

Under section D of Figure 19-5 the responsibilities of the individual assigned to call for emergency medical assistance are presented. This section also includes space for entering site-specific information for the location of the nearest telephone, emergency telephone number, directions to the injured athlete, and the location of the flag person. If known, the person calling for assistance should report the nature of the injury to the receptionist. After

Figure 19-2.

Medical Release Form

I hereby give permission for any and all medical attention necessary to be administered to my child in the event of an accident, injury, sickness, etc., under the direction of the people listed below until such time as I may be contacted. My child's name is _____.
This release is effective for the time during which my child is participating in the _____
_____ football program and any tournaments for the 19___/19___
season, including traveling to or from such tournaments. I also hereby assume the responsibility for payment of any such treatment.

PARENTS' OR GUARDIANS' NAMES: _____

HOME ADDRESS: _____

	Street	City	State	Zip

(___)_____(W)

HOME PHONE: (___)_____   (___)_____(W)

INSURANCE COMPANY: _____

POLICY NUMBER: _____

FAMILY PHYSICIAN: _____

PHYSICIAN'S ADDRESS: _____ PHONE NO. (___)_____

In case I cannot be reached, either of the following people is designated:

COACH'S NAME: _____ PHONE NO. (___)_____

ASS'T. COACH OR OTHER: _____ PHONE NO. (___)_____

SIGNATURE OF PARENT OR GUARDIAN _____

SUBSCRIBED AND SWORN BEFORE ME THIS _____ OF _____, 19 ___

SIGNATURE OF NOTARY PUBLIC _____

Figure 19-3.

Athlete's Medical Information Summary

(important medical information to be transcribed by the coach or designee
from the Athlete's Medical Information form)

Athlete's Name: _____ Athlete's Birthdate: _____

Parents' Names: _____ Date: _____

Address: _____

Phone No's.: (____)_____ (____)_____ (____)_____
　　　　　　　　(Home)　　　　　　　(Work)　　　　　　　(Other)

Who to contact in case of emergency (if parents cannot be immediately contacted):

Name: _____ Relationship: _____

Home Phone No.: (____)_____ Work Phone No.: (____)_____

Name: _____ Relationship: _____

Home Phone No.: (____)_____ Work Phone No.: (____)_____

Hospital preference: _____ Emergency Phone No.: (____)_____

Doctor preference: _____ Office Phone No.: (____)_____

MEDICAL HISTORY

Part I. Transcribe Part I.

	Date	Doctor	Doctor's phone no.
1. Last tetanus shot?	_____		
2. Last dental examination?	_____	_____	_____
3. Last eye examination?	_____	_____	_____

Part II. This athlete has or has had the following:

A. **General Conditions:**	Circle one or both		B. **Injuries:**	Circle one or both	
_____	Past	Present	_____	Past	Present
_____	Past	Present	_____	Past	Present
_____	Past	Present	_____	Past	Present
_____	Past	Present	_____	Past	Present
_____	Past	Present	_____	Past	Present
_____	Past	Present	_____	Past	Present

Part III. Summary of Part III responses that have present implications: _____
_____
_____
_____
_____

Part IV. This athlete has or has had the following personal habits:

Personal Habit	Circle one or both		Indicate extent or amount
_____	Past	Present	_____
_____	Past	Present	_____
_____	Past	Present	_____

Part V. Responses in Parts II, III, and IV or any other concerns that have present implications for my coaching. Also describe special first aid requirements, if appropriate. _____
_____
_____
_____
_____
_____
_____
_____

Figure 19-4.

On-Site Injury Report Form

Name _____ Date of injury ____/____/____
         (Injured Player)   mo   day   yr

Address _____
            (Street)   (City, State)   (Zip)

Telephone _____
              (Home)   (Other)

Nature and extent of injury: _____

_____

How did the injury occur? _____

_____

Describe first aid given, including name(s) of attendee(s): _____

_____

Disposition: to hospital   to home   to physician

Other _____

_____

Was protective equipment worn?   _____ Yes   _____ No

Explanation: _____

_____

Condition of the playing surface _____

_____

Names and addresses of witnesses:

Name	Street	City	State	Tel.
Name	Street	City	State	Tel.
Name	Street	City	State	Tel.

Other comments: _____

_____

Signed	Date	Title-Position

Emergency Plan Form*

Essential Items:

1. Well-stocked first aid kit
2. Medical forms for each athlete (Athlete's Medical Information, Athlete's Medical Information Summary, and Medical Release)
3. On-Site Injury Report form

PROCEDURES

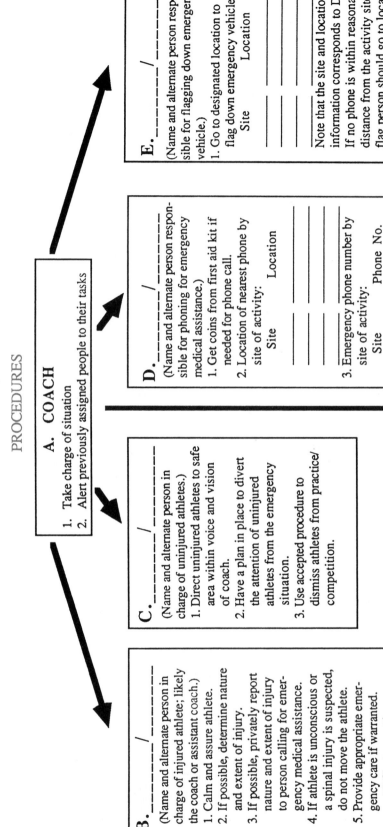

A. COACH

1. Take charge of situation
2. Alert previously assigned people to their tasks

B. _____ / _____

(Name and alternate person in charge of injured athlete; likely the coach or assistant coach.)

1. Calm and assure athlete.
2. If possible, determine nature and extent of injury.
3. If possible, privately report nature and extent of injury to person calling for emergency medical assistance.
4. If athlete is unconscious or a spinal injury is suspected, do not move the athlete.
5. Provide appropriate emergency care if warranted.
   a. ABC's (open Airways, restore Breathing, and restore Circulation)
   b. Control bleeding by direct pressure.
   c. For heat stroke, immediately cool body by cold sponging, immersion in

C. _____ / _____

(Name and alternate person in charge of uninjured athletes.)

1. Direct uninjured athletes to safe area within voice and vision of coach.
2. Have a plan in place to divert the attention of uninjured athletes from the emergency situation.
3. Use accepted procedure to dismiss athletes from practice/competition.

D. _____ / _____

(Name and alternate person responsible for phoning for emergency medical assistance.)

1. Get coins from first aid kit if needed for phone call.
2. Location of nearest phone by site of activity:

   Site   Location
   _____   _____
   _____   _____
   _____   _____

3. Emergency phone number by site of activity:

   Site   Phone No.
   _____   _____
   _____   _____
   _____   _____

4. Report the nature of the injury and calmly respond to questions.

E. _____ / _____

(Name and alternate person responsible for flagging down emergency vehicle.)

1. Go to designated location to flag down emergency vehicle.

   Site   Location
   _____   _____
   _____   _____
   _____   _____

   Note that the site and location information corresponds to D.6. If no phone is within reasonable distance from the activity site, flag person should go to location where a vehicle can be flagged down.

2. Direct emergency medical personnel to injured athlete.

Figure 19-5 (continued)

cold water, and cold packs.
d. For shock, have athlete lie down, calm athlete, elevate feet unless head injury, control athlete's temperature, loosen tight fitting clothing, and control pain or bleeding if necessary.
e. For allergic reaction, use ana-kit if available.
6. Transfer care to emergency medical personnel. (Note that the Medical Release Form and one individual whose name appears on the form must accompany athletes to medical center unless parents or guardians are available.)
7. Provide Athlete's Medical Information Summary to emergency medical personnel.

5. Directions to sites:

Site	Directions
_____	_____
_____	_____
_____	_____

6. Location of flag person by site:

Site	Location
_____	_____
_____	_____
_____	_____

7. Remain on the phone until the other person hangs up.
8. Return to person attending to injured athlete and privately report status of emergency medical assistance.

A. COACH, cont.

3. Use the information on the Roster Summary of Contacts in an Emergency to phone the injured athlete's parents (guardians) or their designees.
4. Complete the On-Site Injury Report form.

*A minimum of 4 completed copies of this form is needed; one for each of the individuals with assigned tasks. Make sure that information is included on all practice and competition sites.

completing the call for assistance, this individual should privately report the status of emergency medical assistance to the person attending the injured athlete.

Whether or not someone is needed to flag down and direct the emergency vehicle will depend on the site of the team's activities. The procedures for the flag person are described in Figure 19-5 under section E. In rare situations, where there is no telephone near the site of the injury, the flag person will be responsible for securing emergency medical assistance.

After the injured player is released to emergency medical personnel, the coach should complete the On-Site Injury Report form. Also, if the injured athlete's parents or guardians are unaware of the emergency situation, information on either the Athlete's Medical Information form or its Summary should be used to contact them.

PROVIDE FIRST AID

Aids for Proper Care

If the injury is less serious and does not require assistance from trained medical personnel, you may be able to move the player from the field to the bench area and begin appropriate care. Two important aids to properly care for an injured player include a first aid kit and ice.

• First Aid Kit

A well-stocked first aid kit does not have to be large but it should contain the basic items that may be needed for appropriate care. This checklist provides a guide for including commonly used supplies. You may wish to add and subtract from the kit on the basis of your experience and/or local policies or guidelines.

A good rule of thumb for coaches is, "If you can't treat the problems by using the supplies in a well-stocked first aid kit, then it is too big a problem for you to handle." You should be able to handle bruises, small cuts, strains, and sprains. When fractures, dislocations, back, or neck injuries occur, call for professional medical assistance.

_____ white athletic tape	_____ plastic bags for ice
_____ sterile gauze pads	_____ coins for pay telephone
_____ Telfa no-stick pads	_____ emergency care phone numbers
_____ elastic bandages	
_____ Band-aids, assorted sizes	_____ persons to contact in an emergency
_____ foam rubber/moleskin	_____ scissors/knife
_____ tweezers	_____ safety pins
_____ disinfectant	_____ soap

• Ice

Having access to ice is unique to every local setting. Thus, every coach may have to arrange for its provision in a different way. Ice, however, is very important to proper, immediate care of many minor injuries and should, therefore, be readily available.

Care of Minor Injuries

• R.I.C.E.

Unless you are also a physician, you should not attempt to care for anything except minor injuries (e.g., bruises, bumps, sprains). Many minor injuries can be cared for by using the R.I.C.E. formula.

R = Rest: Keep the player out of action.

I = Ice: Apply ice to the injured area.

C = Compression: Wrap an elastic bandage around the injured area and the ice bag to hold the bag in place. The bandage should not be so tight as to cut off blood flow to the injured area.

E = Elevation: Let gravity drain the excess fluid.

Most minor injuries can benefit from using the R.I.C.E. formula for care.

When following the R.I.C.E. formula, ice should be kept on the injured area for 15 minutes and taken off for 20 minutes. Repeat this procedure three to four times. Icing should continue three times per day for the first 72 hours following the injury. After three days, extended care is necessary if the injury has not healed. At this time, options for care include:

• stretching and strengthening exercises
• contrast treatments

- visiting a doctor for further diagnosis
- **Contrast Treatments**

If the injured area is much less swollen after 72 hours, but the pain is subsiding, contrast treatments will help. Use the following procedure:

1. Place the injured area in an ice bath or cover with an ice bag for one minute.
2. After using the ice, place the injured area in warm water (100° - 110°) for three minutes.
3. Continue this rotation for five to seven bouts of ice and four to six bouts of heat.
4. Always end with the ice treatment.

Contrast treatments should be followed for the next three to five days. If swelling or pain still persists after several days of contrast treatments, the player should be sent to a physician for further tests. Chapter 20 of this section deals with the rehabilitation of injuries. Read it carefully, because proper care is actually a form of rehabilitation.

COMMON MEDICAL PROBLEMS IN FOOTBALL

Information about 24 common medical conditions that may occur in football is presented in this section. The information about each condition includes: (1) a definition, (2) common symptoms, (3) immediate field treatment, and (4) guidelines for returning the player to action.

Abrasion

Definition:
- superficial skin wound caused by scraping

Symptoms:
- minor bleeding
- redness
- burning sensation

Care:
- Cleanse the area with soap and water.
- Control the bleeding.
- Cover the area with sterile dressing.
- Monitor over several days for signs of infection.

Return to Action:
- after providing immediate care

Back or Neck Injury

Definition:
- any injury to the back or neck area that causes the player to become immobile or unconscious

Symptoms:
- pain and tenderness over the spine
- numbness
- weakness or heaviness in limbs
- tingling feeling in extremities

Care:
- Make sure the player is breathing.
- Call for medical assistance.
- Do not move the neck or back.

Return to Action:
- with permission of a physician

Blisters

Definition:
- localized collection of fluid in the outer portion of the skin

Symptoms:
- redness
- inflammation
- oozing of fluid
- discomfort

Care:
- Put disinfectant on the area.
- Cut a hole in a stack of several gauze pads to be used as a doughnut surrounding the blister.
- Cover the area with a Band-aid.
- Alter the cause of the problem when possible (e.g., proper size and/or shape of the football shoes).

Return to Action:
- immediately, unless pain is severe

Contusion

Definition:
- a bruise; an injury in which the skin is not broken

Symptoms:

- tenderness around the injury
- swelling
- localized pain

Care:

- Apply the R.I.C.E. formula for first 3 days.
- Use contrast treatments for days 4-8.
- Restrict activity.
- Provide padding when returning the player to activity.

Return to Action:

- when there is complete absence of pain and full range of motion is restored

Cramps

Definition:

- involuntary and forceful contraction of a muscle; muscle spasm

Symptoms:

- localized pain in contracting muscle

Care:

- Slowly stretch the muscle.
- Massage the muscle.

Return to Action:

- when pain is gone and full range of motion is restored

Dental Injury

Definition:

- any injury to mouth or teeth

Symptoms:

- pain
- bleeding
- loss of tooth (partial or total)

Care:

- Clear the airway where necessary.
- Stop the bleeding with direct pressure.
- Make sure excess blood does not clog the airway.
- Save any teeth that were knocked free; store them in the player's own mouth or a moist, sterile cloth.

- Do not rub or clean tooth that has been knocked out.
- Transport player to a hospital or dentist.

Return to Action:

- when the pain is gone (usually within two to three days)
- with permission of a dentist or physician

Dislocation

Definition:

- loss of normal anatomical alignment of a joint

Symptoms:

- complaints of joint slipping in and out (subluxation)
- joint out of line
- pain at the joint

Care:

- mild
  —Treat as a sprain (i.e., R.I.C.E.).
  —Obtain medical care.
- severe
  —Immobilize before moving.
  —Must be treated by a physician.
  —Obtain medical care. Do not attempt to put joint back into place.
  —R.I.C.E.

Return to Action:

- with permission of a physician

Eye Injury—Contusion

Definition:

- direct blow to the eye and region surrounding the eye by a blunt object

Symptoms:

- pain
- redness of eye
- watery eye

Care:

- Have the player lie down with his/her eyes closed.
- Place a folded cloth, soaked in cold water, gently on the eye.
- Seek medical attention if injury is assessed as severe.

Return to Action:

- for minor injury, player may return to action after symptoms clear
- for severe injury, with permission of a physician

Eye Injury—Foreign Object

Definition:

- object between eyelid and eyeball

Symptoms:

- pain
- redness of eye
- watery eye
- inability to keep eye open

Care:

- Do not rub the eye.
- Allow tears to form in eye.
- Carefully try to remove loose object with sterile cotton swab.
- If object is embedded in the eye, have the player close both eyes, loosely cover both eyes with sterile dressing, and bring the player to an emergency room or ophthalmologist.

Return to Action:

- with permission from a physician

Fainting

Definition:

- dizziness and loss of consciousness that may be caused by an injury, exhaustion, heat illness, emotional stress, or lack of oxygen

Symptoms:

- dizziness
- cold, clammy skin
- pale
- seeing "spots" before one's eyes
- weak, rapid pulse

Care:

- Have the player lie down and elevate his feet or have the player sit with his head between the knees.

Return to Action:

- with permission of a physician

Fracture

Definition:

- a crack or complete break in a bone [A simple fracture is a broken bone, but with unbroken skin. An open fracture is a broken bone that also breaks the skin.]

Symptoms:

- pain at fracture site
- tenderness, swelling
- deformity or unnatural position
- loss of function in injured area
- open wound, bleeding (open fracture)

[Note that a simple fracture may not be evident immediately. If localized pain persists, obtain medical assistance.]

Care:

- Stabilize injured bone by using splints, slings, or bandages.
- Do not attempt to straighten an injured part when immobilizing it.
- If skin is broken (open fracture), keep the open wound clean by covering it with the cleanest available cloth.
- Check for shock and treat if necessary.

Return to Action:

- with permission of a physician

Head Injury—Conscious

Definition:

- any injury that causes the player to be unable to respond in a coherent fashion to known facts (name, date, etc.)

Symptoms:

- dizziness
- pupils unequal in size and/or non-responsive to light and dark
- disoriented
- unsure of name, date, or activity
- unsteady movement of eyeballs when trying to follow a finger moving in front of eyes
- same symptoms as noted for back or neck injury may be present

Care:

- If above symptoms are present, player may be moved carefully when dizziness disap-

pears. Players with head injuries should be removed from further practice or competition that day and should be carefully observed for a minimum of 24 hours.
- Obtain medical assistance.

Return to Action:
- with permission of a physician

Head Injury—Unconscious

Definition:
- any injury in which the player is unable to respond to external stimuli by verbal or visual means

Symptoms:
- player is unconscious
- cuts or bruises around the head may be evident

Care:
- ANY TIME A PLAYER IS UNCONSCIOUS, ASSUME AN INJURY TO THE SPINAL CORD OR BRAIN.
- If necessary, clear the airway keeping the player's neck straight.
- Do not move the player.
- Call for medical assistance.

Return to Action:
- with permission of a physician

Heat Exhaustion

Definition:
- heat disorder that may lead to heat stroke

Symptoms:
- fatigue
- profuse sweating
- chills
- throbbing pressure in the head
- nausea
- normal body temperature
- pale and clammy skin
- muscle cramps

Care:
- Remove the player from heat and sun.
- Provide plenty of water.

- Rest the player in a supine position with feet elevated about 12 in.
- Loosen or remove the player's clothing.
- Fan athlete.
- Drape wet towels over athlete.

Return to Action:
- next day if symptoms are no longer present

Heat Stroke

Definition:
- heat disorder that is life-threatening

Symptoms:
- extremely high body temperature
- hot, red, and dry skin
- rapid and strong pulse
- confusion
- fainting
- convulsions

Care:
- Immediately call for medical assistance.
- Immediately cool body by cold sponging, immersion in cool water, and cold packs.

Return to Action:
- with permission of a physician

Lacerations

Definition:
- a tearing or cutting of the skin

Symptoms:
- bleeding
- swelling

Care:
- Elevate area.
- Direct pressure with gauze (if available) to the wound for 4 or 5 minutes usually will stop bleeding.
- Continue to add gauze if blood soaks through.
- Clean the wound with disinfectant.
- Use the R.I.C.E. formula.
- If stitches are required, send to a doctor within 6 hours.

Return to Action:

- as soon as pain is gone, if the wound can be protected from further injury
- with permission of a physician, if stitches are required

Loss of Wind

Definition:

- a forceful blow to mid-abdomen area that causes inability to breathe

Symptoms:

- rapid, shallow breathing
- gasping for breath

Care:

- Check player to determine if other injuries exist.
- Place player in a supine position.
- Calm the player in order to foster slower breathing.

Return to Action:

- after 5 minutes of rest to regain composure and breathing has returned to normal rate

Nose Bleed

Definition:

- bleeding from the nose

Symptoms:

- bleeding
- swelling
- pain
- deformity of nose

Care:

- Calm the athlete.
- Get the athlete into a sitting position.
- Pinch the nostrils together with fingers while the athlete breathes through the mouth.
- If bleeding cannot be controlled, call for medical assistance.

Return to Action:

- minor nosebleed—if no deformity and no impairment to breathing, pack nose with gauze before athlete continues competition—when bleeding has stopped for several minutes

- serious nosebleed—no more competition that day; doctor's permission if a fracture has occurred

Plantar Fasciitis

Definition:

- inflammation of the connective tissue (fascia) that runs from the heel to the toes

Symptoms:

- arch and heel pain
- sharp pain ("stone bruise") near heel
- gradual onset of pain, that may be tolerated for weeks
- morning pain may be more severe
- pain may decrease throughout day

Care:

- Rest the foot.
- Stretch the Achilles tendon before exercise.
- Use shoes with firm heel counter, good heel cushion, and arch support.
- Use of a heel lift may reduce shock to the foot and decrease the pain.
- Use adhesive strapping to support the arch.

Return to Action:

- when pain is gone

Puncture Wound

Definition:

- any hole made by the piercing of a pointed instrument

Symptoms:

- breakage of the skin
- minor bleeding, possibly none
- tender around wound

Care:

- Cleanse the area with soap and water.
- Control the bleeding.
- Cover the area with sterile dressing.
- Consult physician about the need for a tetanus shot.
- Monitor over several days for signs of infection.

Return to Action:

- with permission of a physician

Shin Splints

Definition:
- pain in the anterior-lateral (front-side) region of the shin associated with running activities that may be caused by a tearing of the muscle (tibialis anterior) away from the tibia (shin), overuse of the muscle, fallen arches or excessive and repeated pronation (turning inward) of the ankle

Symptoms:
- generalized pain in the anterior-lateral region of the shin
- usually night and morning pain
- pain may subside with activity

Care:
- R.I.C.E.
- Have athlete engage in ankle flexibility exercises if pain free.
- If severe pain, see physician.

Return to Action:
- when athlete no longer experiences pain
- when running no longer produces post activity pain

[Note that mild pain may be tolerated. However, if post activity pain is pronounced, the athlete should continue the R.I.C.E. process and refrain from running types of activity.]

Shock

Definition:
- adverse reaction of the body to physical or psychological trauma

Symptoms:
- pale
- cold, clammy skin
- dizziness
- nausea
- faint feeling

Care:
- Have the athlete lie down.
- Calm the athlete.
- Elevate the feet, unless it is a head injury.
- Send for emergency help.
- Control the player's temperature.
- Loosen tight-fitting clothing.
- Control the pain or bleeding if necessary.

Return to Action:
- with permission of a physician

Sprain

Definition:
- a stretching or a partial or complete tear of the ligaments surrounding a joint

Symptoms:
- pain at the joint
- pain aggravated by motion at the joint
- tenderness and swelling
- looseness at the joint

Care:
- Immobilize at time of injury if pain is severe.
- Use the R.I.C.E. formula.
- Send the player to a physician.

Return to Action:
- when pain and swelling are gone
- when full range of motion is reestablished
- when strength and stability are within 95 percent of the non-injured limb throughout range of motion
- when light formal activity is possible with no favoring of the injury
- when formal activity can be resumed with moderate to full intensity with no favoring of the injury

Strain

Definition:
- stretching or tearing of the muscle or tendons that attach the muscle to the bone (commonly referred to as a "muscle pull")

Symptoms:
- localized pain brought on by stretching or contracting the muscle in question
- unequal strength between limbs

Care:
- Use the R.I.C.E. formula.
- Use contrast treatments for days 4-8.

Return to Action:
- when the player can stretch the injured segment as far as the non-injured segment
- when strength is equal to opposite segment

- when the athlete can perform basic football tasks without favoring the injury

[Note that, depending on the severity of the strain, it may take from 1 day to more than 2 weeks for an athlete to return to action.]

MAINTAINING APPROPRIATE RECORDS

The immediate care you provide to an injured player is important to limit the extent of the injury and to set the stage for appropriate rehabilitation. However, immediate care is not the end of prudent action when an injury occurs. Two additional brief but valuable tasks should be completed. The first of these is to fill out an On-Site Injury Report form (see Supplement 19-1) and the second is to log the injury on the Summary of Season Injuries form (see Supplement 19-2).

On-Site Injury Report Form

It is important for you to maintain a record of the injuries that occur to your players. This information may be helpful to guide delayed care or medical treatment and may be very important if any legal problems develop in connection with the injury. Supplement 19-1 includes a standard form that will help guide the recording of pertinent information relative to each injury. These records should be kept for several years following an injury. You should check on legal requirements in your state to determine how long these records should be kept.

Summary of Season Injuries Form

Supplement 19-2 lists each of the common medical conditions that occur in football and also provides a space for you to record when each type of injury occurred. At the end of the season, you should total the incidences of each injury type to see if there is any trend to the kind of injuries your team has suffered. If a trend exists, evaluate your training methods in all areas of practices and games. Try to alter drills or circumstances that may be causing injuries. Review Chapter 18 for techniques that may help you prevent injuries. Perhaps your practice routine ignores or overemphasizes some area of stretching or conditioning. Decide on a course of action that may be implemented for next season, and write your thoughts in the space provided or note the appropriate changes you wish to make on your season or practice plans.

SUMMARY

This chapter attempts to acquaint you with various injuries associated with football and how you should be prepared to deal with these injuries. If you have prepared your first aid kit, brought along the medical records, and familiarized yourself with the different types of injuries, you should be able to handle whatever situation arises. Follow the steps that are outlined for you, and remember—you are not a doctor. If you are in doubt about how to proceed, use the coins in your first aid kit and call for professional medical help. Do not make decisions about treatments if you are not qualified to make them.

Remember, react quickly and with confidence. Most injuries will be minor and the injured players will need only a little reassurance before they can be moved to the bench area. Injuries cannot be completely avoided in football. Therefore, you must prepare yourself to deal with whatever happens in a calm, responsible manner.

REFERENCES

American Red Cross. (1981). *Cardiopulmonary resuscitation.* Washington, D.C.: American Red Cross.

Tanner, S.M., & Harvey, J.S. (1988). How we manage plantar fasciitis. *The Physician and Sportsmedicine,* 16(8), 39-40, 42, 44, 47.

Whitesel, J., & Newell, S.G. (1980). Modified low-dye strapping. *The Physician and Sportsmedicine,* 8(9), 129-131.

SUGGESTED READINGS

American College of Sports Medicine, American Orthopaedic Society for Sports Medicine & Sports Medicine Committee of the United States Tennis Association. (1982). *Sports injuries—An aid to prevention and treatment.* Coventry, CT: Bristol-Myers Co.

Hackworth, C., Jacobs, K., & O'Neill, C. (1982). *Prevention, recognition, and care of common sports injuries.* Kalamazoo, MI: SWM Systems, Inc.

Jackson, D., & Pescar, S. (1981). *The young athlete's health handbook.* New York, NY: Everest House.

Rosenberg, S.N. (1985). *The Johnson & Johnson first aid book.* New York: Warner Books, Inc.

On-Site Injury Report Form

Name _____ Date of injury ____/____/____
        (Injured Player)   mo   day   yr

Address _____
        (Street)   (City, State)   (Zip)

Telephone _____
        (Home)   (Other)

Nature and extent of injury: _____

_____

How did the injury occur? _____

_____

Describe first aid given, including name(s) of attendee(s): _____

_____

Disposition: to hospital   to home   to physician

Other _____

_____

Was protective equipment worn?   _____ Yes   _____ No

Explanation: _____

_____

Condition of the playing surface _____

_____

Names and addresses of witnesses:

Name	Street	City	State	Tel.
Name	Street	City	State	Tel.
Name	Street	City	State	Tel.

Other comments: _____

_____

Signed	Date	Title-Position

Supplement 19-2.

Summary of Season Injuries Form

Injury Type	First 4 Weeks	Middle Weeks	Last 4 Weeks	Total
1. Abrasion				
2. Back or Neck Injury				
3. Blisters				
4. Contusion				
5. Cramps				
6. Dental Injury				
7. Dislocation				
8. Eye Injury— Cintusion				
9. Eye Injury— Foreign Object				
10. Fainting				
11. Fracture				
12. Head Injury Conscious				
13. Head Injury Unconscious				
14. Heat Exhaustion				
15. Heat Stroke				
16. Lacerations				
17. Loss of Wind				
18. Nose Bleed				
19. Plantar Fascitis				
20. Puncture Wound				
21. Shin Splints				
22. Shock				
23. Sprain				
24. Strain				
25. Others:				

Do you see a trend?   YES   NO

Steps to take to reduce injuries next season:

(1) _____

(2) _____

(3) _____

SUMMARY OF SEASON INJURIES

(4) _____

(5) _____

(6) _____

(7) _____

(8) _____

(9) _____

(10) _____

(11) _____

(12) _____

(13) _____

(14) _____

(15) _____

(16) _____

(17) _____

(18) _____

(19) _____

(20) _____

(21) _____

(22) _____

(23) _____

(24) _____

(25) _____

(26) _____

(27) _____

(28) _____

(29) _____

(30) _____

(31) _____

(32) _____

(33) _____

(34) _____

20
Rehabilitation of Common Football Injuries

Rich Kimball, M.A.
Eugene W. Brown, Ph.D.
Wade Lillegard, M.D.

QUESTIONS TO CONSIDER

- What are the important components of a rehabilitation program?
- How can a coach tell when athletes are trying to "come back" too fast?
- Is it necessary to obtain permission from parents and a physician before returning an injured athlete to competition?
- Following an injury, what determines if an activity is too stressful?

INTRODUCTION

Decisions about the rehabilitation of injuries and re-entry into competition must be made according to a flexible set of guidelines; not hard and fast rules. Every individual on your team and each injury is unique. Therefore, rehabilitation techniques and re-entry criteria will differ for each injured player.

GENERAL PROCEDURES

Most injuries suffered by your athletes will not be treated by a physician. Therefore, you, the athlete, and the athlete's parents will determine when the athlete returns to action.

Athletes, coaches, and parents realize that missing practices will reduce the athlete's ability to help the team. Pressure is often exerted on the coach to return injured athletes to action before they are fully recovered, especially if they are the stars of the team. If an athlete has been treated by a physician for an injury, written clearance by both the physician and the parents should be obtained before permitting the athlete to return to practices and games. Also, clarification as to any limitations on participation should be obtained from the physician.

Chances of an injury recurring are greatly increased if an athlete returns too soon. The following five criteria should be met, in order, before allowing an injured athlete back into full physical activity:

1. absence of pain
2. full range of motion at the injured area
3. normal strength and size at the injured area

233

4. normal speed and agility
5. normal level of fitness

If a physician is not overseeing an injured athlete's rehabilitation, the task of rehabilitation will probably fall upon the coach. Stretching activities, calisthenics, and possibly weight training exercises should form the basis of a rehabilitation program. Start with simple stretches. Presence of pain during movement is the key to determining if the activity is too stressful. The onset of pain means too much is being attempted too soon. When athletes can handle the stretching, then calisthenics and possibly weight training can be added to the program. The principles of training included in Chapter 17 should guide all phases of the rehabilitation program.

Absence of Pain

Most injuries are accompanied by pain, although the pain is not always evident immediately when the injury occurs. Usually, the pain disappears quickly if the injury is a bruise, a strain, or a minor sprain. For more serious injuries such as dislocations or fractures, the pain may remain for days or weeks. Once the pain is gone, the athlete can start the stretching portion of a rehabilitation program.

The main goal of a rehabilitation program is to re-establish range of motion, strength, power, and muscular endurance at the site of the injury. As long as athletes remain free of pain, they should proceed with their program. If pain recurs, they should eliminate pain-producing movements until they are pain-free again. The athletes should be in close contact with their physicians during any rehabilitations from injury.

The chance of an injury recurring is greatly increased if an athlete returns to action too soon.

Full Range of Motion

Injuries generally reduce the range of motion around a joint. The more severe the injury, the greater the reduction in range of motion, particularly when the injured area has been immobilized. As soon as they are able to move an injured area without pain, athletes should be encouraged to progressively increase the range of movement until a normal range is achievable. For example, if the athlete has strained a groin muscle, a fairly common injury early in the season, the muscle should be stretched as much as possible without causing pain. Initially, the movement may be slight if the injury was severe. With stretching, the full range of motion will eventually return. The athlete's physicians must be involved at this stage of rehabilitation. Physicians often prescribe specific exercises to safely increase range of motion. When the athlete can move the injured joint through its normal range, strengthening exercises should begin.

Normal Strength and Size

After a body part has been immobilized (by cast, splint wrap, or disuse), muscles become smaller and weaker than they were before the injury. Just because a cast is removed and the injuries have "healed" does not mean that athletes are ready to practice or play at full speed. Loss of muscle mass means a loss of strength. Letting athletes resume a normal practice schedule before their strength has returned to pre-injury levels could lead to re-injury. Strengthening the injured area should be done conservatively and under a physician's direction. If weights are used, start with light weights and perform the exercise through the entire range of motion. If the exercise causes pain, then lighter weights should be used. To determine when full strength and size has been regained, compare the injured area to the non-injured area on the opposite side of the body. When both areas are of equal size and strength, then the athletes may progress to the next phase of recovery.

Your goal is to have the athletes regain full strength through the entire range of motion before allowing them to return to competition.

Normal Speed and Agility

When a physician gives written clearance for an athlete to return to practice, incorporate progressively greater levels of intensity of activity. You should be careful to gradually challenge the previously injured body part. In your observation of injured athletes, try to detect any favoring of an injured part or inability to smoothly perform a skill at increasing intensities. When athletes can move at pre-injury speed and agility, they are almost ready to play. However, they must still establish their pre-injury level of fitness.

The main goal of a rehabilitation program is to reestablish range of motion, strength, power, and muscular endurance to the injured area.

Normal Level of Fitness

Every extended layoff reduces the level of muscular fitness. While recovering, the athlete may be able to exercise other body parts without affecting the injured area. For example, someone with a sprained ankle may not be able to run and catch the ball, but he may be able to swim. Someone with a broken wrist may be able to do a variety of lower body activities such as jog, play defense, or walk through plays. Cautiously encourage this type of activity, because it helps to maintain portions of the athlete's pre-injury levels of fitness. Athletes who have missed long periods of time due to an injury should practice for several days after meeting the previous criteria before being allowed to play in a game. Their cardiovascular system and the endurance of the injured musculature need time to adjust to the demands of the game. The longer the layoff, the more conditioning work the athlete will need.

SUMMARY

When the pain is gone, and the range of motion, strength, agility, and conditioning are back to normal, your athlete is ready to reenter practice and competition. The entire process may have taken 2 days for a bruise to 12 or more weeks and assistance from physicians for a fracture. In either case, if you have followed the general guidelines of this chapter, you know you have acted in the best long-term interest of the athlete. Participation is important, but only if participation is achieved with a healthy body. Resist the pressure and the temptation to rush athletes into a game before they are ready. Your patience will be rewarded in the games to come.

21
Nutrition for Successful Performance

Elaina Jurecki, Ph.D.
Glenna DeJong, M.S., M.A.

QUESTIONS TO CONSIDER

- What is a proper diet for young football players?
- Do young athletes need protein, vitamin, and mineral supplements?
- Should there by any restriction on the amount of water consumed before, during, and after games and practices?
- Should salt tablets be provided for the players during practices and games?
- Are ergogenic aids important in improving football performance?
- When should a pre-game meal be eaten and what should it contain?

INTRODUCTION

All children have the same nutritional needs, but young athletes use more energy and, therefore, usually need to consume more calories. Good performance does not just happen; it requires training sessions to improve techniques, increase endurance, and develop game strategies. Good nutrition is another important factor that affects an athlete's performance, but it is less frequently understood and practiced. Studies have shown that good overall eating habits are more beneficial to the athlete than taking vitamin or protein supplements or eating special foods at a pre-competition meal.

Food consists of all the solid or liquid materials we ingest by mouth, except drugs. Breads, meats, vegetables, and fruits, as well as beverages—even water—are considered food, because they contain essential nutrients for the body. These nutrients include energy (calories from fat, protein, and carbohydrates), carbohydrates, protein (amino acids), fat, vitamins, salts (electrolytes), minerals, trace elements, and water. Water constitutes more than half the body's weight and provides the medium within which other nutrients are delivered to different body parts to perform their important functions.

What impact could you have on your athletes' diets? How can you influence what your athletes eat when you do not cook their meals? When you meet with the team's parents during an orientation meeting, explain to them how good nutrition can aid their children's performance. This information can be reinforced by giving your athletes similar nutritional advice.

Frequently, your athletes will listen more closely to your advice than that of their parents and use the tips you suggest on improving their diets because they believe these tips will also improve their performance.

PROPER DIET

A good diet is one that provides adequate energy (calories), proteins, carbohydrates, fats, vitamins, minerals, and water in the amounts needed by the body in order to perform its normal daily functions. A variety of foods needs to be eaten to provide the 40 plus nutrients essential for good health. This can be achieved by eating the specified number of servings from each of the four food groups (see Table 21-1).

Calories

Calories are the energy content of food used to satisfy the needs of the energy body so it can properly function. Energy obtained from food is temporarily stored as glycogen in the liver and muscle, as fat in various deposit sites, and as protein in muscle and other places although protein is used as an energy source only during extreme situations. Foods vary in calorie and nutrient content. Foods to avoid are those that are high in calories and low in nutrient content. Foods that are high in sugar (candy, cakes, soda pop, cookies) or fat (fried foods, chips, salad dressings, pastries, butter) supply "empty calories," meaning they do not contribute to the essential nutrients discussed earlier but do contribute many calories. These foods should be used with discretion.

The energy cost of physical activity, or amount of calories burned, depends upon (a) the intensity of the physical activity, and (b) the length of time of exertion. A young football player, about 120 pounds in body weight, burns approximately 375 calories per hour of practice. During a game or training session, ranging from 45 to 90 minutes, your players burn up to 25 percent more energy than they do on a day in which they don't practice. Hence, heavy training may require an additional 280 to 560 calories per day intake to compensate for the calories burned during the activity.

An average adolescent burns differing amounts of calories during the various activities listed in Table 21-2.

When your players reach exhaustion, most of their bodies' energy stores are depleted and their blood sugar decreases, causing fatigue. This situation is remedied with appropriate rest and calorie ingestion—preferably from carbohydrate sources since these foods can replenish energy stores more efficiently.

Carbohydrates

Carbohydrates are a group of chemical substances which includes sugars and starches. They are widely distributed in many foods. As stated previously, carbohydrates can be stored as liver and muscle glycogen or can be found in the blood as glucose. During moderate to high intensity exercise, carbohydrates supply the majority of the energy needed in the body (see "Energy Production Systems" in Chapter 17). However, the carbohydrate storage capacity of the body is limited and can be greatly decreased by skipping meals or with exercise. Since car-

Table 21-1. Recommended daily intake of each of the four food groups.

Dairy Products	3-4 servings (milk, cheese, yogurt) to provide calcium, phosphorus, vitamin D, protein, and energy.	1 serving = 1 cup of milk or 2 oz. of cheese
Protein Products	2 servings (meat, fish, poultry, or vegetable protein foods such as beans and whole grains) to provide amino acids, B vitamins, iron, essential fatty acids, energy, and more.	1 serving = 2 to 3 oz. of meat
Fruits and Vegetables	4 servings (oranges, apples, pears, broccoli, carrots, green beans) to provide vitamin A and C, and electrolytes.	1 serving = 1/2 cup of vegetables or fruit
Grain Products	4 servings (bread, cereal, pasta, rice) to provide B vitamins and protein.	1 serving = 1 slice bread or 1 cup of cereal, pasta, or rice.

Table 21-2. Caloric expenditure during various activities.

Activity	Calories/minute*	Activity	Calories/minute
Sleeping	0.9	Football	5-7
Sitting, normally	1.0	Calisthenics	4
Standing, normally	1.2	Skipping rope	8-12
Class work, lecture (listen to)	1.4	Running (10 mph)	16
		Football (game)	6-8
Walking indoors	2.5		

*Based on an average adolescent, 120 lbs. Add 10 percent for each 15 lbs. over 120, subtract 10 percent for each 15 lbs. under 120.

bohydrates can be digested easily and quickly, they are the most readily available sources of food energy for storage energy replacement.

A diet high in carbohydrate (55-60 percent of total caloric intake) helps maintain adequate stores in the body. Most of the dietary carbohydrates should come from complex carbohydrate sources such as pasta, rice, fruits, and kidney beans. Refined sugars found in candy, cookies, and syrup should be avoided.

Carbohydrates are easily digested and are the most readily available source of food energy.

Fat

Fat is the most concentrated source of energy. It contains twice as much energy (calories) per unit weight as either carbohydrate or protein. Fats have many important functions in the body including carrying vitamins A, D, E, and K to perform their necessary functions, building blood vessels and body linings, and providing a concentrated store of energy (calories).

During mild to moderate exercise, fats are an important energy source along with carbohydrates (see "Energy Production Systems" in Chapter 17). The storage capacity for fat is much greater than that for carbohydrate and only in extreme cases are fat stores depleted. Therefore, dietary intake of fat should be 30 percent or less of total caloric intake since replenishment isn't normally necessary. In fact, high levels of fat in the diet have been implicated in diseases such as coronary artery disease and cancer.

Foods high in fat content are digested at a slower rate than foods high in carbohydrates or protein. If players have high fat meals (ham-

burger, fries, pizza, etc.) before their game, chances are good that such meals will not empty completely from their stomachs for 3-5 hours, and this may adversely affect their play. Foods having a high concentration of fat include butter, margarine, vegetable oils, peanut butter, mayonnaise, nuts, chocolate, fried foods, chips, and cream products.

Figure 21-1 lists the percent of fat from a variety of food sources.

Protein

Proteins are important as structural components of all body tissues (e.g. muscle, skin, brain, etc.), regulators of metabolism (e.g. hormones and enzymes), and as an energy source during starvation and exercise although its contribution is minor as compared to fats and carbohydrates (see "Energy Production Systems" in Chapter 17). Amino acids are the "building blocks" which comprise all proteins. Of the 20 amino acids necessary for protein synthesis in the body, 11 can be manufactured in the body and are considered nonessential amino acids. The other nine are considered essential amino acids as they must be supplied in the diet. In a balanced diet, 12-15 percent of the total caloric intake should come from protein.

Foods from animal sources (e.g., meat, fish, poultry, eggs, milk, and cheese) provide the body with all of the essential amino acids. Vegetable foods (dried peas, beans, nuts, cereals, breads, and pastas) are also important sources of protein, but most vegetables are lacking in certain essential amino acids. Therefore, a combination of foods from animal and vegetable sources assures meeting the body's requirement for essential amino acids, as well as other nutrients.

Because of an increased rate of muscular growth, athletes have a *slightly* larger protein requirement than non-athletes. Studies on the dietary habits of athletes show that this increased requirement can be easily met by the athlete's normal diet; no protein supplement is necessary. During training, at most, an additional 9 grams of protein (which can be provided by 1 cup of milk or 2 ounces of meat or cheese) is sufficient to meet increased demands. In fact, too much protein can place undo stress on the body.

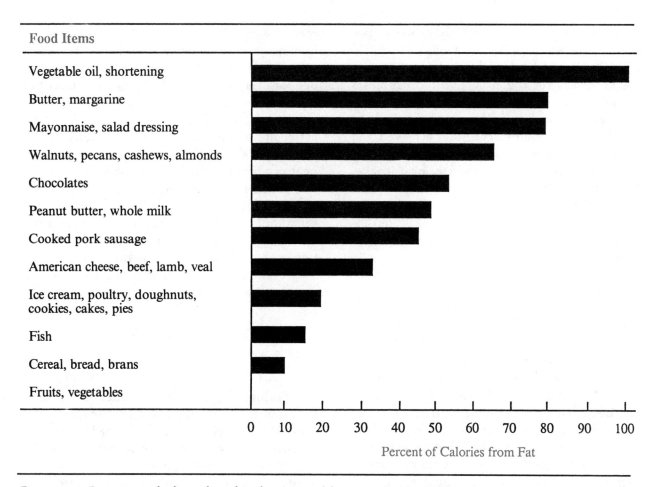

Figure 21-1. Percentage of calories from fat when ingested from specified food items.

Eating a high-protein diet could lead to dehydration of the body, which could actually decrease athletic performance.

Excessive amounts of ingested protein—greater than the body's needs—are converted into body fat. The waste products from this conversion must be excreted by the kidneys, placing a greater strain on these organs. Water also is excreted with the protein-waste products in the urine. Thus, eating a high-protein diet could lead to dehydration of the body, which could actually decrease athletic performance.

It is a myth that building muscle requires a high-protein diet featuring large quantities of meat. Another myth is that a steak dinner eaten before an athletic event will help team members improve their performance. This type of meal may actually work against them if consumed less than 3 or 4 hours before playing time. These meals, as well as any high protein meal, are also usually high in fat. Players cannot digest this

type of meal as easily as a high-carbohydrate meal and may suffer from cramps and/or feel weighted down and sluggish.

Vitamins and Minerals

Vitamins and minerals are found in varying quantities in many different kinds of foods, from a slice of bread to a piece of liver. Vitamins and minerals are nutrients required by the body in very small amounts for a larger number of body functions. They do not contain calories or give the body energy. When an athlete feels "run down," *this is usually not caused by a vitamin deficiency.*

We need vitamins and minerals in only minute quantities. Requirements of most vitamins and minerals are in milligram (1/1000 gram) amounts. These substances taken in excess of the body's need will either be stored in the body or excreted in the urine. The extra amounts will not provide more energy or enhance performance; however, they can be toxic or interfere with normal metabolism.

Vitamin and mineral supplementation is not necessary for the athlete who consumes a balanced diet. However, in certain sports such as wrestling, bodybuilding, and ballet, where weight loss through starvation is achieved, the athlete may not be obtaining adequate amounts solely due to the diminished caloric intake. Therefore, in situations where the athlete's diet is not balanced or caloric intake is low, supplementation may be advised. A much better approach, however, would be to encourage proper eating habits.

Vitamins and minerals do not supply energy; high levels of vitamins and minerals can hinder the athlete's performance.

Some vitamin and mineral supplements contain 10 or more times the Recommended Daily Allowance (RDA), which is sometimes just below the level of toxicity. If vitamin and mineral supplements are used, a single daily multi-vitamin/mineral tablet that provides 100 percent of the RDA or less for each nutrient is preferable to therapeutic level supplements providing greater than 100 percent of the RDA. The RDAs of vitamins and minerals are listed in Table 21-3.

Water

Water plays a vital role in the health and performance of an athlete. Your football players may lose more than 2 percent of their body weight due to dehydration from playing a fast-moving game or during a long workout. A player's performance significantly deteriorates after dehydration of more than 2 percent of his/her body weight. Drinking plenty of water is necessary for football players who are physically active in hot, humid weather (see Figure 21-2).

Physical exercise increases the amount of heat produced in the body. If sufficient water is not available for cooling of the body through perspiration, the body temperature may exceed safe limits. The individual will become tired more rapidly and in severe cases, heat exhaustion and heat stroke may result (see Chapter 19). A temperature/humidity guide for fluid and practice time is included in Table 21-4.

Maintenance of adequate body water levels is necessary to help prevent heat illness.

Feeling thirsty is not an adequate indication that the body needs water. In fact, by the time athletes feel thirsty, they already may have reached a dangerous level of body water depletion. It takes several hours to regain water balance once water loss has occurred. There is no physiological reason for restricting water intake before, during, or after athletic contests and practices. Players should drink 8-16 ounces of water 30 minutes before the game and 8 ounces every 20 minutes during the game.

Athletes should be encouraged to drink water before, during, and after each game and practice session.

Table 21-3. Recommended daily dietary allowances.*

Age (Years)	Children 7-10	Males 11-14	Females 11-14
Weight (pounds)	62	99	101
Height (inches)	52	62	62
Energy (calories)	2,400	2,700	2,200
range of calories	1,650-3,300	2,000-3,700	1,500-3,000
Protein (grams)	34	45	46
Vitamin A (mg RE)	700	1,000	1,000
Vitamin C (mg)	45	50	50
Calcium (mg)	800	1,200	1,200
Iron (mg)	10	18	18

*Adapted from Food and Nutrition Board, National Academy of Sciences—National Research Council, Revised, 1980.

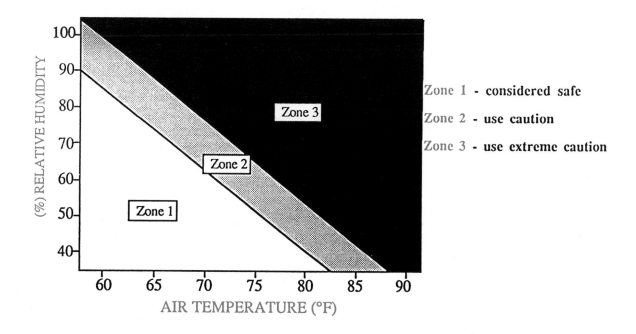

Figure 21-2. Guide for preventing heat illnesses associated with participation in physical activities under various conditions of temperatures and humidity.

Salts and Electrolytes

Another common myth is that salt (sodium) tablets and electrolyte solutions (solutions containing the elements sodium, potassium, and chloride are needed by the athlete. These are not only unnecessary but can be harmful.

Salt tablets are irritating to the stomach and intestine and can increase the danger of dehydration by causing diarrhea when taken before a practice or game. Although the body needs to replace both water and sodium, the need for water is more critical.

Some coaches provide 0.2 percent salt solutions (drinking water containing small amounts of salt) during an athletic event, but research has shown that plain water is just as effective. The body needs water immediately to replace the water lost during a game or practice, but any sodium lost can easily be replaced by eating salted foods after the event. Most Americans get more sodium than they need from salt already in their diet; therefore, excessive salting of food is unnecessary and not recommended.

The best replacement fluid is water.

ERGOGENIC AIDS

Ergogenic is derived from the Greek words ergon meaning work and gennan meaning to produce. In sports, ergogenic aids are agents thought to increase potential for work output. Various mechanical, psychological, physiological, nutritional, and pharmacological aids exist which purportedly improve performance. This discussion will focus on nutritional and pharmacological aids.

Nutritional Aids

Ergogenic foods are those substances that claim to "give you more energy," "improve your performance," and/or "enhance your endurance." There is no scientific evidence supporting any of these claims. Most of these foods and dietary practices are harmless to the athlete. The only danger these foods pose occurs when they replace necessary foods that the athlete needs for normal bodily functions. Some

Table 21-4. Temperature/humidity guide for taking precautionary action during football practices and games.

Temperature	Precautions to Take
Under 60° (F)	No precaution is necessary.
61-65° (F)	Encourage all players to take fluids. Make sure water is available at all times.
66-70° (F)	Take water breaks every 30-45 minutes of playing or practice time.
71-75° (F)	Provide rest periods with water breaks every 30-45 minutes of playing time—depending on the intensity of exercise. Substitute players during the game, so all may receive appropriate rest and fluids.
76° (F) and up	Practice during coolest part of the day. Schedule frequent rest breaks. Force water intake.
	Tell players to wear light, loose clothing that allows free circulation of air. Remove outer clothing when it gets wet because wet clothing reduces evaporation, thus hindering one of the body's cooling mechanisms.
	Move to the shade if possible.
	Drink water before, during, and after practice sessions and competition.
Relative humidity greater than 90%	Similar precautions should be taken as those listed for 76° (F) and up.

examples of these foods are bee pollen, pangamic acid, honey, lecithin, wheat germ oil, phosphates, alkaline salts (e.g., sodium bicarbonate, tomato juice, or organic juice), and gelatin.

Inform your athletes that these substances do not improve performance contrary to advertiser's claims. Encourage them to eat healthy diets and explain that this is the key to improving their performance.

Pharmacological Aids

• Steroids

Anabolic steroids (Dianabol, Anavar, Winstrol, etc.) have structures similar to the male sex hormone, testosterone. They are referred to as anabolic because, under certain circumstances, they promote tissue-building via increases in muscle mass and decreases in muscle breakdown. This effect is most evident in males when great increases in muscle mass and strength are seen at puberty. A 20-fold magnification in circulating testosterone levels accom-

panies these increases at this time. However, muscle mass and/or strength gains following steroid administration on already sexually mature subjects are questionable or at best show only moderate improvements.

In addition to their anabolic effects, steroids used in athletics also have androgenic or masculinizing effects. Males and females both may experience increased facial and body hair, baldness, voice deepening, and aggressiveness while using these drugs. Anabolic steroids also produce many reversible and irreversible side effects that are of great concern to the medical community as described in Table 21-5.

Steroid abuse is a major problem in athletics today even at the junior high and high school levels despite cases of well-known athletes who have been negatively affected by such abuse. In the 1983 Pan American games, 7 of the 19 athletes tested were disqualified for steroid use and many more withdrew from competition to prevent detection. Ben Johnson, the great Canadian sprinter, had his gold medal rescinded at the 1988 Olympic games following discovery of steroid abuse. Not only is steroid use unethical, it is dangerous. Your athletes should be informed of the dangerous and potentially fatal effects of steroid usage. The risk of infertility, liver damage, immune dysfunction, and aggressive behavior far outweighs any possible advantages of taking steroids.

• Amphetamines

The use of pep pills or amphetamines is on the rise in athletics. These drug compounds cause reactions similar to adrenaline in that they increase heart rate, blood pressure, metabolism, breathing rate, and blood sugar levels. They may also cause headaches, dizziness, confusion, and sometimes insomnia, all of which could actually be detrimental to good physical performance. In fact, research suggests that amphetamines have little or no positive effect on exercise performance. Urge your athletes to stay clear of amphetamines as evidence for their potential detriment far exceeds any known benefits.

The best prescription for increased strength and improved performance is hard practice, plenty of rest, a good diet, healthy eating habits, and plenty of fluids.

Table 21-5. Harmful effects of anabolic steroids.*

Body System	Reversible Effects	Irreversible Effects
Cardiovascular (heart/blood vessels)	High blood pressure, changes in blood fats, predisposing to heart disease, sticky platelets	Abnormal heart muscle, heart disease, stroke, heart attack
Skeletal	Minor changes in height	Early closure of the growth plates, making you shorter than you would be otherwise
Muscular	Increased water in muscle	Abnormal muscle cells, tendon rupture
Reproductive—male	Shrunken testicles, decreased sperm production, breast development, increased size of the prostate gland	Cancer of the prostate, increased breast development, abnormal testicles
Reproductive—female	Decreased breast size, increased body hair (facial also), menstrual problems	Increased size of clitoris, deepening voice, baldness, use during pregnancy may cause fetal deformity or death
Liver	Increased leakage of liver enzymes, abnormal growth of liver cells, turning "yellow" from backup of bile in liver	Cancer of liver, blood-filled sacs in liver
Endocrine (hormones)	Too much insulin secreted, decreased thyroxine, decreases hormone secretion from pituitary gland in brain	Do not know which effects are permanent
Skin	Acne, increased facial hair	Severe acne, baldness
Mental Attitude	Irritability, aggressiveness, mood swings, problems getting along with people, change in sex drive	Relationships with people damaged, possible personality changes
Immune	Decreased functioning of the immune cells and antibody formation	Serious infections, cancer

*This table comes from a paper entitled "What the High School Athletes, Coaches and Parents Should Know About Anabolic-Androgenic Steroids." This paper is available upon request from the Michigan State University Sports Medicine Clinic, Clinical Center, East Lansing, MI 48824.

• Caffeine

A stimulant commonly found in coffee, tea, cola, and chocolate is caffeine. Its ingestion has been found to improve physical performance in such long duration events as cycling and running. Therefore, its use may be warranted in endurance events and if used should be consumed 1 hour prior to the event. However, caffeine may cause headache, insomnia, and/or irritability in persons who normally avoid this drug. These people should avoid caffeine as these symptoms may be detrimental to performance. Don't rely on caffeine as a miracle performance drug, as it is not! Sensible training and proper diet are the best prescriptions that can't be beat for improving performance.

MEAL PATTERNS

Preadolescents and adolescents should eat at least three meals daily. Nutritional snacks may be added to the regular breakfast-lunch-dinner pattern if extra calories are needed. Most active athletes tend to skip meals, grab quick-fix meals, or depend on fast food restaurants and vending machines for meals on the run. This practice could lead to diets low in vitamins and minerals and high in fat and sodium. For example, a meal consisting of a hamburger, fries, and soda would provide 571 calories or approximately one-fourth of the energy requirement of a 15- to 18-year-old athlete, but less than one-tenth of the other nutritional requirements. Nutritional foods with good ratios of nutrients to calories are listed in Table 21-6. To maximize performance during periods of intense daily training, an athlete should consume approximately 500 grams (2000 Kcal) of carbohydrates per day.

Pre-Game Meal

One of the biggest concerns of athletes and coaches is what the team members should eat for the pre-game meal. Unfortunately, there are no foods that contain any special, magical properties that can improve your football players' performances if eaten before the game. Performance during an event or workout is dependent more on food consumed hours, days, or

Table 21-6. Contributions of nutritional snacks.

Food	Amount	Calories	Vit A	Vit C	Calcium	Iron
			\multicolumn{4}{c}{—— % Recommended Daily Allowance ——}			
Fresh orange	1 med. size	65	8	150	7	5
Orange juice	1 cup	110	14	200	3	5
Peanut butter	1 tablespoon	95	—	—	0.5	3
2% Milk	1 cup	120	14	4	37	1
Cheese and crackers	1 oz. cheese, 4 crackers	175	9	—	27	7
Carrot sticks	8 or 1 carrot	30	70	13	3	5
Ice cream	1 cup	270	15	2	22	1
Fruit-flavored yogurt	1 cup	230	14	2	43	2
Raisins	1/4 cup pressed	120	—	—	56	15
Applesauce	1/2 cup	115	1	3	—	7
Banana	1 med.	100	6	27	—	7
Ready-to-eat cereal	1 ounce	110	29	27	—	36

even weeks before the event. The most important consideration should be to select foods that can be digested easily, tolerated well, and liked by the players.

Pre-game stress causes an athlete's stomach and intestine to be less active. Minor food intake is recommended before vigorous exercise to delay exhaustion, but should be eaten 2 or 3 hours before the competition to give the stomach and intestines sufficient time to empty. Meals eaten before a practice session should be given the same general consideration as the pre-game meal, except there is no need to compensate for nervous stress.

Carbohydrates leave the stomach earlier and are digested more readily than either fats or protein. Foods that are easily digested include cereals, bread, spaghetti, macaroni, rice, potatoes (baked, not fried), and fruits. Examples of high-fat foods which should be avoided include cake, peanut butter, nuts, luncheon-type meats, gravy, yellow cheese, butter, and ice cream. Gas-forming foods (e.g., cabbage, cucumbers, cauliflower, and beans) and foods high in fiber and roughage (e.g., whole wheat bread, bran cereal, and raw vegetables) may cause discomfort to the player if eaten the day of competition.

Those athletes who have difficulty digesting solid foods before competition may prefer a liquid meal. These products should not be confused with instant powdered meals or "instant breakfasts," which have too much fat, protein, and electrolytes to be eaten before athletic contests. Liquid meals have the following advantages: (a) they leave the intestine rapidly, (b) they provide substantial calories, and (c) they are more convenient than preparing a solid meal. However, liquid meals do not provide any greater benefits for improving performances than do easily digested, well-tolerated meals.

Lunch should be eaten about 3 hours prior to afternoon practices or games. Possible choices for lunch include: spaghetti with tomato sauce; sandwich of white bread with a thin spread; chicken noodle or vegetable soup; low-fat yogurt or cottage cheese; fresh or canned fruits and fruit juices; crackers with white cheese or cheese spread; low-fat milk; baked potato sprinkled with white cheese and bacon bits (not real bacon but the soybean-flavored brand); or pizza—heavy on the tomato sauce and light on the cheese. If the team has an early morning practice or game, (8:00 A.M.) athletes should eat breakfast about 5:00 A.M. to ensure plenty of time to digest their meal before playing time. If they do not wish to eat breakfast that early, they could eat a lighter meal (e.g., liquid meals or juice and a piece of white toast with jelly—no butter or margarine) an hour before playing time. However, eating the larger meal two or three hours before playing time would delay feelings of fatigue and hunger and would be recommended when the team has to play a football tournament lasting more than four hours. Possible selections for breakfast would include: cereal with low fat milk, pancakes, French toast, fruit juice, oatmeal or cream of wheat, white toast with jelly or cinnamon sugar, soft- or hard-boiled eggs, and fresh or canned fruit.

Pre-game meal:
- *Eat carbohydrate-rich foods*
- *Avoid fatty foods*
- *Avoid gas-forming and high-fiber foods*
- *Eat three or four hours before the game*
- *Drink plenty of fluids hourly*
- *Avoid concentrated sweets*

Candy bars are not a good source of quick energy and will not help your players perform better. A candy bar eaten right before the game may give your athletes a sudden burst of energy, but this energy boost is only temporary. The body over-compensates for the increase in blood sugar that results from eating a simple sugar (such as candy), causing feelings of tiredness and hunger. Your athletes will be full of energy for only a short time, then they will become sluggish and weak. Therefore, candies and anything high in sugar should be avoided especially just prior to activity.

Nutritional Support During Competition

Intense prolonged activities such as football and distance running require significant fluid and energy replacement during the event. Water is the most important replacement, but performance and endurance may be enhanced with proper carbohydrate replacement.

In a study of elite soccer players (Williams 1983), muscle glycogen (carbohydrate) stores were assessed after a 90-minute soccer match. The groups of players that drank 1 liter of a 7 percent sugar solution during the game had 63 percent more glycogen in their muscles than the group that drank plain water. In other words, the group that drank the sugar solution had much more "reserve" energy stores.

A 7 percent carbohydrate solution easily can be made by dissolving 70 grams (4.5 tablespoons) of glucose (sugar) in 1 quart (32 ounces) of water. Athletes should drink about 8 ounces of this mixture every 20 minutes during a match to maintain normal blood glucose levels. Many commercial carbohydrate replacement "sport drinks" are available with similar concentrations.

WEIGHT CONTROL

Each of your football players is different in height and build and, therefore, they have different ideal body weights. Rather than suggesting that your players weigh a specific number of pounds, you should work at improving their skill and physical fitness.

Weight Loss

Athletes who have too much fat will tend to be slower and tire more easily. For those individuals, some weight loss could improve their performance. In order to lose weight, energy output must exceed energy intake. Because of this, the more active athletes have an easier time losing weight than their less active peers.

One pound of fat has the energy equivalent of approximately 3,500 calories. Reducing food intake by 500 calories per day will result in a loss of about 1 pound per week. Increasing the athlete's activity or training may also result in extra weight loss. Because fat cannot be lost at a rate faster than 1 or 2 pounds per week, weight loss greater than this amount could result in loss of body protein and not body fat. Hence, crash diets are not recommended because loss of valuable body protein (muscle mass) can occur.

Sauna baths, cathartics, and diuretics are methods used to lose weight by dehydration. These methods are not recommended because body fluids, not body fat are lost which reduces strength and endurance. The key to losing weight is to begin months before the season starts, follow a healthy diet, avoid high-calorie foods, eat three balanced meals, and increase activity level.

Important points to consider when attempting to lose weight:
- *Start early*
- *Lose at a slow pace*
- *Lose fat, not fluid or muscle*
- *Avoid excessive weight loss, especially during growing periods*
- *Avoid use of saunas, diuretics, or cathartics*

Weight Gain

The goal for athletes trying to gain weight is to add more muscle, rather than fat. Eating an extra 500 calories per day should result in gaining 1 pound of muscle per week. This increase in caloric intake must be accompanied with intensive exercise, at a level that is slightly less than full exertion. A good way to add those extra calories is by adding a daily snack such as dried fruit, nuts, peanut butter sandwich, juice, milk shake, or oatmeal-raisin cookies. Trying to gain weight at a faster rate will result only in more body fat in the wrong places, rather than muscle in the right places.

Important points to consider when attempting to gain weight:

- *Start early*
- *Gain at a slow pace*
- *Eat nutritious foods, and not foods high in fat content*

As a coach, you can give your players some tips on how to gain or lose weight properly— eating the right foods and gaining/losing weight at the proper pace. Encourage your players to eat a healthy diet because they should naturally achieve their ideal body weight by eating balanced meals and snacks and exercising. Most of your athletes will still be growing and will require additional calories to meet the demands of their growing bodies.

If you have athletes who are excessively over- or underweight, you may tactfully approach their parents and suggest that they seek medical attention for their child.

At the ideal body weight, the athlete performs best.

Many teenagers eat a lot of junk foods— high in calories and low in nutrients—but the motivated athletes would prefer foods high in nutrients if they realized that these foods could help them in performing their best.

SUMMARY

Your group of football players is a motivated group of individuals who want to improve their performances to become a successful team. As their coach, you can provide them with the necessary information on how they can play their best. Providing your team with the nutritional advice presented in this chapter will assist them in obtaining maximum performance through eating a healthy diet and avoiding unsafe habits.

REFERENCES

Ivy, J.L. (1988). Muscle glycogen storage after different amounts of carbohydrate ingestion. *Journal of Applied Physiology,* 65, 2018-2023.

Ivy, J.L. (1988). Muscle glycogen synthesis after exercise: Effect of time on carbohydrate ingestion. *Journal of Applied Physiology,* 64, 1480-1485.

Mathews, D., & Fox, E. (1976). The physiological bases of physical education and athletics. Philadelphia: W.B. Saunders.

Williams, M.H. (1983). *Ergogenic aids in sports.* Champaign, IL: Human Kinetics.

SUGGESTED READINGS

American College of Sports Medicine. (1987). Position stand on the use of anabolic-androgenic steroids in sports. *Medicine and Science in Sports and Exercise,* 19(5), 534-539.

Clark, N. (1981). *The athlete's kitchen: A nutrition guide and cookbook.* Boston: CBI Publishing.

Darden, E. (1976) *Nutrition and athletic performance.* Pasadena, CA: The Athletic Press.

Food and Nutrition Board: Recommended dietary allowances. Rev. Ed., 1980. Washington, D.C.: National Academy of Sciences.

Higdon, H. (1978). *The complete diet guide for runners and other athletes.* Mountain View, CA: World Publications.

Katch, F.I., & McArdle, W.D. (1977). *Nutrition, weight control, and exercise.* Boston: Houghton Mifflin.

National Association for Sport and Physical Education. (1984). *Nutrition for sport success.* Reston, VA: American Alliance for Health, Physical Education, Recreation and Dance.

Smith, N.J. (1976) *Food for sport.* Palo Alto, CA: Bull Publishing.

Williams, E.R., & Caliendo, M.A. (1984) *Nutrition, principle issues, and application.* New York, NY: McGraw-Hill.

Williams, M.H. (1983) *Nutrition for fitness and sport.* Dubuque, Iowa: Wm. C. Brown.

Section IV
Rules of Play

22
Basic Football Rules With Modifications for Youth Players*

Vern Seefeldt, Ph.D.

QUESTIONS TO CONSIDER

- What modifications could be made to the rules of football to meet the developmental needs of youth players?
- How should the rules of football be applied in order to promote safety, enjoyment, and fairness?

INTRODUCTION

Football is generally regarded as a sport played by powerful, aggressive males who enjoy body contact and risk-taking behavior. However, modifications of football rules that result in elimination or reduction of body contact can make the sport more acceptable to younger athletes, females, and to all who love to run, kick, throw, and catch a football but who have an aversion to blocking, tackling, and the aggressive play that is generally associated with tackle football.

The modifications of football rules that are suggested in this handbook were selected because their implementation influences the opportunities that are available to younger players and those who want to avoid or reduce the bodily contact of regulation football. The primary purposes of these rule modifications are to:

1. permit young players to develop the skills of passing, receiving, kicking, punting, and centering a football without the fear of injury due to bodily contact
2. enable players to become involved in all the fundamentals of football except blocking and tackling at young ages
3. permit individuals to learn a sport that has life-long carry-over value, if played without blocking and tackling
4. reduce the risk of injuries when children of varying sizes play football
5. emphasize the motor skills of football rather than strength, power, and body size

The rule modifications that have the greatest impact on the way football is played pertain to the:

---

*The rules for regulation football are modifications from a variety of sources. Among them are the **1991 High School Rules,** National Federation of State High School Associations, 11724 Plaza Circle, P.O. Box 20626, Kansas City, MO, 64195; **Official's Manual: Touch and Flag Football,** by J. Reznik and R. Grambeau, 1978; **Physical Education Handbook,** Prentice Hall, 1983; and **Youth League Football, Coaching and Playing,** The Athletic Institute, 1991.

1. size of the playing field
2. elimination or reduction of body contact
3. number of players per team and the positions played
4. length of the contest
5. equipment and attire
6. offensive and defensive tactics

The following rules describe the regulation game of football.

THE GAME OF FOOTBALL

Football (interscholastic and regulation) is played by two teams on a field 360 by 160 feet. The team in possession of the ball attempts to advance the ball by carrying, kicking, or passing it. If a foul occurs, the penalty loss, if not declined, is measured during the period between downs. Penalties that include loss of down indicate that the offending team has lost the right to replay the down. The team on offense has four downs to advance the ball to the line-to-gain, which is 10 yards in advance of the spot where the first down starts. Points are scored by touchdown, a successful try for point after a touchdown, field goal, or safety.

Teams are composed of 11 players, but if a team does not have substitutes to replace injured or disqualified players, it may continue with fewer players.

Ideally, the regulation game is administered by four officials (a referee, umpire, linesman, and line judge). A greater or lesser number of officials is permitted. The referee's decisions are final in all matters pertaining to the game.

The referee has authority to rule promptly, and in the spirit of good sportsmanship, on any situation not specifically covered in the rules.

The Football Field and Its Markings

The field shall be a rectangular area with dimensions, lines, zones, goals, and markers as shown in Figure 22-1.

To ensure safety in equipment, the yard line markers, if placed on the ground and within 5 yards of the sidelines, shall be constructed of soft, pliable material.

Yard lines and other markings:

The yard lines shown in Figure 22-1 shall be marked with a noncaustic material. Hydrated lime or lime oxides, or caustic material of any kind may not be used.

Lines that mark the ends and sidelines should be at least four inches wide. Other field dimension lines should also be four inches in width.

Advertising and/or commercial markings on the field should be discouraged.

Goal lines and the team box boundaries should be marked in a color that contrasts with other field markings. The area between the sidelines and the team box boundaries should be solid white or marked with diagonal lines.

To aid game officials with an obstructed operating area, a four-inch wide broken restraining line may be placed around the outside of the playing field, two or more yards from the sidelines and end lines, as an extension of the line limiting the team box area.

All boundary lines are out-of-bounds. Thus, measurements shall be from the inside edges of the boundary marks.

Goal line marks shall be entirely in the end zones so the edges toward the field of play and their vertical planes are the actual goal line.

A soft, flexible pylon at least 18 inches high, orange or red in color, shall be placed at the inside corner of each of the intersections of the sidelines with the goal lines and the end lines, as well as with each intersection of the inbounds lines extended and the end lines.

When goal posts are part of the field of play, the goal is the vertical plane extending above the crossbar and between the inner edges of the goal posts. The top edge of the crossbar shall be 10 feet above ground. The crossbar shall be 23 feet, 4 inches long and the distance between the outside edges of the uprights above the crossbar shall not exceed 24 feet. The goal posts shall extend at least 10 feet above the crossbar.

No decorative material may be attached to the crossbar or goal posts.

Equipment

Football is played with an inflated ball that shall meet the following specifications:

A cover consisting of 4 panels of a pebble-grain, tan cowhide or approved composition

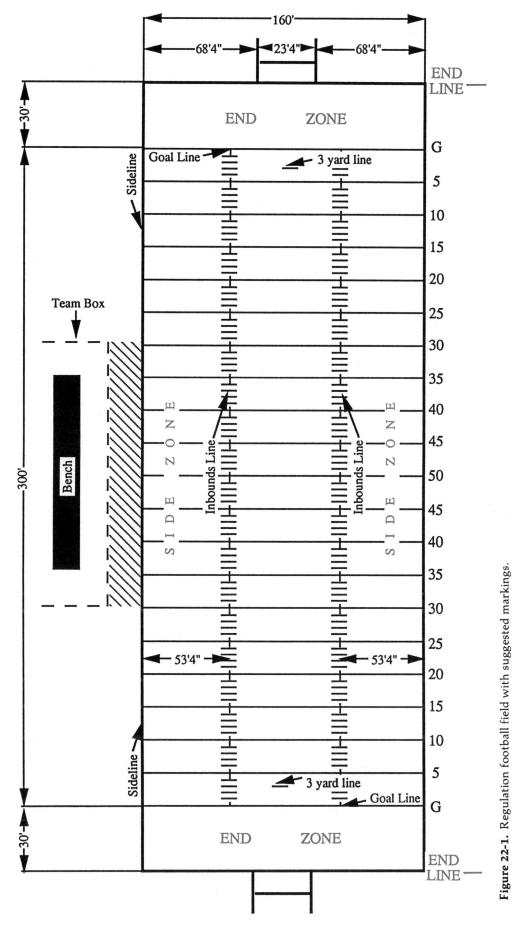

Figure 22-1. Regulation football field with suggested markings.

Note: Both team boxes may be on one side between the two 45- and 20-yard lines. End lines and sidelines should be at least 4 inches wide. Other field dimensions should be 4 inches wide.

Note: Recommend the area between team boxes and sidelines be solid white or marked with diagonal lines.

Note: Recommend the field slope from center to each sideline at 1/4-inch per foot.

Note: A 4-inch wide broken restraining line may be put around the entire field, 2 or more yards from boundaries.

without grooves other than those formed by the natural seams and the lace on one of the panels.

One set of either 8 or 12 evenly spaced laces. The length of the lace shall be confined within the outer extremities of the stripes.

Two 1-inch white stripes 3-3¾ inches from each end of the ball, measured to the nearest edge of the stripe.

The ball should conform to the shape and dimensions as shown in Figure 22-2. It should weigh between 14 and 15 ounces and be inflated to a pressure of 12½ to 13½ pounds.

Teams may use any legal ball approved by the referee during those downs in which it free kicks or snaps. If the field is wet, the referee may order the ball changed between downs.

The line-to-gain and the measurement of distances shall be accomplished with the use of a yardage chain joining 2 rods that are exactly 10 yards apart. A down marker to indicate the number of the down and a competent crew to operate this equipment shall be provided by the game management. The chain and down marker will be operated outside and within 6 feet of the sideline on one side of the field throughout the game. The yardage chain is not used when the line-to-gain is the goal line.

A game clock shall be provided by the home team. The operator shall be approved by the referee unless time is kept on the field by a designated official.

The Players

Each team shall designate a player as field captain and only he/she may communicate with officials. The captain's first choice of any of-

fered decision is final. Decisions involving penalties shall be made before any charged time-out is granted either team.

Figure 22-3 shows one of the offensive formations and the recommended numbering of players according to position. Each player shall be numbered 1 through 99 inclusive.

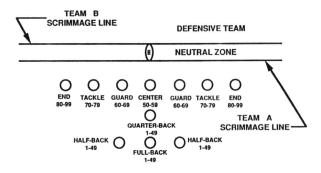

Figure 22-3. Diagram showing one of the offensive formations and the recommended numbering of players according to position. Each player shall be numbered using 1 through 99 inclusive.

The Player's Equipment

Each player shall wear:

A helmet that meets NOCSAE test standards and has a visible exterior warning label regarding the risk of injury. A chinstrap should properly secure the helmet.

Each helmet shall be equipped with a face protector (the multiple bar type is recommended). The face protector shall be made of nonbreakable material with rounded edges. Those constructed of metal shall have the surface covered with resilient material designed to prevent chipping, burrs, or abrasiveness that may endanger players.

Intraoral (within the mouth) mouth and tooth protectors shall include an occlusal (protecting and separating the biting surfaces) and a labial (protecting the lips) portion. The mouth protector should be constructed from a model made from an impression of the individual's teeth or constructed and fitted to the individual by impressing his/her teeth into the mouth and tooth protector itself.

Knees of players should be protected by soft knee pads at least ½-inch thick or ⅜-inch

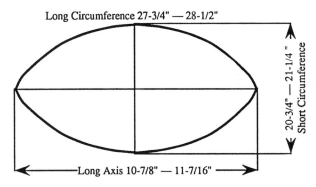

Figure 22-2. Dimensions of a regulation football.

thick if made of an approved shock-absorbing material.

Hip pads with tail bone protector should be worn by all players.

Shoulder pads, fully covered by a jersey, are required.

Thigh guards are also required equipment for all players.

Thigh and shin guards must have any hard surface covered with material such as closed-cell vinyl foam that has a minimum compression resistance of 4 to 8 pounds for 25 percent compression or other material with equivalent specifications and is at least ¼-inch thick on the outside surface and at least ⅜-inch thick on the inside surface and the overlap of the edge.

Other items of equipment include approved shoes, a jersey with Arabic block or modern Gothic numerals on the front and back, and pants that cover the knees.

The numbers on the jersey shall be at least 10 inches high in the back and 8 inches high in the front. The color of the number shall contrast with the jersey color and have numeral bars or strokes about 1½ inches wide.

Jerseys of opposing teams should be of contrasting colors. The home team shall wear its dark color and the visiting team its light color. Avoidance of similarity of colors is the responsibility of the visiting team, but if there is doubt, the referee may request the home team to change jerseys.

Any equipment that, in the opinion of the umpire, is dangerous or confusing shall not be permitted. The use of artificial limbs, that are no more dangerous to players than the corresponding human limb and do not place an opponent at a disadvantage may be used.

Equipment or substances that shall always be declared illegal include projecting metal or other hard substance on clothes or person; elbow, hand, wrist, or forearm guard or brace made of sole leather, plaster, metal, or other hard substance even though these devices may be covered with soft padding; knee braces made of hard unyielding material, unless hinges are covered on both sides and all of its edges overlapped. Any other hard substance across the front of the leg must be covered with at least ½-inch of closed-cell slow recovery rubber or other material of the same minimum thickness

and having similar physical properties. Also prohibited are forearm pads, hand pads, or gloves, unless sanctioned by the umpire as being made entirely of soft nonabrasive, nonhardening material which poses no danger to the wearer or other players.

Any tape or bandage on the hand or forearm, unless sanctioned by the umpire as being nonabrasive and necessary to protect an existing injury is not permitted. Nonhardening, nonabrasive tape or bandage (not to exceed three thicknesses) and sweatbands, when any of these are worn on the wrist beginning at the base of the thumb (proximal end of the metacarpal bone) and extending not more than 3 inches toward the elbow, may not be worn. Shin or thigh guards of any hard substance must have the outside surface and all edges covered with soft material at least ½-inch thick or ⅜-inch thick if made of an approved shock-absorbing material.

Shoes should meet the following specifications:

The shoe shall be made of canvas, leather, or synthetic attached to a firm sole of leather, rubber, or composition material that may have cleats that comply to specifications listed below, or which may be cleatless. Among the items that do not meet these requirements are gymnastic slippers, tennis shoes cut so low that protection is reduced, ski and logger boots, and other apparel not intended for football use.

Removable cleats that do not conform to the following specifications are not permitted. Cleats must be constructed of a material which does not chip or develop a cutting edge. Legal material includes leather, nylon, certain plastics, and rubber. The use of aluminum is not permissible. The base and the tip of the cleat must be parallel. The free end may be rounded in an arc with a radius of not less than ⁷⁄₁₆ inch provided the overall length is not more than ½ inch measured from the tip of the cleat to the shoe. A single toe cleat does not require a raised platform that extends across the width of the sole. The raised platform of the toe cleat is limited to ⁵⁄₃₂ inch or less. The ⁵⁄₃₂ inch platform is measured from the lowest part of the shoe's sole.

Exposure of the metal posts to which cleats

are fastened must be prevented by an effective locking device.

Players may not wear nonremovable cleats, studs, or other projection which exceed ½-inch in length, made with or that may develop a cutting edge or made with other than a non-abrasive rubber or rubber-type synthetic material.

Ball-colored helmets, jerseys, patches, or pads without stripes of contrasting colors may not be worn. Items of a reddish tan color or sleeves with stripes similar to those on the ball should not be purchased. Any transverse stripe on the sleeve below the elbow is illegal.

Players may not apply any slippery or sticky substance of a foreign nature on equipment or exposed part of the body.

Other illegal equipment includes plastic material covering protective pads whose edges are not rounded with a radius equal to ½ the thickness of the plastic, computers or any electronic or mechanical devices for communication, and tear-away jerseys.

The head coach shall be responsible for verifying to the referee that all of his/her players are equipped in compliance with these rules. Questions regarding legality of a player's equipment shall be determined by the umpire. If required player equipment is missing or when illegal equipment is found, correction must be made before the contest may begin or resume. An official's time-out shall be declared to permit prompt repair of equipment that becomes illegal or defective through use.

The required equipment shall be properly worn by all players while the ball is alive.

RULES GOVERNING SCORING PLAYS AND TOUCHBACKS

The game is won by the team that accumulates the most points. Points are scored as follows:

Touchdown	6 points
Field Goal	3 points
Safety—Points awarded to the opponent	2 points
Successful Try For Point	
a. After Touchdown	2 points
b. Field Goal or Safety	1 point

In Case of a Forfeited Game the Game Score is Offended Team . . . 1; Opponent . . . 0

If offended team is ahead at the time of the forfeit, that score stands.

Touchdown

A touchdown occurs when a runner advances from the field of play so that the ball touches the opponent's goal line (vertical plane).

A touchdown also occurs when a loose ball is caught or recovered by a player while the ball is on or behind his/her opponent's goal line, or when a backward pass or fumble is declared dead in the end zone of the opponent of such passer or fumbler while no player is in possession, other than because of an inadvertent whistle.

Try For Point

After a touchdown, the scoring team shall attempt a try for point during which the ball is snapped on the defensive team's 3-yard line anywhere between the inbounds lines. This involves a scrimmage down that is neither numbered nor timed.

The try for point begins when the ball is ready-for-play. It ends when either of the following occurs: the defensive team secures possession, it is apparent that a drop kick or placekick will not score, the try for point is successful, or the ball becomes dead for any other reason.

If during a successful try the offensive team incurs a loss of down foul, no points are scored and there is no replay.

If during a successful kick try, a foul by the defensive team occurs, the offensive team is given the choice of accepting the penalty and replaying the down following measurement, or of accepting the result of the play and enforcement of the penalty from the succeeding spot. If the defensive team fouls during a successful 2-point try, the penalty is automatically declined. If the offensive team fouls, the down may be replayed after measurement.

If the offensive team fouls during an unsuccessful try for point after touchdown, the penalty is obviously declined, the results of the play stand and there is no replay. If the defensive team fouls, the down is replayed after measurement.

If a double foul occurs, the down is replayed. When a try for point down is replayed, the snap may be from any point between the inbounds lines on the yard line through the spot of the ball.

After a try for point the defensive team shall designate which team will kick off.

Field Goals

A field goal may be scored in the following ways:

1. the field-goal attempt shall be a placekick or a drop kick from scrimmage, or from a free kick following a fair catch, or an awarded fair catch
2. the kick shall not touch any player of the kicking team beyond the neutral zone, or the ground before passing through the goal
3. the kick shall pass between the vertical uprights or the inside edges of the uprights extended and above the crossbar of the opponent's goal.

After a field goal, the opponent of the scoring team shall designate which team will kick off.

Definition of the Terms Force, Safety, and Touchback

Responsibility for forcing the ball from the field of play across a goal line is attributed to the player who carries, snaps, passes, fumbles, or kicks the ball. Muffing or batting of a pass, kick, or fumble in flight is not considered a new force, because the original force has not been spent.

A safety is scored when a runner carries the ball from the field of play to or across his/her own goal line, and it becomes dead there in his/her team's possession.

Exceptions to the previous rule occur when a defensive team player intercepts a forward pass or catches a scrimmage kick or free kick between his/her 5-yard line and the goal line and his/her original momentum carries him/her into the end zone where the ball is declared dead in his/her team's possession or it goes out-of-bounds in the end zone. In such situations the ball belongs to the defensive team at the spot where the pass was intercepted or the kick was caught.

Another exception to scoring a safety occurs when a player who is either in the field of play or in his/her end zone forces a loose ball from the field of play to or across his/her goal line by his/her kick, pass, fumble, snap, muff, or bat and provided the ball becomes dead there in his/her team's possession, or the ball is out-of-bounds when it becomes dead on or behind their goal line. This rule does not apply to a legal forward pass that has become incomplete.

A safety is not scored when a player on offense commits any foul for which the penalty is accepted and measurement is from a spot in his/her end zone; or throws an illegal forward pass from his/her end zone and the penalty is declined in a situation which leaves him/her in possession at the spot of the illegal pass and with the ball having been forced into the end zone by the passing team.

A touchback is scored when:

1. any scrimmage kick or free kick touches anything while the ball is on or behind the receiving team's goal line, unless a field goal is scored or unless the receiving team chooses a spot of first touching by the kicking team.
2. any scrimmage kick or free kick becomes dead on or behind the kicking team's goal line with the ball in possession of the kicking team and the force is the receiving team's muff or bat of the kick after it has touched the ground.
3. a fumble, or muff, or bat of a backward pass or a fumble after either has touched the ground is the force which sends the ball to or across the opponent's goal line and provided such opponent is in possession or the ball is out-of-bounds when it becomes dead on or behind its goal line.
4. a forward pass is intercepted in the defensive team's end zone and becomes dead there in the defensive team's possession.

The team whose goal line is involved shall put the ball in play anywhere between the inbounds lines on its 20-yard line by a snap after a touchback and by a free kick after a safety.

RULES GOVERNING SERIES OF DOWNS, NUMBER OF DOWN, AND TEAM POSSESSION AFTER PENALTY

Series of Downs

Four consecutive downs are awarded the team that next puts the ball in play by scrimmage following a free kick, touchback, or fair catch. Each awarded first down starts a new series of four downs.

When a scrimmage down ends with the ball in the field of play or out-of-bounds between the goal lines, a new series is awarded to Team A, if the ball belongs to A on or beyond the line-to-gain, or to Team B, if the ball belongs to B at the end of any down, and to Team B, if at the end of the fourth down, the ball belongs to A behind the line-to-gain. A new series of downs is awarded to the team in possession at the end of the down if there is a change of team possession during the down, unless the penalty is accepted for a foul that occurred before the change of possession. A new series of downs is awarded to Team R (the receiving team), if K (the kicking team) kicks during any scrimmage down and the ball is recovered by R or goes out-of-bounds. A new series of downs is awarded to the team in possession at the end of the down if the receiving team is the first to touch a scrimmage kick while it is beyond the neutral zone, unless the penalty is accepted for a foul that occurred before the kick ended.

The lost of down aspect of a penalty has no significance following a change of possession or if the line-to-gain is reached after enforcement.

When a free kick down ends with the ball in the field of play or out-of-bounds between the goal lines, a new series is awarded to the receiving team at the inbounds spot if the receiving team is the last to touch the kicked ball before it goes out-of-bounds. A new series of downs is awarded to the team in possession of the ball when the down ends if the ball is recovered beyond the receiving team's free kick line. A new series of downs is awarded to the receiving team at the spot of recovery if the kicking team recovers the kicked ball before it travels the 10 yards to the receiving team's free kick line and before the receiving team has touched the ball. A new series of downs is awarded to the receiving team at the spot of first touching by the kicking team if the kicking team is the first to touch the kicked ball before it has gone 10 yards. If the kickers recover a scrimmage kick in or behind the neutral zone that has not been touched first by the receiving team beyond the neutral zone, the ball belongs to the kicking team and the down counts.

Rules Governing Down and Possession After Penalty

When a penalty is declined, the number of the next down is the same as if the foul had not occurred. If a double foul occurs during a down, the number of the next down is the same as that of the down in which the foul occurred. After a distance penalty, the ball belongs to the team in possession at the time of the foul. Team possession may then change if a new series is awarded.

A series of downs end when, following a foul, any of the following occurs:

1. the acceptance of the penalty includes the award of a first down
2. acceptance or declination of any penalty leaves a team in possession beyond the line-to-gain
3. declination of any penalty leaves team B in possession of the ball
4. there is acceptance or declination of the penalty for any foul that occurs after team possession changes during the down, or after the receiving team is first to touch a scrimmage kick while it is beyond the neutral zone, unless the foul occurs before the kick ends and the penalty is accepted
5. acceptance of a penalty on fourth down which carries a loss of down leaves team A in possession behind the line-to-gain.

After a series of downs end, a new series with first and 10 yards to gain is awarded unless one of the following is involved: a try for point; a field goal; or a free kick after a safety or fair catch or awarded fair catch. The first down is awarded to the team in possession when the foul occurs unless declining the penalty leaves the other team in possession of the ball.

Descriptions of the Line-to-Gain and Measurements

The line-to-gain is established at the end of the down in which a new series is awarded and after considering the effect of any act that occurs during that down. The line-to-gain then remains fixed until the series ends and a new line-to-gain is established.

The referee may call for the linesman to bring the yardage chain or other measuring device on the field for a measurement. Measurement shall be parallel with the sideline and from a convenient yard line to the yard line through the foremost point of the ball when it became dead. The ball shall be placed with its long axis parallel with the sideline before measurement. The inside edge of the foremost rod marks the line-to-gain when the traditional yardage chain is used.

A measurement may be requested by the captain prior to the ball being declared ready-for-play, but it may be denied if, in the referee's opinion, it is obvious the line-to-gain has not been reached.

To start a new series of downs, the inside edge of the rod nearest the goal of the team that is to snap the ball is set on the yard line through the ball's foremost point. The foremost point of the ball at the time it became dead becomes the rear point when the direction of the offense is changed. After a fourth down incomplete forward pass, the ball is placed as it was at the start of the down. After a safety or touchback, the foremost point of the ball is placed on the 20-yard line

A ball touching the goal line plane, when it becomes dead is in the end zone, even though it is moving away from the nearer end line and has its foremost point in the field of play. When any kick is touched near the receiver's goal line, the ball becomes dead only if it is on or behind the goal line at the time it is touched. In doubtful cases, the ball should be considered behind the goal line.

RULES OF PLAY

Rules Governing Live and Dead Balls

A *live ball* indicates that the ball has been legally snapped or free kicked and that a down is in progress. *Dead ball* is a term used to indicate that it is a period between downs.

A ball in *player possession* is a ball held or controlled by a player after it has been handed or snapped, or after a player has caught or recovered it.

A *loose ball* is a pass or a fumble or a kick. A loose ball that has not yet touched the ground is in flight. A *grounded loose ball* is one which has touched the ground. Any loose ball continues to be a loose ball until a player secures possession of it or until it becomes dead, whichever occurs first.

Definitions of Blocking and Tackling

Blocking is obstructing an opponent by contacting him/her with any part of the blocker's body. Blocking by a player either on offense or defense is a legal act provided it is not fair catch interference, forward pass interference, a personal foul, or an illegal block.

During legal blocking, teammates of the runner may contact opponents with their arms or hands provided the elbows are entirely outside the shoulders, the hands are closed or cupped with the palms not facing the opponent, the forearms are approximately parallel to the ground, in the same horizontal plane, and extended no more than 45 degrees from the body.

The blocker's hands may not be locked nor may the blocker swing, throw, or flip the elbow or forearm so that it is moving faster than the blocker's shoulder at the time the elbow, forearm, or shoulder contacts the opponent. The blocker may not initiate contact with the arm or hand against an opponent above the opponent's shoulder, but the blocker may use the hand or arm to break a fall or to retain balance.

An offensive player may use his/her hands or arms as a runner, to ward off or push any player; during a kick, to ward off an opponent who is attempting to block him/her; to push or pull or ward off an opponent when the ball is loose if the offensive player may legally touch or possess the ball and such contact is not pass interference, a personal foul, or illegal use of hands.

A defensive player may use unlocked hands, a hand or an arm to ward off an opponent who is blocking him/her or is attempting to block him/her. He/she may push or pull the blocker out of the way in an actual attempt to get at the runner or a loose ball.

When a player on defense uses a hand or arm, the hand must be in advance of the elbow at the time of the contact. When a player pretends to be a runner, reasonable allowance may be made for failure of the defense to discover the deception. This does not cancel the responsibility of any defensive player to exercise reasonable caution in avoiding any unnecessary tackle.

Blocking below the waist is making initial contact below the waist against an opponent other than a runner. Blocking below the waist applies only when the opponent has one or both feet on the ground.

Butt blocking is a technique involving a blow with the face mask, frontal area, or top of the helmet driven directly into an opponent as the primary point of contact either in close line play or in the open field.

A *chop block* is a delayed block at the knees or below, against an opponent who is in contact with a teammate of the blocker in the free-blocking zone.

Tackling is the use of hands, arms, or body by a defensive player in his/her attempt to hold a runner or to bring him/her to the ground.

Face tackling is driving the face mask, frontal area, or top of the helmet directly into the runner.

Definitions of the Terms Catch, Fair Catch, Intercept, Recover

A *catch* is the act of acquiring player possession of a live ball in flight. Catching an opponent's fumble or pass is an *interception*. *Recovery* means securing possession of a live ball after it strikes the ground. If a player attempts a catch, or an interception, or a recovery while he/she is in the air, the ball must be in his/her possession when he/she first returns to the ground inbounds prior to touching out-of-bounds. Catching is always preceded by touching of the ball; thus, if touching causes the ball to become dead, securing possession of the ball has no significance.

A *fair catch* is a catch beyond the kicker's line and between the goal lines of any kick by a receiver under conditions in which the receiver forfeits the right to advance the ball in return for protection against being blocked or tackled by an opponent.

A *valid fair catch signal* is the extension and lateral waving of one arm only, at full arm's length above the head by any member of the receiving team.

An *invalid fair catch signal* is any signal given by a runner that does not meet the requirements of a valid signal. A fair catch signal is invalid after the kick has touched a receiver or after the kick has touched the ground.

An *illegal fair catch signal* is any signal given by a runner after the kick has been caught or after the kick has been recovered.

A *simultaneous catch or recovery* is a catch or recovery in which there is joint possession of a live ball by opposing players who are inbounds.

Definition of Clipping

Clipping is throwing the body across the back of the leg of an opponent or charging or falling into the back of an opponent who is not a runner or pretending to be a runner. Clipping shall not be assessed unless the official sees the initial contact. Doubtful cases involving a side block or the opponent turning his/her back to a blocker are to be judged according to whether the opponent was able to see or ward off the blocker.

The use of the hand or arm on the back is not clipping when it is for the purpose of warding off a blocker or when it is a legal attempt to catch or recover a loose ball which may be legally touched or possessed.

Other Definitions of Play

A *down* is action that starts with a legal snap (beginning a scrimmage down) or a free kick (beginning a free kick down) and that ends when the ball next becomes dead.

Encroachment is used to indicate that a player was illegally in the neutral zone.

Force is the result of energy exerted by a player that provides initial movement of the ball. The term *force* is used only in connection with the goal line and in only one direction, i.e., from the field of play into the end zone. Force may result from a carry, fumble, kick, pass, or snap. On kicks going into the receiver's end zone, force is not a factor because such kicks are always a touchback regardless of who supplied the force. After a backward pass, fumble, or kick has been grounded, a new force may result from a bat, an illegal kick, or a muff.

A *foul* is a rule infraction for which a penalty is prescribed. The following are types of fouls.

Player—a foul (other than unsportsmanlike) by a player in the game

Nonplayer or unsportsmanlike—a noncontact foul during the down that does not involve illegal participation and does not influence the play in progress

Double—one or more live ball fouls (other than unsportsmanlike) committed by each team at such a time that the penalties offset each other

Multiple—two or more live ball fouls (other than unsportsmanlike) committed by the same team at such a time that the offended team is permitted a choice of penalties

Players, coaches, administrators and officials should remember that no foul causes loss of the ball, nor does a live ball foul cause the ball to become dead. Game situations that produce results somewhat similar to penalties, but that are not classified as fouls are: disqualification of a player; first touching of a kick by a member of the kicking team; non-completion of a forward pass; and forfeiture of a game.

The *free-blocking zone* is a rectangular area extending laterally four yards on either side of the spot of the snap and three yards behind each scrimmage line. While in the free-blocking zone an offensive player who is stationary at the snap and any defensive player may contact an opponent below the waist on his/her initial charge provided all players involved in the contact were in the free-blocking zone at the snap, and that the contact is in the free-blocking zone.

Blocking from the rear is not clipping when the contact is in the free-blocking zone, the offensive blocker is on his/her line of scrimmage and is in the free-blocking zone at the snap, and the opponent is in the free-blocking zone at the snap. Blocking from the rear by a defensive player is illegal except to tackle the runner or a player pretending to be a runner.

The free-blocking zone disintegrates and the right to block below the waist and/or clip during close line play is not to continue after the initial line charge, or after the position of the ball is established, or the ball has left the zone.

Definitions of a Fumble, Muff, Bat, and Touch

A *fumble* is any loss of player possession other than by kicking, passing, or handing.

A *muff* is the touching of a loose ball by a player in an unsuccessful attempt to secure possession. A muff includes an accidental kick.

Batting is the intentional slapping or striking with the arm, hand, leg, or knee of a loose ball except in a legal kick, or a ball in player possession by a player of the team in possession.

Touching refers to any contact with the ball either by touching it or being touched by it.

A *goal line* is the vertical plane that separates the field of play from the end zone. When related to a live ball in a runner's possession while the ball is over the out-of-bounds area, the goal line includes the extension beyond the sidelines. A team's *own goal line* is the one it is defending.

Handing the ball is transferring player possession from one player to a teammate in such a way that the ball is still in contact with the first player when it is touched by the teammate. Passing does not constitute handling the ball.

Hurdling is an attempt by a player to jump with one or both feet with knees foremost over a player who is still on his/her feet.

Definition of the Terms Kicker and Kicks

The *kicker* is one who punts, drop kicks, or placekicks the football. This player continues to be the kicker until he/she has had reasonable opportunity to regain his/her balance.

A *placekick* is a legal kick made while the ball is in a fixed position on the ground or on a *pliable tee* that elevates the lowest point of the ball two inches or less above the ground. No material or device may be placed on the ground to improve the kicker's footing. The ball may be held in position by a *placekick holder* who shall be any teammate of the kicker.

A *punt* is a legal kick by a player who drops the ball and kicks it before it touches the ground.

A *drop kick* is a legal kick by a player who drops the ball and kicks it when it touches the ground or as it is rising.

A *kick* ends when a player gains possession or when the ball becomes dead.

Kicks—Kickoff and Free Kicks

A *free kick* is a kick that puts the ball in play to start a free kick down, during which each player of the kicking team other than the kicker and holder for a placekick must be behind his/her free kick line.

A free kick is used for the kickoff and for a kick following a safety. A free kick is also used if a free kick is chosen following a fair catch or awarded fair catch. Either a drop kick or a place-kick may be used for the kickoff and for a kick following a fair catch or awarded fair catch. A safety may be followed by a drop kick, place-kick, or punt.

A *kickoff* is a free kick that puts the ball in play at the beginning of each half of the game, after a successful field goal, and after any try for point.

Kicks—Scrimmage and Formations

A *scrimmage kick* is any legal kick from behind the offense's scrimmage line.

A *scrimmage kick formation* is a formation where at least one player is seven yards or more behind the neutral zone and no player is in position to receive a hand-to-hand snap from between the snapper's legs.

Other Definitions of the Rules of Play

The *scrimmage line* for each team is a vertical plane through the point of the ball nearest the team's goal line. The scrimmage line is determined when the ball is ready-for-play and remains until the official gives the next ready-for-play signal.

An *offensive player* is on the line of scrimmage when facing an opponent's goal line with the line of his/her shoulders approximately parallel thereto and with his/her head breaking the plane of an imaginary line drawn through

the waistline of the snapper and parallel to the line of scrimmage.

An offensive player on the line of scrimmage may stand, crouch, or kneel. At the snap, both feet shall be outside the outside foot of any adjacent player other than the snapper. The snapper and the offensive linemen next to the snapper may lock legs.

An *offensive back* (except for the player under the snapper) is in the backfield, provided his/her head does not break the plane of an imaginary line drawn parallel to the line of scrimmage through the waistline of the nearest teammate who is legally on the line.

A *defensive player* is on his/her line of scrimmage when he/she is within one yard of his/her scrimmage line at the snap of the ball.

The *line-to-gain* is the yard line established when a new series (first down) occurs. Unless there is a penalty, the line-to-gain is 10 yards in advance of the foremost point of the ball when placed for first down. If the 10 yards extend into the end zone, the *goal line* is the line-to-gain.

Definition of Neutral Zone

The neutral zone is the space between the two free kick lines during a free kick and between the two scrimmage lines during a scrimmage down. The neutral zone is established when the ball is placed in the ready-for-play position.

The neutral zone may be expanded following the snap up to a maximum of two yards behind the defensive line of scrimmage during any scrimmage down.

Definition of Out-of-Bounds

A player is *out-of-bounds* when any part of him/her touches anything (other than another player or game official) that is on or outside the sideline (or end line).

A ball in player possession is out-of-bounds when the runner or the ball touches anything (other than another player or game official) that is on or outside a sideline or end line.

A *loose ball* is out-of-bounds when it touches anything (including a player or game official) that is out-of-bounds. *Exception:* A kicked ball is not immediately dead if on a field goal try, it touches a goal post or crossbar and caroms through the goal.

Definition of Passing the Ball

Passing the ball is throwing it. In a pass, the ball travels in flight. The ball's initial direction determines whether a pass is forward or backward. A pass ends when it is caught or not caught, touches the ground, or is out-of-bounds.

A *passer* is a player who throws a forward pass. He/she continues to be a passer until the pass ends or until he/she moves to participate in the play.

A *forward pass* is a pass thrown toward the opponents end line.

A *backward pass* is a pass thrown parallel with or toward the passer's end line.

A *runner* is the player who is in possession of a live ball or simulating possession of a live ball.

Scrimmage is the action of the two teams during a down which begins with a snap.

A *shift* is the action of one or more offensive players who, after a huddle or after taking set positions, move to a new set position before the ensuing snap.

A *snap* is the legal act of passing or handing the ball backward from its position on the ground. The snap begins when the snapper first moves the ball legally other than in adjusting it for snapping. In a *legal snap*, the movement must be a quick and continuous motion of the hand or hands during which the ball actually leaves the hand or hands of the snapper and touches a backfield player or the ground before it touches a lineman. The snap ends when the ball touches the ground or any player. The player who snaps the ball (usually the center) is the *snapper*.

Spearing is the intentional use of the helmet in an attempt to punish an opponent.

The *spot of a player foul* is where the foul occurs. If a player foul occurs out-of-bounds and during a down, the spot of the foul is at the intersection of the inbounds line and the yard line (extended) on which the foul occurs.

A *nonplayer or unsportsmanlike foul* is treated as a dead ball foul, and is administered from the succeeding spot.

Tripping is the use of the lower leg or foot to obstruct an opponent other than a runner below the knees.

Definitions of Players and Teams

The *offense* is the team that is in possession of the ball. At such time, the opponent is the *defense.*

A *player* is one of the 22 team members who is designated to start either half of the game or who replaces another player. A player continues to be a player until a substitute enters the field and indicates to the player that he/she is replaced.

A *substitute* is a team member who may replace a player. He/she becomes a player when he/she legally enters the field and indicates to a player that he/she is replaced.

A *replaced player* is one who has been notified by a substitute that he/she is to leave the field.

A *disqualified player* is a player barred from further participation in a game.

A *nonplayer* is a coach, trainer or other attendant, or a substitute who does not participate by touching the ball, hindering an opponent, or influencing the play.

DEFINITIONS OF PERIODS OF PLAY, TIME, AND SUBSTITUTIONS

Periods of Play

The game of football shall be administered with periods and intermissions as indicated in Table 22-1. If, at the end of the fourth period, the teams have identical scores, the tie may be resolved in any method that has been approved. This may include the extension of playing time.

The officials shall assume authority for the contest 30 minutes prior to the scheduled game time, or as soon thereafter as they are able to be present.

A period or periods may be shortened in any emergency by agreement of the opposing coaches and the referee. By mutual agreement of the opposing coaches and the referee, any remaining period may be shortened at any time. Games interrupted because of events beyond the control of the responsible administrative authorities shall be continued from the point of

Table 22-1. Suggested time intervals for the football game.

Period of Timing	Clock Time		
	Intermediate	7-8 Grade	5-6 Grade
First Half:			
1st period	12 minutes	8 minutes	6 minutes
Intermission for changing goals	1 minute	1 minute	1 minute
2nd period	12 minutes	8 minutes	6 minutes
Intermission			
When Teams Leave Field	15-20 minutes	10-15 minutes	10-15 minutes
15 minutes is normal. It may be increased to a maximum of 20 minutes **for special halftime activities** provided opponents have been properly notified prior to the game.			
Mandatory Warm-Up Activity	3 minutes	3 minutes	3 minutes
(The head coach is responsible for his/her team being on the field for mandatory warm-up at the end of the halftime intermission.)			
Second Half:			
3rd period	12 minutes	8 minutes	6 minutes
Intermission for changing goals	1 minute	1 minute	1 minute
4th period	12 minutes	8 minutes	6 minutes
10-Yard Line Overtime Periods	Untimed	No Playoff of Ties	
Note: Charged Time-outs	1 minute	1 minute	1 minute

interruption unless the teams agree otherwise, or there are conference, league, or state association rules that govern such situations.

When weather conditions are construed to be hazardous to life or limb of the participants, the officials are authorized to delay or suspend the game.

The referee shall have authority to correct obvious errors in timing if discovery is prior to the second live ball following the error.

Starting Each Period

A kickoff begins each half of a game. Prior to the start of a game the referee, in the presence of the field captains, shall toss a coin after designating which captain shall call the outcome of the toss. The winner of the toss shall have first choice of options for either the first or second half. The loser shall have the first choice of options for the half the winner of the toss did not select. The options for each half shall be to choose whether his/her team will kick or receive or to choose the goal his/her team will defend.

The captain not having the first choice of options for a half shall exercise the remaining option.

Between the first and second and between the third and fourth periods, the teams shall change goals. However, the team possession, the number of the next down, the relative position of the ball, and the line-to-gain remain unchanged.

Defining When/How Periods End

Approximately four minutes before the end of each half, the referee shall notify the field captains and their coaches of the time remaining. If time is not out, the referee shall order the clock stopped while notifying the teams. If an electric field clock is the official timepiece, no notification is required.

If time for any period expired during a down, play shall continue until the down ends. No time signal shall be sounded while the ball is alive.

A period must be extended by an untimed down, (except for unsportsmanlike or nonplayer fouls) if, during the last timed down, one of the following occurred:

a. there was a foul by either team and the penalty is accepted, unless it is a defensive foul during a down which results in a score other than a safety

b. there was a double foul

c. there was an inadvertent whistle and the down is to be replayed

If a dead ball foul occurs after time expires for any period, the penalty shall be measured from the succeeding spot.

If a touchdown was scored, the try for point is attempted as part of the same period.

Time-Outs and Intermission

A team has three time outs during each half of a regulation game. Unused first half time-outs may not be used in the second half or in overtime.

A charged team time-out occurs when the ball is dead and:

a. a player's request is legally granted
b. the repair of faulty player equipment requires the assistance of a team attendant or attendants, or which, without the assistance of a team attendant delays the ready-for-play signal for more than 25 seconds
c. a time-out is requested and granted for the purpose of reviewing an official's application of a rule that may have been misapplied or misinterpreted. If no change in the ruling results, the time-out remains charged to the requesting team.

Charged time-outs are of one minute duration. Charged time-outs shall be reduced in length only if both teams are ready to play prior to the 25-second ready-for-play signal by the referee.

The referee shall notify the teams within five seconds after the time-out expires and shall declare the ball ready-for-play.

Successive charged time-outs may be granted during the same dead ball period. An official's time-out may follow a charged time-out if it is for the continuance of a coach-official conference, or if a safety factor is involved. The captain and coach should be notified when a team's permissible charged time-outs during a half have been used.

Requests for subsequent timeouts after a team has used its permissible charged time-outs shall be denied unless they are for (1) an injured player who is identified when the request is made, (2) necessary repair to a player's equip-

ment, or (3) the review of a possible misapplication or misinterpretation of a rule.

When the Ball is Ready-For-Play

An official's time out is assessed in the following situations.

(1) If a request for an injured or improperly equipped player is granted, or (2) if the referee erroneously grants a time-out to which a team is not entitled, or (3) if an official alters a ruling following a properly called conference with a coach. If repair of faulty equipment without the assistance of a team attendant delays the ready-for-play signal for more than 25 seconds, or requires the assistance of a team attendant(s), the player must be replaced for at least one down.

A one minute time-out is allowed during the intermission between the first and second period and the third and fourth period and following a try for point, successful field goal, or safety, and prior to the succeeding free kick. Such time-out is not charged to either team.

An official's time-out occurs when, without any time-out being charged to either team, an official orders the clock stopped or to remain stopped for the following reasons:

- following a change of team possession
- after a foul, to administer the penalty
- to dry or change the game ball
- when a first down is declared
- for any unusual delay in getting the ball ready-for-play
- when captains and coaches are notified of the time remaining
- for a player in need of equipment repair
- for a player who appears to be injured
- when a coach-referee conference concerning the possible misapplication of a rule results in the referee altering his ruling
- for measurement of a possible first down

An official's time-out shall be taken as soon as the ball becomes dead following a change of team possession or whenever the covering official declares the ball dead and it appears to him/her the ball has reached the line-to-gain.

A time-out occurs when an injured or apparently injured player is discovered by the official while the ball is dead and the clock is stopped and for whom the ready-for-play signal is delayed, or for whom the clock is stopped. In such instances the injured player shall be replaced for at least one down unless the halftime or overtime intermission occurs. This time-out, if not charged, is an official's time-out.

Another situation in which a time out occurs is when an unconscious or apparently unconscious player is determined by the game officials. The player may not return to play in the game without written authorization from a physician. This time-out, if not charged, is an official's time-out.

A player, directed by his/her coach, may request and be granted a time-out for the purpose of the coach and the referee reviewing a decision that may have resulted from misapplication or misinterpretation of a rule, provided the request is made prior to the time the ball becomes alive following the play to be reviewed. When a time-out is so granted, the referee will confer with the coach at the sideline in front of his/her team box outside the field of play. If the conference results in the referee altering his/her ruling, the opposing coach will be notified, the revision made, and the time-out shall be an official's time-out. If the referee's original ruling prevails, the time-out remains charged to the team requesting the time-out for the conference.

Delay When the Ball is Ready-For-Play

When the referee gives the ready-for-play signal the ball is ready for play. The 25-seconds begins at that moment.

Action or inaction that prevents promptness in putting the ball in play is **delay of game.** Delay of game includes failure to snap or free kick within 25 seconds after the ball is ready-for-play; unnecessarily carrying the ball after it has become dead or consuming time in failing to unpile at the end of a down; a coach-referee conference after all the permissible charged time-outs for the coach's team have been used, and during which the referee is requested to reconsider the application of a rule and no change in the ruling results; failure of players to properly wear legal or required equipment when the ball is about to become alive; and any other conduct which unduly prolongs the game

When a team attempts to conserve or consume time illegally, the referee shall order the clock started or stopped. Failure of a team to play within two minutes after being ordered to do so by the referee shall result in forfeiture of the game.

Substitutions

No substitute shall enter during a down.

Any number of eligible substitutes may replace players between downs provided the substitutions are completed by having the replaced players off the field before the ball becomes alive. A replaced player, or a substitute who has been unable to complete the substitution, is required to leave the field at the side on which his/her team box is located and go directly to his/her team box.

No substitute shall become a player and then withdraw during the same dead ball interval. No player shall withdraw and reenter as a substitute unless a dead ball foul occurs, or there is a charged time-out or a period ends.

A replaced player or substitute who attempts unsuccessfully to leave the field during a down and who does not participate in nor affect the play, constitutes an illegal substitution.

SNAPPING, HANDING, AND PASSING THE BALL

Rules that Apply Before the Snap

No player shall encroach on the neutral zone after the ball is ready-for-play by touching the ball or an opponent or by being in or beyond the neutral zone. After the snapper has made his/her final adjustment of the ball, it is encroachment for any player to break the plane of the neutral zone, except for the snapper's right to be over the ball. When over the ball, the snapper shall have his/her feet behind his/her line and no part of his/her person other than a hand or hands on the ball may be beyond the foremost point of the ball.

No false start shall be made by any player on the offensive team after the ball is ready-for-play and before the snap. A false start occurs if a shift or feigned charge simulates action of the snap, any act that is clearly intended to cause an opponent to encroach, or any offensive player on his/her line between the snapper and the player on the end of his/her line, after having placed a hand(s) on or near the ground, moves his/her hand(s) or makes any quick movement unless the movement is caused by an irregularity such as calling all players off the line for receiving a new signal or a defensive player stepping into the neutral zone too soon. If the false start causes the defensive team to encroach, only the false start is penalized.

The snapper may make preliminary adjustment of the ball before assuming his/her set position and before the offensive linemen have assumed positions on their line. These preliminary adjustments by the snapper include lifting the ball slightly for lateral rotation without moving the location of the ball but may not involve rotating the nose of the ball end for end; tilting the ball; removing his/her hand(s) from the ball.

The snapper, after gripping the ball following preliminary adjustment, and prior to the snap and with the ball resting on the ground with the long axis at right angles to the line of scrimmage, may not fail to clearly pause before the snap, remove both hands or slide his/her hand(s) along the ball, make any movement that simulates a snap, and lift or move the ball in other than a legal snap.

An illegal snap or other infractions of the snap cause the ball to remain dead.

Rules Governing Position and Action at the Snap

Prior to the snap the player numbering requirements include having at least seven offensive players, five of whom must be numbered 50-79 on their line at the snap. Defensive players may be anywhere on or behind their line. Exceptions to this rule are: during the down in which the offensive team sets or shifts into a scrimmage kick formation, any offensive team player number 1-49 or 80-99 may replace and take the position of linemen numbered 50-79. A player in the game under this exception must assume an initial position on his/her line of scrimmage between the ends, This player remains an ineligible receiver during the down.

Not more than one offensive player may be in motion at the snap and then only if such motion is not toward his/her opponents— goal line. Except for the player under the snapper, the player in motion shall be at least five yards behind his/her line at the snap if he/she started from any position not clearly behind the line and did not establish him/herself as a backfield player by stopping for at least one full second while no part of his/her body is intersecting the vertical plane through the waistline of his/her nearest teammate who is on the line.

Before the ball is snapped all eleven players of the offensive team shall come to an absolute stop and shall remain stationary simultaneously without movement of hands, feet, head, or body for at least one second.

A legal snap requires that the ball leave the hand or hands of the snapper and touch a backfield player or the ground before it touches an offensive lineman. Each scrimmage down must start with a legal snap. An illegal snap causes the ball to remain dead.

The player on each side of and next to the snapper may lock legs with the snapper, but any other offensive lineman must have both feet outside the outside foot of the player next to him/her at the snap.

Handing the Ball

Any player may hand the ball backward at any time.

During a free kick down, no player may hand the ball forward to a teammate.

During a scrimmage down, an offensive player may not hand the ball forward in or beyond the neutral zone. However, the ball may be handed forward behind the neutral zone only to any lineman who has clearly faced his/her goal line by moving both feet in a half-turn and is at least one yard behind his/her line when he/she receives the ball, or to a teammate who, at the snap, was behind his/her line or on an end of his/her line and was not the snapper nor adjacent to the snapper.

During a scrimmage down after a change of team possession, no player may hand the ball forward to a teammate.

The Fumble and Backward Pass

Any player in possession of the ball may make a backward pass or may lose player possession through a fumble. If a fumble or a backward pass is caught or recovered by any player, he/she may advance the ball.

If a fumble or a backward pass goes out-of-bounds between the goal lines or becomes dead inbounds while no player is in possession or while opponents are in joint possession, the ball belongs to the passing or fumbling team unless lost after fourth down. If a fumble or a backward pass is out-of-bounds behind a goal line, the ball belongs to the team defending that goal and the result is either a touchback or a safety.

Definition of Forward Passes

A legal forward pass is defined as a ball thrown during a scrimmage down and before team possession has changed by a player on the offensive team who has both feet in or behind the neutral zone when the ball is released. More than one forward pass may be thrown during the down.

Illegal forward passes are defined as follows:

1. a pass thrown from beyond the neutral zone
2. a pass that is purposely incomplete or thrown into an area not occupied by an eligible offensive receiver to save loss of yardage
3. a pass caught, batted, or muffed by an ineligible receiver who is in or behind the neutral zone
4. a pass after team possession has changed during the down.

A forward pass (legal or illegal) is complete and the ball may be advanced when caught by any player of the offensive or defensive team. If a forward pass is caught simultaneously by two opponents, the ball becomes dead and belongs to the passing team.

A forward pass, legal or illegal, is incomplete and the ball becomes dead when the pass touches the ground or goes out-of-bounds. A forward pass is also incomplete when a player in the air possesses the pass and alights so that his/her first contact with the ground or with anything other than a player or game official is on or outside a boundary. When an incompletion occurs, the down counts unless the pass is after a series has ended. If the incomplete pass is legal, the passing team next snaps the ball

Table 22-2. Descriptions of the forward pass.

Legal Forward Pass	Illegal Forward Pass (Ball Remains Alive Until Declared Dead by Rule)
From in or behind the neutral zone.	a. From a point beyond the neutral zone.
	b. Purposely incompleted.
	c. Caught, batted, or muffed by an ineligible receiver.
	d. After team possession has changed during the down.

Completed Forward Pass	Incomplete Forward Pass
a. Pass caught by the passer's eligible or ineligible receiver; ball remains alive. (Acceptance of a penalty may nullify the catch by the ineligible receiver.)	a. Pass which touches the ground.
b. Any intercepted pass; ball remains alive.	b. Pass which goes out-of-bounds.
c. Pass simultaneously caught by opponents; ball becomes dead.	c. Pass tossed by a player who is in the air, but first touches the ground out-of-bounds.
	Ball becomes dead in all of these cases.

(unless lost after fourth down) at the spot of the previous snap.

If the penalty for an illegal pass is accepted, measurement is from the spot of such pass. If the offended team declines the distance penalty, it has the choice of having the down counted at the spot of the illegal incomplete pass; or if the illegal pass is caught or intercepted, of having the ball put in play as determined by the action that followed the catch.

The following players are eligible to receive a forward pass.

1. Each offensive player who, at the snap, was on an end or legally behind his/her scrimmage line. A possible total of six players, numbered 1-49 or 80-99, are eligible to receive forward passes.
2. After the defensive team touches the pass, all offensive players then become eligible.
3. All defensive team players are eligible to receive forward passes.
4. A player who is eligible at the start of the down remains eligible throughout the down.

No player on the offensive or defensive

team shall interfere with an eligible opponent beyond the neutral zone during a legal forward pass play. For the offensive team, this restriction begins at the time of the snap, and for the defensive team, when the ball leaves the passer's hand. The restriction does not apply if the pass does not cross the neutral zone. Interference occurs if any player on the offensive or defensive team is beyond the neutral zone and interferes with an eligible opponent's opportunity to move toward, catch, or bat the ball. It is also interference if an ineligible offensive team player touches a forward pass beyond the neutral zone before a player of the defensive team has touched it. If there is more than one legal forward pass, the restrictions end when the last pass has been touched by the defensive team.

The following situations are exceptions to the rules on interference. Interference does not occur if:

1. Unavoidable contact occurs when two or more eligible receivers are making a simultaneous attempt to move toward, catch, or bat the ball.
2. The ball has been touched by the defensive team.
3. The ball has been touched by the offensive team. In this situation restrictions end for eligible offensive and all defensive players.
4. The ball has been touched by the offensive team. Ineligible offensive players may not use their hands or arms other than in a legal block to ward off an opponent, because they may not legally touch the ball.
5. In both (3) and (4), if there is more than one legal forward pass. The restrictions for the defensive team end when the first pass is touched, but restriction for the offensive team end when the last pass is touched.
6. Contact by the offensive team is immediately made on a defensive team lineman and the contact does not continue beyond the expanded neutral zone.

An ineligible offensive player is illegally downfield on a legal forward pass play if he/she has gone beyond the neutral zone before any legal forward pass (or the last pass if there is more than one), which goes beyond the neutral zone, is thrown. An ineligible receiver is not illegally downfield if, at the snap, he/she immediately contacts a defensive lineman and the contact does not continue beyond the expanded neutral zone.

DEFINITIONS OF BALL IN PLAY, DEAD BALL AND OUT-OF-BOUNDS

Putting the Ball in Play

The ball shall be put in play by a kickoff to start each half and to resume play after a field goal or after a try for point.

A free kick shall also put the ball in play after a safety, when a free kick down is replayed, and when a free kick is chosen following a fair catch, or an awarded fair catch, or the replay of a down that follows a fair catch or an awarded fair catch.

A snap shall put the ball in play when a free kick is not specified. A snap or free kick shall be started between the inbounds lines.

If a snap or free kick is attempted before the ball is ready-for-play, or there is an illegal snap or other infraction of the rules governing snapping, the ball remains dead.

Definition of a Dead Ball and End of the Down

An official shall cause the ball to remain dead by sounding a whistle immediately when a foul occurs before a snap or free kick. The ball becomes dead and the down is ended when a runner goes out-of-bounds, or is held so his/her forward progress is stopped, or allows any part of his/her person other than hand or foot to touch the ground.

Exceptions to the dead ball rules are as follows:

The ball remains alive if, at the snap, a placekick holder with his/her knee(s) on the ground and with a teammate in kicking position catches or recovers the snap while his/her knee(s) is on the ground and places the ball for a kick, or if he/she rises to advance, hand, kick, or pass the ball, or if the holder rises and catches an errant snap and immediately returns his/her knee(s) to the ground and places the ball for a kick or again rises to advance, hand kick, or pass the ball. However, the ball becomes dead if the placekick holder fumbles or muffs the snap

Table 22-3. Summary of rules relating to the forward pass.

Legal Forward Pass	Penalty	Enforcement Spot
1. Illegal Forward Pass		
a. Pass after team possession has changed.	Loss of 5	
b. Pass from beyond the neutral zone.	Loss of 5	
c. Pass purposely incompleted.	And	End Of Run
d. Pass caught, batted, or muffed by ineligible receiver in or behind the neutral zone.	Loss of Down	
2. Forward Pass Interference		
Restriction applies only to a pass which crosses the neutral zone and interference may occur only beyond the neutral zone.		
a. Ineligible offensive team touches the pass beyond the neutral zone before the pass touches the defensive team.	Loss of 15 and Loss of Down	Previous Spot
b. Offensive team hinders defensive team (restriction begins with the snap of the offensive team).		
c. Defensive team hinders offensive team (restriction begins with the snap of the offensive team).	Loss of 15 and "Automatic" 1st Down for Offensive Team	
d. Intentional pass interference.	Additional 15 Yards	Succeeding Spot
3. Ineligible Receiver Downfield		
Ineligible offensive player illegally advances across the neutral zone before the pass which crosses the neutral zone is in flight.	Loss of 5	Previous Spot

and recovers after his/her knees have been off the ground, and he/she then touches the ground with other than hand or foot while in possession of the ball.

The ball also becomes dead and the down is ended when a live ball goes out-of-bounds, when any forward pass (legal or illegal) is incomplete or is simultaneously caught by opposing players, and when any legal kick (scrimmage or free) touches anyone or anything while the kicked ball is on or behind the receiver's goal line (plane). An exception to this rule occurs if a drop kick or placekick from scrimmage, or a free kick following a fair catch or awarded fair catch, touches an upright or crossbar or a player on the receiving team in the end zone and caroms through the goal. In such a situation the touching is ignored, and the attempt or try is considered successful.

The ball is dead and the down is ended when any loose ball is simultaneously caught or recovered by opposing players, when a loose ball is on the ground motionless and no player attempts to secure possession of it or when any loose ball touches, or is touched by anything inbounds other than a player, an official, the ground or authorized equipment. If any of the previous situations occur the ball will be put in play in accordance with the procedure for an inadvertent whistle.

The ball is dead and the down ends in the following situations:

a. when the kickers catch or recover any free kick anywhere
b. when the kickers catch or recover a scrimmage kick beyond the neutral zone
c. when the kickers are first (i.e., before any touching by the receivers) to touch a scrimmage kick after it has come to rest beyond the neutral zone and between the goal lines

The ball is dead and the down ends in the following situations: following a valid or invalid fair catch signal given by any member of the receiving team when the kick is caught or recovered by any member of the receiving team, when a touchdown or field goal occurs, during a try for point if the defensive team secures possession or as soon as it is apparent that a kick has failed to score, and when an official sounds his/her whistle inadvertently.

Rules Governing an Inadvertent Whistle

If an inadvertent whistle occurs while a legal forward pass or snap is in flight, or during a legal kick, the down shall be replayed. If an inadvertent whistle blows while the ball is loose following a backward pass, fumble, illegal forward pass, or illegal kick, the team last in possession may choose to put the ball in play where possession was lost, or replay the down. If an inadvertent whistle occurs while the ball is in player possession, that team may choose to accept the play at that point, or replay the down.

Rules Governing Out-of-Bounds and Inbounds Spots

When the out-of-bounds spot is between the goal lines, the ball shall be put in play at the inbounds spot unless a forward pass is involved. If the out-of-bounds spot is behind a goal line, it is a safety, field goal, or touchback. If the ball touches a pylon, it is out-of-bounds behind the goal line.

When a runner goes out-of-bounds, the inbounds spot is fixed by the yard line through the foremost point of the ball at the time the runner crossed the plane of the sideline.

When the ball becomes dead in a side zone or is awarded to a team there or is left there by a penalty, play is resumed at the inbounds spot. This rule does not apply to an incomplete forward pass, a replayed try for point, or a free kick or snap which follows a fair catch or awarded fair catch in a side zone.

In the case of an uncompleted forward pass, the ball is returned to the spot of the snap if the pass is legal, and to the spot of the pass if it is illegal.

Whenever a team may designate the spot along the proper yard line from which the ball is to be put in play, it shall have the same privilege if the down is to be replayed or a dead ball foul occurs.

RULES GOVERNING KICKING THE BALL AND FAIR CATCHES

The Kickoff and Other Free Kicks

A free kick line corresponding to a scrimmage line is established for each team during any free kick. These lines are always 10 yards apart. Unless moved by a penalty, in interscholastic play the kicker's free kick line is its 40-yard line for a kickoff; its 20-yard line after a safety; the yard line through the spot of the catch after a fair catch; and the yard line through the spot of an awarded fair catch.

A free kick shall be made from any point between the inbounds lines and on the kicker's free kick line. Once designated, the kicker must kick from that spot. When a punt is used following a safety, the ball must be kicked within one step behind the kicker's free kick line. The referee has authority to move the ball to a playable line if the ball is in an unplayable spot on the field; in which case, both free kick lines are moved to compensate.

A free kick infraction occurs if at least five of the receiving team's players are not within five yards of their free kick line after the ball is declared ready-for-play and until it is kicked.

After the ball is ready for play and until it is kicked, it is encroachment for any player other than the kicker and the holder for a placekick to be beyond the free kick line.

Any receiver may catch or recover a free kick in the field of play and advance, unless any member of the receiving team has given a valid or invalid fair catch signal.

If any kicker recovers or catches a free kick, the ball becomes dead. It belongs to him/her unless fair catch interference occurs and the receiver chooses an awarded fair catch or unless first touching occurs. The kickers may recover the ball before it goes beyond the receiver's free kick line if it is touched first by any receiver. Any kicking team member may recover a free kick if it has both touched the ground and gone beyond the plane of the receiver's free kick line. These two requirements may occur in any order. The ball is awarded to the receivers if a free kick becomes dead inbounds between the goal lines while no player is in possession, or inbounds anywhere while opponents are in joint possession.

"First touching of the kick" occurs if any kicker touches a free kick before it crosses the receiver's free kick line and before it is touched there by any receiving player. Receivers may take the ball at the spot of first touching, or any spot if there is more than one spot of first touching, or they may choose to have the ball put in play as determined by the action which follows first touching. The right of the receiver to take the ball at the spot of first touching by the kicker is canceled if the receiver touches the kick and thereafter during the down commits a foul or if the penalty is accepted for any foul committed during the down.

A free kick is not repeated unless a foul occurs prior to a change of possession and the penalty is accepted or if there is a double foul.

A foul has occurred if a free kick that goes out-of-bounds between the goal lines is untouched inbounds by the receivers, or not last touched inbounds by the receivers. If the penalty for this foul is declined, or the free kick is last touched inbounds by the receivers, it is put in play by the receivers at the inbounds spot.

Description of Scrimmage Kicks

The offensive team may punt, drop kick, or placekick from or behind the neutral zone before team possession has changed.

Any receiver may catch or recover a scrimmage kick while it is behind the neutral zone and advance the ball, unless it is during a try for point, or unless any member of the receiving team has given a valid or invalid fair catch signal.

Any kicker may catch or recover a scrimmage kick while it is in or behind the neutral zone and advance the ball unless the kick is during a try for point.

Any kicker may catch or recover a scrimmage kick while it is beyond the neutral zone or the neutral zone expanded, provided such kick has been touched by a receiver who was clearly beyond the neutral zone at the time of touching. Such touch is ignored if it is caused by the kicker who pushes or blocks the receiver into contact with the ball.

"First touching of the kick" occurs when any kicker touches a scrimmage kick between the goal lines and beyond the neutral zone expanded before it is touched beyond this zone by a receiver and before the ball has come to rest. Such touching is ignored if it is caused by a receiver who pushes or blocks the kicker into contact with the ball.

The touching of a low scrimmage kick by any player is ignored if the touching is in or behind the expanded neutral zone. The neutral zone may not be expanded into the end zone.

When any scrimmage kick is out-of-bounds between the goal lines or becomes dead inbounds between the goal lines while no player is in possession, or inbounds anywhere while opponents are in joint possession, the ball is awarded to the receiving team. The ball is put in play at the inbounds spot following an out-of-bounds unless the receiving team chooses a spot of first touching.

Description of a Touchback

If any free kick or scrimmage kick touches anything while the kicked ball is on or behind the receiver's goal line or goal line plane, it becomes dead and is a touchback, unless a drop kick or placekick from scrimmage, or a free kick following a fair catch or awarded fair catch touches an upright, crossbar, or receiving player and caroms through the goal. If any kick becomes dead in the kicker's end zone while no player has possession, it is either a safety or touchback.

Rules Governing the Fair Catch

Any receiver may signal for a fair catch while any legal kick is in flight and is beyond the kicker's free kick line if it is a free kick, or beyond the neutral zone if it is a scrimmage kick. Any receiver who has given a valid or invalid fair catch signal in the end zone or in the field of play is prohibited from blocking until the kick has ended.

The ball becomes dead if any receiver gives a valid signal for a fair catch, and he/she catches the kick beyond the neutral zone and between the goal lines.

Only the receiver who gives a valid fair catch signal is afforded protection. If, after a receiver signals for a fair catch, the catch is made by a teammate beyond the neutral zone, it is not a fair catch but the ball becomes dead.

After a fair catch is made, the captain may choose to free kick or snap anywhere between the inbounds lines on the yard line through the spot of the catch. When a fair catch is awarded

Table 22-4. Summary of scrimmage kick and free kick activities.

Scrimmage Kick	Free Kick
1. Kick recovered beyond the neutral zone may be advanced only by the receiving team.	1. A kickoff, including the kick following a safety, cannot score a field goal.
2. Kick recovered in or behind the neutral zone may be advanced by either team.	2. A free kick following a fair catch or awarded fair catch may score a field goal.
3. Kick not recovered by either team belongs to the receiving team.	3. A free kick may not be advanced by the kicking team.
	4. A free kick not recovered by either team belongs to the receiving team.

Note: The kicking team is in team possession during a kick. A kick ends when a player gains possession or when the ball becomes dead by rule.

If the Kick Becomes Dead in the Receiving Team's End Zone: Touchback in all cases unless a field goal is scored.

If the Kick Becomes Dead in the Kicking Team's End Zone:	
If the force is:	Then the ruling is:
a. The kick or any other force by the kicking team	Safety, if the kick is out-of-bounds or the kicking team has possession including when the ball is loose.
	Touchdown, if the receiving team is in possession.
b. By the receiving team	Touchback, if the kick is out-of-bounds or the kicking team has possession, including when the ball is loose.
	Touchdown, if the receiving team is in possession.

at the spot of interference, the captain may choose to free kick or snap anywhere between the inbounds lines. These choices remain if a foul occurs and the down is replayed.

If a valid or invalid fair catch signal has been given by any member of the receiving team no receiver may advance the ball.

While any free kick is in flight or any scrimmage kick is in flight beyond the neutral zone, the kicking team shall not touch the ball or the receiver, unless to ward off a blocker, nor obstruct the receiver's path to the ball. This prohibition applies between the goal lines even when no signal is given, but it does not apply if the act is after the kick has been touched by the receiver.

Receivers or runners shall not give an invalid fair catch signal.

RULES GOVERNING THE ENFORCEMENT OF PENALTIES

Procedure After a Foul

The referee shall, at the end of the down, notify both captains when a foul occurs during a live ball. He/she shall inform the captain of the offended team regarding the rights of penalty acceptance or declination and shall indicate to him/her the number of the ensuing down, distance to be gained, and status of the ball for each available choice. The captain's choice of options may not be revoked. Decisions involving penalties shall be made before any charged time-out is granted either team.

When a live ball foul by one team is followed by a dead ball foul by the opponent, the penalties are administered separately and in the order of occurrence. When the same team commits a live ball foul followed by one or more dead ball fouls, all fouls may be penalized. The penalty for a foul by the opponents of the scoring team is automatically declined when it occurs during the down in which a touchdown or 2-point try is scored.

Double and Multiple Fouls

It is a double foul if both teams commit fouls, other than unsportsmanlike fouls, during the same live ball period in which:

1. there is no change of team possession
2. there is a change of team possession, and the team in possession at the end of the down fouls prior to final change of possession
3. there is a change of possession and the team in final possession accepts the penalty for its opponent's foul. In all of the above situations the penalties cancel each other and the down is replayed

Penalties for dead ball fouls are administered separately and in the order of their occurrence. A dead ball foul may not be coupled with a live ball foul or another dead ball foul to create a double or multiple foul.

A foul during a try for point is not paired

with a dead ball foul to create a double or multiple foul.

Types of Play and Basic Enforcement Spots

If a foul occurs during a down, the basic enforcement spot is fixed by the type of play. There are two types of play:

1. A loose ball play is action during a free kick or scrimmage kick or a legal forward pass or a backward pass or a fumble made by the offensive team from in or behind the neutral zone or the run or runs that precede such legal pass, kick, or fumble.
2. A running play is any action not included in item 1.

If a foul occurs during a loose ball play, the basic enforcement spot is the previous spot.

If a foul occurs during a running play, the basic enforcement spot is the spot where the related run ends. The run ends where the player loses possession if his/her run is followed by his/her fumble or pass. If the runner does not lose possession, his/her run ends where the ball becomes dead.

Administering Penalties

The penalty for any deal ball foul, any non-player foul, or any unsportsmanlike foul, is administered from the succeeding spot. A non-player or unsportsmanlike foul is administered as a dead ball foul. The penalty for a foul that occurs simultaneously with a snap or free kick is administered from the previous spot.

The penalty for a foul during a running play or a loose ball play is administered from the basic spot unless the foul is by the offense and occurs behind the basic spot. In that case, it is administered from the spot of the foul.

Special Enforcements

A measurement cannot take the ball more than half the distance from the enforcement spot to the offending team's goal line. If the ordinary distance penalty is greater than this, the ball is placed halfway from the spot of enforcement to the goal line.

If there is a foul by the defensive team dur-ing a successful kick try, the offensive team has the choice of accepting the penalty and replaying the down or accepting the results of the play with the penalty enforced from the succeeding spot.

If the offensive team throws an illegal forward pass from its end zone or commits any other foul for which the penalty is accepted and measurement is from on or behind its goal line, it is a safety.

For a defensive team foul, if the enforcement spot is on or behind the offended team's goal line any measurement is from the goal line.

If there is a player foul by the offensive team that is not unsportsmanlike, during a down which results in a successful field goal, touchdown or try, the acceptance of the penalty nullifies the score.

Fouls by the offensive team that include loss of down are illegally handing the ball forward, an illegal forward pass and forward pass interference.

Fouls by the defensive team that give the offensive team an automatic first down are roughing the kicker of a scrimmage kick, roughing the placekick holder of a scrimmage kick, forward pass interference and roughing the passer who has thrown from in or behind the neutral zone

A disqualified player must always be removed from the field of play.

The referee's decision to forfeit a game is final.

RULES PERTAINING TO THE CONDUCT OF PLAYERS AND OTHERS

Helping the runner is a foul. An offensive player shall not push, pull, or lift his/her teammate, the runner.

Illegal Use of Hands and Holding

An offensive player (except the runner) shall not: use an illegal blocking technique, use interlocked blocking by grasping or encircling the body parts of a teammate or use his/her hands, arms, or legs to hook, lock, clamp, grasp, encircle, or hold in an effort to restrain an opponent.

The runner may not grasp a teammate.

A defensive player shall not use any technique that is illegal. This includes using his/her hands to strike a blocker's head, using his/her hands or arms to hook, lock, clamp, grasp, encircle, or hold in an effort to restrain an opponent other than the runner or contacting an eligible receiver who is no longer a potential blocker.

Definition of Illegal Blocking

A player shall not block an opponent below the waist except when such action is used to tackle the runner. For an exception to this rule, see the free-blocking zone rule.

A receiver who has given a valid or invalid fair catch signal may not block an opponent until the kick has ended.

The kicker or placekick holder of a free kick may not be blocked before he/she has advanced five yards beyond his/her free kick line, or the kick has touched the ground or any other player.

A player shall not clip an opponent who is not a runner. For an exception to this rule, see the free-blocking zone rule.

A player shall not use a delayed block at the knees or below against an opponent who is in contact with a teammate of the blocker in the free-blocking zone.

A player shall not trip an opponent who is not a runner.

Rules Governing Illegal Personal Contact

No player shall strike an opponent with his/her fist, locked hands, forearm, or elbow, nor kick or knee him/her.

Other actions of personal contact that are illegal are:

- hurdling an opponent
- butt blocking, face tackling, or spearing
- intentionally using his/her helmet to butt or ram an opponent
- hiding the ball under a jersey
- swinging the foot, shin, or knee into an opponent, or extending the knee to meet a blocker
- charging into or throwing an opponent to the ground after he/she is obviously out of the play, or after the ball is clearly dead either in or out-of-bounds
- throwing a helmet to trip an opponent
- grasping an opponents face protector or any edge of a helmet opening
- piling on any player who is lying on the ground
- making any other contact with an opponent that is deemed unnecessary and which incites roughness
- positioning him/herself on the shoulder or body of a teammate or opponent to gain an advantage

Defensive players must make a definite effort to avoid charging into a passer who has thrown the ball from within or behind the neutral zone. No defensive player shall charge into the passer who is standing still or fading back after the pass is thrown, because the passer is considered out of the play after the pass.

No defensive player shall block, tackle, or charge into the kicker of a scrimmage kick, or the placekick holder, other than under the following situations:

1. when contact is unavoidable because it is not certain that a kick will be attempted
2. when the defense touches the kick near the kicker and contact is unavoidable
3. when contact is slight and is partially caused by movement of the kicker
4. when contact is caused by the defensive player being blocked into the kicker

No player or nonplayer shall intentionally contact an official.

Rules Governing Noncontact Unsportsmanlike Conduct by Players

No player shall act in an unsportsmanlike manner during either a period or an intermission. Examples of unsportsmanlike conduct are:

1. intentionally kicking at the ball, other than during a legal kick
2. using disconcerting acts or words prior to the snap in an attempt to interfere with the offensive team's signals or movements
3. using profanity, insulting, or vulgar language or gestures

4. leaving the field between downs to gain an advantage unless replaced or unless with permission of the referee
5. using words or acts to taunt or engender ill will
6. intentionally kicking at any opposing player
7. intentionally swinging an arm, hand, or fist at any opposing player

When the ball becomes dead in possession of a player, he/she shall not intentionally kick, spike, throw or fail to place the ball on the ground or immediately return it to a nearby official.

Rules Governing Illegal Participation

No replaced player or substitute shall hinder an opponent, touch the ball, influence the play, or otherwise participate.

Unless blocked or pushed out-of-bounds, no player of the offensive team or the kicking team shall participate by touching the ball or hindering an opponent after having been out-of-bounds during the down.

Illegal participation consists of:

1. having twelve or more players participating at the snap or free kick
2. not replacing an injured player for at least one down, unless the halftime or overtime intermission occurs
3. using a replaced player or substitute to deceive opponents at or immediately before the snap or free kick
4. deceiving opponents at or immediately before the snap or free kick by having a player pretend to be injured
5. having a disqualified player reenter the game.

Illegal Kicking and Batting of the Ball

No player shall intentionally kick the ball other than as a free kick or a scrimmage kick.

No player shall bat a loose ball other than a pass or a fumble in flight, or a low scrimmage kick in flight which he/she is attempting to block in or behind the neutral zone. Exceptions to illegal kicking and batting are:

1. A player on the kicking team may bat toward his/her own goal line a grounded scrimmage kick that is beyond the neutral zone.

2. Any pass in flight may be batted in any direction, unless it is by an ineligible player or it is a backward pass batted forward by the passing team.
3. A ball in player possession may not be batted forward by a player of the team in possession.

Noncontact Unsportsmanlike Conduct by Nonplayers

No coach, substitute, trainer, or other team attendant shall act in an unsportsmanlike manner during either a period or intermission. Examples of such unsportsmanlike conduct are:

- attempting to influence a decision by an official
- disrespectfully addressing an official
- using a mechanical devise to coach or to attract attention
- holding an unauthorized conference. Communications between players and coaches near the sideline between downs is not an unauthorized conference
- using profanity, insulting, or vulgar language or gestures
- indicating objections to an official's decision
- using an artificial aid to coach or direct play
- the use of mechanical visual-aid equipment, including computers, television and video tape for monitoring, replay, for coaching purposes during the game, including intermissions
- be outside the team box but not on the field
- being on the field except as a substitute or replaced player
- failure of the head coach, following verification, to have his/her player(s) wear legal and/or required equipment
- the failure of a team to be ready to start either half

Rules Governing Unfair Acts

A player or nonplayer or person not subject to the rules shall not hinder play by an unfair act that has no specific rule coverage.

No team shall repeatedly commit fouls which halve the distance to the goal line.

Neither team shall commit any act which, in the opinion of the referee, tends to make a travesty of the game

23
Rules for Flag Football*

Vern Seefeldt, Ph.D.

QUESTIONS TO CONSIDER

- What are the advantages of flag football over tackle football?
- Why is the 10-yd. chain not required in flag football?
- What is the advantage of having 8 rather than 11 persons per team?
- What constitutes a legal block?
- What constitutes illegal de-flagging?

INTRODUCTION

The objective of flag football is to provide an opportunity for children, youth, and adults to learn and experience the game of football in a non-tackle environment.

Personal Equipment

The equipment for flag football is relatively inexpensive, consisting of a football, football jersey or shirt, and flag belts. Players are expected to furnish their own shoes.

Field Equipment

Proper zone and down markers are required. Soft pylons serve this purpose.

Age Groups

Age groups of no more than two years are recommended. The following age divisions have

proven to be compatible with developmental progressions in rules and playing strategy.

Recommended Age Groups:

6 and 7 years
7 and 8 years
9 and 10 years
11 and 12 years
13 and 14 years
15 and 16 years

SUMMARY OF FLAG FOOTBALL RULES

1. Every player on the roster must play a minimum of 10 downs per game.
2. Two or three flag belts may be used. Belts and flags must be uniform for both teams.
3. Every player on the offense is eligible as a pass receiver.
4. Tackling is not allowed.
5. Aggressive play, including collisions with the

---

*These rules are excerpts from *Offical Rules and Regulations*, Pop Warner Football, Pop Warner Little Scholars, Inc., 1315 Walnut Street, Philadelphia, PA, 19107.

ball carrier prior to securing the flag, is not permitted.

6. Blockers must have both feet on the ground at all times. Leaving the ground for a block is illegal.
7. All kickoffs and punts are free kicks.
8. Fumbles are dead balls. No recovery is permitted.

FLAG FOOTBALL RULES IN DETAIL

Players

A game is played between two teams consisting of eight players each.

Each team roster shall have a maximum of 16 players, and a minimum of 10 players must be present and ready to play each game. A forfeit will result when the minimum number of players is not present.

Each team shall designate one player as "captain" and only he/she shall represent the team and address an official on matters of interpretation of rules or to obtain essential information.

The offensive team must have five players on the line and three in the backfield. The defensive team may choose any formation except in kicking situations, when five persons must be on the line of scrimmage.

Team Player Designations

The following designations are for statistical purposes only. A defensive team may use any alignment. The offensive line must have five persons at all times but may use any formation:

a. **Offensive Team Line**
   1. right and left ends
   2. right and left guards
   3. center

b. **Offensive Team Backfield**
   1. left halfback
   2. right halfback
   3. tailback

c. **Defensive Team Line**
   1. two defensive ends
   2. two defensive tackles
   3. one linebacker

4. two defensive backs
5. one safety

Mandatory Play Rule: All players will play a minimum of 10 plays. Failure to abide by this rule will result in a forfeiture of that game.

Game Termination—Lopsided Score

Once a team is ahead in any game by 30 or more points, that game will be terminated. Once a differential of 20 points exists in a game, coaches should exercise prudence by substituting liberally to avoid termination of the game.

Playing Fields:

The field shall be rectangular with lines and zones and shall conform to either of two designs (see Figures 23-1 and 23-2).

a. Major Field (commonly called "100-Yard Field"):

   This field measures 120 yds. in length, divided into five zones of 20 yds. each between two end zones of 10 yds. each. It is 53-1/3 yds. wide.

b. Minor Field (commonly called "80-Yard Field"):

   This field measures 100 yds. in length, divided into four zones of 20 yds. each between two end zones of 10 yds. each. It is 40 yds. wide.

c. Goalposts are unnecessary as points after touchdown (conversion) are made only by passing or running, and there are no field goals kicked.

d. A conversion line will be marked 3 yds. from the goal line and at an equal distance from each sideline.

e. A kickoff area will be marked (usually by an "X") as follows:
   1. Major Field: from the 40-yd. line
   2. Minor Field: from the 30-yd. line (middle of second zone and equal distance from the sidelines)

The following field equipment will be used:

a. A down marker will be used to indicate the number of the down.
b. A zone marker will be used to indicate the

Major Field
(100 yds.)

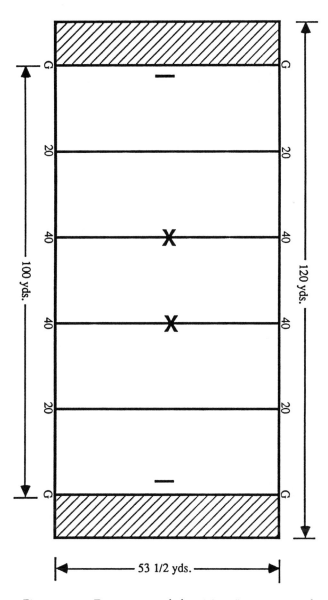

Figure 23-1. Dimensions of the "Major" or "100-Yard" field.

distance to go for a first down (placed at the forward zone line).

c. Corner flags with flexible staffs will be placed at the four sections of the end zones and the sidelines. Soft pylons may be used if flags are unavailable.

Equipment

The *game ball* shall be of a good grade of

Minor Field
(80 yds.)

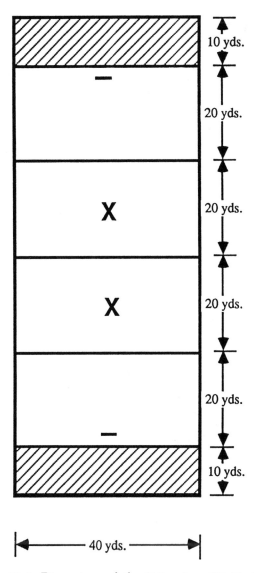

Figure 23-2. Dimensions of the "Minor" or "80-Yard" field.

leather with specifications as described in Table 23-1.

Flags

a. Each player must wear a belt with the number of flags designated as "standard" by the league, that being either two or three flags.

b. The flags will be attached to a belt and extend or hang there from each side of the player's body. In case of three flags, the third will hang from the rear of the player's body.

c. Flags will be 14-20 in. long and 3 in. wide.

Table 23-1. Dimensions of the game ball for various age groups.

	Junior Ball (inches)	Intermediate Ball (inches)	High School Ball (inches)
Length, Long Axis Circum.	10¼-10½	10⅝-10¾	11-11¼
Short Axis Circum.	18¼-18½	19½-20⅛	21¼-21½
Long Axis	25-25⅛	26¼-26¾	28-28¼
Weight	12-13 oz.	14-15 oz.	14-15 oz.

d. The belt must be tight to prevent being turned around during a de-flagging.
e. The home team will wear dark flags and the visitors will wear light flags.
f. The securing of flags to the body, waist, or belt, other than provided above, is illegal.
g. Jerseys cannot be worn over flags.
h. If a player's flag is inadvertently lost, he/she is ineligible to handle the ball.

Game Uniforms

a. All team members must wear the same color jersey.
b. All jerseys will be numbered, front and back, for proper identification by officials and statisticians.
c. Any type of pants may be worn.
d. Jerseys will be tucked in at all times.
e. Soft-soled shoes such as those worn in basketball, tennis, or other court games are the preferred shoe; however, non-detachable rubber-cleated shoes (soccer style) are allowed. No other footwear is acceptable.

Eye Glasses

a. Eyeglasses, when worn, shall be of athletically approved construction with non-shattering glass (safety glass).
b. Contact lenses may be worn.

Prohibited Equipment

a. Spiked or street shoes.
b. Padding of any kind, including hard surface padding such as shoulder pads, hip pads, and helmets.
c. Hard metal or any other hard substance on a player's clothing or person.
d. Anything that conceals the flags.
e. Sticky substances such as grease or glue on a player's clothing.

f. Any equipment, in the opinion of the referee, that will endanger or confuse players.

Referees

a. There will be at least two referees appointed prior to the game.
b. More than two referees may be assigned for a game.
c. Each game official will carry a yellow handkerchief and drop it when an infraction occurs.

PLAYING RULES

Players

The free substitution rule is always in effect and a player may enter the game any time the ball is dead.

Team Captains

a. Each team will have at least one captain on the field at all times during the game.
b. The captain will address the referees only on matters of interpretation and to obtain information.

The Game

There will be:

a. Two 15-minute halves for the 6-7, 7-8, and 9-10-year-old players
b. Two 20-minute halves for the 11-12, 13-14, and 15-16-year-old players
c. Three time-outs per half
d. 10 minutes between halves

Each half will start with a kickoff.

a. The Major Field kickoff will be from the 40-yd. line.
b. The Minor Field kickoff will be from the 30-yd. line. (Although this yard line is not diagramed, the kickoff line will be marked with an appropriate symbol, usually an "X.")
c. The referee will call the team captains together for a toss of a coin to decide a choice of kicking or receiving. The winning captain has the choice.
d. The losing captain has the same choice at the beginning of the second half.

e. There shall be no onside kickoffs.
f. Out-of-bounds kickoffs shall automatically go to the:
   1. 40-yd. line (Major Field)
   2. 20-yd. line (Minor Field)
g. With the above modifications, other kickoff rules are the same as those of the National Federation of State High School Associations.

Punting

a. The offensive team may punt at any time.
b. A punt is always a free kick.
c. Punting intentions are announced to the referee by the captain or acting captain.
d. Rushing the punter is prohibited. No offensive or defensive player may move across the line of scrimmage until the kick has been made.
e. There shall be a free catch of a punt. The receiver shall signify his/her intentions for a free catch by waving his/her hand clearly over his/her head.

Downs (First Down and Zone to Go)

a. Each team will have four consecutive downs to advance the ball into the next zone or to score a touchdown.
b. Once a team enters into the next zone, it is a first down and a new series of downs begins.
c. A team failing to move the ball into the next zone will lose possession. The opposing team takes over at the point where the ball is declared dead and begins its series of first down and zone-to-go.
d. The forward part of the ball touching any line will be the determining factor in measuring for a first down.
e. A down will be repeated if provided for by the rules (see "Penalties").
f. When the offensive team is within the last zone and has a first down, it will be first down and goal-to-go.

De-flagging

a. There shall be no tackling of the ball carrier, passer, or kicker.

b. The player carrying or having possession of the ball is down when the flag is removed from his/her waist (de-flagging). After a de-flagging, the defensive player will hold the flag above his/her head and stand still.
c. The defensive player cannot hold or push the ball carrier down to remove his/her flag. An accidental touch of the body or shoulder while reaching for the flag will not be considered a violation; however, touching of the head or face will be considered a violation.
d. Defensive players may not run over, push, or pull a blocker away from them. Defensive players may push offensive players sideways if they get past the defensive players, but the blocker may not be pushed down.
e. A defensive player must go for the passer's flag. He/she may not touch the passer's arm.

Blocking

a. A blocker must be on his/her feet at all times while blocking. All linemen except the center must not assume the three-point stance or otherwise spring from a coiled or crouching start. Instead, they must simply stand at the line of scrimmage and await the snap. The center, though crouching if he/she is to block, must first stand straight up.
b. Cross-body and roll blocking are not permitted.
c. A blocker cannot use his/her hands.
d. Blocking shall be with the arms down and the body, in the form of shoulder and brush blocking only.
e. A defensive player cannot block or push a ball carrier out of bounds.
f. Butting, elbowing, or knee blocking are not permitted.
g. There will be no two-on-one blocking for the ball carrier beyond the line of scrimmage.
h. Blocking a player from behind is not permitted (clipping).
i. There will be no interlock blocking.
j. A defensive player will be restricted in the use of his/her hands to the blocker's body and shoulders.

Ball Carrier

a. The ball carrier cannot use his/her hands or arms to protect his/her flags. The defensive player must have the opportunity to remove the ball carrier's flags.

b. The ball carrier cannot lower his/her head to drive or run into a defensive player.
c. Stiff-arming by the ball carrier is illegal.
d. The ball carrier cannot spin or hurdle to prevent a defensive player from removing his/her flags.
e. The ball carrier may run in any direction until the ball is declared dead.

Center

a. The center must snap the ball between his/her legs.
b. The center must have both feet on the scrimmage line with no part of his/her body beyond the forward point of the ball.
c. The center may adjust the long part of the ball at right angles to the scrimmage line for one time only.

Passing

a. All backfield players are eligible passers.
b. Passing will be attempted from behind the line of scrimmage only.
c. A lateral pass is a pass thrown parallel to the line of scrimmage or back toward the passer's own goal line. A lateral pass is not considered a forward pass.
d. A forward pass is a pass thrown from behind the line of scrimmage toward the defensive team's goal line.

Receiving

a. All players are eligible to receive forward passes.
b. A receiver may catch a ball even if he/she steps out of bounds or out of the end zone as long as he/she comes down with one foot inbounds.
c. Two or more receivers may touch a ball in succession resulting in a completed pass.
d. If an offensive and defensive player catch a pass simultaneously, the ball is declared dead at the spot of the catch and the passing team is awarded possession.
e. An offensive player cannot be out of bounds and return inbounds to catch a pass. This will be ruled an incomplete pass.

Dead Ball

All balls touching the ground are immediately dead (except kickoffs and punts). For example, the ball is declared dead at the following times:

a. When the ball carrier touches the ground with his/her body, other than hands or feet.
b. When the ball carrier's flag has been pulled.
c. If a pass receiver or ball carrier has a missing flag (ball is dead at that spot).
d. Following a touchdown, safety, or touchback.
e. When the ball goes out of bounds for any reason.
f. If the center snap hits the ground before reaching a backfield person.
g. When the ball hits the ground as a result of a fumble or muffed ball—**there are no fumble recoveries in flag football.**
h. If a lateral pass touches the ground (ball is declared dead at that point)—if a lateral pass goes out of bounds, the ball is ruled dead at the point it crosses the boundary line.
i. If a forward pass strikes the ground or is caught at the same time by an opposing player(s).
j. When a player on the kicking team touches a punt before a player on the receiving team touches it.
k. A free catch (cannot be advanced).

Scoring Values

Touchdown	six points
Safety	two points
Points after touchdown:	
Passing	one point
Running	two points
Forfeit (offended team wins by)	1-0

Tie Game

a. Team with the greatest number of first downs is declared the winner.
b. If both teams have an equal number of first downs:
1. The ball will be placed in the center of the field. The referee will toss a coin in the presence of the two team captains. The winning captain will have the option of putting the ball in play at the centerline.

2. Each team will have four consecutive downs and the winner will be the team gaining the most yardage in its series of downs.
3. Each team will have its four downs even if one of those downs results in a touchdown.
4. Penalties will count as plus or minus yardage.
5. Intercepted passes will count as incomplete passes.
6. If the yardage is still the same at the end of the eight-down series, the series will be repeated.

Injured Players

Once removed from a game because of injury, a player must sit out at least one series of downs.

Once treated for injury off the field, a player requires permission of one parent or legal guardian to resume playing football in the same season.

Schedules

Maximum number of games suggested for each age group per season is shown in Table 23-2.

Penalties

Because two football field sizes can be used, penalties are adjusted accordingly. The Major Field will be assessed the standard 15- and 5-yd. penalties. The Minor Field will be assessed 9- and 3-yd. penalties. With this in mind, references to penalties will be given as (15-9) and (5-3) in the following listings.

The offended team will always have the choice of accepting or declining a penalty. If the penalty is declined, the down will remain the same as if no infraction occurred. Also, when

Table 23-2. Suggested number of games, by age group.

Age Group	Pre-season	Regular Season
6-7	0	8
7-8	1	8
9-10	1	9
11-over	1	10

the penalty is greater than the distance to the goal line, the penalty shall be half the distance to the goal line.

Kickoffs

If either team is offside on the kickoff, the penalty will be (5-3) and the ball will be kicked again.

Line of Scrimmage—Centering

a. Offsides, defensive or offensive (5-3).
b. Illegal snap (5-3).
c. Failure to observe 25-second rule (5-3).
d. Illegal motion—more than one backfield person in motion (5-3).
e. Illegal formation, offense (5-3).

Punting

a. Failure to announce to the referee (5-3) and punt is repeated, or the receiving team may take the ball at the spot where the ball is declared dead.
b. If the kicking or receiving team enters the neutral zone before the punt—(5-3) from the spot where the ball is declared dead after the kick.
c. Less than five players on the line of scrimmage for the offensive or defensive team—(5-3) from where the ball is declared dead after the kick.
d. De-flagging a receiver after a fair-catch signal—(15-9) from the spot of the foul.

Passing

a. If an illegal forward pass is thrown and intercepted, the play will continue until the ball is declared dead. The intercepting team has the option of possession from that spot or accepting the penalty (5-3).
b. Passer crosses line of scrimmage—(5-3) and loss of down.
c. Intentional grounding—(5-3) and loss of down.
d. Offensive pass interference—(15-9) from line of scrimmage and loss of down.
e. Defensive pass interference—first down from spot of infraction for the offensive team.

Delay of Game

a. Continuing to play after the ball is dead—(5-3) from where the ball is dead.

b. Recovering a fumble or falling on the ball (5-3).
c. Advancing a fair catch (5-3).
d. Unnecessary delay of game for any reason (5-3).

Flag Wearing and De-flagging

a. Tackling (15-9).
b. Wearing the flags illegally (5-3).
c. Ball carrier using his/her hands to prevent a defensive player from de-flagging (15-9).
d. Holding, pushing, or hitting the ball carrier while de-flagging—(15-9) from spot of foul.
e. Leaving one's feet while de-flagging—(15-9) from spot of foul.
f. Wearing one flag (5-3).

Illegal Handoff

a. If the ball is handed forward beyond the scrimmage line—(5-3) and loss of down.
b. Handing or snapping a ball to a lineman (5-3).

Illegal Substitutions

a. More than eight persons per team on the field—(5-3).
b. Substitution(s) while the ball is in play or before it is declared dead (5-3).
c. Disqualified player entering game (15-9).

Blocking

a. Leaving feet to block (15-9).
b. Cross-body blocking or roll blocking (15-9).
c. Illegal use of hands by blocker (15-9).
d. Holding a defensive player (15-9).
e. Defensive player blocking or pushing the ball carrier out of bounds (15-9).
f. Butting, elbowing, or knee blocking (15-9).
g. Defensive player using hands illegally (5-3).
h. More than two blockers for the ball carrier (on one defensive player) beyond the line of scrimmage (5-3).
i. Clipping (15-9).
j. Interlock blocking—(5-3) from spot of foul.

Ball Carrier

a. Stiff-arming—(15-9) from spot of foul.
b. Lowering head to drive or run into defensive player (15-9).
c. Use of head to butt defensive player (15-9).
d. Use of hand or arms to protect flags (15-9).
e. Spinning or hurdling (5-3).

Unnecessary Roughness

a. Offensive and defensive (15-9).
b. Disqualification of guilty player or players if repeated.

Unsportsmanlike Conduct

a. Fighting—(15-9) offenders ejected from game.
b. Defensive player pulling offensive player's flag to make him/her ineligible for play (15-9).
c. Insulting and abusive language (15-9).
d. Interference with progress of the game by coaches or any other team personnel (15-9).
e. Illegal play (15-9).
f. Team leaving field before game is completed (15-9). Failure to return—forfeit. Win for team remaining on field.
g. Failure of home team to control players or fans (15-9). Forfeit if not controlled.

Penalties other than those herein listed will, in the judgment of game officials, follow the guidelines for penalties under the National Federation of State High School Association rules.

24
Rules for Touch Football*

Vern Seefeldt, Ph.D.

QUESTIONS TO CONSIDER

- How do the dimensions of a touch football field differ from a flag football field?
- What constitutes a legal touch?
- Who is eligible to throw or catch the ball in touch football?
- In what ways may teams score points in touch football?

INTRODUCTION

The object of the game of touch football is to advance the ball over the opponent's goal line without being touched. Points are awarded for a touchdown (six points), a point after touchdown (one point by kicking, two points by running), a field goal (three points), a safety (two points), a forfeit (one point), and by penetration toward the opponent's goal in event of a tie (one point).

A regulation football field equipped with goalposts and yard lines may be used. Players are prohibited from wearing the heavy official football equipment because tackling is not permitted. Runners are stopped by a touch of one or both hands about the waist, instead of a tackle. A touch football team is usually composed of seven players, but variations (from five to eight players) may be used with few modifications to the rules.

GAME RULES

Playing Field

An official touch football field is 40x100 yds. long (see Figure 24-1). The field is divided into four 20-yd. zones and two end zones, each 10 yds. in depth.

Goals

Goalposts are not necessary. However, lack of goalposts eliminates points after touchdown by kicking and field goals. In these cases, points after touchdown are gained by running or passing.

Uniform

No special uniform is required. The use of football helmets and pads is prohibited. Tennis type shoes or soccer shoes with molded rubber cleats may be used.

---

*These rules were gleaned from a variety of sources but primarily from *Physical Education Handbook*, 7th ed. Seaton, C., Schmoltlach, N., Clayton, I., Leible, H., & Messersmith, L. Englewood Cliffs: Prentice Hall, Inc.

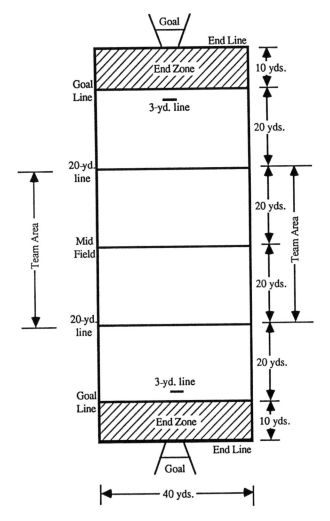

Figure 24-1. The 100-yd. touch football field.

Ball

A regulation leather or rubber-coated football may be used. A junior-size football should be used by younger children.

Periods

Four 10-minute periods constitute a game with a 1-minute rest between periods and a 5-minute rest between halves. Games may also be divided into two 20-minute halves with a 5-minute rest period.

Overtime

Tie games may be decided by one of the following methods:

a. award the game to the team with the greatest number of penetrations inside the opponent's 20-yd. line

b. award the game to the team with the greatest number of first downs

c. give each team four downs from the 20-yd. line and award the game to the team advancing the ball the farthest

Time-out

Each team is allowed two time-outs per half. Time-outs are also taken under the following conditions:

a. when the ball goes out of bounds
b. after a score
c. while a penalty is being enforced
d. at the discretion of the referee
e. at the end of each period

Players

A team consists of seven players, although fewer or more players may be used by mutual consent. The offensive team must have at least three persons on the line of scrimmage when the ball is put in play.

Substitutes

Any number of substitutions may be made at any time during the game while the ball is dead.

Starting the Game

A toss of a coin by the referee determines which team has the choice of kicking off, receiving, or goals. The loser of the toss has the choice of the remaining options. Privileges of choice are reversed at the beginning of the third period.

Putting the Ball in Play

The ball is put in play at the start of the game, after a score, and at the beginning of the third period by a placekick from the kicker's 40-yd. line. Defensive team members must be 10 yds. away when the ball is kicked, and members of the kicking team must be behind the ball. If the ball does not go 10 yds., it must be kicked again. If the ball goes out of bounds after 10 yds., the opponents have a choice of beginning play where it went out of bounds or on their own 20-yd. line. If the ball is kicked into the end zone and the opponents elect not to run it out, play begins on their 20-yd. line.

First Downs

A team has four chances to move the ball from one 20-yd. zone to the next. If a team does not advance the ball from one zone to the next in four downs, the ball goes to the opponents at that spot.

Passing

The following regulations govern passing:

a. All players on both teams are eligible to catch passes.
b. Forward passes may be thrown from any point in back of the line of scrimmage, and lateral passes may be thrown anywhere on the playing field.
c. Any number of passes may be thrown in a series of downs.

Penalties

5-yd. Penalty Infractions (from line of scrimmage):

a. Offside.
b. Delay of game.
c. Less than three players on line of scrimmage.
d. Illegal motion or shift.
e. Illegal forward pass.

15-yd. Penalty Infractions (from spot of foul):

a. Illegal use of hands.
b. Illegal block.
c. Unnecessary roughness (push, tackle, shove, trip, hold).
d. Unsportsmanlike conduct.
e. Clipping.
f. Pass interference.

25
Football Rules for Special Populations and Situations*

Vern Seefeldt, Ph.D.

QUESTIONS TO CONSIDER

- What are the advantages and disadvantages of limiting the contest length to the number of plays rather than to a specific length of time?
- What precautions are provided to reduce rough or aggressive behavior?
- What changes in defensive play are mandated by permitting the offensive team to pass the ball at any time?
- What changes are introduced to football by permitting every player to throw and receive the ball?

INTRODUCTION

Modifications to the regulation game of football are generally designed to meet the specific needs of a special population. Factors such as age, ability, physical condition, gender, and environment have all contributed to the modifications of rules that are described in this chapter. Sponsors of organized competition are urged to consider the impact of specific modifications on the safety and enjoyment of the participants prior to determining the rules that will govern play.

MODIFIED FLAG FOOTBALL

Playing Area: Field 30x60 yds.

The field is divided into three zones by lines marked off at 20-yd. intervals. There also should be two end zones, from 5-10 yds. in width, defining the area behind the goal in which passes may be caught. Modified Flag Football is played with two or three flags on each player. The flag is a length of cloth that is hung from the side at the waist of each player. To down (stop) a player with the ball, one of the flags must be pulled.

---

*These rules were gleaned from a variety of sources. Special recognition is given to *Dynamic Physical Education for Elementary School Children*, 8th ed. New York. Dauer, V. & Paugrazi, R. New York: Macmillan Publishing Co.

Players: Six to nine on a team

Modified Flag Football should rarely, if ever, be played with 11 players on a side. This results in a crowded field and leaves little room to maneuver. If six or seven are on a team, four players are required to be on the line of scrimmage. For eight or nine players, five offensive players must be on the line.

The Game

The game consists of two halves. A total of 25 plays makes up each half. All plays count in the 25, except the try-for-point after a touchdown and a kickoff that goes out of bounds.

The game is started with a kickoff. The team winning the coin toss has the option of selecting the goal it wishes to defend or choosing to kick or receive. The loser of the toss takes the option not exercised by the first team. The kickoff is from the goal line, and all players on the kicking team must be on the goal line at the time of the kick. The kick must cross the first zone line or it does not count as a play. A kick that is kicked out of bounds (and is not touched by the receiving team) must be kicked over. A second consecutive kick out of bounds gives the ball to the receiving team in the center of the field. The kickoff may not be recovered by the kicking team unless first touched by the receivers.

A team has four downs to move the ball into the next zone, or they lose the ball. If the ball is legally advanced into the last zone, then the team has four downs to score. A ball on the line between zones is considered in the more forward zone.

Playing Time

Time-outs are permitted only for injuries or when called by the officials. Unlimited substitutions are permitted. After any play, the team has 30 seconds to put the ball into play after the referee gives the signal.

Blocking is done with the arms close to the body. Blocking must be done from the front or side, and blockers must stay on their feet.

A player is down if one of his/her flags has been pulled. The ball carrier must make an attempt to avoid the defensive player and is not permitted to run over or through the defensive player. The tackler must attempt to secure the flags and not run over the ball carrier. Good officiating is needed to avoid having defensive players attempt to hold or grasp the ball carrier until they are able to remove one of his/her flags.

Advancing the Ball

All forward passes must be thrown from behind the line of scrimmage. All players on the field are eligible to receive and intercept passes.

All fumbles are dead at the spot of the fumble. The first player who touches the ball on the ground is ruled to have recovered the fumble. When the ball is centered to a back, he/she must gain definite possession of it before a fumble can be called. Players are allowed to pick up a bad pass from the center when they do not have possession of the ball.

All punts must be announced. Neither team can cross the line of scrimmage until the ball is kicked. Kick receivers may run or use a lateral pass. They may not make a forward pass after receiving a kick.

A pass caught in an end zone scores a touchdown. The player must have control of the ball in the end zone. A ball caught beyond the end zone is out of bounds and is considered an incomplete pass.

Scoring

A touchdown scores six points, a completed pass or run after touchdown scores one point, and a safety scores two points. A point after touchdown is made from a distance of 3 ft. from the goal line. One play (pass or run) is allowed for the extra point.

Any ball kicked over the goal line is ruled a touchback and is brought out to the 20-yd. line to be put into play by the receiving team. A pass intercepted behind the goal line can be a touchback if the player does not run it out, even if he/she is tagged behind his/her own goal line.

Penalties

A penalty of 5 yds. is assessed for the following:

1. being offside
2. delay of game (too long in the huddle)
3. passing from a spot not behind line of scrimmage (this also results in loss of down)
4. stiff-arming by the ball carrier, or not avoiding a defensive player
5. failure to announce intention to punt
6. shortening the flag in the belt, or playing without flags in proper position
7. faking the ball by the center, who must center the pass on the first motion

The following infractions are assessed a 15-yd. loss:

1. holding, illegal tackling
2. illegal blocking
3. unsportsmanlike conduct (this also can result in disqualification)

Advantages of Modified Flag Football

Specifying 25 plays per half eliminates the need for timing and lessens arguments about a team's taking too much time in the huddle. Using the zone system makes the first-down yardage point definite and eliminates the need for a chain to mark off the 10 yds. needed for a first down.

AIR FOOTBALL OR PASS BALL

Air Football or Pass Ball is a more open game than Flag Football. The game is similar to Flag Football with these differences:

1. The ball may be passed at any time. It may be thrown at any time beyond the line of scrimmage, immediately after an interception, during a kickoff, or during a received kick.
2. Four downs are given to score a touchdown.
3. A two-handed touch anywhere above the waist is used instead of pulling a flag.
4. If the ball is thrown from behind the line of scrimmage and results in an incomplete pass, the ball is placed at the previous spot on the line of scrimmage. If the pass originates other-

wise and is incomplete, the ball is placed at the spot from which this pass was thrown.

5. Because the ball can be passed at any time, no downfield blocking is permitted. A player may screen the ball carrier but cannot block (make contact). Screening is defined as running between the ball carrier and the defense.

FOURTH DOWN FOOTBALL

Players: Four to six on each team

Supplies: A football

Skills: All football skills except kicking, blocking, and tackling

Every play is a fourth down, which means that the play must score or the team loses the ball. No kicking is permitted, but players may pass at any time from any spot and in any direction. There can be a series of passes on any play, either from behind or beyond the line of scrimmage.

Ball in Play

The teams line up in an offensive football formation. To start the game, the ball is placed in the center of the field, and the team that wins the coin toss has the chance to put the ball into play. The ball is put into play by centering. The back receiving the ball runs or passes to any of his/her teammates. The one receiving the ball has the same privilege. No blocking is permitted. After each touchdown, the ball is brought to the center of the field, and the opposing team puts the ball into play.

To Stop Play

To down a runner or pass receiver, a two-handed touch above the waist is made. The back first receiving the ball from the center has immunity from tagging, provided that he/she does not try to run. All defensive players must stay 10 ft. away unless he/she runs. The referee should wait for 25 seconds for the back to pass or run. If the ball is still held beyond that time, the referee should call out "Ten seconds." The back must then throw or run within 10 seconds or be vulnerable to defensive pressure.

The defensive players cover the receivers

using one-on-one defense, with each player covering an offensive player; a zone defense may also be used.

Because the team with the ball loses possession after each play, the following rules are used to determine where the ball should be placed when the other team takes possession:

1. If a ball carrier is tagged with two hands above the waist, the ball goes to the other team at that spot

2. If an incomplete pass is made from *behind* the line of scrimmage, the ball is given to the other team at the spot where the ball was put into play

3. Should an incomplete pass be made by a player *beyond* the line of scrimmage, the ball is brought to the spot from which it was thrown

Glossary

This glossary contains a listing of terms and definitions that are common to the game of football. It is intended to familiarize coaches, players, and parents with the vocabulary that is used so that they may gain a greater understanding of the game and may communicate better with others about football. The terms are listed alphabetically and are accompanied by common variations of the defined term, when appropriate.

Backfield in motion   One offensive back moving forward, or more than one offensive back moving in any direction before the ball is snapped (illegal).

Ball carrier   The player who runs with the ball.

Blocking   The act of impeding the progress of a defensive player.

Center   The offensive player who snaps the ball backward to start a play.

Clipping   Contacting any part of a defensive player from the back (illegal).

Coach   The individual who instructs and trains the players in the various fundamentals and techniques of the game. This individual is also in charge of the strategy employed in the game.

Defense   Attempting to impede the progress of the team possessing the ball.

Defensive team   The team not in possession of the ball.

Double team   A coordinated block by two offensive players.

Down   A unit of the game that starts after the ball is ready for play with a snap or free kick and ends when the ball next becomes dead.

Downfield   The part of the field toward which the offensive team is headed.

Fake   Any movement of the body which deceives an opponent.

Field goal   Place-kicking the ball over the crossbar from scrimmage (score 3 points).

First down   The first play in a series. A team must gain 10 yds. in four plays or less to be awarded a first down.

Flanker   An offensive back lined up outside the end.

Flat pass   A ball thrown into the area outside the ends toward the sidelines.

Forward pass   A ball thrown toward or beyond the line of scrimmage.

Free kick   An unhindered kick.

Fullback   An offensive back who normally lines up behind the quarterback and in front of the tailback.

Fumble   The accidental loss of control or possession of the ball.

Goal line   A vertical plane extending the width of the field separating an end zone from the playing field.

Guards   Players positioned on either side of the center.

Halftime   The time between each half of the game.

Handing the Ball   The act of transferring the ball from one teammate to another without throwing, fumbling, or kicking it.

Hash mark   The inbounds marking on field for ball placement.

Holding   To impede the progress of an opposing player by grasping that player with the hands or arms.

Huddle   Two or more offensive players grouped together, after the ball is ready for play, to receive assignments before assuming a scrimmage formation.

Illegal motion When an offensive player is moving forward or more than one offensive player is moving backward or laterally at the snap.

Illegal use of hands Holding or pushing by offensive players.

Incomplete pass A pass that is not caught or intercepted.

Interference A screen of blockers; or, illegally preventing a pass receiver from catching the ball.

Kick The act of propelling the ball by striking it with the foot.

Kicker The player who kicks or is designated to kick the ball.

Kickoff A place-kick which starts each half and follows each try-for-point, safety, or field goal.

Lateral A pass that is thrown in any direction other than towards the opponent's goal line.

Linebacker A defensive player aligned behind defensive linemen.

Lineman Any player on either the offensive or defensive team who plays on the line of scrimmage.

Line of Scrimmage See "Scrimmage Line."

Man-for-man A method of individual coverage on pass defense.

Neutral zones An imaginary area the width of the football. It is the space between the two lines of scrimmage and is established when the ball is ready for play.

Offense The team in possession of the ball; the act of advancing the ball.

Offensive team The team in possession of the ball.

Official One of the individuals (referee, linesman, umpire or field judge) who administers the rules of the game.

Offside Crossing the line of scrimmage before the ball is snapped.

Out of Bounds Any area outside the designated playing area (the lines bounding the sidelines and end zones.)

Passer The player who has thrown a legal forward pass.

Pass patterns The routes run by eligible receivers.

Penalty A loss imposed by rule upon a team that has committed a foul.

Pivot A footwork technique where a player keeps one foot in contact with a spot on the ground while moving the other foot.

Power play An offensive play concentrating blockers at one point.

Punt The act of kicking the ball by a player who drops it and kicks it before it strikes the ground.

Quarterback The backfield player who usually handles the ball on the snap from center and usually calls plays in the huddle.

Red dog (blitz) Linebackers shooting through gaps in the offensive line in pursuit of the quarterback. Usually occurs on passing-down situations.

Referee The principal official on the field who assumes a position in the offensive backfield.

Roughing the kicker Making body contact with the punter (illegal).

Safety When a ball is downed by the offensive team behind its own goal line or is forced out of the end zone (scores 2 points for the defense).

Screen pass A forward pass behind the line of scrimmage to a receiver who is positioned behind a screen of blockers.

Scrimmage A practice session including plays, blocking, and tackling.

Scrimmage line The scrimmage line for each team is the yard line and its vertical plane which passes through the point of the ball nearest the team's own goal line.

Secondary The defensive players aligned behind linebackers.

Series Four consecutive downs to advance the ball to the next zone.

Shift A simultaneous change of position by two or more offensive players after they have lined up for the snap.

Signals The verbal calls made prior to the snap of the ball.

Snap The method of putting the ball in play from scrimmage with the center handing the ball between his legs to a back positioned behind him.

Snapper The player who snaps the ball.

Soccer kick A method of kicking off or attempting a field goal.

Stance A term that applies to the position of all players on either side of the center.

Stunting The movement up and down the scrimmage line by defensive players to confuse the offensive linemen prior to the start of a play.

Tackles   The offensive players positioned outside of the guards.

Tackling   The technique used to knock the ball carrier to the ground or to stop his forward progress.

Tailback   An offensive running back who lines up deepest in the backfield.

Touchback   Occurs when a punted or kicked ball goes into the end zone, or when an intercepted pass is recovered in the end zone by the defense. (No points are scored and the ball is placed on the 20-yard line.)

Touchdown   Occurs when a team has possession of the ball in the end zone of the defending team (scores 6 points).

Trap (mousetrap)   Allowing a defensive player to advance across the line of scrimmage and then blocking him from the side.

Try-for-point   an attempt awarded a team after they have scored a touchdown, to try to score an additional 1 or 2 points.

Unbalanced line   An offensive line having more players on one side of the center than on the other.

Unnecessary roughness   Excessive contact with an opponent (illegal).

Unsportsmanlike conduct   Conduct that is not characteristic of good sportsmanship. For example: fighting, using profanity, striking an official, etc. (illegal).

Wide receiver   A player eligible to receive a pass who lines up wide to the outside away from the ball.

Yard line   A line in the field of play parallel to the endline between the goal lines.

Zone defense   When the secondary defense protects a specified territory rather than a designated opposing player.

Index